MW01012388

PLEAS *and* PETITIONS

PLEAS *and* PETITIONS

Hispano Culture and Legislative Conflict in Territorial Colorado

Virginia Sánchez

Foreword by Ken Salazar

UNIVERSITY PRESS OF COLORADO
Louisville

Published by University Press of Colorado
245 Century Circle, Suite 202
Louisville, Colorado 80027

 The University Press of Colorado is a proud member of
the Association of University Presses.

The University Press of Colorado is a cooperative publishing enterprise supported, in part, by Adams State University, Colorado State University, Fort Lewis College, Metropolitan State University of Denver, University of Colorado, University of Northern Colorado, University of Wyoming, Utah State University, and Western Colorado University.

∞ This paper meets the requirements of the ANSI/NISO Z39.48–1992 (Permanence of Paper).

ISBN: 978-1-60732-913-8 (cloth)
ISBN: 978-1-60732-914-5 (ebook)
DOI: https://doi.org/10.5876/9781607329145

Library of Congress Cataloging-in-Publication Data

Names: Sánchez, Virginia, 1953– author.
Title: Pleas and petitions : Hispano culture and legislative conflict in territorial Colorado / Virginia Sánchez.
Description: Louisville : University Press of Colorado, [2018] | Includes bibliographical references and index.
Identifiers: LCCN 2019007282 | ISBN 9781607329138 (cloth) | ISBN 9781607329145 (ebook)
Subjects: LCSH: Hispanic American legislators—Colorado—History—19th century. | Hispanic Americans—Colorado—History—19th century. | Hispanic Americans—Colorado—Social conditions—19th century. | Racism—Colorado—History—19th century. | Colorado—Politics and government—To 1876. | Colorado—Race relations—History—19th century.
Classification: LCC F785.S75 S635 2018 | DDC 978.8/00468—dc23
LC record available at https://lccn.loc.gov/2019007282

Cover illustrations (left to right): Celedonio Valdez, from Denver Public Library, Western History and Genealogy Department; José Anastacio de Jesús Valdez, from Denver Public Library, Western History and Genealogy Department; Francisco Sánchez, courtesy Connie Rodriguez; José Víctor García, courtesy Francisco Gallegos; Pedro Rafael Trujillo, courtesy Charlene Garcia Simms. Background: "Map of Colorado Territory, Shewing the System of Parks," 1865, courtesy David Rumsey Map Collection (www.davidrumsey.com).

Tony and Eric—I love you lots!

Contents

Figures

Tables

Foreword

Ken Salazar

FORMER US SECRETARY OF THE INTERIOR,
US SENATOR, AND COLORADO ATTORNEY GENERAL

The history of the Spanish and Mexican descendants of southern Colorado has been a forgotten history. In *Pleas and Petitions: Hispano Culture and Legislative Conflict in Territorial Colorado*, Virginia Sánchez helps fill this void by telling the story of the rich history and brave struggles of our ancestors in southern Colorado.

Most natives of Colorado do not know precisely how and why the northern part of New Mexico became a part of Colorado. Virginia introduces us to the congressional discussions that took place regarding the change, the number of Hispanos affected, and the fact that these Hispanos had no say in the matter.

I grew up right on the New Mexico–Colorado border, in the San Luis Valley, on a ranch established by my ancestors in Los Rincones in Conejos County. There my family had made a living as farmers and ranchers for over 150 years. As a young boy and throughout my life, I admired the Sangre de Cristo and San Juan mountain ranges. I cherished our rivers with the names of Río Grande, Conejos, and San Antonio. And beyond the landscapes,

DOI: 10.5876/9781607329145.c000a

I celebrated the culture and language that had been part of my family for over 400 years—since the founding of the city of Santa Fe. Yet I was puzzled as to why the border between Colorado and New Mexico existed.

In schools in the Valley, no one ever taught the history of the northward migration of New Mexicans into southern Colorado. Nor were we taught about the history and struggles for recognition of the former Mexican citizens after the Mexican-American War in 1848 as they became citizens of the United States. Virginia's book, for the first time, factually describes the conflicts and struggles of our ancestors as territorial Colorado became the state of Colorado.

Historians have written that Lafayette Head led the first settlers into southern Colorado. Today we know this is not correct. And from territorial governor William Gilpin's first meeting with Lafayette Head, historians have written that Head was well regarded by the Hispanos. Virginia's research tells us a strikingly different story, and the early petitions she discusses tell us that was not the case.

Until Virginia's book, no other author has explained the early territorial law from the Hispanos' point of view and how unjust laws affected the Mexican American population of the area. Her story tells us that they wanted to be returned to New Mexico; however, Congress and the territorial executives would not hear their pleas.

Nativist intolerance occurred in Colorado and occurs today. Virginia's discussion of the first legislative discussion of English-only is important because Hispanos have been citizens of the United States since 1848. This precedes the entry of many other immigrants.

During my time as Colorado attorney general, US senator, and secretary of the interior, I found great strength and purpose from my heritage. As secretary of the interior, I was custodian of America's natural resources and cultural heritage and recognized that much of the history of our nation, especially regarding women and minorities, has simply not been told. In all my time in public life, I worked to celebrate diversity and an inclusive America. In my view, every person's history is equally important, no matter what that person's background might be. Everybody is entitled to know and celebrate his or her history and heritage.

Because of the importance of celebrating an inclusive America, as US senator I championed the creation of the Sangre de Cristo National Heritage

Area because it helped tell the story of the San Luis Valley and northern New Mexico. That history includes our Native American heritage, the 250 years before the signing of the Treaty of Guadalupe Hidalgo, when our ancestors were citizens of Spain and Mexico, and the history after the Mexican-American War. The story of the Sangre de Cristo National Heritage Area will now be more fully told because of Virginia Sánchez's contributions to the history of Colorado in *Pleas and Petitions: Hispano Culture and Legislative Conflict in Territorial Colorado*.

Acknowledgments

The Honorable Richard Thomas Castro had researched the histories of some Hispanos who served in Colorado's territorial and state assemblies. He had hoped to compile the histories of all Colorado Hispano/a legislators into a published book. Sadly, he died before completing his work. However, he sparked a public interest in the history of Hispanic Colorado and the role these legislators played in shaping Colorado's future. To help fulfill a part of his dream, I combined my research of early Colorado to present this book about the Hispano assemblymen of the Colorado territorial legislature, the *dons* (gentlemen) of southern Colorado. This book would not have happened without Castro's vision.

I was unable to locate records for each of the Hispano territorial legislators. In most cases where I did find information, I have included information about their children in order to show family connections to other political families. Legislative-session photos did not begin until 1880; therefore, there are no early photos for some assemblymen. In some cases, the photos are of a later date, but due to their historical value, I include them here. I am extremely thankful to Jerome de Herrera, Antonio Gallegos, Francisco Gallegos, Connie Rodriguez, Claire Ortiz Hill, and Charlene Simms for sharing their family stories, photos, and information. A thorough research of genealogical, historical, church, and civil records helped verify details and provide corrections and new information. All errors are my own.

Primary sources for this book include records from the National Archives and Records Administration; specifically, the records in the District of Columbia and Maryland centers. These records include the US Department of the Interior Territorial Papers (Record Group 48), the Department of State General Records Files (Record Group 59), the Records of the Office of Territories (Record Group 126), and the Territorial Letters Received (Record Group 217). Additional sources came from the Center for Southwest Research at the University of New Mexico (Albuquerque), Stephen H. Hart Library of the History Colorado Center (Denver), New Mexico State Records Center and Archives (Santa Fe), Colorado Archives (Denver), Western History and Genealogy Department of the Denver Public Library, as well as church and civil records in New Mexico and Colorado. Unfortunately, key historical information about Conejos County no longer exists due to a 1980 fire that destroyed the courthouse and its precious records. Huerfano County's early records ended up in an unprotected shelter. Sadly, after their whereabouts were discovered, many had to be destroyed due to mold and extreme water damage. Additionally, no Spanish-language newspapers for this time have survived to present a Hispano view of early Colorado.

During my research, I also accessed information via various Internet websites. Enacted session laws and the House and Council journals for Colorado Territory are available from the William A. Wise Law Library of the University of Colorado Boulder. I used Ancestry.com for information on territorial tax assessments and censuses and FamilySearch.com for microfilmed church records. I located US congressional bills and resolutions through the THOMAS website of the US Library of Congress. I researched information about certain US congressional-chamber debates through the *Congressional Record* website. English-language newspapers that I accessed were available on the Colorado Historic Newspaper Collection website. I cite all paraphrased articles but do not directly quote them in the endnotes. The Colorado Legislator Biographies website provided such information about each assemblyman as date of birth, spouse, committees, and political party.

I am grateful to Molly Otto and Gay Roesch of the Colorado Legislative Library for their efforts on behalf of the website and for their helpfulness.

I am extremely grateful to the following people for sharing their expertise, knowledge, and friendship: Rosemary Evetts of the Auraria Campus Library; Virginia Castro; Robert J. Tórrez; Rodney Ross of the National Archives and Records Administration (NARA) for Legislative Archives, Washington, DC; the staff of the Office of the Historian of the US House of Representatives, NARA, Washington, DC; the staff of the Center for Legislative Archives, NARA, Washington, DC; the staff at the branches for Textual Records and Microfilm, NARA II, College Park, MD; Maggie Coval of Colorado Humanities; Senior Archivist Emily R. Brock, Melissa Salazar, and the staff of the Archives and Historical Services, New Mexico State Records Center and Archives, Santa Fe; Adrienne Leigh Sharpe of the Beinecke Rare Book and Manuscript Library at Yale University; Ann Massman of the Center for Southwest Research at the University of New Mexico; Cecily Nicewicz of the Colorado Supreme Court Library; Keith Schrum and the staff of the Stephen H. Hart Library of the History Colorado Center; the staff of the Colorado Springs Pioneers Museum; and the staff of the Nielsen Library at Adams University in Alamosa, CO; and Coi Drummond-Gehrig and James Jeffrey of the Denver Public Library's Western History and Genealogy Department. Coi helped with many of the images in this book, and James piqued my curiosity about a letter requesting the removal of Indian Agent Lafayette Head.

I am thankful to authors Marianne Stoller, Thomas J. Steele, and others for their work in providing an important transcription of the original *Diary of the Jesuit Residence of Our Lady of Guadalupe Parish, Conejos, Colorado, December 1871–December 1875*. I am also very thankful to authors Jerry Thompson, Malcolm Ebright, Charles F. Price, David L. Erickson, and Jami L. Vigil. Jerry sent me a working copy of his manuscript for *A Civil War History of the New Mexico Volunteers and Militia*. Charles furnished me with his book *Season of Terror: The Espinosas in Central Colorado, March–October 1863*, plus three reels of microfilm of the archive Letters Received by the Military Department of New Mexico. David shared some of his research for his book *Early Justice and the Formation of the Colorado Bar*. Jami sent me a copy of her article "Language Restrictionism Revisited: The Case against Colorado's 2000 Anti-Bilingual Education Initiative," coauthored with René Galindo and published in the *Harvard Latino Review*. You guys rock!

A special note of thanks goes to María Clara Martínez, an author, genealogist, and editor of the newspaper *La Sierra* in Costilla County; the Library of the Colorado Society of Hispanic Genealogy; and Maggie Coval of Colorado Humanities and its Huerfano County Oral History Project. A sincere thank-you goes to Lorenzo Trujillo for recommending articles about language restrictionism and nativity and to Deborah Quintana for sharing information about the Trujillo Homestead. I especially want to recognize Rick Martinez, formerly of the Fort Garland Museum, for his helpful comments regarding Fort Garland and the Espinosas of Conejos; may you rest in peace. A special note of thanks goes to Mario Medina, who located a newspaper endorsement, published in Spanish, of candidates running for territorial offices in 1864. I am very thankful to Phillip Gonzales for helping me decipher information about the Colorado annexation petitions submitted to the US Congress. I also want to thank the press's editor, who helped me make this a better history book. I am heartfully grateful to my husband, former Colorado state representative Tony Hernandez, and our son Eric for their love and support. I thank my parents for sharing their pride in our southwest history and Spanish language and culture. *Mil gracias a todos*.

PLEAS *and* PETITIONS

Introduction

On February 28, 1861, the US Congress approved the act establishing the territory of Colorado; the following month, on March 22, it annexed a rectangular portion of land from the territories of New Mexico, Kansas, Nebraska, and Utah for the new territory. Congress had designated specific meridians of longitude and parallels of latitude, just so the territory would appear as a rectangle on a map.[1] By this action, it automatically placed 7,000 *nuevomexicanos* in a new territory. The history of their annexation to the new territory is told here. It is a story that many southern Colorado natives do not know and one they certainly did not learn in school. By examining legislative records and the biographies of Hispano assemblymen, I provide a historical account of how politics, policies, and laws affected Hispano regional life in territorial southern Colorado.

This book is a brief introduction to territorial law and jurisprudence in Colorado Territory. It addresses ethnic history, political issues, cultural conflict, and institutional racism experienced in the region by Hispano assemblymen and their constituents. It also discusses how certain territorial legislation

DOI: 10.5876/9781607329145.c000b

affected the regional life of the Hispano settlers already living in the area that became Colorado. I begin, in chapter 1, by discussing a chronology of settlement in Colorado and explaining how the northern part of New Mexico Territory became the southern part of Colorado Territory, which is key to understanding why southern Colorado is deeply embedded in Hispano norms, culture, religion, language, and tradition.

As discussed in chapter 1, miners began to swarm the area and worked to establish the Territory of Jefferson. Although the US Congress paid no attention to their new territory's name, it did hear the need for a new congressionally formed square territory. As discuss in this chapter, Congress failed to consider the dire consequences of placing 7,000 nuevomexicanos in Anglo-dominated Colorado Territory.

The cultural conflict between the Hispanos and the Anglo majority is further illustrated in the loss and acquisition of land. I briefly introduce several Mexican land grants in present-day Colorado that are of historical significance in order to provide a frame of reference and to document a history for land issues as well as a history of the areas in which the settlers lived. The congressional confirmation process worked for those lands that were granted to individuals such as Charles Beaubien, but not for the Hispano grantees of the Conejos Land Grant.

I introduce Wilbur Fisk Stone as an early Anglo newspaper correspondent who wrote biased opinions of the Hispanos in southern Colorado but yet became a justice on the Court of Private Land Claims, which denied Hispano settlers confirmation of the Conejos grant. Also in this chapter, I explain why the US Congress placed a part of northern New Mexico Territory into the newly established Territory of Colorado. The New Mexico Territorial Assembly had not requested, petitioned, or approved any annexation of its people or its land. More important, the nuevomexicanos and their land were annexed without their desire or consultation; thus, they had no opportunity to discuss, amend, propose, or protest the actions of Congress. Their liberties had been disregarded by a republic that was supposed to represent and uphold their rights. As stated by New Mexico delegate José Francisco Perea, "a great wrong" had been done "to a large population." Because the histories of the Conejos and Sangre de Cristo grants are unique yet similar, I chose to separate them into their own sections within chapter 1. Here I provide an introduction to the different types of grants and their locations in different parts of the San Luis Valley. The nuevomexicanos in Colorado were often separated from their families in northern New Mexico. Ecclesiastical records show that many of them wished to be returned, with their land, to New Mexico. Many families traveled between territories to be with relatives, to help them celebrate family additions, or to comfort them in their sorrow. Many families chose to marry and have their children baptized into the Catholic faith on the New Mexico side in Ojo Caliente, Arroyo Hondo, Taos, or, on the eastern side of the Sangre de Cristo Mountains, Mora. Relatives from New Mexico came into Colorado to assist in harvests or pasture their herds. They were supported by the labor of each family member. The Hispanos were tied to the land and across territorial borders by kinship and economy. This unity continues today.[2]

The new laws and social order that were brought to southern Colorado further impacted Hispano life. As explained in chapter 2, the federal and territorial governments made no provisions for translating and printing the territorial laws passed by the legislature. The federal and territorial governments also made no provisions for interpreters, so Hispano assemblymen could not effectively take part in the legislative process; in effect, their Hispano constituents were forced to accept taxation without representation.

Additionally, none of the Colorado executives met with their counterparts in New Mexico or California to discuss and determine how to meet the needs of its Spanish-speaking citizens. Passing laws through a legislative body with representation from all citizens was and still is essential in any democratic society. Anglos in the US Congress and territorial legislature created obstacles to the political participation of the Spanish-speaking assemblymen by failing to provide them with a Spanish translation of the enacted laws. Because the territorial government refused to provide the Spanish-speaking representatives with a translation of the House journals and the enacted laws, the Hispano citizens had no actual representation when the laws were being made. All legislative discussion and deliberations were entirely in English.

Despite requests by the Hispano representatives, the laws of Colorado Territory were published only in English. Colorado had no money in its treasury, and Congress refused to appropriate any funds because it considered the Hispanos alien and noncitizens. The Hispano assemblymen were unable to participate in any discussion or deliberations because of language issues. The Spanish-speaking assemblymen were denied any real voice in territorial legislation. And when they requested translated copies of legislative documents, policy, or laws, they ran into funding obstacles on the federal and territorial levels. Without knowing the rules, the Hispano assemblymen could not participate in the legislative game. As they had limited or no English-language abilities, they were forced to work through unqualified and inexperienced interpreters who were unfamiliar with the issues and needs of Hispano southern Colorado.

Legislative actions by the Anglo and Republican-led assemblymen worked to keep members of their majority party in political and economic control. By refusing to approve payment for translating the all-important rules of a chamber, territorial treasurer Samuel Hitt Elbert denied the Spanish-speaking assemblymen access to understanding the internal legislative process. By keeping the rules from them, the territory kept them from participating in the legislative process. A single translated copy could have been shared among the Hispano representatives serving in current and future sessions, but, to Elbert, they were not real citizens. From the very beginning, the Spanish-speaking settlers of southern Colorado were not kept informed as to the character of laws under which they were expected to live; they understood neither the new statutes nor "the rights conferred or obligations the new laws imposed," and they were excluded from every part of the legislative process. These Hispanos had only recently been annexed from New Mexico Territory, and despite their pleas to be restored to New Mexico along with their land, wealthy Anglos secured legislative and congressional support to keep them in Colorado.

In chapter 3 I highlight the struggles experienced by Hispano territorial assemblymen while they tried to create opportunities and better lives for themselves and their constituents in the face of cultural conflict. The people I discuss are generally unique to each grant. I also discuss certain laws that affected *comunidád*. Those who could not pay taxes, even because of an inability to afford them, were seen not just as delinquent but as un-American. The impact the territorial real estate law had on the Sangre de Cristo settlers is also discussed in this chapter.

During this time, the Indian Wars and the US Civil War were being fought simultaneously. A discussion of militiamen and soldiers appears in chapter 4. A military census had been ordered by the New Mexico Military Department to determine the number of Hispanos in southern Colorado who could serve in the Union Army and to record the stores and livestock they owned should the army need them. The Civil War began a month and a half after the US Congress established the Territory of Colorado. Governor William Gilpin quickly learned that many miners in his new territory had emigrated from the southern states and were Confederate sympathizers. He feared that Confederate forces from Texas would make their way north to Colorado for its gold, so companies of soldiers were routinely posted at Fort Garland, a US Army post in Costilla County in southern Colorado. There they were given their marching orders against the Confederates.[3] Soldiers and other new settlers arrived from the East, bringing with them preconceived notions about the American Southwest and its peoples and cultures.

In chapter 5, I provide information about the Conejos Indian Agency, its agent Lafayette Head, and the various hearings held to remove Head from office. Here I also introduce the important Ute Treaty that was being discussed in Conejos the same time many other events discussed in this book occurred. I think you see find that the early Colorado territorial period was definitely a frontier-wild time.

I review, from a Hispano perspective, the collective violence that occurred in southern Colorado in chapter 6. Hispano boys and adult males were lynched after verdicts passed down by all-Anglo miners' courts. The Espinosa brothers, Felipe and Vivián of Conejos County, were hunted down and killed in 1863 without trial or legal process. Although derived from a biased perspective, stories about their escapades have been published in books, aired on television programs about western desperados, and posted on the website Legends of America. These stories tell the same sensationalized version of the alleged murders. Briefly, Felipe de Nerio Espinosa, his brother José Vivián Espinosa, and a supposed nephew named Vicente Espinosa allegedly committed a series of murders throughout southern Colorado. Although I do not focus here on the crimes the Espinosas were popularly charged with, a review of prior research—combined with military records and oral histories I discovered—provides an alternative explanation about where and when the murders occurred and why the Espinosas were violently hunted down and killed. Although I do not present a smoking gun, I review a Hispano perspective about the collective violence that was directed against certain Hispano settlers in southern Colorado.

Throughout the territorial period, Hispano legislators faced numerous hurdles to effecting legislative change on behalf of their Spanish-speaking constituents, as I discuss in chapter 7. Powerful Anglo legislators living in the northern half of the territory helped enact a series of laws and taxes that affected the Hispano citizens living in the southern half of Colorado Territory. The Hispano way of life was so impacted by the new order that the Hispanos living in Conejos and Costilla Counties soon submitted petitions to both territorial and national legislators asking to be reannexed to New Mexico Territory. Anglo authors of Colorado's territorial history have erroneously attributed taxation and peonage as the main issues of Hispano discontent during this period. Then, following the Homestead Act of 1863, men with money filed false claims to obtain more land.

In chapter 8, I address institutional racism used as a weapon and tool by certain Anglos to suppress the use of the Spanish language. The elected Hispano assemblymen had a difficult time protecting, supporting, representing, and advocating for their Spanish-speaking constituents against the impact of prejudice and discriminatory laws and policies of Anglo assemblymen in the majority party. This is not an in-depth study of territorial law, nor does it expound on every piece of legislation; however, the select laws discussed in chapter 8 exemplify the basic sociological issues regarding Hispanos' interactions with their new Anglo neighbors, who spoke a different language, had a different religion, and lived by different customs. The examples, in chapter 8, of certain legislative discussions held in the Territorial House and Territorial Council (Senate) chambers reveal the prejudicial language some assemblymen used to promote bias, impose assimilation, and maintain power and control over the Hispanos and indigenous nations in Colorado Territory. (The Hispanos in southern Colorado far outnumbered immigrant Chinese laborers and African Americans; thus, those other minority groups are not discussed here.)

In chapter 9, I introduce the statehood initiatives and explain how the Hispano vote challenged the power in the northern part of the state. When Hispanos tried to return to New Mexico, Congress failed to hear their pleas or address their petitions. Yet without them, Colorado would not have a large enough population to seek statehood.

I conclude this book with a discussion of the use of language, attempts to restrict its usage, and what nativism and nationalism really mean to minorities. Water law is probably the most important law passed in Colorado

Territory. It is also an important law that other territories and western states have implemented. For this reason, I chose to discuss it in the conclusion. I also present the question, Was a square territory (and state) really necessary? After you have read about the immense impact the Territory of Colorado had on the Hispano settlers, consider the fact that the congressional leaders would not listen to facts and to the people. Hopefully, we all can learn from the settlers' point of view.

This book adds to the growing list of Hispanos who have in some way influenced the course of Colorado's history. The biographies presented in appendix A introduce historical members of Colorado's colorful legislative past. They acknowledge the struggles and efforts of notable Hispano assemblymen who represented southern Colorado during the territorial period as well as the vital roles their family members played to help create Colorado and its cultural diversity. I identify and refer to the assemblymen by their names as recorded on ecclesiastical records. Church and civil records used various spellings of some names; I use those that occur most consistently in these records. To help sort through the various events, readers may want to refer to the timeline in appendix B.

Readers should note that throughout the book the county name appears in parenthesis after the first instance of an assemblyman's name to indicate the county (or counties) he represented. As women's suffrage was not granted in Colorado until after statehood, all voters and elected officials during this period were male. In *Política: Nuevomexicanos and American Political Incorporation, 1821–1910*, Phillip B. Gonzales found one account in 1858 when Gertrudis Mora, a Hispana living in Taos County, served on a county nominations committee. Gonzales wrote, "Nationally women were excluded from the electorate but had begun to utilize such instruments as the petition to voice their political opinions and social concerns."[4] Because there are very few historical records about Hispanas for this period, the only females addressed here are daughters or wives of the Hispano assemblymen.

I use the term "Anglo" rather than "whites" or "European Americans" to refer to people of British descent and native English speakers from the eastern part of the United States. I use the term *nuevomexicanos* to denote Hispanos as those who were born in New Mexico under the Mexican (or even Spanish) and US regimes and/or who became Colorado citizens when Congress established the southern border of the territory in 1861. I use this term because, even though they lived in Colorado, their sentiments still turned to New Mexico. I include the territory and state of California in the discussion of legislative policies. When I mention California during this period, I refer to Alta California and I denote its Hispano peoples as *californios* to distinguish them from nuevomexicanos in the two areas of the northern Mexican frontier. I do not include a discussion of Texas statutes as Tejas was a part of Nueva Viscaya and had become a state of the Union by 1845.

I also interchangeably use the term "Hispanos" to refer to the Spanish-speaking settlers of southern Colorado and northern New Mexico. I use this term over the more familiar "Mexican American," "Spanish American," or "Chicano," as these terms were not used during the territorial periods of either New Mexico or Colorado. Although many cited historical documents use the term "Mexican," its purpose was to separate the nationalities and typically implied a questionable patriotism or loyalty to the United States. This "we" versus "them" mentality ultimately led to a lower-level class of US citizenship. Historian Frances Leon Quintana explained it very well when she wrote, "Through military service starting in the Civil War [Hispanos] were well aware of their American citizenship and had ceased to think of themselves as Mexicans in terms of national affiliation."[5] The Honorable Celestino Domínguez, whom I introduce as one of the few Hispanos who served in the Territorial Council (Senate), was born, raised, and educated in Spain. He fully affiliated with, supported, and represented his Hispano constituents; therefore, for the sake of consistency here, he is a Hispano.

Regarding the use of diacritics, accents in Spanish geographic names appear only if the discussion or event occurred before 1848. Spanish terms appear in italics when the term is first introduced. Diacritics are used in all Spanish terms and names.

Readers cannot expect to understand southern Colorado without knowing the history of New Mexico, as the cultural and historical roots of the two territories were so interwoven. These were frontier communities. What impacted New Mexico impacted the Hispanos of southern Colorado. Some Hispano and Anglo assemblymen had *peones* (laborers) and indigenous slaves working and living in their households; however, peonage and slavery arose as contentious issues as a result of the US Civil War and not a result of Colorado's territorial legislation. For this reason, I do not discuss this issue in great detail here.[6]

Through the years my research has led me to a substantial amount of historical information that needed to be told from a Hispano/a perspective. Much of the history of southern Colorado Territory has been written by Anglos who, unfortunately, did not deeply consider the cultural and racial motivations of military and government officials that greatly impacted the lives of the Hispano settlers and their descendants. The more I learned about these motivations and Colorado's early public policies, and about the subsequent social injustices and the skewed advantages in the legislative process, the more determined I became to relate this history from a Hispano/a viewpoint.

Notes

1. Keleher, *Turmoil in New Mexico*, 127. For a detailed discussion of why western states have geometric boundaries or artificial lines rather than natural divisions such as rivers or mountains, refer to Everett, *Creating the American West*: 171–72, 174, 184.

2. Deutsch, *No Separate Refuge*, 9.

3. Fort Garland, established in 1858, was under the jurisdiction of the Military Department of New Mexico until 1862.

4. Gonzales, *Política*, 330–31.

5. Quintana, *Pobladores*, 226.

6. Paxson, "Territory of Colorado," 62. Technically, Colorado is not a rectangle but an isosceles trapezoid. Colorado's north and south borders (along lines of latitude) are parallel and of equal length, but because its east and west borders are defined by lines of longitude, which are not parallel but converge toward the poles, its north border is slightly shorter than its south border.

I

Competing Claims on the Land

Spanish explorers were the first Europeans to enter the southern portion of what is now the state of Colorado. They found the land already occupied by indigenous peoples, including Utes, Apaches, and Comanches. Colorado at that time was part of New Mexico, a province on the far northern frontier of New Spain. With the Louisiana Purchase, acquired from France in 1803, the territorial claims of the United States overlapped with Spanish New Mexico in the region of the Arkansas River drainage, including southeastern Colorado. Those competing claims were settled by treaty in 1819.

On its independence from Spain in 1821, the new republic of Mexico also ratified the 1819 treaty with the United States. However, in the 1830s Texas declared and asserted its own independence from Mexico and was annexed as a new state by the United States in 1845. Due to encroachment, Spanish and later Mexican military expeditions, with orders from Santa Fe, also traveled north from Taos in search of the French and English. Early settlement into the same area occurred by French and North American fur trappers and later by miners seeking precious ores, mainly gold or silver, in the Rocky Mountains.

DOI: 10.5876/9781607329145.c001

On this frontier different cultures relied on warfare, raids, and retaliation to redeem property (stolen sheep, cattle, horses, and even family members). Many Hispano settlers who had migrated farther north maintained close relations with the Utes, and languages and culture were shared. Honest and fair trade enabled permanent settlement. With peace came settlement, and Mexican citizens petitioned for land from the Mexican government. Two land grants are briefly discussed in this chapter: the Guadalupe, later known as the Conejos, and the Sangre de Cristo. The history of these grants is sad to relate as it does not end well for the Hispano settlers.

Charles Beaubien, a Mexican citizen of French Canadian descent, acquired 100,000 acres of free land from the Mexican government in exchange for his loyalty and defense of the country from encroaching Americans. He became a traitor to his government in 1846 when he assisted US Army major Stephen W. Kearny in establishing an American system of laws in New Mexico.

The war between the United States and Mexico followed in 1846 with disastrous results for Mexico. Additionally, the Mexican government could not arrest Beaubien as he was on US soil and now a US citizen. In addition to the challenges of frontier life, the Hispanos were now introduced to a new culture and new legal system. Mexican land grants would emerge as a locus of confusion and cultural conflict, to say nothing of outright fraud, under American frontier governance.

In 1860 the US Congress confirmed Beaubien's title to land on the Sangre de Cristo grant. Meanwhile, the Guadalupe grantees would have a much more difficult time proving to the surveyor general that they had in fact tried several times to settle Los Conejos after being forced to return to New Mexico due to incursions by indigenous bands.

In accordance with the 1848 Treaty of Guadalupe Hidalgo, Mexico ceded to the Americans about half of its former territory—including Mexican California and Nuevo México, and thus southern and western parts of modern Colorado. The combination of the rush of miners to Colorado and the distance of territorial government led miners to found the extralegal Territory of Jefferson, with its own assembly, laws, and taxes. Anglo miners ravaged mountains, rivers, and forests and overran Ute lands to find gold. Their sudden intrusion and their itinerant and destructive search for new digs contrasted with the commitment to the land characteristic of the long-established nuevomexicano *pobladores* (farmers). Population in the region grew substantially enough that, by an "organic act" of 1861, Congress organized the Territory of Colorado as a strategic step toward eventual statehood. When Congress drew Colorado on the map as a right-angled quadrilateral, its southeast corner was squared off by incorporating a "notch" of land in northern New Mexico. That adjustment of the border—such that a strip of land in the northeast corner of New Mexico Territory was transferred to Colorado—did not simply make a neatly squared shape of the newly created territory. It involved significant cultural dislocations and adjustments for those residents, the Hispanos, who historically were colonists of New Spain and then citizens of Mexico before becoming citizens of the United States by terms of the 1848 treaty. Family and friends and familiar cultural patterns—of laws, taxes, language, religion, land tenure, community affairs—were now split along an arbitrary boundary line.

The north-south separation was not necessarily defined in terms of physical inaccessibility, but the Hispanos in southern Colorado, without having moved themselves, were now subjected to an unfamiliar, intimidating, and sometimes hostile social order. The new territory brought with it a flood of Anglo settlers and officials into Colorado, along with new sets of laws and customs that redefined Hispano life on the northern side of the Colorado–New Mexico border. This chapter outlines those competing claims to the land that became the Territory (and ultimately the State) of Colorado.

Spanish Exploration and Colonization

As early as 1642, Spanish explorers recorded the Royal Gorge near present-day Cañon City, Colorado. During their exploration they named the rivers they crossed, including the Napeste,[1] Rojo, San Lorenzo, Jesús María, Chato, and Las Ánimas del Purgatorio. In 1776 Francisco Domínguez and Silvestre Escalante explored an overland route to the California missions with cartographer Bernardo de Miera y Pacheco. Captain Pacheco also participated in the expedition into southwestern Colorado and mapped the Four Corners region where present-day New Mexico, Colorado, Utah, and Arizona meet. He documented and described the fertile valleys and available water near what became Carracas (near Pagosa Springs) on the San Juan River.[2]

Three years later, in 1779, Juan Bautista de Anza traveled into the far northern frontier of the Spanish borderland with Ute and Apache allies and about

FIGURE 1.1. Miera y Pacheco's map of the San Luis Valley, 1779 (AGI, Torres Lanzas, México, 577). Archivo General de Indias, Sevilla, Spain. Reproduced in Kessell, *Kiva, Cross, and Crown*. https://www.nps.gov /parkhistory/online_books/kcc/contents.htm.

800 soldiers (figure 1.1). In search of the Comanche, this retaliatory expedition marched through what today is known as the San Luis Valley toward La Agua Gerbidora (Manitou Springs). According to his records, they moved north from Taos along the western ridge of the Sangre de Cristo Mountains to the South Platte River. Then they turned east toward the east side of Pikes Peak and returned home traveling along the Front Range. The map created by Captain Pacheco includes the names the Spanish attached to the land formations they encountered.

Spanish settlement increased and expanded in all directions, as did exploration by the French and English. Due to the foreign encroachment, in 1818 Second Lieutenant José de Arce of the Spanish presidio in Santa Fe traveled north from Taos with orders to form an expedition to protect land located in the far northern frontier of New Mexico. The following day at Taos, de Arce's expedition included 120 settlers and indigenous auxiliaries.[3] At 6:00 p.m. on September 3, de Arce and his men stopped on the Río de la Culebra (Culebra [Snake] River), a tributary of the Rio Grande named for the snake-like pattern in which it flowed.[4] The next day the expedition reached the Sierra de los Yutas (Ute Mountains), then crossed the Sierra de Sangre de Cristo (Sangre de Cristo [Blood of Christ] Mountains). The Sangre de Cristo Mountains were named by the Spaniards for the reddish color at sunset evocative of the blood of Christ. Then the expedition camped along the Río Huérfano (Huerfano [Orphan] River), near its namesake, Huerfano Butte.

On September 12, de Arce ordered twenty-five horsemen under the command of Taos settler José Antonio Martínez to reconnoiter at Sierra Blanca (Mount Blanca, north of present-day San Luis). From there they would reconnoiter at the Río Napeste (Arkansas River). By September 15 his command included 429 horsemen and 117 infantrymen from the Taos and Santa Cruz de la Cañada settlements and pueblos. Five days later it traveled south and camped along the Río de las Ánimas (Purgatoire River). Finding no foreign intruders, the expedition began its return trip toward Santa Fe.[5]

The following year, in 1819, the United States and Spain clarified the border at the Arkansas River by virtue of the Adams-Oñis Treaty. At the time, the western boundary of New Mexico extended to California and included the present areas of Arizona, much of Nevada north into southern Utah, and part of southeastern Colorado.

Colonization of the Conejos

In 1821, after Mexico gained its independence from Spain, the northern boundary of New Mexico stretched north into the southern part of present-day Utah and southern Colorado. Mexico then opened its northern borders to outside trade between Santa Fe and the United States along what became the Santa Fe Trail. The Mountain Branch of this trail entered southern Colorado near Bent's Fort, northeast of present-day La Junta (The Junction). (Bent's Fort was a trading post established by fur traders Charles Bent, William Bent, and Ceran St. Vrain. It was in existence from 1833 to 1849.) Between 1866 and 1876, goods continued to arrive via the trail into Pueblo along the Arkansas River, then north to Colorado Springs and Denver. Goods transported into Trinidad (Trinity) were transferred west into the San Juan Mountains.

The Mexican government issued several land grants along the rivers encountered by Lieutenant de Arce's campaign. The first attempted settlement in southern Colorado during the early 1830s began at the settlement named San Francisco. On behalf of the interested settlers, in 1833 José Seledonio Valdez and other Hispanos petitioned the Mexican governor to colonize land along the Conejos River.[6] Theirs would be a community grant called the Guadalupe Land Grant, later the Conejos Land Grant. They were issued the grant and received a title document. By law the grantees, as settlers, had five years to make improvements upon any lands granted; they had to prove they worked the land and obtained subsistence from it, lest the grant become null and void.[7] Unfortunately, due to continuous raids by the Apache, Navajo, Comanche, Ute, and Kiowa Nations, the settlers were forced to abandon the area.

Hispano frontiersmen and French Canadians continued to venture into Mexico's northern frontier to trap beaver and establish trade with the various indigenous nations. To protect its far-northern border from continued foreign invasion, during the 1830s and 1840s the Mexican government encouraged settlement of the frontier and considered citizens' petitions for land. In time, Hispano settlers migrated into Ute lands at Los Conejos (The Rabbits) and into the northern district along the Culebra and Costilla (Rib) Rivers. Their pattern of settlement promoted equality, for land was apportioned according to the size of the family and its ability to utilize the arable land, pasture, and wasteland.[8] They named the Conejos area for the rabbits they encountered or because the river's lively waters resembled quick-running rabbits, and the Costilla area for the nearby rib-like mountain range.

José Seledonio Valdez and three other Hispanos from the Taos area sought a revalidation of their shares in the Guadalupe grant. Rather than submitting their request to the New Mexico governor, they petitioned a revalidation of the Guadalupe land document with the Taos prefect, Juan Andrés Archuleta. Because some of the original grantees had died at Conejos in skirmishes with indigenous bands of Utes and Arapahoes and others had died of natural causes, the grantees hoped the prefect would allow the addition of new families.[9]

On October 12, 1842, Andrés Archuleta approved the resettlement attempt of the Guadalupe grantees and ordered the district's justice of the peace to place the land in their possession (figure 1.2).[10] At Conejos, Justice Cornelio Vigil met the grantees to survey the boundaries and place them in legal possession. The land within the grant lay north to Garita Hill, east to the Rio Grande, south to the San Antonio Mountains, and west to the Sierra Montosa.[11] It covered the present-day counties of Conejos and Rio Grande and portions of Alamosa and Saguache Counties.[12] The judge then measured off lots between the San Antonio and La Jara Rivers. This action gave each family access to irrigatable land. Once again, after the Hispanos had settled in the area, indigenous raiders forced them to return south.[13] Governor Manuel Armijo led his troops on an expedition to the Arkansas River the following spring to view the situation for himself,[14] but no further attempt at settlement in Conejos took place for another four years.

Many Hispano settlers maintained close relations with the Utes, and languages and culture were shared through the medium of amicable trade. Atanacio Trujillo, for example, regularly ventured north from El Rito to Conejos to trap beaver and trade with the Utes.[15] Hunters and *comancheros* (unlicensed traders) who visited Ute lands frequently became fluent speakers of Ute, and many Utes, who had frequently served as auxiliaries during various Spanish, Mexican, and US campaigns against the Navajos, spoke Spanish. Trujillo requested the band's permission to settle the area. Through dialog and trade, the two cultures formed friendly relations, which resulted in the permanent settlement in Ute country by Hispanos.[16]

In 1846 the three original grantees sent a letter to interim governor Charles Bent, asking his permission to resettle the Conejos. Interestingly, Bent replied that he did not have a legal right to grant them possession. However, by "virtue of their former claim" he thought they should go and settle on the land if that is what they wished to do.[17] The grantees traveled north again, only

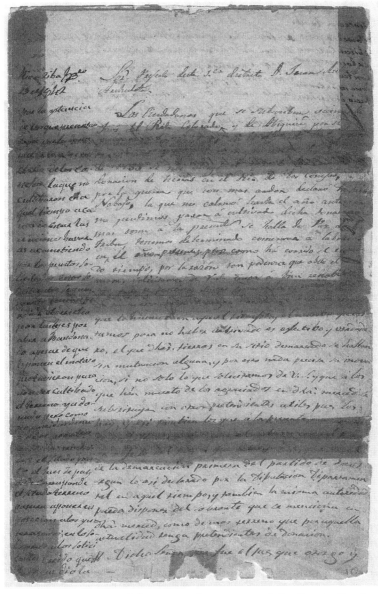

FIGURE 1.2. First page of the petition for a regrant of the Conejos Land Grant, October 12, 1842, addressed to the prefect of Taos, Don Juan Antonio Archuleta; his confirming reply is written in the left margin. Hart Library, History Colorado Center, Land Grant Collection 374, Conejos Grant—Transcripts, Correspondence, Manuscripts, Map, FF29:15.

to be driven back south by the hostiles. An attempt to resettle the Conejos would not occur for another eight years.

By 1848 the United State had acquired, as the negotiated spoils of its war with Mexico, a vast amount of land. By terms of the Treaty of Guadalupe Hidalgo, the United States acquired land in the Mexican northwest. Those residents who remained on seized land became US citizens. Here in the notch area of northern New Mexico, however, frontier culture and customs continued to thrive. Legal and illegal trade expeditions created economic opportunities for all the frontier cultures. At the frontier the different cultures (French, Spanish, Anglo, and indigenous) relied on warfare, raids, and retaliation to redeem property (stolen sheep, cattle, horses, and even family members). The cycle of raid-to-acquire and retaliate-to-redeem resulted in yet further raids by both indigenous and nonindigenous groups. In times of conflict, the indigenous peoples and the Hispanos "frequently destroyed life and property"; however, they "developed a system of mutual survival in the harsh environment."[18] This system resulted in the trade of hides, deer and bison meat, and captured women and children.

To discourage illicit trading, the US government relied on Indian agents to issue trade licenses to reputable applicants. From his agency at Abiquiú, New Mexico, agent Kit Carson issued licenses to several Hispano and Anglo males who had ties to southern Colorado.[19] To obtain a license, an applicant had to be a US citizen, produce testimonies of good character, provide one or more sureties, and post a bond of $500. By making his mark or signing the license, each man agreed to conform to and observe all government trade and communications laws and regulations with indigenous nations. Traders were forbidden to sell any liquor, guns, or ammunition. Any violation of these terms risked revocation of the license.[20]

On February 21, 1858, forty-four-year-old José Celedonio (Seledonio) Valdez paid a $500 bond for a three-month license to trade with the "Utahs within the limits of New Mexico" (figure 1.3).[21] Carlos Beaubien's name appeared on six known licenses between 1855 and 1858 authorizing trade with the "Muache Utahs" and other indigenous nations within the boundaries of New Mexico. He was not listed as *mayordomo* (leader of the expedition), but Beaubien presumably posted money for the bonds, likely in return for a share in the profits. These trading expeditions enabled Beaubien, or his men, to monitor the progress of the settlers living on his Sangre de Cristo Land Grant. In addition,

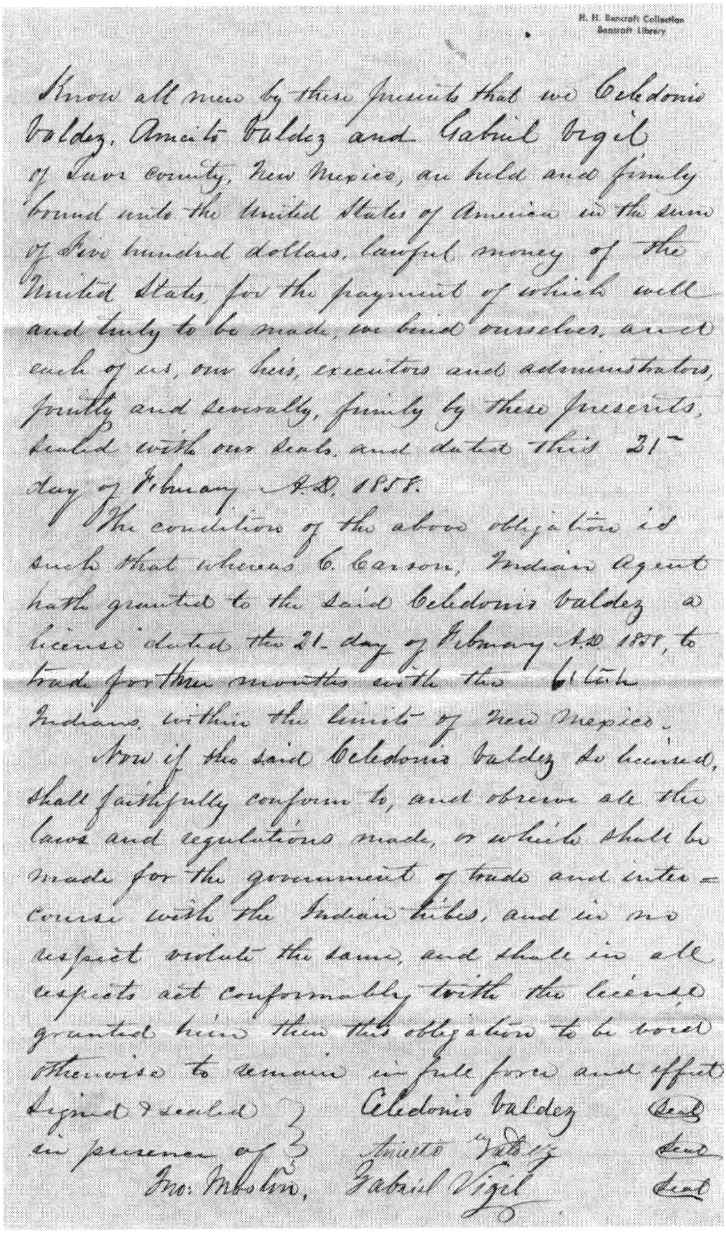

Know all men by these presents that we Celedonio Valdez, Ameto Valdez and Gabriel Vigil of Taos county, New Mexico, are held and firmly bound unto the United States of America in the sum of Five hundred dollars, lawful money of the United States, for the payment of which well and truly to be made, we bind ourselves, and each of us, our heirs, executors and administrators, jointly and severally, firmly by these presents, sealed with our seals, and dated this 21 day of February A.D. 1858.

The condition of the above obligation is such that whereas C. Carson, Indian Agent hath granted to the said Celedonio Valdez a license dated the 21 day of February A.D. 1858, to trade for three months with the Utah Indians, within the limits of New Mexico.

Now if the said Celedonio Valdez so licensed, shall faithfully conform to, and observe all the laws and regulations made, or which shall be made for the government of trade and intercourse with the Indian tribes, and in no respect violate the same, and shall in all respects act conformably with the license granted him then this obligation to be void otherwise to remain in full force and effect

Signed & sealed in presence of
Jno. Mostin,

Celedonio Valdez (Seal)
Ameto Valdez (Seal)
Gabriel Vigil (Seal)

FIGURE 1.3. Trade bond of Celedonio Valdez, February 21, 1858. Bonds of Traders, 1856–1860, Kit Carson Papers, Bancroft Library, University of California at Berkley, BANC MSS P-E 64, Box 3.

trade in captives likely supplied his settlers with much-needed laborers. This frontier custom would end, however, once the US military promoted the extermination of the bison and forcibly removed the remaining western indigenous nations onto reservations.

The settlers finally established permanent settlement on the Conejos in 1854. As more settlers entered the area, the Guadalupe Land Grant became known as the Conejos Land Grant, with farm settlements along the San Antonio, Los Pinos, and Conejos Rivers.[22] They constructed their homes and a makeshift Catholic church and laid out systems of *acequias* or *'cequias* (irrigation ditches). Between 1867 and 1875 there would be thirty-six acequias and their laterals using water from the tributaries of the Alamosa and La Jara Rivers.[23]

On July 22, 1854, the US Congress established three offices of surveyor general that took their instructions from the secretary of the interior. The office in New Mexico was located at Santa Fe. There William Pelham was responsible for ascertaining the "origin, character and extent of all claims to land under the laws, usages and customs of New Mexico."[24] Surveyors general were "authorized to issue notices, summon witnesses, administer oaths, etc., and to make full report to the Secretary of the Interior." The secretary then presented the information to Congress for final action or confirmation.

Because the Guadalupe settlers could not settle on the grant eight years ago due to incursions by indigenous bands, they needed to have their Guadalupe Land Grant revalidated. The settlers submitted a petition along with their copy of the title to the grant. At some point between this date and August, the original title went missing. To assist the settlers in obtaining congressional confirmation of their grant, Charles Beaubien gave written testimony to the New Mexico surveyor general on August 4, 1855, stating that he had accompanied and witnessed the initial customary act of endowing possession upon the Guadalupe grantees (figure 1.4).[25] As they impatiently waited for the surveyor general to make his decision, the settlers continued with their busy lives. Between 1855 and 1857 they hand-dug several acequias that they put to productive use.[26]

In approximately 1856, Father Gabriel Ussel of Taos offered the first Roman Catholic mass at the Guadalupe settlement in a small *jacal* (hut) constructed of upright cedar logs. Father Ussel described the settlement as a "baby town, small [with] few and modest houses."[27] The plaza was enclosed as a defensive circle with two *zaguanes* (entrances), one on the south end and the other on

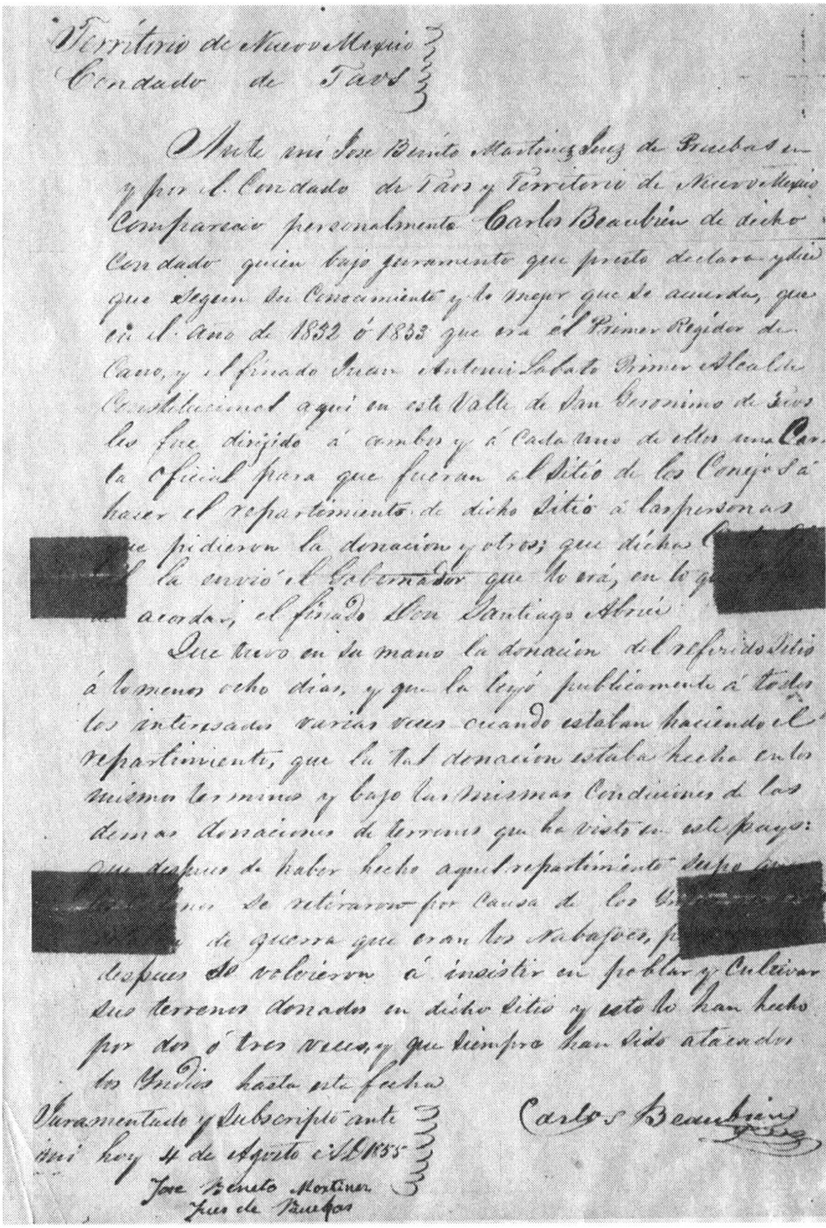

FIGURE 1.4. Affidavit of the Conejos claim sworn by Carlos (Charles) Beaubien, August 4, 1855. Land Grant Collection 374, Conejos Grant—Transcripts, Correspondence, Manuscripts, Map, Hart Library, History Colorado Center, FF29:2.

the north. To protect their livestock from raiders and wolves, the settlers herded the animals through these two entrances.[28]

Unfortunate news arrived in Conejos. Surveyor General William Pelham rejected the Conejos Land Grant on January 13, 1858. Because there was no official land grant title, he rejected the settlers' application for congressional confirmation. This disastrous news rendered the Conejos community grant land vulnerable to outside interests. To further complicate matters, Congress was in the process of creating the new Territory of Colorado. However, they would attempt to stay connected to the land in the same spirit of religion and comunidád. Again, Charles Beaubien gave written testimony about the grant on January 18, 1858 (figure 1.5).[29]

Thankfully, the Catholic parish was formed on June 10, 1858, with Father José Vicente Montaño as its first permanent pastor.[30] Likely they prayed to San Antonio (Saint Anthony), the patron saint of missing articles, and asked for his help in locating their copy of the land grant title. Father Montaño went on to found Colorado's second-oldest Catholic church at San Luis in 1860. This church, named for the Sangre de Cristo, became a parish with its own pastor in 1869.[31] At Conejos the following year, in 1861, the new priest, Father José Miguel Vigil, dedicated the still-unfinished church to Nuestra Señora de Guadalupe (Our Lady of Guadalupe). The church is named in honor of the Virgin Mary and the miracle she performed in 1531 in Mexico City.[32] It was the oldest Catholic parish in Colorado.[33] Unfortunately, an overflow of the Conejos River destroyed many structures, including the newly constructed church. Some settlers moved to the south side of the river, establishing there the settlement of Conejos.[34] Within three years, these two settlements would compete for an important place in local government.

On February 20, 1859, twelve settlers met under the leadership of Father Montaño to discuss the construction of the new parish church and to fix the annual price for services of a cantor and organist.[35] Parishioners donated labor and materials, and Jesús María Sanches managed the construction of the adobe church.[36] José Seledonio Valdez, Jesús María Velásquez, and Lafayette Head[37] collected "every available material" to make its first bell.[38] In addition to collecting various metals from the parishioners. Juan Francisco Luján and Pedro Antonio Lobato worked to cast a bell for the church.[39] Whether they included gold in the bell is not known. However, during this time Anglos were mining for gold in the area's mountains and working to create a federal territory.

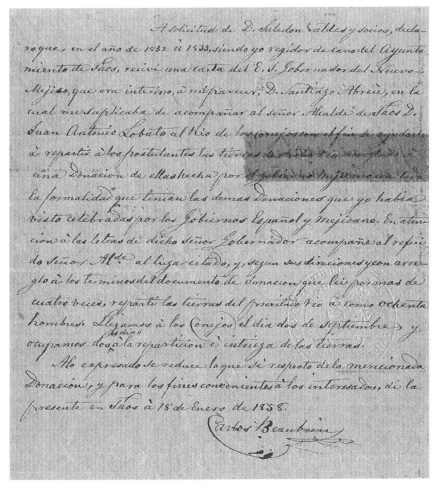

FIGURE 1.5. Affidavit of the Conejos claim sworn by Carlos (Charles) Beaubien, January 18, 1858. Land Grant Collection 374, Conejos Grant—Transcripts, Correspondence, Manuscripts, Map, Hart Library, History Colorado Center, FF29:3.

The medium-sized church bell rang out when calling settlers to mass, advising them of deaths in the community, or proclaiming a blessed event. It also sounded an alarm when the settlers' lives, crops, and livestock were in danger, as indigenous raiders remained a threat during this time. That year, for example, a band of Utes destroyed José Víctor García's crops and killed five cows. Three years later some Arapahoes killed thirteen of his cows.[40]

The legal battle to secure confirmation of the Conejos Land Grant continued well into Colorado's statehood period. In a deposition before the court,
José María Chávez commented on the settlers' reaction once they learned
that again the surveyor general of New Mexico had denied their application.

> About 400 American soldiers were called to put down a disturbance among
> the people. I presented myself to the commander [who] finally agreed . . . to
> reduce his force with the exception of one company; they killed several peo-
> ple at his very door. [One of the men killed was named Lopez.] They had a
> meeting and the people . . . said they would control themselves; the troops left
> that one company; they left as commander of that company a man who knew
> Spanish who had been in Albuquerque.[41]

By February 1861 the Hispano settlers and their land on the Conejos grant
was now in the English-speaking Territory of Colorado. For them, not much
had changed so far; they continued speaking Spanish and tending to their
crops and stock. But this peaceful pace would soon change. On July 3, 1861,
the Conejos grantees petitioned a third time for confirmation. Filing a claim
and seeing it through to confirmation by Congress was a long and expensive
process that was beyond the means of most Hispano settlers.[42] This time,
working through Santa Fe attorney Joab Houghton,[43] they attached a list of
the settlers' names and letters of support. Cornelio Vigil, whom the settlers
had known back in 1850s as the Taos justice of the peace; Charles Beaubien;
and Taos prefect Juan Andrés Archuleta were well aware of their resettlement efforts and submitted affidavits on their behalf.[44] In a cover letter to
the surveyor general, Houghton explained that although the original land
donation document was lost, they wished to present oral proof.[45] Meanwhile,
the settlers would have to continue their lives as they waited for the surveyor
general's response.

The following year, 1862, Congress passed the Homestead Act opening
land in the West for settlement. Under the act the General Land Office surveyed and distributed frontier lands to settlers. The land was divided into a
north-south and east-west grid. Each survey township was six miles square,
subdivided into sections that were each one mile square. Each section could
be further subdivided by halving or quartering, perhaps several times. Under
its provisions, any head of a household, including single women and men,
was entitled to a quarter section (a half-mile by half-mile square, or 160 acres)

of federal land. Within six months of an initial application, the prospective homesteader was required to have begun construction of his or her permanent home among other improvements on the land. The homestead claim was to be the settler's legal residence for the next five years. After this period, the settler and two witnesses answered questions regarding the legality by which the settler made his claim ("proved up on his land").[46] The owner had five years in which to make usable improvements on the land; otherwise, the land reverted to the government.

Six years later, in 1867, the Conejos settlers finally heard from Pelham, who informed them that he had forwarded the claim to the assigned surveyor general for Colorado Territory. Francis M. Case had been appointed the Colorado surveyor general on February 18, 1862. Obviously, the Spanish-speaking settlers had not been informed, in their language, that the territory now had its own surveyor general! Why Pelham took so long to forward their application to Case is unknown; although his office was busy working on other land grant applications. Houghton certainly could have found out about Case to follow up on their application. Apparently, he considered his contract completed once he filed the application. It is not known when Case received the application, but it appears that he took no action. The grant would remain under threat of public domain.

One letter to the editor published in 1871 represents a reader's opinion relating to the surveyor general's decision on the Conejos Land Grant:

> To deprive actual settlers from their homes which were located and settled upon prior to a confirmation is unfair. The officers of the government appointed to execute these laws seem doubtful and uncertain, and their dilatory action in the matter indicates that they are desirous of shirking the responsibility of the adjudication of claims arising under the law.[47]

Meanwhile, the Colorado surveyor general still had taken no action on the Conejos Land Grant claim. In 1875, when the government opened a land office in Del Norte, many grantees feared they could lose their granted land and some Conejos grantees applied for a homestead patent. Purnee A. McCourt, who researched the Del Norte book's patent entries for 1875 to 1878, found that many of those applicants having Spanish surnames applied for homesteads. The township and range of some of these applications corresponded to the area in which land donations were originally made by Taos justice

Cornelio Vigil in 1842. Among the applicants were José Víctor García and José Seledonio Valdez.[48] Unfortunately, Valdez could not produce the paper denoting ownership, and the government interpreted Valdez's homestead application as confirmation that land on the Conejos grant was public domain.

By 1876 the Conejos settlement had not changed much, and neither had the opinions of Anglo news correspondents (figure 1.6). According to a Pueblo newspaper, Conejos now had two settlements divided by the Conejos River:

> [It] is exclusively Mexican in smell, appearance and enterprise . . . The houses are all of adobe with glazed windows and low flat dirt roofs and dirt floors, which in a few cases are covered with course [sic] matting or blankets that supply the place of carpets. No chairs are used, and the visitor must either squat upon the floor or remain standing. The interior is exceedingly neat, however, no dirt or filth is visible, and the walls are whitewashed with some preparation which preserves its whiteness and purity for years . . .
>
> Every few miles we would pass a Mexican collection of huts and obtain a view of the squalid inmates who would gape upon us in open mouthed astonishment as we passed.[49]

The Conejos settlers believed they had a right to the land, established over the years and generations in which they and their ancestors had struggled to build homes, raise crops and livestock, and improve the land: "Not only are there affidavits to such intent and fact from the Mexican officials as well as letters of the grantees themselves, but in the testimony of witnesses before the court, many stated they had been told by parents and relatives of finding on each renewed attempt to settle, old acequias covered with weeds, broken down corrals, and jacals—evidence of prior occupation attempts."[50]

In 1891 Congress established the Court of Private Land Claims for Spanish and Mexican land claims in New Mexico, Colorado, Arizona, and Wyoming. Author Sarah Deutsch claims that Congress established the court to "depoliticize the land issue,"[51] for Hispanos wished to see their claims confirmed, while some Anglos hoped the court would open the land for Anglo settlement. Although regular sessions of the court were to be held in Denver, Santa Fe, and Tucson, most of the cases were New Mexican and most of the hearings were therefore held in Santa Fe.

On March 3, 1891, Congress established the Court of Private Land Claims to investigate land grant claims. Of the five justices selected by President William

FIGURE 1.6. Store, village of Conejos, 1874. Library of Congress, Prints and Photographs Division, Stereographic Cards Collection, Timothy H. O'Sullivan, photographer, LOT 3427-4, No. 15.

Henry Harrison to serve on the court, only two were living west of the Mississippi River. Wilbur Fisk Stone, of Colorado, was one of these justices.[52]

In February 1893 the Court of Private Land Claims accepted a Conejos Land Grant petition from Crescencio Valdez, son of original grantee José Seledonio Valdez.[53] The younger Valdez included a description of the papers filed with the surveyor general in 1861 and provided a sketch map of the grant. He was the owner in fee of an undivided interest in the said land grant.[54] On March 1, 1900, at Abiquiú, New Mexico Territory, Crescencio attended the adjudication proceedings of the US Court of Private Land Claims. There José María Chávez, now age ninety-nine,[55] gave a deposition on the Conejos grant. Chávez testified that during the early days he had herders at Los Conejos who pastured his stock. He also added that he had a house at Los Cerritos in La Isla.[56] More importantly, Chávez testified that he had "personally registered the grant and deposited the original [title] in the office of the Surveyor General in Santa Fe, giving a copy to [a] Jesús Velásquez."[57] In 1900 a court of five justices denied the claim and dismissed the Conejos petition due to lack of acceptable evidence that the grant had ever been made as claimed in 1833.

According to Stoller, the Conejos Land Grant was "the one grant that seemingly conformed best in purpose and in personnel to the Spanish-Mexican traditions and laws for awarding lands, [yet it] is the only one that ended up totally disallowed."[58] Wilbur Fisk Stone would play a role in the disposition of the Conejos case. He arrived in Colorado in 1860 to join the gold rush at the Tarryall Mine in South Park. Stone is also credited as one of the early settlers of Cañon City. While there, he helped establish rules of the people's court, a miners' court system. Stone and his partner, George A. Hinsdale, were the first two editors of the *Pueblo Chieftain*. In this capacity they were able to publish their biased opinions and elaborate on various news reports. Stone's "expressions" promoted the Denver and Rio Grande Railroad while writing that the Hispanos who currently owned the land could be bought out for little money.

Between 1863 and 1866, Stone served as an assistant attorney under Samuel E. Brown,[59] the attorney general for Colorado Territory. Stone rose to become an associate justice of the Colorado Supreme Court and was selected to serve on the Court of Private Land Claims. He was named to this court because he knew Spanish and was familiar with southern Colorado. However, due to his prejudicial views about Mexicans and their land, his recommendation that Congress not confirm the Conejos Land Grant was not issued in good faith. He should have recused himself from such position.

Malcolm Ebright, a noted author and researcher, has written that because land grants were established under the Spanish or Mexican legal system and then adjudicated by the US legal system, "the Court of Private Land Claims failed to recognize the system" of customary law of the land followed by the Hispanos and obligations assumed by the United States under the Treaty of Guadalupe Hidalgo. "[The court] lacked the essential element of all true adjudication—due process."[60] Colorado land grant activists, who were deeply rooted in New Mexican soil, continued to resent the annexation of a portion of northern New Mexico to Colorado, such that a hundred years later, community leaders approached Roberto Mondragón, the nuevomexicano lieutenant governor of New Mexico, and members of the New Mexico legislature for assistance in redressing their land complaints. In 1973 New Mexico state representative Bobby Durán (Taos) and twenty-two other state representatives introduced House Joint Memorial 12 to Washington, DC, asking President Richard Nixon to establish a federal boundary commission "to arrange for the return of Conejos and Costilla (Counties) of Colorado to their rightful status as an integral part of New Mexico." The memorial finally passed the New Mexico State Senate on March 17, 1973. The memorial cited historical rights and the purpose of bestowing the Conejos and Sangre de Cristo grants "upon native New Mexicans to encourage the settlement of land [as] a logical extension of the centuries of old Spanish civilization centered at Taos."[61] For this plan to work, it would have needed the approval of Colorado and the US Congress. However, nothing came of this effort.

Colonization on the Sangre de Cristo

The earliest known petition for a grant of land to colonize along the Río Culebra was issued in 1829 to Taos residents Miguel García, Julián (William) Gordan, and Manuel Copas. Foreigners who settled in New Mexico also sought to obtain land grants in the northern frontier. A document dated June 6, 1829, shows that a commission of the Mexican government denied the request because Gordan and Copas were not Mexican citizens (figure 1.7). The trio made no further attempt to legally colonize the area.

Colonization required sworn allegiance to the Mexican government; in addition, foreign settlers had to have lived in Mexico for at least two years, convert to Roman Catholicism, learn Spanish, become Mexican citizens, be employed and of good character, and promise to bring into the area additional settlers who would defend the land against "outside aggression."[62]

In 1841 New Mexico governor Manuel Armijo unwisely granted land to foreign Anglo men. These grants were made to individuals rather than to communities. The governor's intent was that the new settlers would help protect the northern borderland from incursion by the United States, but the

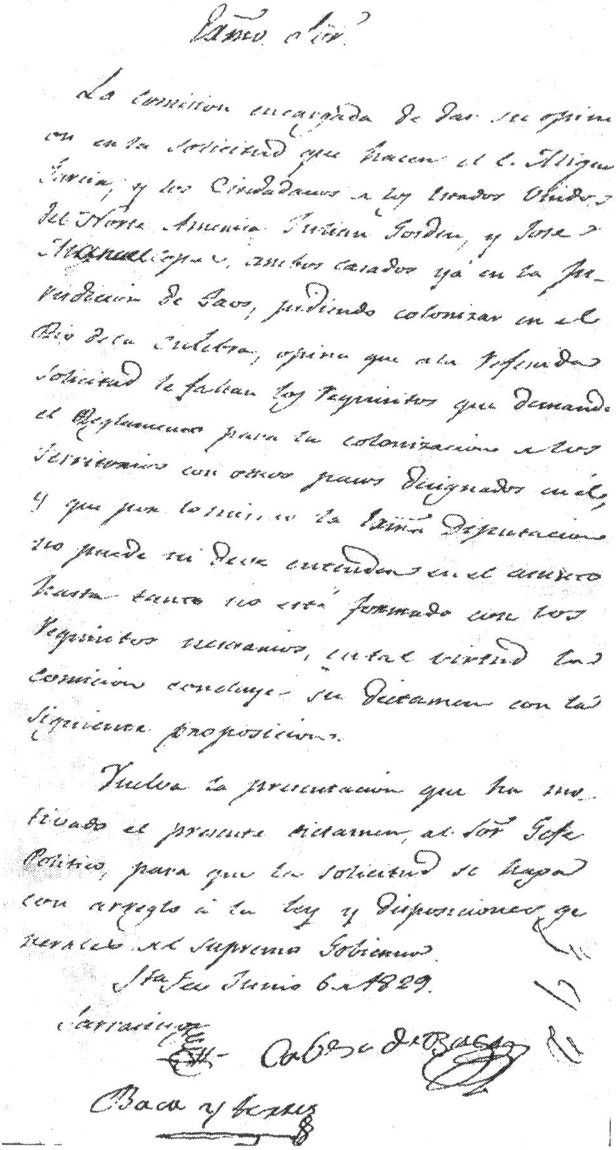

Exmo. Sor.

La comision encargada de dar su opinion en la solicitud que hacen el C. Miguel Garcia, y los Ciudadanos de los Estados Unidos del Norte America Julian Gordon, y Jose Manuel Copas, ambos casados ya en la jurisdiccion de Taos, pidiendo colonizar en el Rio de la Culebra, opina que a la referida solicitud le faltan los requisitos que demanda el Reglamento para la colonizacion de los territorios con otros puntos designados en él, y que por lo mismo la Exma. Diputacion no puede ni debe entender en el asunto hasta tanto no esté formado con los requisitos necesarios, en tal virtud la comision concluye su dictamen con las siguientes proposiciones.

Vuelva la presentacion que ha motivado el presente dictamen, al Sor. Gefe Politico, para que la solicitud se haga con arreglo á la ley y disposiciones que tiene dadas el Supremo Gobierno.

Sta Fee Junio 6 de 1829.

Carrasco

Cabeza de Baca

Baca y Terrus

FIGURE 1.7. Mexico's denial of a petition by García, Gordan, and Copas to settle lands along the Rio de la Culebra, 1829. Spanish Archives of New Mexico I (also known as the Land Grant Records of New Mexico), Collection 1972-007, Bureau of Land Management Series I, NARA, RG 49, Item 392.

departure from strict Spanish land policies consequently led to the sale of Mexican land to Anglo speculators and investors.[63]

Other grants that Governor Armijo approved, and that would later be in present-day Colorado, included the Gervais Nolan, located near the head-waters of the Arkansas, and the Vigil–St. Vrain, in present-day Las Animas County. The Nolan grant was the smallest of the allotments issued by Armijo, and it was the farthest north from Santa Fe. The Vigil–St. Vrain, named for Cornelio Vigil and French Canadian Ceran St. Vrain,[64] extended north to the Arkansas River. It included the valleys of the Huerfano, Cucharas, Apishipa, and Purgatoire Rivers and was the largest of the lands Armijo granted. Another French Canadian to receive a private or individual grant of land was Charles Hypolite Beaubien.

Charles Beaubien arrived in Taos, learned Spanish, and blended into the Hispano community as Carlos Hipolito Beaubien. He married a local Hispana in 1827,[65] and two years later he became a Mexican citizen.[66] By 1834, he was a Taos *alcalde* (mayor).[67] In time he amassed much land and became well connected with other land grant barons, including Ceran St. Vrain and Lucien Maxwell, his sons-in law. By Mexican law, no one person was eligi-ble to be granted more than one grant of land. However, to acquire more land, José Narciso Beaubien applied for a grant of land with his father's former employee and liquor dealer, Stephen Louis Lee. On December 30, 1843, Governor Armijo awarded these two men a grant of land in present-day southern Colorado (figure 1.8). This grant, called the Sangre de Cristo, included the San Luis Valley in present-day Costilla County. It encompassed over a million acres of land within the Culebra, Costilla, and Trinchera watersheds.[68] To obtain individual land from the Mexican government, these three men became Mexican citizens. Ultimately, they each acquired free land from a government they swore to protect. Although each had com-mitted treason, the Mexican government could not punish them because they now lived on US soil and, by the Treaty of Guadalupe Hidalgo, were US citizens.

On September 22, 1846, even as the United States was at war with Mexico, Brigadier General Stephen W. Kearny entered Santa Fe and established a sys-tem of laws known as the Kearny Code. In addition to the challenges of fron-tier life, the Hispanos were now introduced to a new culture and new legal system. These laws provided for a republican form of government, a bill of

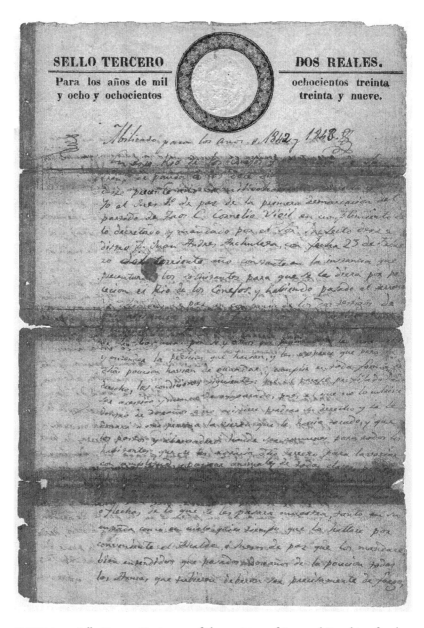

SELLO TERCERO · DOS REALES.
Para los años de mil · ochocientos treinta
y ocho y ochocientos · treinta y nueve.

FIGURE 1.8. *Sello Tercero.* First page of the petition of Lee and Beaubien for the Sangre de Cristo Land Grant, December 27, 1843. Land Grant Collection 374, Conejos Grant—Transcripts, Correspondence, Manuscripts, Map, Hart Library, History Colorado Center, FF29:15.

rights, laws of governance, and the appointment of select males to civil offices in New Mexico. One of these officials was Charles Bent, of Bent's Fort fame. Kearny named Bent, who was originally from Virginia, interim governor of New Mexico. Kearny named Charles Beaubien and Joab Houghton justices of the New Mexico supreme court.[69] Charles Beaubien was a Mexican citizen who had taken an oath to protect Mexico from incursion by the United States. By providing aid to General Kearny, he had committed treason against the Mexican government, the government he swore to protect!

The increased inequities, forced by Kearny's new order and his appointment of Anglos to civil offices, plus the continued loss of land resulted in much discontent among Hispanos and the indigenous Pueblo people. The Taos Revolt of 1847 resulted in the deaths of Governor Bent, teenager José Narciso Beaubien, Cornelio Vigil, and several others. Friends and family of the murdered men—including Charles Beaubien, Ceran St. Vrain, Lucien Bonaparte Maxwell, Joab Houghton, Antoine LeRoux, Thomas Tate Tobin, and Charles Autobees—aided in the arrest of fifteen Hispano and Pueblo males accused of responsibility for the deaths. The accused were brought before an "American" court held in Taos in which Joab Houghton served as judge and Ceran St. Vrain as the interpreter.[70] George Bent, brother of the deceased Governor Bent, served as the foreman of a jury composed of the decedents' Anglo peers. The court session lasted fifteen days. Each of the accused was found guilty, and an Anglo mob "promptly carried out" their executions by hanging.[71] The fifteen accused men had been tried in an unfamiliar court system in which the proceedings were conducted mainly in English.

José Narciso's death in 1847 enabled his heir and father, Charles Beaubien, to acquire the Sangre de Cristo Land Grant, located in the southeastern portion of the San Luis Valley in south-central Colorado. Charles Beaubien purchased Lee's undivided half of the Sangre de Cristo grant for one hundred dollars, thereby becoming the sole owner of a vast amount of land.[72]

To protect his holdings should the United States lose its war against Mexico, Beaubian encouraged more settlers to move north by invitation. After he established the town of Costilla in 1848, he sought to thwart any type of insurrection as that of the year prior. The town of Costilla was on his Sangre de Cristo grant; as owner, he established four rules of conduct in the new town and delegated the responsibility to keep his town civil and clean to the local sheriff. These four *reglas* (rules) were as follows:

Inasmuch as no civilized society can endure in good order, peace and union, which constitutes the happiness of the civilized peoples and establishes the superiority and advantages which Christian people enjoy over the manners of the barbarians, we come to propose to establish the following rules: viz. [*sic*]:

First: To maintain the cleanliness of the town and not consent that there be placed therein any nuisance.

Second: That drunken revels will not be permitted in the presence of the families of the town, nor fights; nor similar disorders.

Third: That no person from outside will be admitted to live in the town without having previously presented himself before the Judge or Justice of the Peace, and received his permission whether or not he may acquire property in the town.

Fourth: Everyone who wishes to take a dwelling or lots in the town will have to request it of the Judge, paying its value which will remain for the benefit of the chapel.

(Signed) Charles Beaubien
Witnesses: J. L. Gaspar [and José] Nasario Gallegos[73]

In 1848 the United States won its war with Mexico and acquired an extraordinary amount of land that included the present states of Arizona, California, Colorado, New Mexico, Nevada, Utah, and part of Wyoming. In accordance with the Treaty of Guadalupe Hidalgo, Mexican citizens who remained on the seized land became US citizens.

By terms of the treaty, the United States had agreed to respect the property of the Mexican citizens, but it did not specify how it would determine ownership. The US could have learned from the California experience to prepare for a means to determine ownership. For example, during the gold rush of the early 1850s, California's Hispano settlers had experienced problems holding on to their granted lands once Anglo miners, prospectors, and settlers entered the area. Adjudicating land grant titles among Anglos and Hispanos eventually but necessarily became a government priority. In 1851, a year after California had already become a state, Congress established a three-member land commission to investigate the legalities of California's land titles and settle land claims.[74]

On July 22, 1854, the US Congress named William Pelham as surveyor general of New Mexico. From his office in Santa Fe, Pelham and his staff attempted to gather evidence from land grant documents and field investigations (surveys) and subpoenaed witnesses for scheduled hearings. Due to general mistrust and language miscommunication, many Hispanos hesitated to turn over their land title documents.

In 1855 Beaubien filed his claim on the Sangre de Cristo grant. The surveyor general's office in Santa Fe then reviewed all claims for authenticity and heard testimony. Pelham found no encumbrances and recommended that Congress confirm the Beaubien claim, which it did on June 21, 1860. Now, under US law and decree, the Sangre de Cristo land was his free and clear; he was free to do whatever he wanted with the land. As will be seen, his future decisions would impact the 1,600 Hispanos settlers living and farming on his land.[75] As discussed later, these decisions would directly impact the settlers he had invited onto his land, their descendants, and those Hispanos settlers who had recently arrived.

Anglo Miners and the Territory of Jefferson

Because Spain had, for so long, rejected trade with the French and Anglos, the Spanish colonists in this northern borderland of New Mexico province remained relatively isolated. Due to the vast and rugged terrain and its hostile indigenous population, this isolation resulted in limited changes to language, less circulation of money, and fewer upgraded tools, arms, and equipment. Once Mexico obtained its freedom from Spain and opened its borders to the United States to the east, more Anglos entered the area, bringing with them money and newer tools.

Beginning in 1858, Anglos from the United States illegally entered onto Indian territory. They were motivated initially by furs, but they also discovered gold. Intent on protecting their land, indigenous nations attempted to thwart migration by destroying mining camps and engaging in skirmishes. However, their efforts could not stop the tide of merchants, lawyers, and land agents in search of wealth. The US Army, responsible for safeguarding the indigenous nations from illegal encroachments on their lands, failed to arrest and fine miners for illegal trespass.

The lure of finding valuable ores brought more Anglos into locations, including Cherry Creek (in Denver), Pikes Peak, and later the Sierra de las

Grullas (San Juan Mountains). By 1859, more than 100,000 unmarried Anglo males had made their homes in the area.[76] According to their research on mob violence, historians William Carrigan and Clive Webb wrote that tensions with Anglo miners often revolved around whether Hispanos should be allowed into or near the mines.[77] Some miners hired them as guides, peones, and *fleteros* (freighters).[78] Hispanos used an *arrastra* (ore-grinding mill) to crush refractory ores. It consisted of two large stones slowly rotated by oxen, horses, or mules to pulverize a circular bed of smaller, ore-bearing rocks. In time, these Colorado miners—who began by kneeling alongside a stream panning for any type of gold nugget or flake—would become familiar with the terms derived from Spanish and Mexican mining practices used throughout the Americas. (In his travel guide George A. Crofutt defined about 650 of these Spanish mining terms.[79])

As more settlers entered the area, the indigenous nations lost access to the once plentiful waterfowl, bison, and other wildlife, which greatly impacted their way of life. During this time, too, very few established farming communities could manage to feed the hungry miners. Many Hispanos living in New Mexico Territory offered to help. From his farm and mill at Guadalupita in Mora County, Felipe de Jesús Baca freighted four wagonloads of coarsely ground wheat flour to sell to miners at Cherry Creek, a tributary of the South Platte River.[80] This grain, which was hand-sickled and likely threshed by sheep, was in much demand in the new territory as miners could not readily purchase it.[81]

At the confluence of Cherry Creek and the South Platte River, miners created the town companies of Auraria and Denver in 1858. As more miners arrived, more mining districts developed throughout the region. Because the miners were so far removed in distance from the territorial governments of Kansas, Nebraska, Utah, and New Mexico, mining quickly developed from an individual economic endeavor to one based on group effort.[82] The first major ore strike near the San Luis Valley was at the Summit Mine on South Mountain in the Summitville District. There miners found gold, silver, and copper.[83] Problems began as they did not understand the isolation these Hispanos had experienced while living in the northern frontier. The miners criticized Hispano customs, language, religion, dress, and tools. Their prejudice created struggles over power and property. Unlike Anglo miners who traveled from digging to digging in search of wealth, the Hispano settlers had set down roots in what would become known as the "notch" of New Mexico Territory.[84]

By 1860, close to 60,000 unmarried Anglo males had overrun Ute land to extract the rich ores so coveted by the US government.[85] These miners had their own ideas regarding the use of natural resources to gain personal wealth and power. The gold they found was not as easily accessible as panning it from streambeds or screening it from loose soil. The gold in quartz veins inside solid rock required additional manpower, blasting, and better equipment to pulverize broken ore from the lode. Because the miners altered stream flows for their sluice mining, they polluted the rivers and washed out the protective topsoil. Deforestation occurred due to the amount of lumber needed for the miners' buildings and houses, fuel, mine supports, tools, and wagon parts.

In 1859 Denver newspaper editor William Newton Byers wrote, "[Here we have] nothing but ourselves to depend upon. . . . the business of our intended State will be principally mining—of the other, entirely agriculture—two means so different as to be under the circumstances incompatible. The prices of labor are and will be so different that no laws that apply to one [territory] will apply to the other." Knowing their effort was neither authorized nor sanctioned by the US Congress, Byers recommended to the region's miners that they press ahead nonetheless and "form a new and independent State." After all, "the U.S. courts of a Territory are the only ones competent for a trial . . . what criminal will be deterred . . . when his judge is separated from him by seven hundred miles of arid waste . . . Shall it be a government of the knife and revolver [or] a new and independent State?"[86]

In his editorial Byers proposed the boundaries of the new territory extend south into New Mexico Territory. The S. A. Mitchell map of 1846 and the Disturnell map of 1847 each showed Taos positioned north of the 37th parallel north.[87] Wishing to protect their existing mineral claims, the Anglo miners, known as "Pikes Peakers," rushed to include the far northern frontier of New Mexico within the southern portion of the rectangular territory they called Jefferson. Wasting no time, in November 1858 the quick-minded miners elected Hiram J. Graham as Jefferson's territorial delegate to represent them in the US Congress. Graham then submitted two petitions to the US Congress for the organization of a new federal territory in the Pikes Peak region. One petition suggested the name of Jefferson; the second petition recommended "Colona." The US Senate, however, paid no attention to either petition.[88]

Hoping to skip the traditional territorial stage, the residents of Fountain City initiated a movement for statehood.[89] On April 11, 1859, like-minded Aurarians asked the citizens of Denver to join them in a meeting on the 15th at "Uncle Dick" Wootton's store in Auraria, to call a convention for the State of Jefferson.[90] News spread quickly. Organizers in and around the Rocky Mountains were primarily from western Kansas Territory. Delegates, including those from New Mexico—from the Huerfano and, presumably, the Costilla, Culebra, and Conejos River settlements—were invited to attend a May 6, 1859, meeting in Denver to prepare a petition for a new state in the Pikes Peak region.[91] One of their major concerns was the miners' need for roads to and from the mountains.

When the delegates elected from the thirteen precincts met in convention the following month on June 6 at 2:00 p.m., they decided to forgo the temporary statehood status and voted for the organization of a new federal territory. Byers reported the attendance of Hickory Rodgers and Levi Ferguson,[92] delegates from Huerfano.[93] In Denver on August 1, 1859, 167 delegates from the thirteen mining districts reconvened in convention to form a state constitution and a memorial to the US Congress (figure 1.9). When the vote was taken on September 7, voters rejected the state proposition.[94] Presumably, one of these delegates was from Taos County, New Mexico.[95]

With no authority from Congress or communication with New Mexico's territorial officials, the miners automatically included Conejos, Costilla, and Huerfano, which were formed from Mexican land grants, as counties in their new territory. Conejos County stretched from the Rio Grande to Utah. Costilla County lay within the Sangre de Cristo Land Grant claimed by Charles Beaubien. These newly created counties were situated along the rivers of the same name. Although the land within these three counties officially belonged to New Mexico (in Taos and Mora Counties), no extant historical documents report discussion by the territorial legislative assembly about concern that its land would come under the miners' jurisdiction.

On September 24, 1859, miners of the Cherry Creek settlements met to organize a territorial government. During an election held on October 3, 1859, male voters selected the territorial delegate to represent them in Congress. Seven days later, voters approved a revised constitution formulated back in August for the State of Jefferson and elected territorial administrators and members of the legislative assembly.[96] It was during this meeting that the

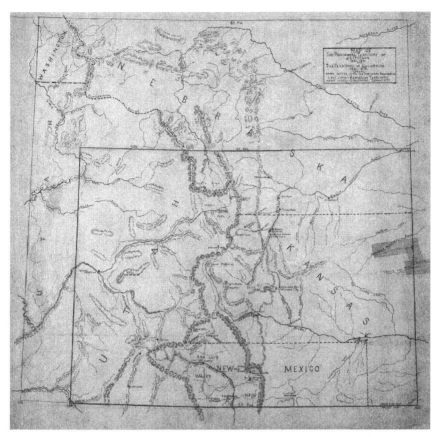

FIGURE 1.9. Map of Jefferson and Colorado Territories. The larger Jefferson Territory extends north into Nebraska; Colorado Territory is the smaller, dark-bordered rectangle within it. The "notch" is represented by the dashed line at the bottom. Map by Albert B. Sanford, History Colorado.

delegates determined the names of the thirteen mining districts or counties and their designated boundaries.[97] The names of the thirteen counties bring up some interesting issues, as some were named for Anglo male politicians of considerable clout in the northern part of the region during this early period. For example, Chaffee County was named for mining investor and Denver banker Jerome Bunty Chaffee; Douglas County for US senator Stephen A. Douglas, a Democrat from Illinois; Gilpin County for author William Gilpin, who fought in the US-Mexican War and learned much about the region and the Mexican land grants; Larimer County for Kansas territorial senator William Larimer Jr., who also founded the town of Denver; and Weld County for Denver and the Gregory mining district's lawyer, Lewis Ledyard Weld.

Due to the lack of information received in their Spanish language, presumably no Hispano males from the southern counties voted in this election. Or perhaps they were not allowed or encouraged to cast their votes. On October 24, Anglo "settlers again marched to the polls," approved the constitution for the Territory of Jefferson, and elected legislators "from the various districts."[98] They voted for a provisional government because "they had no courts; there was no protection of life or property except lynch law; and the laws of Kansas did not extend over the region known as Indian Lands referred to in Section 19 of the Organic Act of Kansas."[99]

For the office of governor of the new Territory of Jefferson, the voters elected Robert Williamson Steele. Governor Steele opened the first session of the new legislature two weeks later on November 7, 1859. Representing nine of the thirteen counties, the elected members of the still-unsanctioned Jefferson Assembly adopted a system of laws that defined the boundaries of each mining district and adopted the laws of Kansas as its grounds of jurisprudence,[100] which was based on English common law. The Jefferson Assembly passed several civil and criminal codes, established a court system, and enacted a poll tax and a tax to improve roads and provide transportation to and from the mountains.

On January 25, 1860, the assembly adopted a territorial seal. It was at least two inches in diameter with the mountains appearing in the distance. At the base of the mountains on the plains was a wagon filled with immigrants carrying mining tools. Near the top edge appeared the inscription "The people are the government." Along the bottom edge appeared "The great seal of the Territory of Jefferson."[101] It is not known whether the seal was ever purchased due to the lack of money in the newly created territory's treasury.

When Jefferson's second territorial assembly convened on November 12, 1860, it had problems keeping a quorum, as the legislators would not get paid for their time and effort during the session. There was no money in the territorial treasury. Further, the miners had successfully forced the first assembly to rescind the poll tax and "pledged . . . to resist any tax collection by the provisional government." By this time some miners now wished to be represented by the Kansas Territorial Assembly.[102] The Jefferson Assembly was beginning to fall apart. Due to political party friction, southern sentiments, and the slavery issue, the US House of Representatives killed the bill to create Jefferson Territory.

Deliberation in the US Congress

As Hispano settlement patterns continued to be formed in the far northern frontier of New Mexico Territory, the US Congress deliberated the possibility of establishing and organizing new western territories and whether slavery should be extended there. In February 1860 the first memorial requesting the recognition of the Territory of Jefferson as a legal government was presented to the president and the US Congress. Discussion centered on the 1851 Fort Laramie Treaty and that this treaty precluded any survey of the land. Senator Stephen A. Douglas (Illinois) reminded the chamber that "intruders into the Pikes Peak region would be removed by the United States" if requested by the indigenous nations. Douglas continued proclaiming "every man in the Pikes Peak region was in violation of the law and each of them had incurred a penalty of one thousand dollars and six months' imprisonment for violation of the Indian intercourse law." Unfortunately, no one explained this part of the Fort Laramie Treaty to the nations. However, "any attempt to remove the [miners] would be resisted."[103]

Senator Douglas submitted an amendment to keep the New Mexico notch in New Mexico, stating that the inhabitants of the notch were "mostly Mexicans" (figure 1.10). In accord with the Compromise of 1850, passed by Congress and signed into national law by President Millard Fillmore, New Mexico Territory accepted slavery in its borders. Douglas complained that the Colorado boundaries violated the 1850 compromise. Reassigning land from New Mexico, where slavery by law was acceptable, into the free territory of Colorado, where slavery was not permitted, would effectively and unfairly abolish slavery in the notch, negating the larger national compromise over where slavery was and was not to be permitted. Senator James Stephen Green (Missouri) pointed out that the recent census showed only twenty-four slaves in the whole of New Mexico, and none in the notch. The reallotment of that portion of New Mexico to Colorado, Green said, would "not cut off five inhabitants . . . and not a single 'nigger.'"[104]

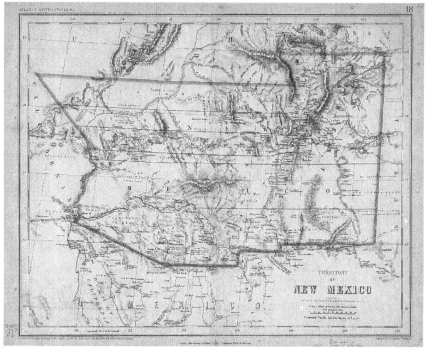

FIGURE 1.10. Map of New Mexico Territory, 1857. New Mexico at the time included what would later become Arizona. The "notch" appears as the territory's protruding northeast corner. Denver Public Library, Genealogy and Western History Department, Map_2017_1278, 1857.

During the Thirty-Sixth Congress in late 1860 two US senators, Green, a Democrat, and Republican Benjamin Wade (Ohio), collaborated with the Republican chair of the House Committee on Territories, Representative Galusha Aaron Grow (Pennsylvania), to have a bill passed establishing the new Territory of Colorado.[105] The bill passed in the Senate, then it continued for deliberation in the House. Unfortunately, Senator Douglas, who was ill and not in attendance during the Senate meeting, voiced his concern regarding the land presently owned by the Hispanos, including their indigenous slaves. Douglas well understood that the Sangre de Cristo and Vigil–St. Vrain grants had been confirmed by the US Congress the previous year in June, and he asked important questions regarding public domain and the transcontinental railroad.[106] Unfortunately, he was too late.

During discussion of the bill in the US House on February 18, 1861,[107] Chairman Grow attempted to expedite passage of the bill. He moved to suspend the rules, limited debate, prohibited amendment to the bill, and moved members directly to a vote. Grow then worked to keep Miguel Antonio Otero, delegate from New Mexico Territory, from proposing his amendment to keep the notch in New Mexico.

Referring to the miners, Grow claimed there were more "people" in the notch—"who had no other governance" than the "bowie-knife and revolver"— than Hispanos. Further, Grow diminished the demographic importance of the New Mexico notch by understating the number of "Mexicans" living in the area. Otero corrected the number, stating the population was 7,000.[108]

Historian Patrick C. Stauter wrote that, according to an 1870 Fort Garland report to the surgeon general's office in Washington, DC, the population of the San Luis Valley in Conejos County was 5,853 people. They were "all strong and hardy frontiersmen." Stauter also wrote that by 1871, 3,000 parishioners lived within the twenty-five settlements that belonged to the Guadalupe Roman Catholic parish alone.[109] Based on this information, Otero's population estimate was more accurate than Grow's.

Representative Thomas S. Bocock (Virginia) then spoke:

> I admit that the lines as the gentleman from Pennsylvania would run them, exhibit more beauty and grace; but if they cannot be preserved consistent with usefulness and justice to the people concerned, I think we ought to change them. I . . . prefer . . . in this matter, to sacrifice beauty and grace to right and justice.[110]

Grow answered that the boundaries had been fixed through three previous congressional sessions. He believed they were the "proper" boundaries as the "social relations and political community" of the Hispanos in the notch had already been "cut off" from New Mexico Territory. Further, he continued, "[Th]ere is certainly no reason for not detaching them from New Mexico, when the geography of the [new] Territory requires it shall be done, and every other consideration corresponds."[111]

Although Congress did not allow territorial delegates to speak on the floor of the House, Grow finally allowed Otero that rare opportunity. Otero was concerned that the bill would violate the protections accorded Hispanos by the Treaty of Guadalupe Hidalgo, by which Mexico had ceded much of its land to the United States. Otero reminded the chamber that the Hispanos were "satisfied with their present [New Mexico] government." "They have lived under that territorial organization ever since they have been under the Government of the United States." Referring to the Treaty of Guadalupe Hidalgo, he attempted to emphasize that these Hispanos had settled and labored much on land that was a part of New Mexico Territory. Reading from a section of the treaty, Otero stated, "[They] shall be free to continue where they now reside." To the committee, Otero intended to stress the notch Hispanos' deep cultural roots, which Grow so readily dismissed. "This Government is bound to give them their preference in that respect." Otero closed, saying, "They are a part of the people of New Mexico; they are a homogenous people."[112]

Officers of the federal government used language as a position of power to control actions affecting all nuevomexicanos, including Hispanos in the notch. Otero called attention to the prejudice certain members of the House expressed about the people of New Mexico:

> It has been the custom, on the part of gentlemen on the other side of the
> House [i.e., Republicans] . . . since this Congress began, to bring up New
> Mexico and her people . . . and try to hold it up to the ridicule of the nation.
> I protest mostly solemnly against such a course of conduct. And gentlemen
> think now they are at liberty to cut it [New Mexico] up in any shape they
> please. I have listened to these aspersions on the people whom I represent
> with a great deal of calmness. I have stood all sorts of opprobrium cast upon
> them; but I cannot sit here quietly and see the people of that Territory, who,
> as I have said, are a homogeneous people, cut in pieces and a portion of them
> transferred to another jurisdiction, when I know it is against their wishes.[113]

Grow again argued that there were more "Americans" in the notch "than Mexicans." Otero immediately interjected that he had "personal knowledge" and this was not correct.[114] He then advised the members of the House that if the bill passed as presented, the notch Hispanos would soon petition to be reinstated to New Mexico Territory. Democratic representative Daniel Sickles (New York) agreed with Otero and called the bill a violation of the 1848 treaty.[115]

Grow refused Otero's amendment to the bill to keep the notch in New Mexico Territory; and, by a Republican majority vote of ninety to forty-four, the US House passed the bill to establish the southern boundary of Colorado

Territory at the 37th parallel of north latitude,[116] naming the new territory for the Colorado River.[117]

Because the act to create the new territory was similar to a bill the Congress had previously considered, no debate took place and the bills for the territories of Colorado, Dakota, and Nevada passed in the House and Senate. The organic act that had established the Territory of Wisconsin in 1836 was considered a model for all new territories. Nearly every word in the judicial sections of Colorado's organic act came from that established for Wisconsin.[118]

Based on an arbitrary boundary line, the US Congress had redefined the system on which their Hispano society structure was founded. The southeast corner of the Colorado Territory was now squared off by incorporating a "notch" of land in northern New Mexico to southern Colorado. The nuevomexicanos living in the notch instantly became citizens of the Colorado Territory, but not as a matter of choice.

Notes

1. I use the more common spelling here. It has also been spelled "Nepestle." Juan Bautista de Anza called it the Napeste.

2. Lambert, *Wooden Canvas*, 14. To recognize Captain Pacheco's important and historic efforts to map early Colorado, a stained-glass window stands in his honor in the state capitol in Denver.

3. Of these, twenty-nine were mounted. The twenty-three infantrymen were armed with 33 guns, 39 lances, 224 cartridge belts, and scores of bows and arrows. Rodriguez, "Procession and Sacred Landscape in New Mexico," 21.

4. While camped there, ten settlers from Santa Cruz de la Cañada arrived with two boxes of ammunition. Because the expedition was not sufficiently armed or mounted, de Arce ordered Matias Ortíz, alcalde of the jurisdiction of Santa Cruz de la Cañada, to send 50 of his 300 men with firearms.

5. Sánchez, *Early Hispanic Colorado*, 137–40.

6. Colorado Historical Records Survey, Works Progress Administration, Division of Women's and Professional Projects, *Inventory of the County Archives of Colorado, No. 11, Conejos County (Conejos)* (Denver: Historical Records Survey, 1938), 4–5. See also Sánchez, *Early Hispanic Colorado*, 186.

7. Stoller, "Grants of Desperation," 22.

8. Abbott, Leonard, and McComb, *Colorado*, 37.

9. McCourt, "The Conejos Land Grant," 37–38. Eighty-three families participated in this resettlement.

10. Affidavit of Charles (Carlos) Beaubien, October 12, 1842, Land Grant Collection, 1866–1954, Conejos Grant—Transcripts, Correspondence, Manuscripts, Map, Hart Library, History Colorado Center, Denver, MSS.374, FF29:15. See also Colorado Historical Records Survey, Works Progress Administration, Division of Women's and Professional Projects, *Inventory of the County Archives of Colorado, No. 11, Conejos County (Conejos)* (Denver: Historical Records Survey, 1938), 4–5.

11. Sánchez, *Early Hispanic Colorado*, 186.

12. McCourt, "The Conejos Land Grant," 35.

13. Stoller, "Grants of Desperation," 22.

14. For details, see Sender Collection, 1697–1884, New Mexico Archives and Records Center, Santa Fe, Roll 2, Documents No. 286 and No. 287, Frames 552, 556.

15. Trujillo, "History of Atanacio Trujillo," 55–58.

16. Ibid.; Quintana, *Pobladores*, 190.

17. McCourt, "The Conejos Land Grant," 37–38. See also *Records of Private Land Claims Adjudicated by the United States Surveyor General*, New Mexican Land Grant Microfilm Collection, Case No. 109, 160, Denver Public Library.

18. Oliva, *Fort Union and the Frontier Army*, 115.

19. Including such men as José Celedonio (Seledonio) Valdez, Antonio José Vallejos, Charles Beaubien, James Fullerton, John Lawrence, Thomas Tate Tobin, and the brothers Frederick William Posthoff and William F. Posthoff. No trade licenses issued by Conejos agent Lafayette Head or Colorado territorial governor and superintendent William Gilpin have survived.

20. For more information about the Conejos owners and their indigenous slaves by name and settlement, and for information about known trade routes from southern Colorado, see Sánchez, "Survival of Captivity: Hybrid Identities, Gender, and Culture in Territorial Colorado," in *Nación Genízara: Ethnogenesis, Place, and Identity in New Mexico*: 183, Tables 8.2 and 8.3: 197–219. This chapter also names the eight men from Conejos County and the one man from Huérfano County who participated in the 1867 raid on the Oraibi in Arizona Territory.

21. Bonds of Traders, 1856–60, Kit Carson Papers, Bancroft Library, University of California at Berkeley.

22. Trujillo, "History of Atanacio Trujillo," 55–58.

23. "Complete List of Water Appropriations, Water District No. 21, Conejos County," Morgan Library, Colorado State University, MSS 296, FF1.

24. Twitchell, *Leading Facts of New Mexican History*, 2:457. Also Carr, "Private Land Claims in Colorado," 13–14.

25. Affidavit of Charles (Carlos) Beaubien, August 4, 1855, Land Grant Collection, 1866–1954, Conejos Grant—Transcripts, Correspondence, Hart Library, History Colorado Center, Manuscripts, Map, MSS 374, FF29:2.

26. McCourt, "The Conejos Land Grant," 39. See also Steinel and Working, *History of Agriculture in Colorado*, 30.

27. Stauter, *100 Years in Colorado's Oldest Parish*, 5.

28. Hart Library, History Colorado Center, Colorado Writers Project, PAM 349/10, 40.

29. Affidavit of Charles (Carlos) Beaubien, January 18, 1858, Hart Library, History Colorado Center, MSS.374, FF29:3.

30. McMenamy, "Our Lady of Guadalupe," 180–81. The article incorrectly named the priest as Jose P. Montano. Stauter, *100 Years in Colorado's Oldest Parish*, 17.

31. Noel, *Colorado Catholicism*, 11.

32. These visions resulted in the Miracle of Tepeyac, a rose-petal-laden *tilma* (cloak) in the Virgin's image. This same *tilma* can still be seen today at the Basilica of Our Lady of Guadalupe in Mexico City. Her blue mantle symbolizes both water and sky. Rodriguez, "Procession and Sacred Landscape," 20.

33. Stauter, *100 Years in Colorado's Oldest Parish*, 17. The parish served parishioners within a narrow, rectangular area, 25 miles long by 120 miles wide, bordered by the Saguache area settlements to the north, Los Pinos to the south, Las Cruces to the east, and Las Mesitas to the west.

34. After the flood Juan María García kept some of the original cedar logs used in the *jacal*. Colorado Writers Project, Hart Library, History Colorado Center, PAM 349/14, 51, 52.

35. McMenamy, "Our Lady of Guadalupe," 180–81. The parish was formed on June 10, 1858, with Father José Vicente Montaño as its first permanent pastor. Stauter, *100 Years in Colorado's Oldest Parish*, 9–10. Members included Juan Gabriel Chacón, Antonio Galves, Rafael Gallegos, Juan Gomez, Quirino Maes, José Gabriel Martínez, Juan Antonio Mascarenas, Salvador Salazar, Vicente Sánchez, Roman Sisneros, Manuel Romero, and José Seledonio Valdez. Lafayette Head served as secretary. Later, other members included Hilario Atencio, Felix Borrego, and Jesús María Velásquez. When Velásquez resigned due to other civic duties, Juan José Gallegos replaced him. For a basic funeral, the cantor, Manuel Ortega, received three dollars a year. For a solemn funeral, he received six dollars. José Quirino Ocaña accompanied Ortega on the organ. For his services Ocaña received ten dollars a year. And to transport his organ to the mission chapels, Ocaña received fifty cents a year. According to the committee's rules, "whether he needed it or not," Ocaña was given one Sunday a year as vacation. The committee also approved that the mayordomo would receive thirty-seven dollars for the purchase of sacramental wine and candles. As part of his responsibilities, he would plan the Guadalupe feast day activities. In lieu of an annual salary for his services, the mayordomo received three burial plots inside the church.

36. Stoller and Steele, *Diary of the Jesuit Residence*, 195–201.

37. Many authors have incorrectly credited Lafayette Head, instead of José María Jáquez, with bringing the first settlers into the area for permanent settlement. Head brought the second group in 1855. Steinel and Working, *History of Agriculture in Colorado*, 29. See also Quintana, *Pobladores*, 155.

38. In keeping with Spanish custom, women of the parish contributed jewelry, plate, and coins. Colorado Historical Records Survey, Works Progress Administration, Division of Women's and Professional Projects, *Inventory of the County Archives of Colorado, No. 11, Conejos County (Conejos)* (Denver: Historical Records Survey, 1938), 7.

39. Colorado Society of Hispanic Genealogy, *Hispanic Pioneers in Colorado and New Mexico*, 28.

40. Castro, "Shaping the Law of the Land," 7. See also Shawcroft, "Biographical Sketches," 29.

41. "Crescencio Valdez vs. United States," Hart Library, History Colorado Center, MSS 374.29.5, Depositions: 12–13.

42. Twitchell, *Leading Facts of New Mexican History*, 2:459. Also Van Ness and Van Ness, *Spanish and Mexican Land Grants*, 10.

43. In 1847 Houghton served as judge during the 1847 Taos Riot court trial. *Records of Private Land Claims Adjudicated by the United States Surveyor General*, New Mexican Land Grant Microfilm Collection, Case No. 109, 98, Denver Public Library.

44. Spanish Archives of New Mexico, New Mexico State Records Center and Archives, Santa Fe, PLC, No. 109, Surveyors General File 80, copy, US Court of Private Land Claims, microfilm, Roll 45. Also McCourt, "The Conejos Land Grant," 43. The application made was made by José Martínez, Antonio Martínez, Julian Gallegos, and Seledon Valdez on behalf of all the settlers.

45. Spanish Archives of New Mexico, New Mexico State Records Center and Archives, Santa Fe, PLC, No. 109, Surveyors General File 80, copy, US Court of Private Land Claims, microfilm, Roll 45. McCourt, "The Conejos Land Grant," 43.

46. Stratton, Pioneer Women, 48.

47. "Letter to the Editor," *Denver Daily Times*, July 14, 1871. Also McCourt, "The Conejos Land Grant," 46.

48. The first governmental township survey of the Conejos grant occurred in 1858. Some of the townships in the exterior area included 33 North through 36 North, Ranges 10 East through 11 East. US Department of the Interior, Bureau of Land Management, *Rectangular Survey Index Field Notes of Book "A,"* https://blm.gov, Book 62, 19. McCourt, "The Conejos Land Grant of Southern Colorado," 39. Saguache County Courthouse, Del Norte Cash Entry Book, April 4, 1876.

49. *Daily Chieftain*, July 6, 1876. See also Tórrez, *New Mexico in 1876–1877*, 93–94.

50. McCourt, "The Conejos Land Grant," 50.

51. Deutsch, *No Separate Refuge*, 20–21.

52. Wesphall, Mercedes Reales, 245–46. The president named Joseph R. Reed of Iowa a chief justice. The two Republican justices he named were Thomas C. Fuller of South Carolina and Henry C. Sluss of Kansas. The two Democratic justices selected were Wilbur Fisk Stone of Colorado Territory and William W. Murry of Tennessee. When Justice Fuller died in 1901, Frank R. Osborne of North Carolina filled his vacancy on the court. The court was given jurisdiction in the states of Colorado, Wyoming, and Nevada and the territories of New Mexico, Arizona, and Utah; however, Justice Reed stated there probably would be no cases in Wyoming, Utah, or Nevada.

53. Denver Public Library Western History and Genealogy Department, MSS, "Papers of the Valdez Family, 1765–1867," 40.

54. McCourt, "The Conejos Land Grant," 47. See also *Records of Private Land Claims Adjudicated by the United States Survey General*, New Mexican Land Grant Microfilm Collection, Case No. 109, 2–5, Denver Public Library.

55. David Gonzales, Bautismos de Nuevo Mexico Mission de Santa Clara 1729–1805 (Pueblo, CO: Genealogical Society of Hispanic America, 1995), 1–4. Also Stoller and Steele, Diary of the Jesuit Residence, December 1871–December 1875, 81n133. In 1900 Chavez was ninety-eight years and eight months old.

56. Spanish Archives of New Mexico, New Mexico State Records Center and Archives, Santa Fe, PLC, No. 109, Surveyors General File 80, copy, US Court of Private Land Claims, microfilm, Roll 45. Also Stoller and Steele, Diary of the Jesuit Residence, December 1871–December 1875, 81n133. Chávez gave his house at Los Cerritos in La Isla to his son-in-law, Antonio María Vigil.

57. Spanish Archives of New Mexico, New Mexico State Records Center and Archives, Santa Fe, PLC, No. 109, Surveyors General File 80, copy, US Court of Private Land Claims microfilm, Roll 45. Also Stoller and Steele, *Diary of the Jesuit Residence*, December 1871–December 1875, 81n133.

58. Stoller, "Grants of Desperation," 37.

59. In 1861 Governor William Gilpin charged Brown with associating with the Confederates. NARA, Washington, DC, Gov. Gilpin to William H. Seward, November 1, 1861, RG 60, entry 9, box 1, folder 5.

60. Ebright, *Land Grants and Lawsuits*, 5, 39.

61. "State Boundary Change Asked; Session Nears End," *Taos News*, March 14, 1975; Simmons, *San Luis Valley*, 264. Fourteen of the twenty-two New Mexico state representatives who introduced House Joint Memorial 12 were Hispano. "A Joint Memorial Requesting Creation of a Federal Boundary Commission to Return the Counties of Conejos and Costilla to New Mexico and to Adjust the Boundary of New Mexico and Colorado," New Mexico Legislature, House of

Representatives, *House Journal*, 31st Legislature, 1st Sess. (1973), 1–3, 358, 615–16, 633, 832–33.

62. Stoller, "Grants of Desperation," 23.

63. Lambert, *Wooden Canvas*, 6.

64. Carr, "Private Land Claims in Colorado," 12.

65. New Mexico Marriages, 1751–1918, film 17022, Carlos Hipolito Beaubien with María Paula Lovato, Taos, New Mexico, September 11, 1827, FamilySearch.com, accessed May 4, 2019.

66. Hafen, *French Fur Traders*, 33.

67. Mexican Archives of New Mexico, New Mexico Archives and Records Center, Santa Fe, 1844 Military Records, No. 3974, March 29, 1830.

69. "Sangre de Cristo Land Grant," MSS 2575, Ralph Carr Papers, FF54, Colorado State Archives, Denver.

69. *Records of Private Land Claims Adjudicated by the United States Surveyor General*, New Mexican Land Grant Microfilm Collection, Case No. 109, 98, Denver Public Library. Hafen, *French Fur Traders*, 25, 36–37.

70. General Stephen Kearny named Houghton a justice of the Supreme Court in 1846. In 1861 Houghton was the attorney for the Conejos grantees in their quest to obtain confirmation of their grant. *Records of Private Land Claims Adjudicated by the United States Surveyor General*, New Mexican Land Grant Microfilm Collection, Case No. 109, 98, Denver Public Library.

71. Frank Blair served as the prosecuting attorney. Members of the jury included Elliott Lee, Lucien Bonaparte Maxwell, Asa Estes, Antoine LeRoux, Charles Towne, and Charles Autobees. Witnesses to the murder of Charles Bent were Bent's wife, María Ignacia Jaramillo; Ignacia's daughter, Rumalda Luna; and Ignacia's sister, Josefa Jaramillo Carson. Broadhead, *Ceran: St. Vrain*, 26.

72. Stoller, "Preliminary Manuscript on the History of the Sangre de Cristo Land Grant," 34.

73. Costilla County Clerk, Public Record, "San Luis Town Reglas," Book I:256.

74. Of the 813 grant claims, its commission recommended 553 for confirmation by Congress. McCourt, "The Conejos Land Grant," 40.

75. Stoller, "Grants of Desperation," 34.

76. Chang, "Leading the Way," 35, col. 1.

77. Carrigan and Webb, *Forgotten Dead*, 33, 42, 43.

78. Other terms used for these hardy men include "teamster," "hauler," and "wagon driver." During the Spanish period freighters played a big part in transporting goods over the Camino Reál (Royal Road) to and from Santa Fe and Mexico and over the Spanish Trail to and from California. During the Mexican period freighters transported goods over the Santa Fe Trail to and from Missouri. And during the

territorial period they transported goods for the US military and hauled mining tools and equipment in and out of the mountains.

79. For a list of these 650 terms, see "Glossary of Mining Terms" in Crofutt, *Crofutt's Grip-Sack Guide*, 169.

80. Andrews and Humphry, "El Patrón de Trinidad," *Colorado Magazine* 21, no. 1 (January 1944): 7. Baca and Pedro Valdez hauled the flour.

81. Simmons, *San Luis Valley*, 133.

82. The governing bodies of Kansas and Nebraska Territories were over 700 miles away. Editor Byers wrote that it was 400 miles to the New Mexico and Utah Territories. "Address of the Preliminary Convention, to the Electors of the Intended State of Jefferson," *Rocky Mountain News Weekly*, May 7, 1859, 1.

83. Simmons, *San Luis Valley*, 176.

84. *Cong. Globe*, 36th Cong., 2nd sess. 1003 (1861).

85. Gundy, "Of Mines and Men," 38.

86. Paxson, "The Territory of Colorado," 58. Baker, *History of Colorado*, 2:485. See also Everett, *Creating the American West*, 171n13.

87. Hafen, "Status of the San Luis Valley, 1850–1861," 48.

88. Hafen, "Steps to Statehood in Colorado," 97.

89. Gonzales and Sánchez, "Displaced in Place," 267. See also "The State of Jefferson" and "Proceedings of the State Constitutional Convention," *Rocky Mountain News*, June 11, 1859, 1; Hafen, *Colorado*, 120, 134–35; and Dale A. Oesterle and Richard B. Collins, *The Colorado State Constitution* (New York: Oxford University Press, 2011), 6–7.

90. Frazier, "Prologue to Colorado Territory," 165. See also Gonzales and Sánchez, "Displaced in Place," 267.

91. "Address of the Preliminary Convention, to the Electors of the Intended State of Jefferson," *Rocky Mountain News Weekly*, May 7, 1859, 1.

92. In 1858 Hickory Rogers was named chair of the Arapahoe County commissioners. Lamar, *Far Southwest*, 184n18.

93. "Proceedings of the State Constitutional Convention," *Rocky Mountain News Weekly*, June 11, 1859, 3.

94. Frazier, "Prologue to Colorado Territory," 166.

95. The names of these delegates are not known. Hafen, *Colorado and Its People*, 204–7; Hafen, "Letters of George M. Willing," 186; Hafen, "Status of the San Luis Valley," 48.

96. Frazier, "Prologue to Colorado Territory," 166; Hafen, "Letters of George M. Willing," 187.

97. Berwanger, *Rise of the Centennial State*, 3; Frazier, "Prologue to Colorado Territory," 167.

98. Frazier, "Prologue to Colorado Territory," 168.

99. *Rocky Mountain News Weekly*, October 20, 1859, 1. See also John Lawrence, "John Lawrence, 'Father of Saguache,' Part 3," *Colorado Magazine* 3, no. 38 (1961): 167–68.

100. Parkhill, *Law Goes West*, 16. See also Lamar, "Colorado," 114.

101. *Provisional Laws and Joint Resolutions Passed at the First and Called Sessions of the General Assembly of Jefferson Territory, Held at Denver City, J.T., November and December, 1859, and January, 1860* (Omaha, N.T.: Robertson and Clark, 1860), January 25, 1860, 264 (joint resolution relating to the seal).

102. Berwanger, *Rise of the Centennial State*, 3; Frazier, "Prologue to Colorado Territory," 169.

103. Frazier, "Prologue to Colorado Territory," 169–70. Frazier refers to the the letter from B. D. Williams to A. G. Greenwood, Commissioner of Indian Affairs; May 18, 1860, NARA, Washington, DC, Letters Received by the Office of Indian Affairs, 1824–1881, Upper Arkansas Agency 1855–64, 475–77. Hart Library, History Colorado Center, Denver, Microfilm copy.

104. Murray, "The Supreme Court of Colorado Territory," 21. *Cong. Globe*, 36th Cong., 2nd sess. 764 (1861); cf. Everett, *Creating the American West*, 172.

105. For discussion of the passage of the bill naming Colorado Territory in the US Senate, see Frazier, "Prologue to Colorado Territory," 172–73; Lamar, *Far Southwest*, 188–89. See also Everett, *Creating the American West*, 171; Gonzales and Sánchez, "Displaced in Place," 273.

106. *Cong. Globe*, 36th Cong., 2nd sess. 1205–6 (1861); Everett, *Creating the American West*, 172n19; Gonzales and Sánchez, "Displaced in Place," 270. For an explanation of Senator Douglas's concerns, see Lamar, *Far Southwest*, 189–90. Peonage and slavery arose as contentious issues as a result of the US Civil War and not a result of Colorado's territorial legislation. For this reason, I do not discuss it.

107. *Cong. Globe*, 36th Cong., 2nd Sess. 764 (1861); cf. Everett, *Creating the American West*, 172.

108. *Cong. Globe*, 36th Cong., 2nd Sess. 1003 (1861); cf. Everett, *Creating the American West*, 172. See also Gonzales and Sánchez, "Displaced in Place," 271.

109. Stauter, *100 Years in Colorado's Oldest Parish*, 16–17. For the plazas as of 1863, see chap. 4, figs. 4.2 and 4.3.

110. *Cong. Globe*, 36th Cong., 2nd Sess. 1003 (1861). See also Everett, *Creating the American West*, 172; Gonzales and Sánchez, "Displaced in Place," 271.

111. *Cong. Globe*, 36th Cong., 2nd sess. 1004 (1861). See also Gonzales and Sánchez, "Displaced in Place," 271–72.

112. *Cong. Globe*, 36th Cong., 2nd sess. 1004 (1861). See also Gonzales and Sánchez, "Displaced in Place," 272–73.

113. *Cong. Globe*, 36th Cong., 2nd Sess. 1004 (1861).

114. Ibid. See also Gonzales and Sánchez, "Displaced in Place," 272–73.

115. *Cong. Globe*, 36th Cong., 2nd Sess. 1005 (1861); Everett, *Creating the American West*, 172. See also Gonzales and Sánchez, "Displaced in Place," 273–74.

116. *Cong. Globe*, 36th Cong., 2nd Sess. 1003–5 (1861); Everett, *Creating the American West*, 172. This area was defined in 1848 when Congress lowered (to the 37° parallel) the northern border of what had been a much larger New Mexico Department in Mexican times to encompass the "notch," a section of range bounded on the east by what had been the New Mexico eastern boundary, extending northward from the 37° parallel up to the 38° parallel, then due west across the Sangre de Cristo and Wet mountain ranges over to the Continental Divide, and then returning south along the ragged divide to the 37° parallel again. See also Keleher, *Turmoil in New Mexico*, 126.

117. *Cong. Globe*, 36th Cong., 2nd sess. 729 (1861). Also see Hafen, *Colorado*, 134–36, 138; Berwanger, *Rise of the Centennial State*, 3.

118. Murray, "The Supreme Court of Colorado Territory," 21.

2

Preparing a Territory

In early 1861, as the James Buchanan administration was replaced by the Abraham Lincoln administration and as the US Civil War loomed, Congress passed an organic act to create the Territory of Colorado. The southern boundary of the new territory was drawn to include a northern projection of New Mexico Territory known as "the notch." What had once been the "far northern frontier" of the Spanish province of Nuevo México now was "southern Colorado." The dishonorable congressional action impacted 7,000 US nuevomexicano citizens living in an area that had long been a part of homogeneous New Mexico Territory. During congressional discussion the chair of the Committee on the Territories deliberately kept Miguel Antonio Otero, delegate from New Mexico, from making an amendment to keep the notch area in New Mexico. Ultimately, Congress redefined the system on which these nuevomexicanos' Hispano social structure was founded.

The Hispanos of Colorado's south-border region had to redirect their political and administrative worldview from Santa Fe to the south and look north instead, to the capital of Colorado, located first in Colorado City (Colorado Springs), then Golden, and finally in Denver.

DOI: 10.5876/9781607329145.c002

The first territorial census in Colorado likely undercounted the Hispano population, a situation that had negatively affected the representation Hispanos were entitled to in the territory's legislative assembly. Although Hispanos ran for offices and voted, in that first election southern Colorado sent only two Hispano representatives to the territorial House.

The two Spanish-speaking representatives arrived at the territorial legislative assembly only to find that the territory had not made preparation for their language needs. The lack of territorial funds would create insurmountable obstacles for the two representatives and their Hispano constituents that would have an unfortunate lasting affect. In the House chamber, they had no translator and no translations of the important legislative documents and statutes. The Hispano assemblymen very soon discovered a disparity when it came to bills that clearly did not benefit their Hispano constituents.

Creating Colorado Territory

On February 28, 1861, President James Buchanan approved the congressional act establishing the Territory of Colorado. The following month Abraham Lincoln began his first term of office as president of the United States. About a month later, on March 22, the US Congress annexed Colorado as a portion of land derived from the territories of Kansas, Nebraska, Utah, and New Mexico that lay between the 102nd and 109th meridians west and the 37th and 41st parallels north.[1] Congress had designated specific meridians of longitude and parallels of latitude just so the territory would appear as a square on a map. Congress defined the territorial boundaries with even and symmetrical lines and right angles, approximating a square, as it also did seven years later when creating Wyoming Territory.[2]

President Abraham Lincoln appointed William Gilpin as Colorado's first governor, Lewis Leydard Weld as territorial secretary, and Copeland Townsend as US marshal. As governor, Gilpin received an annual salary of $1,500, paid by the US Treasury. Because he performed duties as superintendent of Indian affairs, responsible for managing relations among the settlers, miners, and several indigenous nations, Gilpin received an additional annual salary of $1,000. The US Treasury also provided Gilpin with an additional $2,000 to cover office and incidental expenses.[3]

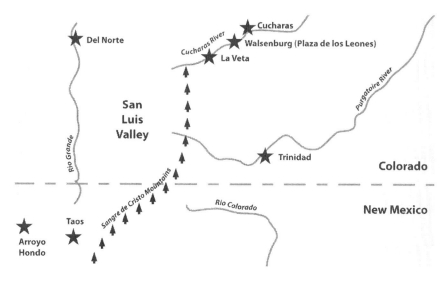

FIGURE 2.1. Map of southern Colorado. Author's map.

Governor Gilpin arrived in Denver on May 21, 1861. Hiram Pitt Bennet, who chaired the governor's reception committee, had citizens distribute hand-bills to announce the new governor's inaugural address. Six days later Gilpin appeared before a large crowd at the Tremont House in "residential West Denver." After his empowering speech a band played the national anthem. During a formal reception held two days later, Robert Williamson Steele, the provisional governor of Jefferson Territory, relinquished his post to Gilpin.[4]

Between May and July, Gilpin attempted to learn more about the needs of the territory. There were judicial districts to create, elections to organize, and new laws to enact; and due to the Civil War, a potential Confederate invasion was looming. Within the next four months, the census he requested had been completed and hence the territorial election. Gilpin became leery of people who did not have strong feelings against slavery, including the territory's Hispano Democrats.[5] According to historian Howard Roberts Lamar, before Gilpin's arrival "a Southern sympathizer had raised a Confederate flag over Wallingford and Murphy's store in Denver." Rumors quickly spread about existing Rebel miners and arrival of more from the southern states. Gilpin believed that southern Colorado was "a hotbed of Confederates—whether miners . . . soldiers at Fort Garland, or settlers at Fountain City,"[6] and even

Hispanos. Unfortunately, during this time, the governor failed to consider the needs of his Spanish-speaking constituents and their Spanish-speaking representatives to the legislative assembly.

The First Territorial Census and Election

Executive office space for Governor Gilpin and Secretary Weld included three rooms on the second floor of the Stettauer Brothers' New York Store, then located on Larimer between E and F Streets.[7] By terms of the territory's organic act, Governor Gilpin asked Marshal Townsend to conduct a territorial population census. To help enumerate the citizens, Townsend appointed "deputies in each settled area." No existing historical records provide the names of those men he appointed; however, by July 1, Townsend reported the territory's five-to-one ratio of males to females twenty-one years or older.[8] Due to the elevation and the Rocky Mountain winters, mining was a seasonal activity, and its miners were an itinerant group who quickly traveled from one dig to another. Townsend's deputies found it impossible to establish an accurate population count in these areas.

Likewise, many nuevomexicanos moved between New Mexico and Colorado Territories to pasture their sheep, bring in the crops, and attend family and religious celebrations. Despite these difficulties, Townsend recorded 25,331 persons, excluding the indigenous nations.[9] Regarding the population of the southern counties, according to the 1860 Taos County census for the Northern District of New Mexico Territory, the number of males named as heads of households in La Costilla was 45, with 152 in the five Conejos precincts and 67 in La Culebra (San Luis) Precinct.[10] These numbers clearly were understated, as the 1860 census for Costilla County, which included the Costilla River plazas, totaled 1,785 alone. An agricultural summary cited 157 farms in Costilla County that year.[11]

From the 1861 census information, the executives determined voting precincts for the House and Council districts. In preparation for the election, the governor's office distributed voting instructions and regulations to the probate judges. Typically, the probate judges appointed the election clerks and poll judges and swore them into office. The election clerks explained voting procedures, signed the voters in, and distributed the ballots. Poll judges were responsible for conducting the elections on the designated voting day, counting the votes after the polls closed, and reporting the results of the election to the probate judge.[12] Free white male citizens of the United States who lived in the new territory and were at least twenty-one years of age were eligible to vote. Likewise, "those recognized as citizens by the treaty with the Republic of Mexico . . . shall be entitled to vote at the first election and shall be eligible to any office within the . . . Territory" (see figure 2.2).

No existing historical documents confirm that ballots and voting instructions had been translated into Spanish for any of Colorado's territorial elections. Spanish-language newspapers, such as the *Anunciador*, *El Progreso*, and *La Opinión Pública*, would have been wonderful resources of the types of news reported to Hispanos; unfortunately, no back issues of these newspapers exist today.

On August 19 families and miners traveled to designated polling places in the southern half of the territory. Hispanos had been familiar with the US electoral process since US occupation of New Mexico in 1846. Throughout Colorado in homes or locations designated as voting or polling locations, Colorado's 9,877 male voters elected men to serve in a bicameral legislature composed of nine members in the territorial Council and thirteen members in the territorial House.

Spanish-surnamed males were nominated for offices in the House and Council in two of the three Hispano-majority southern counties. For two posts in their respective districts, Hispano candidates ran against each other.[13] For the House seats, voters in Conejos County elected José Víctor García,[14] a Republican; Costilla County voters elected Jesús María Barela, a Democrat. Not one Spanish-surnamed candidate appeared on the ballot for a seat in either the House or Council in Huerfano County, which is curious, because Hispanos living in Huerfano County constituted the majority population.[15] However, this omission is curious.

Quirino Crescencio Maes ran against Anglos John Mayes Francisco, Robert Burch Willis, and Harvey E. Easterday for one of the two Council seats in southern Colorado. Easterday was a contractor who supplied the US Army with goods.[16] Of the Anglo candidates, only Francisco was bilingual. According to the district votes for the Conejos, Costilla, and Culebra (San Luis) precincts, Quirino Maes received 342 votes, Francisco 128, and Willis 61. For unknown reasons, Maes's name was not printed on any ballots in seven precincts, some of which were in Huerfano County.[17] Had his

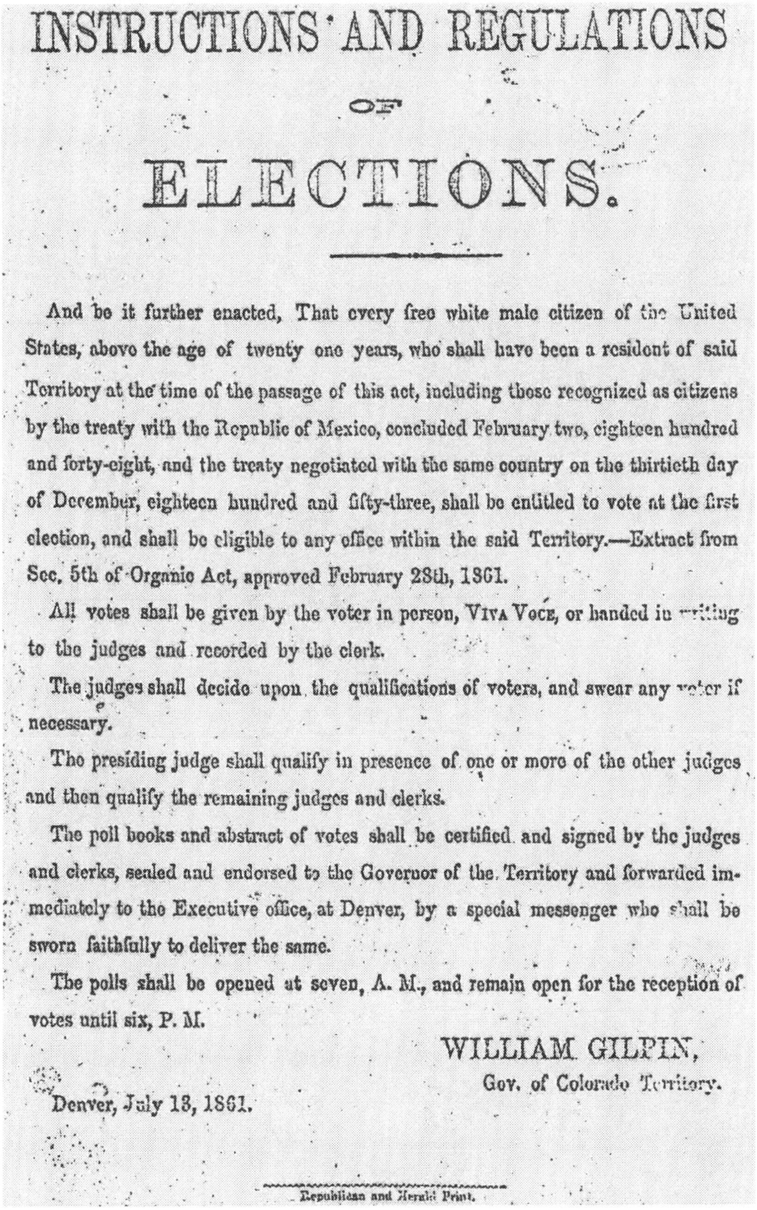

INSTRUCTIONS AND REGULATIONS
OF
ELECTIONS.

And be it further enacted, That every free white male citizen of the United States, above the age of twenty one years, who shall have been a resident of said Territory at the time of the passage of this act, including those recognized as citizens by the treaty with the Republic of Mexico, concluded February two, eighteen hundred and forty-eight, and the treaty negotiated with the same country on the thirtieth day of December, eighteen hundred and fifty-three, shall be entitled to vote at the first election, and shall be eligible to any office within the said Territory.—Extract from Sec. 5th of Organic Act, approved February 28th, 1861.

All votes shall be given by the voter in person, VIVA VOCE, or handed in writing to the judges and recorded by the clerk.

The judges shall decide upon the qualifications of voters, and swear any voter if necessary.

The presiding judge shall qualify in presence of one or more of the other judges and then qualify the remaining judges and clerks.

The poll books and abstract of votes shall be certified and signed by the judges and clerks, sealed and endorsed to the Governor of the Territory and forwarded immediately to the Executive office, at Denver, by a special messenger who shall be sworn faithfully to deliver the same.

The polls shall be opened at seven, A. M., and remain open for the reception of votes until six, P. M.

WILLIAM GILPIN,
Gov. of Colorado Territory.

Denver, July 13, 1861.

Republican and Herald Print.

FIGURE 2.2. Instructions and regulations for elections, July 13, 1861. Denver Public Library, Western History and Genealogy Department, Secretary of State Legislative Records, Abstract of Votes, Colorado Territory, 1861–1876, *Voting Book*, Colorado Voters 1861, Roll 1.

name appeared on the ballot in all ten precincts, Maes might have won the Council seat. Ultimately, in the Council, Francisco was elected to represent Pueblo and Huerfano Counties, and Willis was elected to represent El Paso, Fremont, Huerfano, and Pueblo Counties.[18]

Representatives of the territorial House served a one-year term, while councilmen served two-year terms of office. For each day in attendance during the session, the assembly members earned a salary of three dollars, plus an additional three-dollar stipend for every twenty miles traveled to and from home during the session. In contrast, members of the Jefferson Territorial Assembly had earned ten dollars a day for each day of the 1860 session.[19] By 1866, Colorado's territorial legislators earned five dollars a day for each day worked in a legislative capacity, plus a travel stipend set at fifteen cents per mile.[20]

The returns from the very first territorial election, held in August 1861, conveyed the broad front of nuevomexicano participation in local and territorial government. A total of 546 Hispano voters from Conejos, Costilla, and Huerfano Counties went to the polls. Nuevomexicanos ran for seats in both chambers of the legislative assembly.

The Colorado Territorial Assembly

With the first census completed and the election concluded, Governor Gilpin announced in late August that the first Colorado Territorial Assembly would convene in Denver on September 9, 1861. No historical documents state how the governor's office distributed or circulated this information to the newly elected assemblymen. One by one, each newly elected legislator arrived in Denver, checked into a hotel, and visited the territorial secretary's office to obtain his election certificate.[21]

Now that the executive branch of territorial government had been established, it was time for the legislative branch to begin. On September 9, 1861, twenty of the twenty-two newly elected members appeared for roll call. (Reasons why the two Spanish-speaking representatives failed to appear are explained in chapter 3.) Members of the House assembled in "a grimy room" in the American Auction Furniture Company building at 1451 and 1455 Larimer Street; the Council met nearby in a building across the street from the Broadwell House.[22]

The following day members of the two chambers assembled in the House to hear William Gilpin give his Governor's Message. In his message Gilpin proposed enacting wholesome civil and criminal laws; dividing the territory into counties, townships, and precincts; consolidating some less-populated counties; and establishing a militia to protect the miners and settlers from the 25,000 indigenous "residents."[23] Editors of the *Rocky Mountain News* and the *Colorado Republican and Herald* newspapers published a Spanish translation of the governor's message, prepared by E. B. Smith (figure 2.3). This translation helped Spanish-speaking citizens and their two representatives learn about the governor's plans for the new territory.

According to historian LeRoy Hafen, "No street in Denver ha[d] improved so rapidly [in] two months as Larimer street." He noted that the "lobbies of the two buildings accommodated at least a hundred people. The Post Office, Dave's [David H. Moffat] News Depot, the Executive Department, the Military Head Quarters . . . and the Prison (a sort of necessary accompaniment) are all located on this street."[24] Hotels in operation at the time included the Cherokee House, located at Fifteenth and Blake Streets, and Apollo House, Tremont House, and the Planters, which Anglo miners coming in and out of mountain camps had already rented. Members of both chambers, House and Council, lodged at the Broadwell House. The Broadwell, constructed in 1859, stood on the northeast corner of Sixteenth and Larimer Streets. It was one of the most prominent hotels and boardinghouses in Denver.

When California drafted its first constitution for statehood as a free state in 1849, it created the office of state translator. Its English- and Spanish-speaking delegates recognized the rights of its Spanish-speaking citizens. This step met the legal requirement stipulated by the 1848 Treaty of Guadalupe Hidalgo, in which Mexicans who chose to remain on the conquered lands gained by the United States after its war with Mexico would enjoy "all the rights of citizens of the United States . . . and in the mean time shall be maintained and protected in the free enjoyment of their liberty and property."[25] Furthermore, by terms of the 1849 California constitution, "all laws, decrees, regulations, and provisions, which from their nature require publication, shall be published in English and Spanish."[26]

Likewise, in 1851 the New Mexico Territorial Assembly established the office of translator to assist its non-Spanish-speaking Anglo assemblymen.[27] During this session, few Anglos served in the House and Council. By 1859,

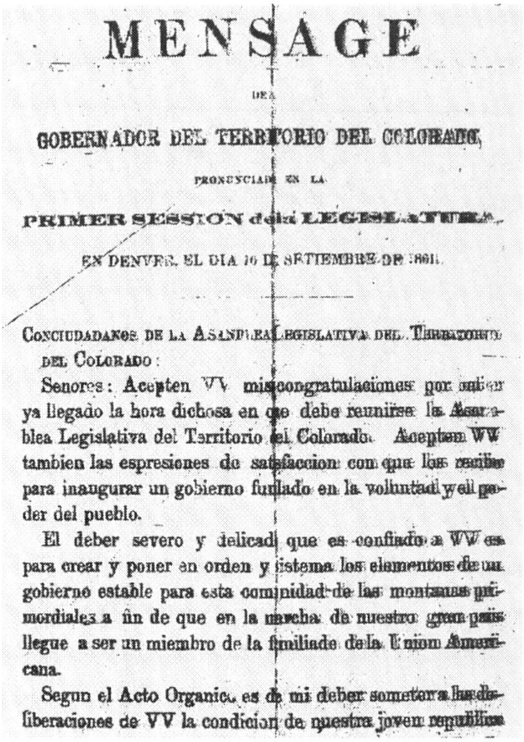
MENSAGE

DEL

GOBERNADOR DEL TERRITORIO DEL COLORADO,

PRONUNCIADO EN LA

PRIMER SESSION de la LEGISLATURA,

EN DENVER, EL DIA 10 DE SETIEMBRE DE 1861.

CONCIUDADANOS DE LA ASAMBLEA LEGISLATIVA DEL TERRITORIO DEL COLORADO:

Senores: Acepten VV mis congratulaciones por haber ya llegado la hora dichosa en que debe reunirse la Asamblea Legislativa del Territorio del Colorado. Acepten VV tambien las espresiones de satisfaccion con que los recibo para inaugurar un gobierno fundado en la voluntad y el poder del pueblo.

El deber severo y delicado que es confiado a VV es para crear y poner en orden y sistema los elementos de un gobierno estable para esta comunidad de las montanas primordiales a fin de que en la marcha de nuestro gran pais llegue a ser un miembro de la familia de la Union Americana.

Segun el Acto Organico es de mi deber someter a las deliberaciones de VV la condicion de nuestra joven republica

FIGURE 2.3. First page of the Spanish translation of Governor Gilpin's message to the First Colorado Territorial Legislature, September 10, 1861. NARA, College Park, MD, State Department and Territorial Records, Colorado, December 28, 1859–April 22, 1874, M3, Roll 1.

two Anglos each served in the House and the Council. According to Lamar, the governor urged the assemblymen to conduct their sessions in English, "to no avail."[28] Yet provision was made to translate bills, resolutions, and other legislative policy documents from Spanish to English and from English to Spanish. The translator was appointed by the governor of New Mexico with the advice and consent of the Hispano-majority assembly. By law, the translator was responsible for furnishing correct translations of all legislative and official documents. For his services, he received an annual salary of $2,000, appropriated by the US Congress from the Legislative Assembly Contingencies Fund. A selected printer then published the rules and journals of each chamber and the enacted laws in both languages. The laws in New Mexico were printed in English and Spanish until 1949.

Colorado had an opportunity to emulate the governmental models of California and New Mexico by translating documents in Spanish and providing for translators, but it did not. By not doing so, the rights of Colorado's Spanish-speaking citizens were at risk.

"Sello del Territorio del Colorado": The Territorial Seal

Since the first territorial legislature, each governor had an opportunity to acknowledge the Hispano and indigenous history and influence in Colorado. The design of the territorial seal presented one such opportunity. Seals were and continue to be used to certify all formal and official city, county, and territorial and state documents.

The majority of legislative representatives and their constituents were Anglo, and many of them were miners. Their interests lay in displacing the Utes, digging gold, and getting rich. They believed that, through their superior economic achievements, they alone deserved Colorado's mineral wealth; in contrast, they viewed the Hispanos as an unintelligent and shiftless conquered people whose slowness in fully embracing Anglo culture and expansion marked them as little better than outlaws.[29] That attitude was latently expressed in the design for the territory's official seal, as approved in the first legislative session.

Governor Gilpin sought a slightly larger seal than the Jefferson territorial seal (described in chapter 1) and asked Secretary Weld to oversee its design. When Weld met with members of the House, Daniel Witter (Park) suggested changing the Latin motto to English, while Speaker Charles F. Holly (Boulder) recommended changing the Latin to Spanish, with the motto *Nada sin la Diedad* and the seal's self-identification as the *Sello del Territorio del Colorado* ("Nothing without God" and "Seal of Colorado Territory"). The House Speaker had recommended a motto that was inclusive of Colorado's Spanish and Mexican history. After a call for a vote, the Spanish motto lost by one vote, and the Latin motto (*Nil sine numine*, "Nothing without Providence") and self-identification (*Sigillum Territorii Coloradensis*) were was adopted.[30]

On November 6, by a joint resolution of the House and Council, the territorial assembly adopted the seal.[31] The main theme of the design of the new seal centered on the importance of mining and the wealth that this industry produced for Colorado. As described by the legislature, the seal included a heraldic shield at its center. On the "red ground" of the shield's upper portion appeared three snow-capped mountains with clouds overhead; on the lower part of the shield, upon "golden ground," appeared crossed miner's tools, a pick and a sledgehammer.[32] The physical seal made to the design specifications was two and a half inches in diameter. When Associate Justice Allen Alexander Bradford took his oath of office, Secretary Weld affixed the territorial seal to the document.

Had the House members viewed the motto as an inclusive, bridge-building opportunity, the Spanish-speaking assemblymen and their constituents might have felt a more welcomed part of the new territory. According to historical accounts, the territorial executives disagreed over who was responsible for guarding the official seal, which led to its eventual loss.

Chamber Journals and Rules

By means of a journal, each chamber recorded the legislative discussion and action that took place each day while in session. There were no funds in the territorial treasury to print the proceedings of each chamber in English, let alone a translated version in Spanish. To keep the Hispanos informed, by September 25, 1861, Denver's *Rocky Mountain News* was selected the assembly's printer. It began printing the journal of the House in English and in Spanish at no cost to the territory.[33] Due to the time involved to translate and publish the English version, it took several weeks for the Spanish-speaking citizens of southern Colorado to receive any translated information about each chamber's proceedings and about how their representatives voted on issues. In addition, southern Colorado was at a disadvantage in receiving important news in a timely manner due to the distance from Denver. By the time key information arrived, it was already outdated, due to slow travel and transport, especially during bad weather.

Unfortunately, then, when conflicts with Secretary Weld arose between newspaper editors over sharing public printing jobs for the territorial government, printing the Spanish translations of the journals in the *News* and the *Herald* became less of a priority.[34] When these newspapers began using more space to chronicle events about the Civil War,[35] the Hispanos received no information and clearly were at a loss.

To establish order in each chamber, the Colorado Council used the same rules of parliamentary protocol as those that had been instituted by the

Jefferson Territorial Assembly, whereas the House adopted the rules used by the Kansas Assembly.[36] Members of the House referred to these rules as the House rules, while the Council referred to them as the Council rules. The standing rules essentially detailed the parliamentary procedure that governed a chamber. Such rules addressed the need for a quorum, defined the means that constituted a majority vote, explained how members were to address each other during discussion and debate, and codified the appropriate ways to make requests or motions. There were at least forty rules used by the Territorial Council.[37]

The Hispano territorial assemblymen consistently requested that the House rules be translated so that they, through an interpreter, could properly take part in the legislative process. Representatives José Víctor García and Jesús María Barela badly needed a Spanish translation of the important House rules in order to understand the internal legislative process under which they were expected to work. Working through E. B. Smith, the assigned interpreter,[38] Barela requested that the House provide two translated copies of the House rules (one copy for him and the other for García) to assist them in understanding and complying with the chamber's rules and common law. As reported by the *Rocky Mountain News*, the House voted to provide them with two copies of the translation: "Resolved . . . that two copies" of the "Rules of the House" be "printed in the Castilian language, for the use of the members from New Mexico, who are seated in this House."[39] The resolution was an interesting play on words as these members were now citizens of Colorado and not New Mexico.

Although members of the House approved the request for a Spanish translation, Speaker Holly still required consent of Secretary Weld, who rejected the appropriation as officially requested by the assembly because the territory had no money in its treasury. Although federal dollars were allocated via a general fund by an act of March 2, 1861, this money was not available until after the next fiscal year ending June 30, 1862.[40] No records indicate that Weld requested an appropriation from the federal government for this needed translation.

For the remainder of the first session, García and Barela were forced to work without a thorough understanding of the House rules. Ironically, because the Spanish-speaking members and their interpreter spoke quietly to each other about the various proceedings taking place, they were in violation of the rule addressing conduct,[41] and some Anglo members were distracted and upset by these ongoing discussions in a foreign language.

During the second session, held the following year, the two Spanish-speaking representatives again requested but did not receive a translation of the important House rules. In fact, the governor canceled the 1863 session because funds in the territorial treasury were limited due to his unauthorized military misuse.

During the third legislative session, held in 1864, García, who had been reelected for a third one-year term, again formally requested two translated copies of the House rules. The members of the House voted to appropriate funds for the translation and printing of two copies, including a translation of the Governor's Message to the current session's assembly. By month's end, García still had not received the translated copies. Growing more impatient, he requested that a special committee visit the newspaper editor to determine when the copies would be available (newspapers were still the only printers available). García, along with two Anglo representatives, learned that again Secretary Weld had not approved the appropriation to translate and print the rules because the territory's citizens did not require or use this internal legislative document. Unfortunately, Weld failed to inform the House members about his decision. He had used his position of authority as yet another barrier for the Spanish-speaking representatives. This type of institutional racism kept these representatives from effectively participating in the democratic process.

The Clout of the Northern Half

The location of the territorial university and capital serves as examples of how politicians of northern Colorado advocated and planned to secure the location of key assets in the northern part of the territory. The success of their actions ultimately placed southern Colorado at a considerable economic disadvantage, whereas northern Colorado became a hub of commercial and economic activity.

In 1861 Speaker Holly named a committee to determine the location for a territorial university. Funds for construction were supposed to be provided by the US Congress and through donations.[42] The three-member committee selected Pueblo, a hundred miles south of Denver, because the weather there enabled year-round access from the settled areas, the town could accommodate growth, and Pueblo was accessible from the "two great highways east to the Missouri River."[43] During the first vote, many of the representatives, including José Víctor García, cast their votes for the seats of the counties they represented. As documented in the journal, this action reflected each representative's support or endorsement of the county he represented. This action also resulted in no one location receiving a majority vote. Speaker Holly then called for a second vote. Working through their interpreter, García and Barela realized that Pueblo would not win a majority, so they voted for Cañon City as the site for the university. Again no one location received a majority vote. When the Speaker called for a third vote, Barela cast the only vote for Cañon City, while García joined other representatives in a sound victory for Boulder, northwest of Denver. Ultimately, the territory still did not have enough money for a university. However, had García and Barela used their collective voting power to support the committee's recommended location (Pueblo) during the first vote—had García not split his vote with Barela in the final vote—Pueblo would have received the majority vote in the House and then possibly a majority vote in the Council as the location of the University of Colorado.[44]

During the second session of the territorial assembly, southern Colorado voters sent four Spanish-speaking representatives to the House; they were incumbents Jesús María Barela and José Víctor García along with José Francisco Gallegos (Costilla) and José Rafael Martínez (Conejos). Representative Gallegos served on a committee to recommend a location for the territorial capital. Towns, cities, and counties competed to serve as the permanent location of the capital. For a brief period, Denver and Pueblo businessmen successfully helped pass bills that benefited their two cities. During its second term, the assembly met in Colorado City (later called Colorado Springs), located north of Pueblo. Because the town seriously lacked sufficient meeting facilities and housing, the members immediately adjourned to Denver, where they completed the legislative session. Golden City (later simply Golden) hosted the legislature from 1863 to 1867, with some sessions adjourning to Denver for reasons not included in extant records. Because the legislature had already selected Cañon City as its site for the territorial prison, that city was not considered for the capital, as the assembly did not want the same city to serve as both capital and prison location.

Most businessmen lobbied instead for Denver, as it had the territory's largest population and was already an incorporated town; therefore, it could attract businessmen and capital. On August 7, 1862, Representative Gallegos submitted a report of the minority (Democratic) committee of the House to reject the bill selecting Denver as the territory's seat of government. Since the bill made no appropriation for public buildings, the House killed it. Gallegos and Barela, both Democrats, were again in the minority party, whereas Representative García was a Republican. The political party to which Representative Martínez belonged is unknown. Ultimately, no selection of the capital city was made, as the session was about to close; however, the minority committee agreed that Colorado Springs possessed important recommendations:

> No general laws of incorporation have yet passed; therefore, there is no need for a vote . . . as there is not enough time during this session to perfect any necessary legislation. The people have not submitted a single petition nor have they demanded that [we approve] a location [this session]. The present location [at Colorado Springs] is near the geographical center of the territory and therefore it is in the right place.[45]

Although representatives from southern Colorado preferred Colorado Springs as the site of the new capital due to its more central location, Denver would be officially named capital of the territory six years later. Pueblo, established in 1846, enabled year-round access from "all settled portions of the Territory." It could accommodate economic growth and was accessible.[46] Additionally, the Anglo assembly members would not have considered Trinidad a prime location for the capital because it was too far south, too close to New Mexico Territory, and too "Mexican." According to author Eugene H. Berwanger, ". . . everything about the town appeared more Mexican than American. The pueblo [adobe] style dominated the architecture and most residents spoke Spanish."[47]

The Hispano assemblymen were discovering that they were not politically, socially, or financially able to overcome Denver's clout when it came to bills that clearly benefited chiefly the northern part of the territory. As is the case even today, the majority party had more legislative power as they were elected by the majority of the territory's citizens. Often bills sponsored by the minority party did not get heard or passed.

In two short months the first Colorado Territorial Assembly completed the organization of government and enacted several taxes and new civil and criminal codes patterned after the laws of the State of Illinois.[48] It enacted forty acts relating to the practice of law, thirty-six private acts, eight joint memorials, and three joint resolutions.[49] And all of this legislation was discussed and voted on as the Spanish-speaking representatives were listening to an English translation provided by an assigned translator. These representatives and their constituents were not familiar with the laws of the State of Illinois. They were unaccustomed to a system of "direct taxation," and they may not have recognized the need to pay as not paying "resulted in the loss of some land, or . . . indebtedness." Former Colorado College professor Marianne Stoller explained the concern:

> For many, simply producing enough surplus to raise cash for texas [sic] was a problem; further, they might not recognize the need or have the opportunity to convert surplus to cash, or doing so might disrupt old systems of social relationships based on trade, kinship and community obligations.[50]

The House journals show no discussion of their concerns regarding taxation. How were the Hispano representatives supposed to know? Had the translator clearly explained this vital information? Neither they nor their county officials back home had received a translation of the enacted civil and criminal codes, and thus they were uninformed as to interpretation of the various laws. The territory's legislative branch had not respected the Hispano's legal right to due process in legislative rules, information, laws, and treatment.

Notes

1. Denver Public Library, *Nothing Is Long Ago*, 42.
2. Keleher, *Turmoil in New Mexico*, 127. For a detailed discussion of why western states have geometric boundaries or artificial lines rather than natural divisions such as rivers or mountains, refer to Everett, *Creating the American West*.
3. Kelsey, *Frontier Capitalist*, 118.
4. Sweig, "Civil Administration of Governor William Gilpin," 180–82.
5. Due to the indigenous servants they had. Berwanger, *Rise of the Centennial State*, 6.
6. Lamar, *Far Southwest*, 197, 257.
7. Hafen, "Colorado's First Legislative Assembly," 42; Sweig, "Civil Administration of Governor William Gilpin," 189n47.

8. Sweig, "Civil Administration of Governor William Gilpin," 184–85.

9. Lamar, *Far Southwest*, 192. See also Hafen, "Colorado's First Legislative Assembly," 42.

10. US Census, Colorado, 1860 Taos County Census, Conejos, Costilla, and Culebra Precincts, ancestry.com.

11. National Park Service, National Register of Historic Places, "The Culebra River Villages of Costilla County, Colorado," sec. 3, 15. Referring to Miller, *Soldiers and Settlers*, 124. According to the government report, two Anglos controlled the supply of grains at Fort Garland. Antonio A. Mondragón was the only Hispano who received a firewood contract, but it was for only one year. For his services, Mondragon received 11 percent less per cord of wood than that paid to Anglo contractors.

12. Gonzales, *Política*, 6. Referring to Harper, "A History of New Mexico Election Laws," 9.

13. John Chandler Clement, ed., *Colorado 1861 Territorial Election* (Denver: Colorado Genealogical Society/Computer Interest Group, 1996), https://history .denverlibrary.org/sites/history/files/Colorado1861TerritorialElection.pdf. See also Denver Public Library, Western History and Genealogy Department, Secretary of State Legislative Records, Abstract of Votes, Colorado Territory, 1861–76, *Voting Book*, Colorado Voters 1861, Roll 1. Karen Mitchell, "Huerfano County Colorado, 1861 Colorado Territorial Election," http://www.kmitch.com/Huerfano/voter1861.htm.

14. According to historian Olibama López-Tushar, García served in the New Mexico Territorial Assembly in 1850. López-Tushar, *People of El Valle*, 40.

15. Denver Public Library, Western History and Genealogy Department, Secretary of State Legislative Records, Abstract of Votes, Colorado Territory, 1861–76, *Voting Book*, Colorado Voters 1861, Roll 1. Also, in 1864, Captain Quirino Crescencio Maes led an independent company of sixty-seven men against the Navajo. Kelly, *Navajo Roundup*, 131.

16. Harvey E. Easterday and Ceran St. Vrain owned the St. Vrain and Easterday Mercantile in Costilla. The company supplied the US Army with goods. In 1862 the company reported its earnings as $4,700. Colorado Territorial Tax, 1863, Division 10, accessed January 3, 2015, at http://www.Amazon.com.

17. Districts 8 and 9 included the Arkansas, Del Norte, and San Juan River settlements. Many misspelled names of Hispano candidates and voters appear on the printed territory's poll results sheets. Denver Public Library, Western History and Genealogy Department, Secretary of State Legislative Records, Abstract of Votes, Colorado Territory, 1861–76, *Voting Book*, Colorado Voters 1861, Roll 1. Also https:// history.denverlibrary.org/sites/history/files/Colorado1861TerritorialElection.pdf, accessed October 13, 2013.

18. Colorado Legislative Biographies, www.leg.state.co.us, accessed October 1, 2017.

19. *Provisional Laws and Joint Resolutions Passed at the First and Called Sessions of the General Assembly of Jefferson Territory, Held at Denver City, J.T., November and December, 1859, and January, 1860* (Omaha, N.T.: Robertson and Clark, 1860), 264.

20. Hafen, "Colorado's First Legislative Assembly," 42, 46.

21. Sweig, "Civil Administration of Governor William Gilpin," 189n48.

22. *Rocky Mountain News*, October 2, 1861, 4. See also Sweig, "Civil Administration of Governor William Gilpin," 205–6.

23. Kelsey, *Frontier Capitalist*, 121; Sweig, "Civil Administration of Governor William Gilpin," 190. See also Hafen, "Colorado's First Legislative Assembly," 44. The number was provided by Agent Head.

24. The first legislative ball, held October 1 in the Broadwell House, was the "grandest and most extensive affair of the kind ever known in this region." Although the governor had previously scheduled the ball for September 26, he rescheduled, as he had previously proclaimed that date a Day of Prayer. The *Colorado Republican* reported the attendance of 108 ladies. "Dancing . . . commenced at an early hour in the evening." The Broadwell served supper at 1:00 a.m., after which dancing resumed until "nearly daylight." Hafen, "Colorado's First Legislative Assembly," 42, 46, 49, 50. See also *Rocky Mountain News*, September 24, 1861; *Daily Colorado Republican and Rocky Mountain Herald*, November 9, 1861.

25. "Treaty of Guadalupe Hidalgo," art. IX, February 2, 1848, Lillian Goldman Law Library of the Yale Law School, Avalon Project, http://avalon.law.yale.edu/19th_century/guadhida.asp, accessed June 28, 2017.

26. Calif. Const. of 1849, art. XI, sec. 21. For its first thirty years, California was a bilingual state. By 1878, when Californians met to revise their state constitution, not one native Spanish-speaking delegate was named to the convention. Subsequently, the Anglo delegates eliminated the 1849 guarantee for Spanish-language publications and limited all official proceedings to English.

27. NARA, Washington, DC, Records of the US Senate, Territorial Papers of New Mexico, RG 46, Tray 1, FF 32nd Congressional List of Accounts and Resolutions transmitted, etc., passed by the Legislature of the Territory of New Mexico in 1851, Enacted in Spanish number 14–11, Enacted in English number 14–12. On June 28, 1851, the Senate approved a joint resolution to provide for and fund office space and supplies for the translator. In 1857 a translator's assistant was employed at three dollars per day for a three-month term. The assistant could only earn his salary for the business of the legislature.

28. Lamar, *Far Southwest*, 81.

29. Carrigan and Webb, *Forgotten Dead*, 52, 53.

30. *House Journal of the Territory of Colorado, 1861*: 89 (relating to Spanish motto).

31. *General Laws, Joint Resolutions, Memorials, and Private Acts Passed at the First Session of the Legislative Assembly of the Territory of Colorado, Begun and Held at Denver, September 9th, A.D. 1861* (Denver: T. Gibson, Colorado Republican and Herald Office, 1861), November 6, 1861, 513–14 (joint resolution regarding territorial seal). Hereafter cited as *General Laws of the Territory of Colorado, 1861.*

32. NARA, College Park, MD, Oath of Associate Justice Allen Alexander Bradford, Colorado Territory, RG 60, Entry 9, Box 1, Folder 6. The eye of God had golden rays extending out from triangular lines. Below the crest and above the shield was a Roman fasces, which symbolized a Republican form of government. On a band of red, white, and blue appeared the words "Union and Constitution." Interestingly, the assembly's joint resolution for a seal mentions specific colors. As necessary for certain territorial documents, officials affixed a blue label, then imprinted the seal onto the label; none of the named colors was visible.

33. Denver Public Library, *Nothing Is Long Ago*, 63.

34. Collins, "Colorado's Territorial Secretaries," 192–95.

35. Everett, *Creating the American West*, 174.

36. Guice, *Rocky Mountain Bench*, 101, 102. Hafen, "Colorado's First Legislative Assembly"; Holly Otto, Colorado Legislative Library, Denver, personal communication. April 3, 2014.

37. *Council Journal of Territory of Colorado, 1861*, 10–13 (standing rules).

38. Hafen, "Colorado's First Legislative Assembly," 46.

39. *Rocky Mountain News Weekly*, Legislature of Colorado, First Session, September 18, 1861, 2, col. 5.

40. Sweig, "Civil Administration of Governor William Gilpin."

41. *House Journal of the Territory of Colorado, 1861*, 10, 13. Hereafter cited as *House Journal of the Territory of Colorado, 1861*; and *House Journal of the Legislative Assembly of the Territory of Colorado, Third Session, Begun at Golden City, on the 1st Day of February 1864, Adjourned to Denver on the 4th Day of February* (Denver: Byers & Dailey, 1864), relating to a request by Mr. Trujillo to have the interpreter speak louder, *House Journal of the Territory of Colorado, 1864*, January 11, 1864, 34; February 9, 1864, 37; March 8, 1864, 153. Hereafter cited as *House Journal of the Territory of Colorado, 1864.* See also Hafen, "Colorado's First Legislative Assembly," 46.

42. Sweig, "Civil Administration of Governor William Gilpin," 192.

43. *House Journal of the Territory of Colorado, 1861*, 230–31.

44. Ibid., 298 (relating to the location of the University of Colorado).

45. *Rocky Mountain News Weekly*, August 14, 1862, 1, col. 5. See also *House Journal of the Territory of Colorado, 1861*, August 7, 1862, 197–98 (report of Gallegos, Committee on Territorial Affairs).

46. *House Journal of the Territory of Colorado, 1861*, 230–31.

47. Berwanger, *Rise of the Centennial State*, 13.

48. Sweig, "Civil Administration of Governor William Gilpin," 192n63.

49. Memorials usually memorialized a person, whereas resolutions were the opinions of the body on some policy. Memorials and resolutions were considered jointly formed when they came from the whole assembly and not from one specific chamber. A private act applied to one or more individuals or corporate entities.

50. Stoller, "Preliminary Manuscript on the History of the Sangre de Cristo Land Grant," 13.

3

Lack of Due Process

Hispano accommodation to life in Colorado Territory continued to be challenging due to the relatively sudden inapplicability of many previous Hispano customs and institutions as well as the need to adjust to unfamiliar statutes and taxes recently enacted by the Anglo-majority legislature. Law and language posed two of the biggest obstacles hindering the mutual adjustment of the Hispano (and indigenous) and Anglo populations.

Confusion in the legislature occurred not simply because Spanish-language rules and journals were not readily available, if at all, to Hispano legislators, but also because they had to work through the legislative process via a translator. Several misunderstandings occurred.

Once a translator was assigned to them, receiving adequate and timely translations of official business remained a flaw in the legislative and administrative functions of the territorial government. In some cases, officials refused to act upon legitimate requests for translations of statutes due to lack of territorial funds or to personal prejudice toward "Mexicans" at the federal level! In one case, Colorado's territorial delegate reported to the

DOI: 10.5876/9781607329145.c003

Lincoln administration that the translations had already been printed when indeed they had not been. Then the federal official denied the request for a translation of the statutes because he believed these Hispanos were foreign-born immigrants when in fact they were US citizens. Colorado's delegate to Congress then failed to help him understand that these Hispanos were neither foreign-born nor recent immigrants.

Even with the diligent efforts of all involved, translation was a slow process, involving months of handwritten effort by the translator before submitting the results for typesetting, publication, and distribution. Hispano assemblymen and their constituents consistently received translated statutes long after their Anglo counterparts had the English publications in hand, and sometimes only after the statutes had already been amended.

Navigating the law is a matter best left to lawyers, but Hispanos were at a disadvantage in the legal realm not only because of language difficulties and unfamiliarity with Anglo law but also because there were relatively few Hispano lawyers. Often unable to provide satisfactory evidence of their legal qualifications, many Hispano lawyers lost the right to practice law in the new territory. Only two Hispano assemblymen were admitted to the bar during the entire territorial period, although other Hispanos were able to practice without licenses as lawyers in lower courts or as justices of the peace.

The US Congress had had three years of experience in dealing with Spanish and Mexican land grants in California; however, this experience was not tapped into when it came to confirming land grants in New Mexico and southern Colorado. In addition to the challenges of frontier life, the Hispanos were now introduced to a new culture and new legal system.

For example, when the US Congress confirmed Charles Beaubien's claim to the land on the Sangre de Cristo in 1860, he received full ownership, free and clear, and was free to do whatever he wanted with the land. But he had given each settler approximately 500 acres as an incentive to move onto his grant. Additionally, those Hispano settlers, via the deeds he had prepared in 1863 and his Beaubien Document of 1864, considered the land they had labored on theirs and the commons to share in *comunidád*. Ultimately, the deeds did not meet the requirements of the territory's 1861 real estate conveyance law. Further, Beaubien then agreed to sell the land grant to former governor William Gilpin, and although Gilpin promised to honor Beaubien's commitment to the settlers, he did not. The settlers could no longer live

under the traditional Hispano settlement and communal system and would
be forced to repurchase their land or leave.

Cultural and Language Challenges

According to historian Howard Lamar, territorial representatives José Víctor
García (Conejos) and Jesús María Barela (Costilla) arrived five days after the
September 9, 1861, session began. Although no historical records explain why
the two were late, several theories are possible. At the time, county governments had no revenue to grade and maintain dirt roads, and travel by carriage
would have been even more difficult and uncomfortable after heavy rains or
snowfall. Also, the distance from San Luis to Denver, about 260 miles, was
actually farther than from San Luis to Santa Fe. Perhaps the governor's office
had forgotten about the two gentlemen and their language needs and thus
García and Barela never received information, in English or Spanish, in time to
prepare for the long trip and the extended time away from their farms and family. In a worst-case scenario, García and Barela could have found out that the
assembly was in session only after southern Colorado received those newspapers that published the translation of the Governor's Message of September 10.

According to Lamar, once García and Barela arrived in Denver, Governor
Gilpin personally escorted them to the building where the House met.[1] Once
seated in the House and presumably introduced to the other members, the
two representatives found that the assembly had not provided an interpreter.
Meanwhile, the Anglo members continued to address bills and pass laws with
no input from the southern Colorado representatives.

Governor Gilpin asked the territorial assembly to extend the county
boundaries of the thirteen established during the Jefferson period. Many
of these were established along the Front Range near heavy mining activity.
On November 1, 1861, the assembly added four more counties and named
the temporary county seats for each of the seventeen counties. San Miguel
became the county seat of Costilla County, and "Guadaloupe" became the
county seat of "Guadaloupe" County.[2] This spelling error was likely based on
the Anglo legislators' mispronunciation of "Guadalupe"—they used a long ē
sound rather than an open e sound.

Colorado Territory had retained the names of the thirteen counties established by the earlier Jefferson Territorial Assembly. Of these, five county

names were in Spanish: Costilla, El Paso, Huerfano, Pueblo, and Guadaloupe. These names, as spelled, appeared in some Jefferson and Colorado territorial maps and legislative records.

Representative García introduced a bill to change the county's name from Guadalupe to Conejos. The purpose of the name change is unknown. His bill, approved by the assembly on November 7, 1861, included the accurate spelling of the town of Guadalupe and recommended the name Conejos as the official name of the county.[3] García's bill was the only bill introduced by a Hispano and passed into law that first session.

Seven days later the assembly officially changed the Conejos county seat from the Guadaloupe [sic] settlement to the Conejos settlement,[4] located a mile southwest. Here again the reason for the change is unknown. According to oral history, there was some "contention as to where [the county's seat] should be located."

> With the office supplies in possession of the group at Guadalupe. . . . It is a matter of whispered history that they were appropriated by night and moved to Conejos where they were held until the matter was officially settled upon.[5]

Unfortunately, Representative Barela had more difficulty getting his bill to change certain names in Costilla County passed. Attempting to adapt to Colorado's legislative culture, during the first session Barela sought to change the name of Costilla County to San Miguel County, in honor of St. Michael, and to establish the Abajo settlement as its new county seat.[6] County seats were typically located in larger, stable communities. The town of Costilla was the site of the San Miguel Catholic Church,[7] where many early settlers were baptized, married, or buried. Its full name was San Miguel de la Costilla. Why Barela wanted to replace Costilla as the county seat is not known.

Working through the interpreter, E. B. Smith, Barela presented his bill. The process to pass a bill into law involved a series of amendments and votes in both chambers to ensure that members of both the House and the Council carefully considered and deliberated the pros and cons of the bill (table 3.1). When members of the House voted on and approved Barela's bill as presented by Smith, the House clerk returned the bill to the Council for concurrence. Historical documents do not reveal why changes were made to the bill at that point, but the resulting bill demonstrates some of the language and cultural issues that occurred between the interpreter and the Hispano assemblymen.

TABLE 3.1. Steps to pass a bill into law

A chamber's clerk records the bill, the name of the member who introduced the bill, and assigns a number to the bill, e.g., H.B. No. 10 or C.B. No. 10, where *H* represents the House and *C* the Council. During 1861, members of the House submitted 193 bills for consideration while members in the Council submitted 35 bills.

In the chamber, the clerk introduced each bill in numeric order. This introduction is the bill's First Reading.

The Speaker of the House or President of the Council as elected by a chamber's members, assigned three members to a committee to review the bill. The Enrolled and Engrossed Bills Committee was the only committee with two members.*

The committee reviews the bill and gathers other relevant information.

On Second Reading of the bill in chamber, the committee presents its recommendation and any amendments.

After debate in chamber, the members vote to pass or defeat the bill. If a bill passes on Second Reading, the clerk lists the bill on the next day's calendar for the Third and final reading in the originating chamber where its members either pass the bill, amend then pass the bill, defeat the bill, table the bill, or return the bill to committee.

The final vote occurs on the Third Reading. If the bill passes on Third Reading, the clerk sends it to the other chamber where the process starts anew (e.g., First Reading, committee assignment and review, to the chamber floor for consideration on Second and Third Readings).

If a bill passes in both chambers without any changes, the originating clerk sends the bill to the territorial governor. If a chamber makes changes to the bill, the clerk returns the bill to the originating chamber where it can concur with or reject the changes. Once the bill passes in both chambers, the clerk sends the bill to the territorial governor for his signature and the bill becomes law. A bill not passed by both chambers dies. A member can revive a bill through a reintroduction of the process.

At the close of each session, a clerk compiles the signed or enacted bills and arranges for a printing of the session laws.

* In 1861 permanent or standing committees included Judiciary; Finance, Ways and Means; Education; Military Affairs; Highway and Bridges; Expenditures; Incorporations; Territorial Library; Elections; Counties; Federal Relations; Agriculture; and Enrolled and Engrossed Bills. *Source: Council Journal of the Legislative Assembly of the Territory of Colorado, First Session, Begun and Held at Denver, September 9, 1861, 13–14,* William A. Wise Law Library, Digital Archive, http://lawcollections.colorado.edu.

By 1861, three main settlements lined the Culebra River in Costilla County. The three plazas were simply known as Arriba (upper or above, meaning the settlement farthest upstream from the Rio Grande, into which the Culebra flowed), Abajo (below, or farthest downstream), and Medio (between the other two settlements on the river). In English these towns would have been named South Culebra, North Culebra, and Culebra, respectively (figure 3.1). Plaza Arriba later became known as San Pedro, Plaza Abajo as San Acacio, and Plaza del Medio as San Luis de la Culebra (San Luis).[8] As presented by

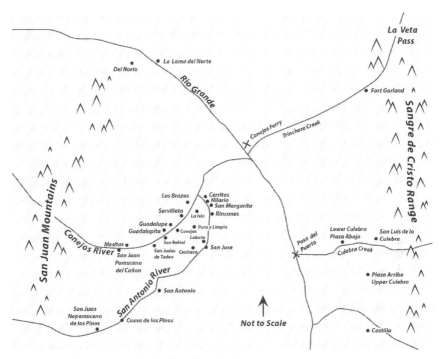

FIGURE 3.1. Settlements in the "notch." Author's map.

Smith, the clerk recorded the county name as San Miguel de la Costilla, and the name of the proposed county seat as En la Plaza de Abajo, which literally translated to "In the Plaza Below." Both names were too long for Anglo Colorado, but more important, they were incorrect. Protestant Anglo assemblymen were not familiar with the cultural and religious significance of the names to the Hispanos, and the interpreter did not comprehend the cultural intent of the changes desired. The plazas San Pedro, San Luis, San Acacio, and San Miguel were named by the early settlers to honor the Catholic saints Peter, Louis, Acacius, and Michael. Perhaps Barela knew that García had requested a land survey that could affect the Costilla plaza.[9] Or because the Costilla plaza was so far south, Barela perhaps thought it best that the county seat be moved twenty miles farther north.

The following month, during the third reading of the bill, the Territorial Council rejected the changes to the bill and returned it to the House. During reading back in the House, Representative García understood Barela's intent to change Costilla County to San Miguel County and to move its county seat north from Costilla plaza to the plaza known as Abajo or Lower Culebra. García immediately moved to reject sections of the bill, but his motion was defeated. Smith's misunderstanding resulted in the assembly's approval of names for a county and a county seat that were neither culturally or historically accurate nor as intended by the Hispano members. Working through Smith, Barela and García were unable to educate Smith or the House members of the cultural or historical significance.[10]

Due to García's disappointment in the bill as it had been passed, Jerome Bunty Chaffee (Gilpin) recommended that the members allow García's protest to be documented in the House journal.[11] By recording a formal protest, García's comments went on public record as having tried to make these important and culturally significant corrections.

Issues with the interpreters continued for many years. During the 1864 session Conejos County citizens reelected José Víctor García to represent them in the House; Costilla County citizens elected José Pablo Antonio de Jesús Ortega. What happened to former Representative Jesús María Barela remains a mystery, and unfortunately there is very little biographical information about him. The House had not yet selected an interpreter or made one available, so House Speaker M. C. White (Summit) appointed three members to recommend "suitable persons" to act as interpreter. Celestino Domínguez, whom García and presumably Ortega favored, was not available, as Conejos County voters had elected him to represent them in the Council. Four days later the committee finally recommended E. P. Parker as interpreter. García and Ortega stressed the need for his immediate services. The Speaker named a committee to find an interim interpreter, and committee members J. E. Leeper (Clear Creek), Norton W. Welton (Costilla, Huerfano), and García selected Parker, who promptly arrived in the House chamber and was "duly elected interpreter *pro tem*." Parker must have had the needed qualifications, as five days later García made the motion to elect him as the official House interpreter.[12]

Translators and Interpreters

Sometime after September 18, 1861, Secretary Weld received a request from the assembly to hire private citizen Celestino Domínguez to translate the statutes and resolutions into Spanish. By May of the following year, Domínguez was close to completing his translation of the 1861 statutes when Weld left for Washington to clarify his responsibility regarding the selection of Colorado's territorial printer. This meant that printing of the translated statutes had to wait until Weld's return.

However, in April, Weld resigned to seek military service. President Lincoln replaced him with Samuel H. Elbert as Colorado's new territorial secretary.[13] The Hispano representatives and Domínguez were "very anxious" for Elbert to arrive in Denver so the translation of the 1861 statutes could be sent "at once" to the printer.[14] But once Elbert arrived, he refused to act because he wanted more direction from the federal government.[15]

On May 30, 1862, Representatives José Víctor García and Jesús María Barela sought territorial delegate Hiram Pitt Bennet's assistance in securing federal funds to print the translated statutes. They asked Domínguez, who was fluent in English, to write a letter to Bennet regarding the "great injustice the people" of Conejos and Costilla Counties were suffering due to not having the laws of the territory printed in Spanish.[16] As requested, Domínguez wrote the letter, in which he reminded Bennet that the elected officials in Conejos and Costilla Counties could not "administer justice, collect taxes or perform any official duty" until they received a Spanish version of the statutes. He also reminded Bennet that the Hispanos constituted one-fifth of the territory's population. In closing, Domínguez asked Bennet to represent these facts to the US treasurer. Domínguez said he would inform the Hispano assemblymen about Bennet's "kind exertion in their favor" and that they would "be indebted" to Bennet for his aid in addressing "their just grievance" (figure 3.2).

Because Bennet had already left the territory,[17] Barela and García submitted the letter to Weld, now a private citizen in Denver, who forwarded the letter to Bennet in Washington. After receiving the letter, Bennet gave the request to the comptroller of the US Treasury, Elisha Whittlesey.

When Bennet asked Whittlesey for an appropriation to print Colorado's translated statutes, Whittlesey denied the request because Hispanos were "foreign-born." Whittlesey, of Ohio, failed to understand, or perhaps did not care, that these Spanish-speakers were in fact citizens of the United States by means of the 1848 Treaty of Guadalupe Hidalgo and that they had been recently annexed from New Mexico Territory to the newly established Territory of Colorado. Whittlesey clearly demonstrated his ignorance of the history, demographics, and needs of these US citizens: "The custom of the Government has been to encourage foreign-born citizens to acquire a knowledge of our own language and hence in the Territories the Laws have been printed in the English language only except in New Mexico where 9/10 of the people are spaniards [sic] and use only their native tongue, and such printing was done by an act of Congress."[18]

Bennet made no attempt to help Whittlesey—who displayed a nativist or nationalist sentiment—understand that these Hispanos were not foreign born or recent immigrants. Bennet also inaccurately reported to President Lincoln's secretary of state, William Henry Seward, that a Colorado newspaper had already printed the laws in both lan-

guages.[19] After discovering this had not been done, Bennet failed to inform Secretary Seward. By this action Bennet had failed to support his constituents in the southern counties, and he gravely insulted the Hispano assemblymen.

Having received no appropriations from Congress, Colorado's second territorial governor, John Evans, held the assembly responsible for either securing territorial funds to print the laws in Spanish or "leaving those citizens uninformed as to the nature and requirements of the laws they are expected both to enforce and to obey." He said, "A portion of our citizens, who are Mexicans, comprising most of the inhabitants of those counties originally belonging to New Mexico, have been unable to understand or properly enforce our laws, because the [laws] have not been printed in the only language which they speak."[20]

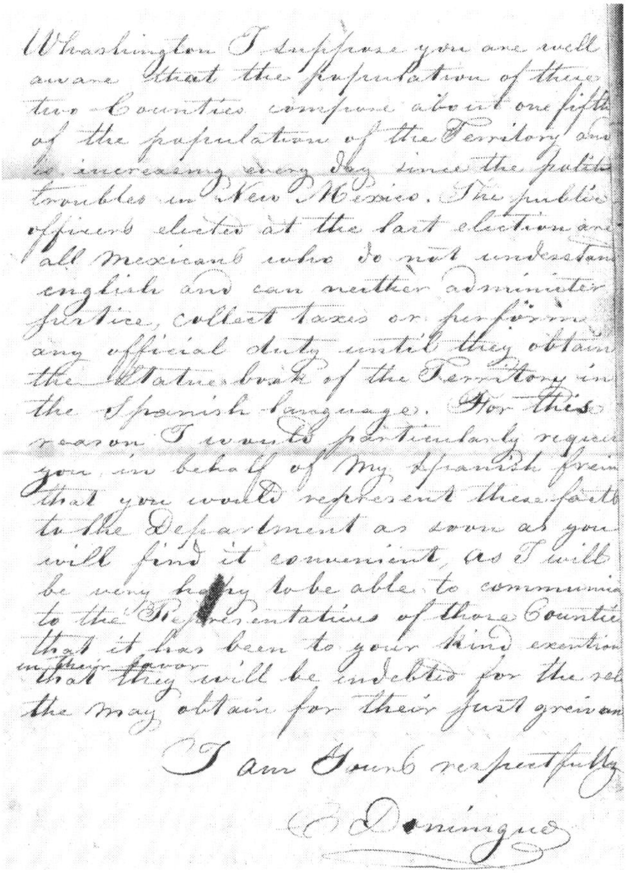

Whashington I suppose you are well
aware that the population of these
two Counties compose about one fifth
of the population of the Territory and
is increasing every day since the polit
troubles in New Mexico. The public
officers elected at the last election are
all mexicans who do not understan
english and can neither administer
justice, collect taxes or perform
any official duty until they obtain
the Statute book of the Territory in
the Spanish language. For this
reason I would particularly reque
you in behalf of my Spanish frien
that you would represent these fact
to the Department as soon as you
will find it convenient, as I will
be very happy to be able to communic
to the Representatives of those Countie
that it has been to your kind exertion
in their favor ~~that they~~ will be indebted for the rel
the may obtain for their just grievan

I am Yours respectfully

C Dominguez

FIGURE 3.2. Letter from Celestino Domínguez requesting Spanish translations of territorial laws, 1862. Celestino Domínguez to H. P. Bennet, May 30, 1862, Territorial Letters, Division of Warrants, Records, and C (Correspondence), First Comptroller's Office, January 1, 1862–December 31, 1862, Vol. 6, 1, 2, NARA, Washington, DC.

On March 1, 1864, the chair of the Territorial Ways and Means Committee, M. C. White (Summit), reported to the House that his committee believed the "Spanish citizens [were] due laws printed in their language," and that doing so would raise more money than the cost to print. White also stated that such an appropriation would save them from "internal dissentions [*sic*] and strife" and enable them to become "acquainted with their duties as citizens."[21] Revenue from the mines helped the territorial treasury as that year the territorial secretary approved $7,000 to translate and print 150 copies of the statutes from the first, second, and third sessions and 500 copies of the Governor's Message. The statutes of the three sessions were printed in one hardbound volume (figure 3.3).[22]

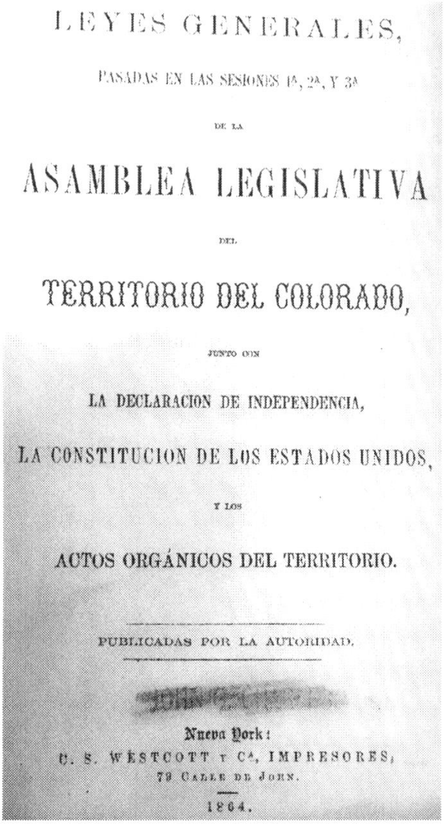

LEYES GENERALES,

PASADAS EN LAS SESIONES 1ª, 2ª, Y 3ª

DE LA

ASAMBLEA LEGISLATIVA

DEL

TERRITORIO DEL COLORADO,

JUNTO CON

LA DECLARACION DE INDEPENDENCIA,

LA CONSTITUCION DE LOS ESTADOS UNIDOS,

Y LOS

ACTOS ORGÁNICOS DEL TERRITORIO.

PUBLICADAS POR LA AUTORIDAD.

Nueva York:
U. S. WESTCOTT y Cª, IMPRESORES,
79 CALLE DE JOHN.
1864.

FIGURE 3.3. Title page of Spanish translation of laws passed in the first through third sessions of the Colorado Territorial Assembly (1861–63), published in 1864. Colorado Supreme Court Library.

It had taken the territory three years to pay Celestino Domínguez an unknown amount for translating the statutes of the First Assembly, and fifty dollars for his translation of the 1861 Governor's Message.[23] This amount did not accrue any interest. Upon receipt of the printed translated materials, Secretary Elbert sent the copies to officers and the representatives in Conejos, Costilla, and Huerfano Counties.

Again, in 1866, the Hispano representatives requested an appropriation for the translation of the statues from the fifth and sixth sessions. Two years later territorial secretary Frank Hall received bids to translate, print, and bind the statutes of the fourth, fifth, and sixth sessions (1865–67). The statutes were translated, and 300 copies were printed in one hardbound volume (figure 3.4).[24] Once the treasurer received the printed copies, he distributed them to

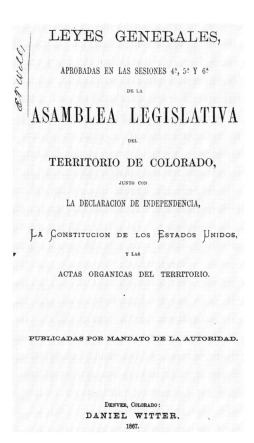

LEYES GENERALES,

APROBADAS EN LAS SESIONES 4ª, 5ª Y 6ª

DE LA

ASAMBLEA LEGISLATIVA

DEL

TERRITORIO DE COLORADO,

JUNTO CON

LA DECLARACION DE INDEPENDENCIA,

LA CONSTITUCION DE LOS ESTADOS UNIDOS,

Y LAS

ACTAS ORGANICAS DEL TERRITORIO.

PUBLICADAS POR MANDATO DE LA AUTORIDAD.

DENVER, COLORADO:
DANIEL WITTER.
1867.

FIGURE 3.4. Title page of Spanish translation of laws passed in the fourth through sixth sessions of the Colorado Territorial Assembly (1865–67), published in 1867. Colorado Supreme Court Library.

the civil servants.[25] On May 2, 1872, the editor of *Colorado Chieftain* still had no sympathy for Hispano citizens who had not received a Spanish translation of the revised statues. The editor wrote, ". . . our Mexican citizens [need] an early and diligent study of the English language, if they wish to become familiar with the revised statues of Colorado."[26]

Five years after publishing the second volume of statutes, Secretary Hall accepted bids to translate, codify (index), and print the revised statutes of all territorial legislative sessions to date (first through ninth). In 1872, 200 copies were printed in an 860-page, hardbound volume (figure 3.5). Upon delivery, the secretary shipped the copies to the southern counties.

Once a translator's bid for the job was accepted, he worked long hours going over the available copies of the English versions of the statutes. Perhaps he

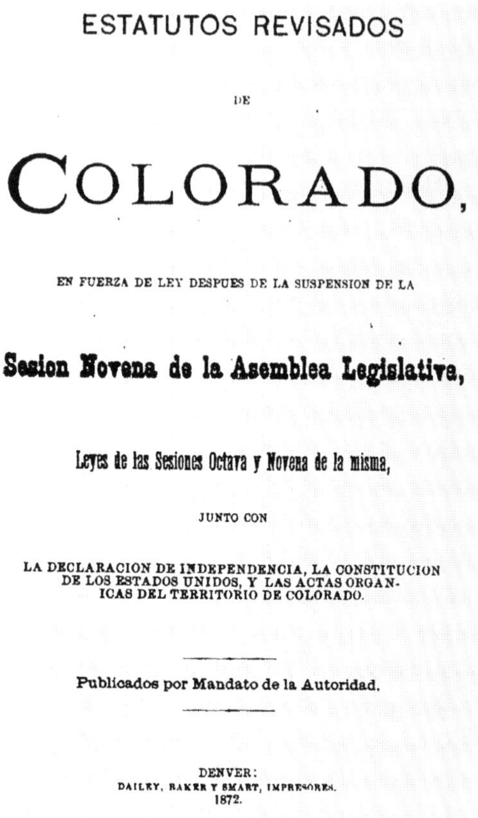

ESTATUTOS REVISADOS

DE

COLORADO,

EN FUERZA DE LEY DESPUES DE LA SUSPENSION DE LA

Sesion Novena de la Asemblea Legislativa,

Leyes de las Sesiones Octava y Novena de la misma,

JUNTO CON

LA DECLARACION DE INDEPENDENCIA, LA CONSTITUCION
DE LOS ESTADOS UNIDOS, Y LAS ACTAS ORGAN-
ICAS DEL TERRITORIO DE COLORADO.

Publicados por Mandato de la Autoridad.

DENVER:
DAILEY, BAKER Y SMART, IMPRESORES.
1872.

FIGURE 3.5. Title page of Spanish translation of laws passed in the eighth and ninth sessions of the Colorado Territorial Assembly (1870 and 1872), published in 1872. Colorado Supreme Court Library.

had to wait until the English version was printed. As in the case of Celestino Domínguez, it took about seven months for him to complete the translation of the statutes of the first session.[27] Upon completing his translation, a translator would have delivered his handwritten copy to the secretary or directly to the printer for typesetting and publication. This was a time-intensive process, for the territory did not have an office dedicated to a territorial translator, as had already been established and in use in New Mexico Territory, for example.

Anglo civil servants had received their English copies of the statutes much earlier than the Hispanos had received their Spanish-language copies. It had taken four years just to get the first volume of statutes translated and printed. The Spanish translation of the crucial territorial statutes had not been made available to the Hispano civil servants until 1864, then again in 1868 and 1872.

By the time these translated statutes were finally received in the southern counties, many of the laws had already been amended.

Getting the laws translated and then printed and shipped took more time than that needed for the English versions. The secretary then sent the translated copies to the southern counties as freight on a stagecoach or wagon. This meant that the Anglo assemblymen and county officials received their copies many months before their Spanish-speaking counterparts even received the statutes of the first three sessions.

Attorneys in the Territory

On October 24, 1861, the territorial assembly passed a law regulating the certification and licensing of attorneys. By law, a man interested in becoming an attorney had to have studied law for two successive years, and one year of that study had to have been with a lawyer in the territory. After this study he was eligible to apply for a license to practice law. To obtain a license, he needed a certificate from a county court attesting to his moral character and a certificate from one or more of the reputable attorneys he studied under for two years.

According to attorney Robert B. Murphy, in 1861 the territory had eighty-nine Anglo lawyers. A committee of three citizens,[28] appointed by the territorial supreme court, examined all applicants to determine their qualifications. Men who formerly practiced law outside the territory had to provide vouchers or licenses as proof of their experience as lawyers. An attorney was then admitted to the bar by meeting the statutory requirements of being a member of the bar of another state or territory and by submitting to the territorial supreme court proof of his license or a satisfactory voucher showing his admission. By the end of 1861, names recorded in the ledger of attorneys admitted to practice in Colorado numbered eighteen.[29]

No documents exist proving that these requirements were translated and disseminated to the Hispano lawyers in the southern counties. Although several Hispanos listed their occupations as lawyers, records about their practice and education are no longer available. Known *hombres buuenos* (learned men, judges, attorneys) served their communities between 1857 and 1871. Six of these were then living in the southern Jefferson–New Mexico border region and served their communities in 1857 and in 1860. Four of these men were from Conejos: José Víctor García (1857), Gabriel Lucero (1857), Marcelino Torres (1859), and

José María Jáquez (1860). In Culebra Juan Andrés Moya practiced law in 1860, and Miguel Antonio Vallejos from Costilla served as a judge in 1860 (table 3.2).[30]

Because the Colorado's "territorial system did not consider their legal training legitimate," many Hispanos lost their practices.[31] Many men who had served as lawyers but who held no license were elected as judges to smaller courts. Most of the justices of the peace had limited or no legal training, and many originally came from other jurisdictions with differing laws.[32] On February 5, 1866, the assembly passed a law allowing male citizens over age twenty-one to practice law in probate court without a license.

Land Law and the Sangre de Cristo Land Grant

Although Congress could have used California's three-year experience, it took very little action to confirm New Mexico's Spanish and Mexican land grant claims. Congress finally named a surveyor general for New Mexico on July 22, 1854. From his office in Santa Fe, William Pelham and his staff attempted to gather evidence from land grant documents and field investigations (surveys) and subpoenaed witnesses for scheduled hearings. Due to general mistrust and language miscommunication, many Hispanos hesitated to turn over their land title documents.

One year after the office of the Surveyor General of New Mexico was established, Beaubien filed his claim on the Sangre de Cristo land grant. The surveyor general's office in Santa Fe then reviewed all claims for authenticity and heard testimony. Surveyor General William Pelham found no encumbrances and recommended that Congress confirm the Beaubien claim, which it did five years later on June 21, 1860. Now, under US law and decree, the Sangre de Cristo land was his free and clear; he was free to do whatever he wanted with the land. By law, the land automatically reverted to Beaubien. But he had enticed the settlers onto his grant by offering them land! What would happen to them? What about their rights to the land?

As an inducement Beaubien offered each settler approximately 500 acres to move onto his granted land. This land was in strips of land, not in one-square-mile measurements used in the East. In addition, Beaubien gave the community of settlers a *vega* (commons). This pastureland still lies on the Sangre de Cristo between the settlements of San Luis, San Pablo, and San Pedro.[33] Once the settlers arrived, they constructed their homes and laid out systems

TABLE 3.2. Hispano judges and attorneys in Colorado Territory
Hombres Buenos *(learned men)* 1857–71

County/Plaza	Name	Year(s) Served	Title
Taos/Conejos	Jose Victor Garcia	1857	Justice of Peace
Taos/Conejos	Gabriel Lucero	1857	Justice of Peace
Taos/Conejos	Marcelino Torres	1859	Justice of Peace
Taos/Conejos	Jose Maria Jaquez	1860	Justice of Peace
Conejos	Jesus Maria Velasquez	1862	Probate Judge
Conejos	Juan Ysidro Lucero	1862	Lawyer
Conejos	Juan Bautista Jaquez	1862–65	Lawyer
Conejos	Antonio Gorgonio Galvez	1864	Probate Judge
Conejos	Juan Jose Gallegos	1864	Justice of Peace
Conejos	Juan Bautista Jaquez	1870	Probate Judge
Conejos	Jose Arcadio Velasquez	1870	Probate Judge
Conejos	Antonio Maria Vigil	1875	Lawyer
Conejos/Cenicero	Jose Pablo Antonio de Jesus Ortega	1864	Justice of Peace
Conejos/La Isla	Juan A. Martin	1864	Lawyer
Conejos/El Brazo	Jose Victor Garcia	1864–66	Lawyer
Conejos/El Cañon	Silverio Suazo	1864–65	Lawyer
Costilla	Miguel Antonio Vallejos	1861	Judge
Costilla	Juan Miguel Vigil	1864	Probate Judge
Costilla	Juan Santos Maes	1864	Justice of Peace
Costilla	Baltazar Quintana	1865	Justice of Peace
Costilla	Vicente Quintana	1866	Justice of Peace
Costilla/Saguache	Jose Antonio Moran	1867	Justice of Peace
Costilla/San Luis	Jose Ygnacio Ortega	1870	Probate Judge
Culebra	Juan Andres Moya	1860	Lawyer
Huerfano/Cucharas	Jose Albino Cordova	1870	Justice of Peace
Las Animas/Trinidad	Juan N. Gutierrez, Sr.	1867–68	Probate Judge
Las Animas/Trinidad	Jesus Maria Garcia	1869–70	Probate Judge
Las Animas/San Francisco	Casimiro Barela	1869–70	Probate Judge
Las Animas	Jose Rafael Sotero Chacon	1870–71	Justice of Peace
Las Animas/Trinidad	Jesus Maria Garcia	1874	Probate Judge

Source: Data compiled from census, voter, and tax assessment records; biographies; bounty land claims; and other documents.

of acequias by which, through gravity and the lay of the land, water from river or streams was diverted to their croplands.

The acequias were a communal venture in which the owners of water rights worked together to build, maintain, repair, and protect the ditches as well as regulate the sharing of water. The first acequia constructed in southern Colorado Territory was the San Luis People's Ditch. According to its Colorado water court record, its settlers completed construction of their ditch on April 10, 1852. The ditch received water from the Costilla Creek to irrigate 5,000 acres of land.[34] This ditch has continuously moved water from the Culebra River to farm fields for well over 150 years, and today this historic ditch has first-priority water rights in Colorado.[35]

Using the flow of gravity and following the curve of the land, the acequia moves water in a snakelike pattern. Its construction required a careful review of the lay of the land and analysis of the soil. Much labor went into constructing an acequia. At the worksite laborers, using wooden shovels, cut through the dirt. They placed the dirt and rocks onto large pieces of rawhide. Then the rawhide was dragged away by mule or oxen. Their construction methods had been passed down from generation to generation.[36] They would labor to clear the land and bring it under cultivation. They would continue to honor the customary land practice that centered on land's agricultural use for subsistence.

For some unknown reason, Beaubien began to consider the consequences to his settlers living along the Costilla, Culebra, and Trinchera Rivers. On May 1, 1863, he gave power of attorney to Costilla County clerk John L. Gaspar,[37] authorizing him to prepare deeds, in Spanish, to the Hispano settlers living among the seven villages within the Sangre de Cristo grant. As directed, Gaspar prepared the 135 deeds, thereby perfecting the document under US law. Beaubien signed the deeds ten days later. Jose Nasario Gallegos, the San Luis alcalde, assisted Gaspar in accepting proof of ownership and likely in helping Gaspar write the deeds in Spanish. According to the Mexican-era alcalde tradition, Gallegos had authority to take this proof.

Then on May 11, 1863, Beaubien wrote a document, known as the Beaubien Document,[38] to protect the settler's right of access to the natural resources on his vega.[39] Beaubien, now ill, had agreed to sell the land grant to former territorial governor William Gilpin, with the agreement that Gilpin would honor Beaubien's covenants and agreements with the settlers.

One of the settlers to receive a deed from Beaubien was José Gregorio Martín. About 1853 Martín had unintentionally settled on the land without Beaubien's permission. Once he learned of his error, Martín approached Beaubien with an offer to trade sheep for land. Reportedly each signed a contract. When Martín was hit by lighting and killed, reportedly Beaubien continued to honor the contract. In 1863 Beaubien, through the Costilla County clerk, "gave a deed for the land to Martín's son José de la Cruz Martín."[40]

Although Beaubien had demonstrated an understanding of the requirements for conveying property use rights under US law,[41] this understanding was later challenged. Someone complained that the deeds Beaubien had Gaspar make did not follow protocol. Specifically, Beaubien and Gaspar had not included the "Christian and surnames" of the settlers; he generally referred to them only as "community members" and "inhabitants" of certain settlements. He also did not include an accurate description of the individual properties.[42] Further, his two witnesses, and San Luis alcalde José Nasario Gallegos were not authorized by law to take the proof of deeds.[43]

Gaspar, who could read English, had access to the published 1861 statutes, including the real estate conveyance law. However, the damage he and Beaubien caused created major obstacles for the Hispano settlers. Now the land they had lived and toiled on was in danger of becoming public lands. Soon the settlers would be forced to purchase the land or leave. How could they pay for the land? Theirs was not a cash society. To obtain the cash, they would have to sell their livestock or obtain a private loan from a willing rico contractor. Both would lead to certain debt. It had been a little over a year since the US Congress placed these Hispanos of the "notch" in Colorado Territory. The land Beaubien gave them upon settlement was now in the dangerous hands of the government. The Beaubien Document did not stand up to the test of the law. It had failed to honor the Hispano customary land practice, centered on land's agricultural use for subsistence.[44]

Beaubien and Gaspar's actions leave many questions: Why had Beaubien deliberately left the settlers vulnerable to such property loss? Although it appears that Gaspar was the only person Beaubien consulted, both men knew other key territorial officials who were aware of the law and the impact to the settlers on his grant. Unfortunately, there are no answers.

The Beaubien heirs now became concerned about the taxes they owed on the vast land grant. Historian Stoller reminds us: "If the heirs had become so concerned about the amount of [territorial and federal] taxes they owed, imagine how the Hispano settlers felt?"[45] On April 7, 1864, about two months after Beaubien's death, the Beaubien heirs sold all but a one-sixth interest in the Sangre de Cristo grant to Gilpin for $15,000, equating to four cents an acre.[46]

Although the land was now in Colorado Territory, Beaubien and the Hispano settlers were still functioning under the traditional Hispano settlement and communal system. Just as Charles Beaubien had done before his death, Gilpin promised to allow the original settlers to continue residing on the land and recognize and confirm their access rights to the vega.[47] The settlers were now confident they could retain their land and commons. But Gilpin had other plans for his land.

Gilpin's plan went into effect. He and his partners decided to divide the land into two estates and develop large farms and planned communities. The company thought the Hispanos would provide a willing labor pool.[48] The Trinchera Estate was eventually developed by the Colorado Freehold Land and Emigration Company, and the Costilla Estate by the United States Freehold Land and Emigration Company (USFLEC).[49] The USFLEC was one of two landholding companies formed by Gilpin and his Anglo partners.

One agreement was intended only for the original settlers, many of whom were now deceased. It also resulted in the settlers receiving less than an acre of land. One company member said:

> As soon as the tract is open for settlement [. . .] the Mexicans will be gradually crowded out. At present nothing could be more painful to them than to be obliged to leave their beautiful settlements.[50]

The Hispano settlers on the Sangre de Cristo land, those who had constructed their adobe homes and churches and who had labored to clear the land and bring it under cultivation, ultimately discovered in 1873 that they now had to purchase their land from the USFLEC. Gilpin worked on a system that scaled the price to the time of occupancy while USFLEC representatives met with leaders from the larger Hispano settlements. Those settlers who could prove that Charles Beaubien had placed land in their care could purchase the land from Gilpin for twenty-five cents an acre. Settlers who had no proof of land ownership but who had cultivated land between five and fifteen years could purchase the land for two and a half dollars an acre. Those who had cultivated the land for two years could purchase the land for twenty to thirty-five dollars an acre. Those who could not produce titles to their land would be ejected.[51] Many Hispanos could not read or understand the English contracts and were deceived into signing over their communal rights to the land. This action resulted in forcing settlers into expensive legal proceedings, repurchasing their holdings, being evicted by court order, or selling their holdings.

The 1870 census recorded 157 farms along the Culebra River; by 1880, there were only 73! To quote Stoller, "The people . . . in the Culebra River [settlements were subsequently] plunged into much greater economic [stress], many forced to abandon the life and land which they love so much."[52]

Gilpin's decisive, unsympathetic, and selfish action was made for the economic good of a handful of Anglo men. This action resulted in the mass migration of Hispanos east toward Huerfano County during the mid-1860s. In the Huerfano they could apply for land patents via the Homestead Act. The move benefited some families; other families would not be so lucky.

Litigation of the land on the Sangre de Cristo continues today. In 1960 Jack Taylor acquired title to La Sierra in Costilla County and began fencing out the locals of 77,500 acres of mountainous common land. In November 1961 Taylor and his employees, Pervis Raley and Al Randolph, "beat and kidnapped" Tomas Rael and Gilbert and Edward Medina for trespassing on the Taylor property. When Taylor took the community to court in 1965, the district court ruled in his favor and took away the community's historic land rights to La Sierra.[53]

In response, a community-based organization, the Land Rights Council, assisted Apolinar Rael and other plaintiffs in bringing a lawsuit against Taylor (*Rael v. Taylor*). Apolinar Rael, relation to Tomas Rael unknown, believed a racist court had produced the 1965 ruling and hoped to present the plaintiffs' case. He pledged to "pick up his rifle and fight" if the courts failed to rule on their behalf. According to an interview by Nicki Gonzales, when eighty-two-year-old Rael asked his neighbors to sign on as plaintiffs, the room filled with silence. Then Agatha Medina steadied her crutches as she rose to her feet and said, "*Bueno cabrones, si ustedes hombres no tienen los huevos para firmar, dejame pasar*" ("Okay, you sons of bitches, if you men don't have the balls to sign, get out of my way").[54] The attendees followed her lead and signed as plaintiffs in the suit.

After decades of litigation, the Land Rights Council prevailed. In 2002, Colorado Supreme Court justice Mary Mullarkey declared it "the height of arrogance and nothing but a legal fiction" for the court not to interpret Charles Beaubien's documents in historical context. Since 2004, many of the descendants of the original heirs to the Sangre de Cristo grant have received legal access to La Sierra: "Those landowners who have access rights to the Taylor Ranch are those residents of Costilla County, Colorado who can trace the settlement of their properties back to at least the time that William Gilpin owned the ranch."[55]

Today the Land Rights Council continues to preserve the rights of the heirs of the Sangre de Cristo grant by allowing access to La Sierra as provided by the Treaty of Guadalupe Hidalgo. The organization is also dedicated to work with its owners to protect and preserve La Sierra's natural resources. Moreover, those who struggled against great odds to keep the heritage land grants viable never forgot their ancestral New Mexico legacy.

Notes

1. Lamar, *Far Southwest*, 204.

2. *General Laws of the Territory of Colorado, 1861*, October 31, 1861, 52–53. This act also spelled Guadalupe as "Gaudaloupe."

3. *House Journal of the Territory of Colorado, 1861*, November 7, 1861, 52 (relating to Conejos County). Hereafter cited as *House Journal of the Territory of Colorado, 1861*.

4. *General Laws of the Territory of Colorado, 1861*, November 7, 1861, 143.

5. Hart Library, History Colorado Center, CWA, Conejos County, Charles E. Gibson Jr., 1933–1934a, 116.

6. *House Journal of the Territory of Colorado, 1861*, October 16, 1861, 192 (relating to CB No. 25, a bill for an act to define county boundaries and to locate county seat in Colorado Territory).

7. Simmons, *San Luis Valley*, 129.

8. By custom, directions were always in relation to river flow with the speaker facing downstream. Ibid., 302, 303, 307; Colville, *La Vereda*, 257.

9. Hall, *Portrait and Biographical Record of the State of Colorado: Containing Portraits and Biographies of Many Well Known Citizens of the Past and Present*. Chicago: Chapman Publishing, 1899: 815. It is not known when García requested the survey or whether he requested it in a legislative capacity as a member of either the New Mexico or Colorado territorial assemblies.

10. La Plaza de Abajo was located east of San Acacio. López-Tushar, *People of El Valle*, 37; Colville, *La Vereda*, 257.

11. *House Journal of the Territory of Colorado, 1861,* 212 (relating to Garcia's protest).

12. *House Journal of the Territory of Colorado,* February 3, 4, 8, and 11, 1864, 11, 27, 29, 30, 42 (interpreter issue).

13. Armstrong, "Clothed with the Authority," 364–70. Elbert was instrumental in the organization of the Second and Third Colorado Volunteers. Collins, "Colorado's Territorial Secretaries," 196.

14. NARA, Washington, DC, Records of the Accounting Officers of the Department of the Treasury, Records of the Division of Territorial Accounts, RG 217, "Letters Sent Relating to Territorial Expenses," December 4 1854–June 30, 1880; "C. Dominguez to Bennet," May 30, 1862, entry 128, vol. 6; "Whittlesey to Bennet," June 16, 1862, entry 129, vol. 7.

15. Ibid. See also Armstrong, "Clothed with the Authority," 367–68.

16. NARA, Washington, DC, Territorial Letters, Division of Warrants, Records, and C. (Correspondence), First Comptroller's Office, January 1, 1862–December 31, 1862, vol. 6, May 30, 1862.

17. Although the Domínguez letter specified these two counties, he was speaking for the Hispanos in all of the southern Colorado counties. Barela, García, and Domínguez had searched for Delegate Bennet to personally deliver their letter and discuss the important issues with him. Some Hispanos in Costilla County, including José Celedonio Valdez of Conejos County, informed Domínguez that he and other Hispanos from Costilla County had seen Bennet in southern Colorado just prior to his departure to Washington. NARA, Washington, DC, Territorial Letters, Division of Warrants, Records, and C. (Correspondence), First Comptroller's Office, January 1, 1862–December 31, 1862, Celestino Domínguez to H. P. Bennet, vol. 6, May 30, 1862.

18. NARA, Washington, DC Territorial Letters, Division of Warrants, Records, and C. (Correspondence), First Comptroller's Office, January 1, 1862–December 31, 1862, vol. 6, June 16, 1862. Whittlesey was expressing an opinion of the "Know-Nothing Party" that began in Ohio and spread throughout the northern states.

19. Bennet incorrectly reported that the statutes were printed in the *Colorado Republican and Rocky Mountain Herald.* Armstrong, "Clothed with the Authority," 368. See also Collins, "Colorado's Territorial Secretaries," 192.

20. *House Journal of the Territory of Colorado,* February 3, 1864, 20 (relating to printing the laws in Spanish).

21. Ibid., March 1, 1864, 151.

22. Ibid., February 8, 1864, 20, 22.

23. Ibid., March 1, 1864, 151 (relating to an appropriation for the printing of the Governor's Message). An 1864 joint resolution recorded his name as C. Dominguez.

General Laws and Joint Resolutions, Memorials, and Private Acts, Passed at the Third Session of the Legislative Assembly of the Territory of Colorado, Convened at Golden City on the 1st Day of February, 1864, Adjourned to Denver on the 4th Day of February (Denver: Byers & Dailey, 1864), March 9, 1864, 258 (joint resolution). Hereafter cited as *General Laws of the Territory of Colorado, 1864*.

24. *Leyes Generales, Aprobadas en las Sesiones 4, 5 y 6 de la Asamblea Legislativa del Territorio de Colorado junto con la Declaracion de Independencia, la Constitución de los Estados Unidos, y las Actas Organicas [sic] del Territorio*, 1867; originals housed in the archives of the Colorado Supreme Court Library, Denver.

25. Conejos and Costilla Counties received one hundred translated copies; Saguache and Las Ánimas Counties fifty copies, Huerfano County seventy-five copies, and Pueblo County twenty-five copies.

26. *Colorado Chieftain*, May 2, 1872, 3, col. 2.

27. NARA, Washington, DC., Territorial Letters, Denver, Colorado Territory, Division of Warrants, Records, and C. (Correspondence), First Comptroller's Office, January 1, 1862–December 31, 1862, Celestino Domínguez to H. P. Bennet, May 30, 1862, vol. 6. Unfortunately, none of these handwritten translations exists today.

28. Sweig, "Civil Administration of Governor William Gilpin," 185–86.

29. Murray, "The Supreme Court of Colorado Territory," 23.

30. US Census, Taos County, New Mexico, Culebra, p. 219, Schedule 1, line 22, Household/Dwelling 1958, ancestry.com.

31. Gonzalez, *Refusing the Favor*, 34.

32. Smaller civil and criminal matters were handled by justice of the peace courts. These courts and the probate courts had jurisdiction to hear cases involving sums of less than $100. On March 2, 1863, this statute was amended to enable justice of the peace courts to hear cases involving sums up to and including $300, and probate courts up to and including sums of $2,000. Probate courts handled decedents' estates, to which the monetary limit did not apply. Judges of both these courts were elected and usually received no legal training. Murray, "The Supreme Court of Colorado Territory," 23, 27.

33. Stoller, "Preliminary Manuscript on the History of the Sangre de Cristo Land Grant," 31–32. Stoller wrote that the list of settlers appears in the Blackmore Papers, SRC, Hart Library, History Colorado Center, Denver; and in the John L. Gaspar Collection, 1864–1925, MSS 1359.

34. Today at least two-thirds of its irrigated land is organized or platted into long lots. Colorado General Assembly, "Session Laws of Colorado 2009," First Regular Session, 67th General Assembly, www.state.co.us/gov_dir/olls/sl2009a/sl_168.htm, accessed August 24, 2014.

35. Ibid., HB 09-1233.

36. Sánchez, *Forgotten Cuchareños*, 69. Also Rivera, *Acequia Culture*, 3.

37. In 1865 Gaspar served in the Colorado Territorial Senate representing Costilla County. He had also served as county clerk and recorder by 1867. Colorado Legislative Biographies, www.leg.state.co.us, accessed January 26, 2015. Gaspar Street in San Luis, on which the present county clerk's office sits, is named for him.

38. Costilla County Clerk, Costilla County, Book 1, 256.

39. La Vega in the San Luis Valley is the largest commons in the United States, measuring 633.32 acres of natural resources.

40. Hart Library, History Colorado Center, Denver, CWA, Interview of Jose Gregorio Martin, Charles E. Gibson, Jr., 1933–1934a, 102.

41. Center for Land Grant Studies, "Landmark Ruling on the Sangre de Cristo Grant," n.17, http://www.southwestbooks.org/sangredecristo.htm, accessed July 18, 2017. *Lobato v. Taylor*, Colorado Supreme Court, case no. 00SC527, *Lobato v. Taylor*, 13 P.3d 821, 830 (Colo. App. 2000).

42. Statutes of the Territorial Assembly of the Territory of Colorado, November 5, 1861, 64–67.

43. Costilla County Records, vol. 1, 256. General Statutes of the Territory of Colorado, November 5, 1861, 64–68.

44. For more information about the old custom of adjoining landowners having first chance of purchasing lands, see Sender Collection, 1697–1884, New Mexico Archives and Records Center, Santa Fe, Roll 2, document no. 275, frame 510.

45. Stoller, "Preliminary Manuscript on the History of the Sangre de Cristo Land Grant," 14.

46. Gilpin had also purchased Ceran St. Vrain's share of the grant and later both interests of Lucien Bonaparte Maxwell and James Quinn. López-Tushar, *People of El Valle*, 33.

47. Costilla County Court Records, County Clerk's Office, San Luis, Book 1, April 7, 1864, 241–42.

48. Gregory A. Hicks, "Memory and Pluralism on a Property Law Frontier," unpublished manuscript, accessed November 14, 2005, http://www.law.bepress.com, 8.

49. Lamar, *Far Southwest*, 248. Stoller, "Preliminary Manuscript on the History of the Sangre de Cristo Land Grant," 35.

50. National Park Service, National Register of Historic Places, "The Culebra River Villages of Costilla County, Colorado," sec. E, 17, 26.

51. Stoller, "Grants of Desperation," 30. López-Tushar, *People of El Valle*, 33–34.

52. Stoller, "Preliminary Manuscript on the History of the Sangre de Cristo Land Grant," 95–96.

53. KOA-TV moving image collection, accession number 87.488.7, History Colorado Center, Denver. See also "San Luis Range War," https://www.youtube.com /watch?v=a0FZQ2J4xYI, accessed September 27, 2017.

54. Gonzales, "La Sierra and the San Luis Land Rights Struggle," 27.

55. Ibid.

4

Protection by Soldiers and Militiamen

Protection against warring indigenous raiders, preparation for armed Southern sympathizers, unruly miners, and incursions by Confederate troops required some form of military presence in the notch and later in southern Colorado Territory. Such a presence included militiamen, enlisted soldiers, and volunteers of the US Army.

In the Southwest the Indian Wars were fought during the same time as the Civil War. The various federal departments involved that were connected to the territories of New Mexico and Colorado included the local superintendent of Indian affairs (the territorial governor), the Indian agent appointed by the president, the military districts of New Mexico and Colorado, the local military post (Fort Garland), and the US Departments of Military Affairs and Indian Affairs. Quite often these individuals and departmental heads disagreed on timely and much-needed action. At Fort Garland there were new recruits en route to Fort Union to muster in and out of military service, indigenous bands arrived to meet with their agent or a Fort Garland commander, and US Army soldiers were called out on peacekeeping missions with the settlers and miners.

DOI: 10.5876/9781607329145.c004

Quite often problems resulted when the left hand did not know what the right hand was doing. This chaos led to problems in timely and fresh rations and government stores for the indigenous bands associated with the agency; communication issues due to language barriers and among the various departments, agencies, and individuals; transportation issues due to weather and road conditions; and the type of action required by unclear military and civil orders. The fear of unfamiliar people and culture clouded many persons' judgment.

In addition, Fort Garland was the most remote post in the New Mexico Military Department. There soldiers commonly relied on whiskey for relaxation, amusement, and as medicine. Soldiers used it to cope with hostilities and relieve boredom. Alcohol was a big problem, and many conflicts arose from its misuse.

Some early Hispano male settlers were familiar with the Ute language and had traded with them for needed goods. They were also familiar with militia duty and expeditions to combat raiding by warring indigenous nations and to redeem stock and captive family members.

Memories of the Taos Riot of 1847 still instilled fear in some of Colorado's Anglo settlers. And due to the Civil War, everyone was on the lookout for Rebel sympathizers, Confederates, and any type of civil disobedience or unusual behavior. This period was a time of uncertainty, caution, and fear.

"Widespread disinformation" about the New Mexico Volunteers and militia during Civil War battles in New Mexico resulted in additional prejudice and bias. Anglo officers and soldiers (regulars) generally treated Hispano males with disrespect and berated them due to their limited command of the English language and their worn-out uniforms and outdated weapons.[1] Volunteers often had to use their own weapons.

Distrust between Hispanos and Anglos further manifested itself in a military census conducted in late 1862 at Conejos. As preparation to meet any Confederate threat, the commander of the New Mexico Military Department ordered an accounting to be made of military-age males as well as stores of firearms and ammunition and of food, including livestock, in Conejos and Costilla Counties. Based on fear of being conscripted, Hispano males failed in large numbers to show up to be counted. The women in Hispano households likewise were evasive in their responses about their male kin, their land, and their crops and livestock. The poor timing of the census coincided with many other significant events taking place at the time. However, the analysis of the Conejos census provides readers with much new information about the people, time, and place.

Indigenous Raiders

Settlement along the Arkansas River began about 1846, when José Benito Sandoval and trapper Mariano Baca established El Pueblo, an outpost on the north end of the Vigil–St. Vrain Land Grant. Settlements in the southern counties of Colorado Territory required protection from indigenous raiders. According to one of the earliest descriptions of El Pueblo, the outpost

> was a wretched species of [a] fort, [and its] most primitive construction [was] nothing more than a large square enclosure, surrounded by a . . . cracked and dilapidated . . . wall of adobe . . . [The] mud room [was] very neatly finished, considering the material and garnished with a crucifix, [with] a looking glass, a picture of the Virgin, and a rusty horse-pistol. There were no chairs, but instead . . . [a] number of chests and boxes [ar]ranged about the room. There was another room beyond, less sumptuously [sic] decorated, and here three or four Spanish girls, one of them very pretty, were baking cakes at a mud fireplace in the corner . . . They brought out a poncho, which they spread upon the floor by way of a tablecloth. A supper, which seemed to us luxurious, was soon laid out upon it, and folded buffalo robes were placed around it to receive the guests.

On Christmas Eve in 1854, bands of Ute and Jicarilla attacked El Pueblo because Ute chief Blanco thought Sandoval traded them blankets infected with smallpox. Two of Sandoval's sons were taken captive: Felix was twelve years old, Isidro was nine. Felix was held in captivity for eight months; Isidro was held for nearly six years. Sandoval's wife and two other sons were in New Mexico at the time and were spared from the killing. The following month, Blanco's band grew in strength and number and attacked a settlement along the Huerfano River.

Some years previous, about 1852, Charles Beaubien had established a friendship with the US Army and encouraged it to establish a military post to protect his settlers and miners and enforce the 1849 Ute Treaty. In response to the attacks by indigenous warriors, the Military District of New Mexico engaged volunteer units and soldiers from Fort Massachusetts and Fort Union.[2] Fort Massachusetts sent out scouting parties to patrol the San Luis

Valley and received its food and supplies from settlements in the far northern frontier of the former New Mexico province and as far south as Taos and Fort Union. During one raid on the settlers in 1855, indigenous warriors killed two Hispanos and captured a small boy. According to oral history, when the men "gave chase, the [warrior] carrying the boy on horseback dropped him, turned [his horse, then] thrust his spear to kill the boy." The spear grazed the boy's side, and he later recovered from the wound.[3] Although the settlers notified the US Army of the raid, by the time the Fort Massachusetts soldiers arrived, the warriors and their plunder were long gone.

However, antagonisms were not directed exclusively at the indigenous nations. The Taos Massacre and the US war against Mexico had occurred only scant years before, and the loss of lives was still felt by the people of both cultures. Accordingly, Hispanos also bore the brunt of Anglo distrust and in return often felt resentment toward the Anglos. Army assistant surgeon DeWitt Clinton Peters reported on the New Mexicans' dislike of American soldiers at Fort Massachusetts and predicted a "reconquest by the Mexican government" or civil unrest: "The Mexicans dislike the Americans and did they dare show it, it would not be long forthcoming in the shape of a civil war."[4] Due to the few munitions available to the settlers during this time, the doctor's fears proved unfounded, but his apprehensions of an unfamiliar people and culture were plain.

The Conejos Militia

In the 1850s and 1860s, each community of sufficient population raised a company for the volunteer service to protect their communities from raids on their family members, food stores, and livestock.[5] By September 1857, over 300 citizens had been killed by the raiding Navajo. In response to raids by indigenous bands, militia units "usually reacted quicker and chased the raiders longer and harder than the U.S. troops did." At the first sign of trouble, all available able-bodied men would muster in the plaza with their weapons Men in militia units elected their leaders. The militia captain, usually over the age of forty-five, was often elected based on his knowledge and experience of frontier warfare and leadership. Sometimes these elected leaders were men of wealth or status. The elected captain then rode out, "often hours after the crimes had been committed."[6]

New Mexicans grew tired of the US Army's attempt to control the indigenous raiders, and the New Mexico Territorial Assembly voted to raise volunteer battalions. It authorized independent campaigns that were under the authority of the governor and "independent of all other military authority."[7] After US occupation, nuevomexicanos were not actively recruited for enlistment in the regular US army; however, many participated in militias and later in volunteer units such as the New Mexico Volunteers. Engagements with indigenous nations were planned and authorized in Santa Fe through the New Mexico Military Department and the New Mexico governor. In contrast to the regular army, militiamen and volunteers were recruited for sixty days, three months, or six months. The New Mexicans may have been called up for recurring and needed expeditions, yet they were home in time to plant and pick their crops.

On January 30, 1859, Jesús María Velásquez, from the Guadalupe settlement, was named captain of the New Mexico Volunteers from Los Conejos, the "Conejos River on the Northern Frontier."[8] The following year on January 17, he led ninety-nine Hispanos in the Conejos Militia, a mounted company, on a campaign against the Navajo (table 4.1). Each militiaman supplied his own horse, arms, and equipment and provisions. Because the Conejos Militia was a large company, it had two musicians, a bugler and a drummer.[9] Unfortunately, records about this unit and its battles no longer exist. Captain Velásquez and his men returned to Conejos and continued to serve their communities. Because Beaubien had arranged protection with the US government seven years earlier, no military records indicate that the settlers from the Costilla River settlements established and maintained a militia.

Fort Garland

Fort Garland was important in the defense of supply routes along the Old Spanish Trail and the Trappers' Trail from Fort Laramie.[10] About 1856, the government approached Beaubien about its need to replace Fort Massachusetts.[11] The following day, construction of the new adobe fort, named Fort Garland, began six miles south between the Ute and Sangre de Cristo Creeks.

When the soldiers moved into the new Fort Garland on June 24, 1858, they brought with them the Mexican "national and regimental banners" that

TABLE 4.1. Members of the Conejos Militia, January 17, 1860

Capitan	Jesus Maria Belasquez	
1° teniente [Lieutenant]	J. Maria Jaquez	
2° teniente	J. Gavriel Marti	
Alferes [Ensign]	Francisco Gayegos	
Sargento [Sergeant]	Antonio G. Galbis	
Sargento	Felis Borrego	
Sargento	Jesus Maria Chabes	
Sargento	Carpio Lovato	
Corporal	Jose Gregorio Pais	
Corporal	Juan J. Mascarenas	
Corporal	J. Maria Martines	
Corporal	Pablo Antonio Ortega	
Armero [Gunsmith]	Francisco Lugan	
Clarin [Bugle]	J. Gabriel Martines	
Tambor [Drum]	J. Turnino Lusero	
Soldados [Soldiers]		
Jesus Maria Lucero	Luis Pacheco	Vitervo Sisneros
Martin Gayegos	Querino Maes	Jesus Maes
Antonio Jose Lovato	Teodoro Maes	Felis Cordova
Juan Manuel Gayegos	Jesus Maria Suasos	Aniseto Martines
Juan Francisco Chacon	Jesus Maria Sanches	Lionides Galvis
Luis Montoya	Vicente Sanches	J. Francisco Archuleta
Jesus Olguin	Francisco Martines	Guadalupe Torres
Manuel Romero	J. de Jesus Chabes	J. Sanches
Albino Gayegos	Seledonio Baldes	Juan Aragon
Juan de Jesus Martines	J. Francisco	Manuel Samora
J. Guadalupe Maes	Sandobal	Juan Pablo Mascarenas
Cornelio Lucero	J. Deciderio Martines	Santiago Manhego
Ylario Atencio	J. Ramon Garcia	Martin Chabes
Manuel Antonio Mestas	Pedro Fernandes	Germin de Jesus Gomes
Manuel Estevan Trugillo	J. Simon Garcia	J. Duran
Francisco Antonio Trugillo	Nasario Baldes	Santiago Sanches
Juan Antonio Martines	Senobio Trugillo	Jesus Maria Quintana
Bicente Belasques	Buenabentura Borrego	Gayego Marques
Antonio Jose Chabes	Buena Bentura Mestas	J. Tomas Sanches

continued on next page

TABLE 4.1—*continued*

Soldados [Soldiers]		
Manuel Sisneros	Juan de Dios Ruibal	Juan de la Crus Espinosa
Francisco Garcia	Juan Salas	Juan Nicolas Martines
Antonio Domingo Gayegos	Luis Lovato	Manuel Chabes
Francisco Gayegos	Bartole Baldes	J. Antonio Lucero
Juan Lenor Sisneros	Julian Gayego	Juan Aragon
Damacio Salas	J. Pablo Martines	Juan Baca
Francisco Antonio Atencio	J. Francisco Maes	Dolores Barela
Deciderio Lovato	Juan Eusebio Lucero	Vitor Garcia
Pedro Aragon	Juan Eusebio Rodrigues	Pedro Martines
Pedro Ortega	Jose Antonio Gonsales	

Source: "Lista de Personas que Forman la Compania de milicianos de los Conejos," January 17, 1860, Territorial Archives of New Mexico, New Mexico Archives and Records Center, Santa Fe, Roll 85.

Company A of the 3rd Infantry of the US Army had seized during the war with Mexico. These banners continued to be on display at Fort Garland as symbols of the victory over Mexico and to build and retain morale among the US Army troops. These symbols reminded the Anglo and Hispano soldiers of their respective places in the present social order. The military had yet to establish a means to unify the winners and the losers.

According to an oral history of post physician Charles Alden, on February 22, 1860, Company A hosted a "great festival" in celebration of George Washington's birthday. Many officers of the New Mexico Military Department, neighboring posts, and regimental companies attended. Some civilians were also present, although Dr. Alden did not indicate their heritage. Near the "native" (Hispano) musicians was a grouping of "American" flags. Opposite them hung the captured Mexican flags. At the south end of the room were three "transparencies [curtains] represent[ing] the national and regimental banners" won by Company A in the Mexican War. It was typical for regimental banners to display on them the names of important engagements in which the units had fought. At Fort Garland that evening the "crowning victory of the war," the "City of Mexico," appeared on a laurel wreath.[12]

According to fort commander Colonel M. L. Crimmins, during this time there were about twenty-five Hispano families growing corn and wheat along the Culebra River; eighteen miles away, along the Costilla River, he estimated another twenty-five families. He reported another fifty families along the Colorado, and along the San Cristobal, a dozen families.[13]

Like Fort Massachusetts, Fort Garland was not prepared and was "too far removed . . . to be of much service in protecting the settlements."[14] By the spring of 1862 Ute chief Blanco and his band were raiding settlements along the Conejos and Costilla Rivers. Sometime later, Muache Ute chief Kaneache led his band on a raid in Conejos. According to author Virginia McConnell Simmons, the settlers met the band east of the Guadalupe Plaza where they battled for "half the day."[15] Ultimately, the settlers fled their homes and hid in the nearby bushes while the band continued their killing and raided the livestock.

Recruiting Soldiers: Miners, No Mexicans

The US Civil War began on April 12, 1861. New US Army recruits began to flow through Fort Garland en route to Fort Union for transition to military life and to prepare for battle against the Confederates. During most of the Civil War, Fort Garland was under the jurisdiction of the New Mexico Military Department. This fort was "the most remote post in the Department . . . and proved to be one of the least desirable duty stations in the Southwest."[16] Alcohol was a big problem, especially at isolated posts, and many conflicts arose from its misuse. Soldiers commonly relied on whiskey for relaxation and amusement and as medicine. Soldiers used it to cope with hostilities and to relieve boredom. In 1862 the Colorado territorial legislature passed an act making it illegal to "sell or give spirituous liquors, or wine of any class, to any non-commissioned officer or soldier in the service of the Army of the United States." Frederick William Posthoff, the post sutler, had been distilling liquor in La Costilla and selling it at Fort Garland, but in November 1862 the post commander forbade Posthoff from issuing whiskey at the post or selling alcohol to his men.[17]

Sometime prior to February 1861, New Mexico governor Abraham Rencher had commissioned José Julián Espinosa of Conejos as a captain (figure 4.1).[18] At his own expense, Espinosa outfitted his entire company of Hispanos from the various settlements for a regiment of the New Mexico Volunteers. His brother, Donaciano Espinosa, served as a company sergeant. On July 4, 1861,

FIGURE 4.1. Captain José
Julián Espinosa. Courtesy
Francisco Gallegos.

they were mustered into service in the US Army. Initially, Captain Espinosa's company would provide military escort for government wagons traveling between Fort Union and Albuquerque. However, his Company D became part of a regiment commanded by Colonel Kit Carson. The regiment participated in the Battle of Valverde in February 1862, fighting Texas Confederates seeking to advance west into New Mexico and possibly as far as California. During the battle all of the horses of Espinosa's company were transferred to another unit, "leaving his men to fight on foot." Espinosa suffered much personal financial loss due to the transfer of his horses and equipment.[19] When Espinosa was released from duty on May 10, 1862, he returned to his farm in southern Colorado.[20]

Other officers in the 1st Regiment who later had ties to southern Colorado included Captain Charles Deus and Major José Rafael Sotero Chacón. Chacón had an exemplary military career; however, he was passed over for promotions. He was mustered out of service on September 2, 1864, and moved north from New Mexico to Trinidad in Las Animas County (figure 4.2).

Deus, a Prussian, came to New Mexico during the US war with Mexico. He was a member of the Missouri Light Artillery, a company composed mostly of German immigrants. By the time of his arrival at Santa Fe, he had

FIGURE 4.2. Major
Rafael Chacón and
Juanita Páiz. Courtesy
Denise Lovato Durán.

changed his first name from Karl to Charles. To supply his men with horses,
Deus sold $3,500 worth of his wagons, cattle, and personal belongings. The
company of Captain Deus mustered at Fort Union on August 4, 1861, and the
following year fought at the Battle of Valverde. He was able to speak English,
Spanish, and some indigenous languages. Deus married a Hispana, and they
later migrated north into what became Huerfano County. They later moved
west to San Luis, where he became a merchant.[21]

Deus had first attempted to enlist men into the Colorado Volunteers, but
Governor Gilpin still had not received permission from Washington for his
already-formed unit. In July 1861 Captain Deus recruited Hispanos from
the settlements along the Culebra and Costilla Rivers for the New Mexico
Volunteers.[22] Gilpin was riled to learn that Deus had enlisted men into the
New Mexico Volunteers rather than his Colorado Volunteers.[23] During the
spring of 1862, when General Edward Canby of the New Mexico Military
Department contacted Governor Gilpin about the need to recruit companies
of New Mexico Volunteers, Gilpin recommended he recruit from the "less
fortunate miners," as there were plenty available.[24]

At Denver, Major Adolph H. Mayer established a recruiting office on
Fourth Street near Front Street. To recruit Anglo men in Denver and on the

eastern plains at Julesburg, Mayer purchased advertisements in the *Rocky Mountain Daily Mail* asking citizens to rescue New Mexico Territory from a Confederate invasion.[25] In a subsequent advertisement, Mayer clarified to readers that regiments already raised were filled with Anglo men—and no "Mexicans."

In May, General Canby suspended all recruitment "among the Mexican population" into the New Mexico Volunteers due to "widespread disinformation" about the volunteers and militia.[26] Rumors about the Hispanos' retreat in key battles fueled additional prejudice throughout the Civil War; however, in his memoir Captain José Rafael Sotero Chacón, who spoke only Spanish, reported that his company fought well, with "valor and activity," and that they had not retreated "until ordered to do so."[27]

Anglo officers and the nonvolunteer regulars generally treated all Hispanos with disrespect. They berated Hispano soldiers because they spoke limited or no English, or fought with outdated weapons, and because only a few wore government-issued uniforms.[28] On May 25 the New Mexico Military Department ordered Major Mayer to close his recruiting office for the 4th Regiment of the New Mexico Volunteers.[29] Canby then rearranged the military district in the Department of New Mexico. Colonel John Milton Chivington was placed in charge of the Military District of Colorado. That August, Captain Deus, who had been recruiting from mining camps at Buckeye Joe, Laurett, and Cañon City, submitted an interesting report about three officers recruiting for the Colorado Volunteers. To dissuade Anglo miners from enlisting in the New Mexico Volunteers, these officers told the miners that Deus's regiment was composed of "greasers" and that the men should not "enlist for Mexico."[30] At Fort Garland during this time Captain Ethan Wayne Eaton's company of New Mexico Volunteers was mostly made up of nuevomexicanos.[31] In a report to Brigadier General James H. Carleton, Eaton asked for proper treatment of his men:

> The policy generally used towards the Mexican people by Americans in my opinion is wrong and not for the best interest of the Country or government. When New Mexico was made a part of the United States, the people were made our own people, entitled to the same privileges [sic] and protection as ourselves. [Keeping] them back . . . continually [stirs] up a feeling of jealousy & animosity between the two people.[32]

The US Military Census of Conejos

The Civil War was into its second year. To determine the number of men available to defend Colorado from a Confederate attack, General James Henry Carleton, commander of the Department of New Mexico, sent Major Archibald H. Gillespie to the southern counties of Colorado Territory to take a military census. As ordered, Gillespie would travel to Conejos to determine the number of males who could be conscripted; the amount of stores of food, guns, and ammunition; and the number of livestock that could be commandeered as needed for Union forces.

Gillespie arrived at Fort Garland in October 1862. He had intended to participate in an inspection of the post, but he got drunk and missed the inspection. On October 23 at the home of W. F. Posthoff near the post, the major was again drunk. Another report stated that he had been seen drunk in Costilla.[33] His addiction plagued him during the entire tour.

On October 30, 1862, post commander Captain Eaton provided Major Gillespie with a nine-man escort.[34] Half of the escort rode on horseback while the remaining men rode in a "miserably disgraceful" wagon led by a six-mule team. According to Gillespie, "The harness [was] so old and rotten it [could] hardly be kept together."[35] The party marched south toward the Culebra River and passed the "Lower Culebra" (Plaza Abajo, or San Acacio). Then they turned west and crossed the Rio Grande into a "bleak and barren plateau [toward] the village of Guadalupe de los Conejos." In a "cutting winter wind," the party covered twenty-eight miles in twelve hours.[36]

Conejos had a total of twenty plazas in fifteen precincts. Eight small plazas formed the precincts of Santiago, Guadalupe, San Rafael, San Antonio, and San Jose. Word traveled fast among the plazas, and many settlers believed Gillespie was there either to forcibly impress men into the service of the United States or to imprison them for nonpayment of the Civil War and miscellaneous territorial taxes unexpectedly imposed upon them.

On the evening of November 1, Gillespie's party crossed the San Antonio River toward the San Jose plaza and the property of José Seledonio Valdez. Gillespie likely camped on the Valdez property for the evening as details of soldiers commonly quartered at ranches and stations when necessary. Valdez may have ridden out to meet Gillespie's party, determine the purpose of the visit, and provide an area for the evening's quarter. Gillespie had learned to speak Spanish while serving in California during the war with Mexico.[37]

Precinct Musters

Gillespie was only visiting the settlements, yet he required a large escort party. On November 3 the military party marched southwest toward Conejos. One can only imagine Major Gillespie's presence on horseback leading a sergeant and nine privates into the small, quiet, and unsuspecting Hispano settlements. During this time, several unexplained murders were taking place in south-central Colorado, for which some Hispanos from Conejos were being blamed. The various events occurring in and around Conejos during this time had everyone on edge (as discussed further in chapter 6).

On November 3, 1862, Gillespie dispatched a message to Indian agent Lafayette Head, instructing him to arrange a meeting with as many of the Conejos "Prefects, Alcaldes, Sub-Alcaldes, Sheriff and Constables" as possible (table 4.2). Gillespie wanted the meeting held at Head's residence the following day.

According to Colorado historian Frank Hall, in 1863 Manuel Lucero was county clerk; Miguel Antonio Martinez, sheriff; Jose Gabriel Martinez, county treasurer; and Pedro Antonio Lobato, chairman of the board of commissioners. During the meeting Gillespie read a Spanish version of General Carleton's special orders for the muster and census: "In the simplest manner, [I explained] that the Census or information desired was for no sinister purpose, for the levying of no tax or inforcement [sic], either of persons or property, but solely for ascertaining the number of inhabitants, the amount of available means for sustaining the Government of the United States."[38]

The Conejos prefect, Captain Jesús María Velásquez, instructed those present to immediately assemble all the men from the plazas of the principal precincts and advise them of the designated time and date of their precinct's muster. In closing, Gillespie instructed them "to use zeal and activity to accomplish the object desired." Although Gillespie did not record the names of the men attending the meeting, he reported that they all agreed that the first muster would take place the following morning.[39]

On November 4, at the home of José Seledonio Valdez of La Isla de San José (the Island of St. Joseph), the first muster of the eight plazas in the

TABLE 4.2. Conejos precincts, town mayors, and constables
As reported by Major Gillespie in 1862

Precinct		Town	Alcalde (Mayor)	Constable (Sheriff)
1	Guadalupe	Guadalupe	Jose Victor Chavis	Cornelio Lucero
		Sirvieta		Jose Maria Martinez
		Guadalupita	Jose Francisco Martinez	
		In front of Guadalupe		
		Mesitas		
2	Santiago	Hilario	Buenaventura Borrego	Luis Rafael [de Jesus] Trujillo
		San Jose		
		Cerritos	Feliz [de Jesus] Borrego	Andres Martin
		Rincones		
		Casas Garcia		
		Lobato		
		Santa Margarita		
		Houses below Garcias		
3	San Rafael	Cañon	[Capt.] Jesus M. [Maria] Valdez	Silverio Suaso
		San Rafael		Fernandez Valdez
			Benigno Mes	
4	San Antonio	Pinos	Francisco Trujillo	Felipe Lusero
		San Antonio		Antonio Maria Sisneros
		Houses below San Antonio	Francisco Martinez	
5	San Jose	Cenisero	Juan Jose Mascarenas	Mariano Montoya
		Plaza Garcia		Miguel Montoya
			(Jose) Pablo (Antonio de Jesus) Ortega	

Source: NARA, Washington, DC., Letters Received, Department of New Mexico, Jesus M. Velasquez to Maj. Gillespie regarding Conejos Precincts, November 5, 1862, M1120, Roll 18.

Santiago precinct began at 8:00 a.m. It was not until 11:00 a.m. that a few men arrived. Gillespie's visits to the plazas of Los Pinos and Cenicero met "with worse success." Although he attempted to explain that his inquiries were "for their benefit and interests," Gillespie became angry and perplexed. The men he needed information from had not appeared for their muster.[40]

The muster called at the Guadalupe precinct the following day met with "little better success, but mostly old men." Gillespie reported that "nearly all the men between the ages of eighteen and forty-five had fled to the mountains or across the Rio Grande" and that "a feeling of disloyalty" existed through-out most of "this part" of southern Colorado.

> Some fifty of them even went across the mountains to the River Huerfano, as they said to avoid impressment into the Army of the United States . . . The people . . . constantly [show] an indisposition [and] pay [no] proper respect to U.S. Officers. [There is] a total disregard of the Civil Authorities of the Territory, which if it does arise from disloyal sentiments, is a spirit of lawless recklessness, which requires the strong arm of Military power to furnish and destroy without delay.[41]

Gillespie did not report how he knew the men had fled; however, from Lafayette Head he learned that laborers constructing Head's large stable "had thrown down their axes and had run."[42] Unfortunately, the muster rolls for the Guadalupe and Santiago precincts no longer exist.

Gillespie decided he would visit "every plaza and house" in the district to obtain information from any and all who might be present. Every house he visited displayed "a feeling of great distrust and suspicion." The people were reluctant to give him any information. Those who met with him used "falsehood . . . to conceal and mislead." He also claimed they were disrespectful. In his report to headquarters, he wrote about the "prejudices of the people" and that they were "disposed and consider themselves beyond the reach of all law." Had not the government, he complained, "always produced the ready fray" and extended its care "to protect their lives and property from an invading foe and the depredatory Indians?"[43]

According to the 1860 Taos County census for San Rafael (Precinct 19), the San Judas de Tadeo (Saint Judas of Thaddaeus) plaza had sixty households, and all but three homes were built of adobe.[44] When Gillespie's military entourage approached, the people there were so scared that when a woman gave the alarm, the men fled.

When he asked about their property and the names of household members, nearly all the women responded that most of their men were in Santa Fe. The women feared forced enlistment of their sons and husbands; all feared losing their land, livestock, and crops to the US government: "The women answered to questions falsely; they denied having any land, and in no instance would they tell the ages of their husbands . . . The widows would not give their names and replied to questions with abusive language." Although

Gillespie reported that "the people are notoriously bad and lawless,"[45] he did not state how he knew this, nor did he provide any names.

According to the 1860 Taos County census for the Conejos precinct, San Juan de Pumeceno del Cañon had ninety-five households. The San Juan de Pumeceno del Cañon plaza was named for the Bohemian saint John Nepomucene (or Nepomuk), who was canonized in 1729. Some settlers often shortened the name of this plaza to San Juan or even Cañon; they also shortened "Nepomuceno" to "Pomuceno."[46] Here only four men appeared for the muster.[47] Twenty-four-year-old resident Jesús María Valdez provided Gillespie with the names and information for eighteen males, three of whom were illegible for service.[48]

Due to the meager attendance at the musters, Agent Head and Captain Velásquez suggested Gillespie use information from the 1861 territorial voter rolls to create a muster roll. To vote in Colorado Territory's first election, male voters had to be over the age of twenty-one. These were exactly the men Gillespie was interested in. Using the voter rolls, he found nineteen men between the ages of twenty-four and sixty-two; thirteen men were under forty-five years of age, but only three could be considered fit for service (figure 4.3). Eight of these men had old rifles, carbines, or fowling pieces that were of no value for military service. To obtain additional names and information, Gillespie interviewed "prominent" Anglo merchants, reliable citizens and neighbors, and "old men, women and children." He eventually created a military roll of the Hispanos from the five precincts that the government could enroll or conscript if needed. For all of Conejos, Gillespie reported 375 men capable of bearing arms; of these, 292 were under the age of forty-five (table 4.3).[49] Gillespie, however, did not enumerate any of the six Anglo men living in Conejos.[50]

MAJOR GILLESPIE'S SUMMARY OF CONEJOS

From the official reports Gillespie submitted to headquarters, we learn new information about Conejos County and its people. In his "Abstract of Military Census for Conejos," Major Gillespie provides key information about the Conejos plazas. For each plaza, he provided the number of families by gender and age. Then he listed information about available arms and ammunition, livestock by type and number, amount of fodder, and the type

TABLE 4.3. Major Gillespie's military roll, District of Conejos, Colorado Territory
Submitted January 3, 1863, from Fort Garland by Archibald H. Gillespie, Maj. US Army, Addl. Aide-de-Camp on Special Assignment to Maj. Genl. H. W. Halleck

Precinct	Plaza	No. of Men	No. of Rifles	No. of Carbines	No. of Pistols	No. of Shotguns	No. of Muskets
Guadalupe	Guadalupe	43	3	4	4	1	
	Sirvieta	32	8	3			
	Guadalupita	16	2	1	1	1	
	In front of Guadalupe	5	1				1
	Mesitas	3	1				
	Hilario	1					
Santiago	Hilario	17	1	2	1	1	
	San José	16	4	1	1		2
	Cerritos	16		3	1	1	
	Rincones	15	1	2	1	1	
	Casas Garcia's	12	1	4	1	2	
	Lobato	6	2	1		1	
	Santa Margarita	5		2	1		
	Houses below Garcia	2		2			
San Rafael	Cañon	31		1	2	1	
	San Rafael	23	3	4	3	2	
San Antonio	Pinos	62	3	9	2	1	3
	San Antonio	20	2	5	3	2	
	Houses below San Antonio	4	2	2			
San José	Cinesero	42	3	4			3
	Plaza Garcia	4	1	1	1	2	
Total	20 plazas [Hilario listed twice]	375	38	57	22	16	9

Source: NARA, Washington, DC, Letters and Telegrams Received, 1860–1880, "General Recapitulation of the Military Roll of the District of Conejos, C.T., 1863," Fort Garland Letterbook, C.T., M1120, RG 393, Part 5, Entry 4, Box 1.

and amount of crops and grains raised. He also determined the number of wagons, houses, and amount of cultivated and uncultivated land per plaza (figure 4.3).

Prect. No.	No. Place	Name	Men	Women	Families	Males 1 to 7	Males 7 to 16	Females 1 to 7	Females 7 to 16	Arms Total	Rifles	Carbines	Pistols	Muskets	Shotguns	Fowling	Powder lbs	Horses	Mares	Mules	Jacks	Oxen	Cows	Goats	Hogs	Sheep	Corn	Wheat	Potatoes	Hay	Fodder in loads	Wagons	Houses	Lands in Varas	Land cult in acre	Mills
1	1	Guadalupe	24	25	19	5	4	15	1	25	3	2	4	1		4	12	15	18	6	1	95	362		1	900	85	2102	373.5	90		13	21	3760	144	1
2	2	Guadalupita	9	10	9	2	5	6	5	18	3	1		1			3.5	7	3	3	1	17	33	10	3		41	568	78	20		2	9	2060	48	1
3	3	Sirvieta [sic]	24	24	21	13	9	15	4	41	10	5	1	1			6	1	4		4	18	64		1	2850	63.5	1496	234	10	23	3	21	2480	73	3
3	4	Hilario	22	61	21	14	17	11	19	61	2	2	1				15.5	6	12	1	15	28	82	6		583	18	860	115.5	3	2	5	20	2810	82	1
4	5	Casas Garcia	13	13	13	5	9	6	8	28		2	3	1	4		6	5	3	1	13	8	44	33		423	6	597	50	3	2	2	12	1260	38	
	6	Mesitas	3	3	3																	8	15					306	31	3	3	3	3	620	16	
5	7	Cerritos	14	16	13	9	8	10	4	31	1	5	1			1	5	7	6	4	1	25	79	153	16	1100	273	953	6	6	3	4	13	2707	39	2
	8	Santa Margarita	7	7	7	5	2	7	2	14	1	1	1				5.5	9	2	2	1	35	70		5	1200	101.5	675	51	6		3	7	1530	29	
6	9	Rincones	18	19	16	10	6	12	8	36	2	4	1	1			2.5	5	5	2	1	25	70		1		100.5	727	21		6	2	16	2980	66	1
7	10	San Jose	17	15	13	4	11	4	5	24	5	4	5	12			9	14	2	13	1	40	265		8	50	61	1211	41	19		8	12	2550	76	1
8	11	Plaza Garcia	7	7	6	4	4	4	5	19	3	2	1					4	1			6	33		12	1700	12	295	7.5				7	72	12.5	1
	12	Lobato	7	4	3	3	6	4	5	18	2	1	1	1	1	1	6	2	1			9	18				30	223	135	6	2	5	5	740	13	1
	13	below Plaza Garcia	3	3	3	3	2	4	3	12	1	2	1			1	2	1				2	14		1		1.5	155	4.5	1	2	3	3	280	9	1
9	14	Cinesero [sic]	30	28	23	12	15	14	15	56	1	6	2	4			2	16	21	5		31	346	63		3555	30	681	2.5	14	4	9	23	4150	65	2
10	15	Plaza Garcia	4	4	4	1			1	10	1	1	1		2		4	6	4			22	39	30		200	60	393		3		4	4	950	18	
	16	on Rd to San Rafael	8	6	4	1	4	3	2								3.5	8	4	4	6	6	150				45	550	129	18		1	4	700	30	
	17	below San Antonio	3	3	3	2	2	2	5	11	2	1	1	1			3	8	4	5		6	15			50	69	564		6		1	4	530	16	
11	18	San Juan de Pumeceno de los Pinos	35	29	29	14	27	24	13	78	4	8	8	5		1	7.5	13	13	3		31	53	10	21		73.5	1017	12	28	3	3	31	2550	63	2
12	19	Cuevas de Los Pinos	13	13	11	8	14	2	2	26	3	4	3				3.5	2	3		4	17	15	23	9	1000	9	611	3	7		1	10	762	28.5	
	20	San Antonio	17	19	16	8	7	7	8	30	3	7	3	4			15	14	9	19	4	30	52	23	9	1000	33	901	21	6		8	16	1820	61	2
13	21	San Rafael	17	19	17	13	16	23	5	58	3	7	5	1	2	3	3	6	6	2		24	39		31	950	30	808	6		3	2	17	2070	61	1
	22	Casas Gallegos	4	6	2	2	1	1	4	7								1	3			4	8			500	15	225	69			2	2	320	13	
14	23	San Judas de Tadeo	18	22	20	17		7	15	39	2	3	2	1	1	1	2.5	7	5	1	3	4	7	20	19		10.5	208	75				20			
15	24	San Juan de Pumeceno del Cañon	13	26	18	8	5	4	9	26	2	3	3	2		1	7	15	4	4		20	28			400	78.5	1065	113		1	1	15	1720	32	
15	24	TOTAL	330	379	294	161	176	186	149	672	50	73	44	29	24	5	135	166	132	75	55	505	1901	371	137	16461	1246.5	17191	1578.5	250	43	76	295	39421	1033	20

FIGURE 4.3. Abstract of Major Gillespie's military census, District of Conejos, January 31, 1863. NARA, Washington, DC, M1120, RG 393, Letters and Telegraphs Received, 1860–1880, "Abstract of Military Census of District of Conejos, General Recapitulation" Fort Garland Letterbook, C.T., Part 5, Entry 4, Box 1.

Although the Hispanos were not so willing to meet with him, he was able to learn this information from on-site visits under a military presence and from their Hispano neighbors or well-informed Anglos. The soldiers assigned to him certainly would have searched wherever necessary to assist their commander in obtaining the information to complete his mission.

Gillespie's report of the San Juan de Pumeceno plaza breaks down the information, from the above report, to an individual family level. He listed the name and age of the head of household and the number and ages of women and children in the household. In addition to an inventory of arms, livestock, and crops, the report also listed the number of wagons, houses, mills, amount of cultivated land owned (figure 4.4). (See figure 6.2 for the abstract for San Judas de Tadeo Plaza.) The number of men and arms Gillespie reported for San Judas de Tadeo and San Juan de Pumeceno, however, does not correspond with the totals he recorded on the "Abstract of Military Census" report.

Gillespie reported about 400 head of sheep as belonging to the widow Maria Concepcion Suazo. Suazo, however, was not a widow; she was the wife of Quirino Crescencio Maes.[51] Gillespie also reported that Suazo owned the only wagon in all of Conejos, which seems unlikely. Gillespie's report about the living conditions of two widows offered no sympathy but rather contempt: "The houses or cabins with but two exceptions are very miserable; the women, save [twenty-eight-year-old] Señora [Maria Concepción] Suazo, were mostly in rags, very dirty, and presented the lowest class of poverty to a sad degree. The widow [thirty-year-old Petra] Chaves was abusive, suspiciou[s] and dissrespectful [*sic*] for [*sic*] public authorities was every where exhibited."[52]

Gillespie estimated that the Conejos population of 2,700 settlers cultivated over 4,000 acres. According to Gillespie's detailed report, José María Jáquez owned the most livestock and grew most of the county's wheat (figure 4.5). There were about "4,000 head of cattle, (200 to 300 beef) and some 35,000 sheep in and around [the] Conejos Valley; horses and mules are not numerous," rather "mares and Jacks [are] being used on account of Indian robberies . . . The number of oxen, wagons, and transportation generally, is correct, good, and available at any time."[53] Major Gillespie also made a notation that Jáquez has just opened a distillery for making whiskey from wheat on January 15, 1863.[54]

No.	Name	Age	Women	Children	Arms	Ammo	Horses	Mares	Mules	Oxen	Cows	Calves	Sheep	Land	Corn	Wheat	Potatoes	Hay	Wagons	Houses	Mills	Misc	Land Cult
1	Manuel Galvez	40	1		rifle / carbine	2 lbs	4	2	1	6	8	5		100	24 bu	45 bu	45 bu			1			2 ac
2	Jose Maria Jaquez	58	3								8	5		200		250 bu				1			4 ac
3	Juan Jaquez	30	1				1			2	4	3	'	100	4.5 bu	9 bu				1			2 ac
4	Donaciano Marquez	25	1	9 females from 7 to 14 years of age 4 females from 2 to 7 years of age 5 males from 7 to 10 years of age 8 males from 1 to 7 years of age												15 bu				1		19 Hogs at large - no owners acknowledging them	
5	Francisco Martin	33	1		musket		1							100		45 bu	6 bu			1				2 ac
6	Gabriel Martin	27	1				1	2	1	4	8	4		200		150 bu	18 bu			1				4 ac
7	Juan Antonio Martin	47	2											100		30 bu	12 bu			1				1 ac
8	Pedro Martin	28	1													15 bu				1				
9	Jose Olaveri	30	1				2							120	24 bu	60 bu	8 bu			1				2 ac
10	Jose Maria Suaso	30	1				2									50 bu	3 bu			1				
11	Antonio Valdez	33	2		rifle	2.5 lbs	2			4	2			220		240 bu				1				4 ac
12	Jesus Maria Valdez	24	1											100	9 bu	45 bu	12 bu			1				3 ac
13	Juan Jaramio	26	1				1							110	3 bu	45 bu	3 bu			1				2 ac
14	Petra Chavez	30	widow																	1				
15	Maria Concepcion Suaso	28	widow		3 pistols / 2 carbines	3 lbs	1	2	2	4	6	5	400	150	12 bu	60 bu	6 bu		1	1			6 ac
	Total		19	26		7.5 lbs	15	4	4	20	28	17	400	1720	78.5	1065	113		1	15		19	32

FIGURE 4.4. Abstract of military census for San Juan de Pumeceno Plaza, 1862. NARA, Washington, DC, M1120, RG 393, Letters and Telegrams Received, 1860–1880, "Abstract of Military Census of District of Conejos, Plaza of San Juan de Pumeceno," Fort Garland Letterbook, C.T., Part V, Entry 4, Box 1.

Jáquez owned the first grist mill in Conejos.[55] Each of the twenty-six mills, of log construction, was eighteen feet square. The grinding stones in each were three feet in diameter. The settlers had brought them down from "the mountains on the south side of the valley near Los Pinos." The small undershot waterwheel ground eighteen bushels in twelve hours.[56] According to author Ruth Marie Colville, settlers living in New Mexico transported their grain to Conejos, *al salir de lucero* (at sunrise), rather than visiting the more convenient San Luis mill, because the Conejos mills "made whiter flour."[57]

Gillespie also noted, "considering the very small amount of seed with which they commenced," the Hispanos had had much luck growing potatoes. To transport them to Fort Garland and Santa Fe, Gillespie wrote, "Parties here . . .

FIGURE 4.5. José María Jáquez. Courtesy Meliton Velasquez.

will contract to freight . . . for two cents [per] pound, 180 lbs. [per] fanega."[58] Most likely he was referring to Hispano freighters. At the time, potatoes sold for three dollars a *fanega* (approximately one and a half bushels).

When Major Gillespie began his mission, he reported about his opinions of the Hispanos and their backward farming techniques. When he reported near the end of his mission, he pronounced them unpatriotic, and only a few "respectable loyal [Hispano] Citizens" had any influence among the people. He failed to acknowledge how far they had come with the little they had:

> The beauty of its location, its salubrity, the fertility of its soil, the great
> and excellent yield of its products . . . [commands] the attention of the

Government. . . . Industrious immigrants will soon [possess] its uncultivated land . . . and what it [will] become [when] more settlers arrive from the East with their improvements and a better knowledge of agriculture.[59]

The valley of the Conejos is very fine for grazing large herds of cattle, and covering immense quantities of very fine hay; wheat grows very well, but is in danger of injury from late frosts . . . There are a few respectable loyal Citizens in the District of Conejos, but their influence is very slightly felt; they attend to their own affairs, mind their own business, and, unless molested, give little heed to occurrences around them; they have no feeling of patriotism towards the United States, and consider that if they conduct themselves properly, they perform their whole duty.[60]

In comparing the Hispanos with the farmers from the East, he neglected to acknowledge the difficulties the people had experienced since being placed in Colorado Territory. There were so many changes affecting them. It was certainly a time of much stress as they attempted to understand the new laws, language, and social order. There was also the continued stress in the potential loss of life, lifestyle, and livelihood. In conducting the Conejos military census, both Major Gillespie and General Carleton had created an uncomfortable environment, and even when Fort Garland was moved out of Carleton's military department, he neglected to cancel any scheduled musters. With the exception of obtaining the names of the females and children, Gillespie's duty, per Special Order 180, had been performed. After preparing the Conejos musters, Gillespie reportedly became ill or drunk. After his recovery, he traveled to Costilla County to prepare similar musters at Plaza Arriba (San Pedro), Plaza del Medio (San Luis), and Plaza Abajo (San Acacio). Unfortunately, none of these muster records have surfaced. After Gillespie submitted his final report, he received absolutely no response from Carleton. General Chivington of the Colorado Military Department and Governor John Evans were also not interested in Gillespie's wonderfully detailed reports that tell us so much about a people, place, and time.

Notes

1. Thompson, *Civil War History*, 37, 62. Treatment also discussed in Meketa, *Legacy of Honor*.

2. Such forces included the likes of Lieutenant Colonel Ceran St. Vrain, Colonel Christopher "Kit" Carson, Major Rafael Chacón, Captains Julián Espinosa, Jesús María Velásquez, Quirino Maes, and others.

3. The two killed were Juan Ángel Vigil and Román Martínez. Hart Library, History Colorado Center, Denver, Colorado Writers Project, PAM 349/28, 104–5, part 2. The following men and their families settled in southern Colorado around 1852: Nasario Gallegos; brothers José (Juan) Ignacio Jáquez and José Salomé Jáquez; Juan Oeracio Jáquez; Juan Pacheco; Mariano Pacheco; José Antonio Martínez; José María Martínez; Juan Julián Martínez; José Hilario Valdez; Desiderio Valencia; brothers Antonio José Vallejos, Francisco Vallejos, Mariano Vallejos, and Miguel Antonio Vallejos; Antonio Vigil; Juan Miguel Vigil; and Ricardo de Jesús Vigil.

4. DeWitt C. Peters to sister, February 15, 1856, microfilm, Bancroft Library, University of California at Berkeley, cited in Vandenbusche, "Life at a Frontier Post," 133–34.

5. Oliva, *Fort Union*, 247.

6. David Poulin, "The New Mexico Volunteers in the American Civil War 1861–1862," 31, http://www.entrada1598.com/books/nmvol/fullbook.pdf, accessed December 3, 2012.

7. Keleher, *Turmoil in New Mexico*, 138n9.

8. Rodgers Library, University of New Mexico at Highlands, James W. Arrott Collection, RG 98, Department of New Mexico Letters, Sender to Receiver, 178–79. Stores for Captain Velasquez's New Mexico Volunteers were to be sent "across from Fort Union to Cant. (Cantonment or Fort) Burgwin."

9. Two other future territorial legislators served in this militia. These men were Privates Pedro Aragón and José Seledonio Valdez. "Lista de Personas que Forman la Compania de milicianos de los Conejos," January 17, 1860, Territorial Archives of New Mexico, New Mexico Archives and Records Center, Roll 85. Muster signed by José María Jáquez, Juez de Paz (Alcalde), Precincto No. 20.

10. Vandenbusche, "Life at a Frontier Post," 133, 139.

11. Marianne Stoller, expert report and trial testimony, Colorado Supreme Court, Case No. 00SC527, *Lobato v. Taylor*, April 28, 2003. Reference to Center for Land Grant Studies, "Landmark Ruling on the Sangre de Cristo Grant," http://southwestbooks.org/sangredecristo003.htm, accessed July 18, 2017.

12. "The Fort and the Fandango of 1860," *La Sierra*, February 11, 2005. US troops entered Mexico City on September 14, 1847. For this reason, the "Marines' Hymn" refers to the "Halls of Montezuma." Moctezuma II (Montezuma) was ruler of the Aztecs with his capital of Tenochtitlan, the site of modern Mexico City.

13. Crimmins, "Fort Massachusetts," 131.

14. Ibid., 134.

15. Simmons, *Ute Indians*, 102.

16. Thompson, *Civil War History*, 377.

17. Ibid., 317–18.

18. Colorado Society of Hispanic Genealogy, *Hispanic Pioneers in Colorado and New Mexico*, 272.

19. Meketa, *Legacy of Honor*, 157.

20. Thompson, *Civil War History*, 556.

21. Ibid., 28–29, 133–34.

22. Ibid., 29. The government reimbursed him only $1,700 of his personal cost to outfit his men. Meketa, *Legacy of Honor*, 190–91; Kelly, *Navajo Roundup*, 36n24.

23. Thompson, *Civil War History*, 28–29.

24. Officers who recruited and later established ties to Colorado include Major Adolph H. Mayer, Captain Charles Deus, Captain James Hobart Ford, Captain Albert Pfeiffer, and Lieutenant R. Howard. Thompson, *Civil War History*, 8, 17.

25. *Rocky Mountain Daily Mail*, April 30, May 1–7, 9–10, 1862.

26. NARA, Washington, DC, General Order No. 41, May 1, 1862, General Orders, 1862, DMN, RG 393, AGO; and Letters Received, Col. Paul to Capt. Nicodemus, May 6, 1862, M1120, Roll 17.

27. Thompson, *Civil War History*, 133–34.

28. Ibid., 37, 62.

29. NARA, Washington, DC, Letters Received, Col. Paul to Capt. Nicodemus, May 6, 1862, M1120, Roll 17.

30. NARA, Washington, DC, Capt. Deus to Maj. Mayer, August 21, 1862, Letters Received, Department of New Mexico, M1120, RG 393, AGO, Roll 16.

31. NARA, Washington, DC, Registers of Letters Received and Letters Received by Headquarters, Department of New Mexico 1854–1865, Whiting to AAG, March 28, 1862, RG 393, AGO.

32. NARA, Washington, DC, Registers of Letters Received and Letters Received by Headquarters, Department of New Mexico 1854–1865, Maj. Gillespie to Capt. Cutler regarding Military Census at Conejos, November 8, 1862, M1120, Roll 18.

33. Thompson, *Civil War History*, 256–57.

34. Two of the privates were from Company H of the Second Colorado Volunteers. The remaining privates were from Companies D and M of the First New Mexico Volunteers. Of these, four Mexicans were in Company D, and three Anglos were in Company M. NARA, Washington, DC, Registers of Letters Received and Letters Received by Headquarters, Department of New Mexico 1854–1865, Whiting to AAG, Letters Received, Department of New Mexico, M1120, RG 393, March 28, 1862.

35. NARA, Washington, DC, Registers of Letters Received and Letters Received by Headquarters, Department of New Mexico 1854–1865, Maj. Gillespie to Capt. Cutler regarding Muster Report of the Escort, November 8, 1862, M1120, Roll 18, 1.

36. NARA, Washington, DC, Registers of Letters Received and Letters Received by Headquarters, Department of New Mexico 1854–1865, Maj. Gillespie to Capt. Cutler regarding Military Census at Conejos, November 8, 1862, M1120, Roll 18, 1.

37. Major Gillespie served as aide-de-camp to Major General H. W. Halleck on special duty by order of Carleton. During the US war with Mexico, Gillespie received injuries to his mouth and jawbone; he wore a beard to conceal his disfigurement. Thompson, *Civil War History*, 255.

38. NARA, Washington, DC, Registers of Letters Received and Letters Received by Headquarters, Department of New Mexico 1854–1865, Maj. Gillespie to Capt. Cutler regarding Military Census at Conejos (second letter), December 8, 1862, M1120, RG 393, Roll 18.

39. NARA, Washington, DC, Registers of Letters Received and Letters Received by Headquarters, Department of New Mexico 1854–1865, Letters Received 1862, E–L, Maj. Gillespie to Capt. Cutler, November 8, 1862, M1120, Roll 18.

40. NARA, Washington, DC, Register of Letters Received and Letters Received by Headquarters, Department of New Mexico 1854–1865, Letters Received 1862, E–L, Maj. Gillespie to Capt. Cutler regarding Graphic idea of the District of Conejos, January 20, 1863, M1120, Roll 18.

41. Ibid.

42. Ibid.

43. Ibid.

44. Denver Public Library, Western History and Genealogy Department, Colorado 1861 Territorial Election, Districts 8 and 9, Precinct 12, Conejos.

45. NARA, Washington, DC, Registers of Letters Received and Letters Received by Headquarters, Department of New Mexico, 1854–1865, "Military Census Final Report," January 31, 1863, M1120, RG 393, Roll 19.

46. Because New Mexico only had about six secular priests serving its vast area, the lay order known as the Third Order of Saint Francis grew in importance in Hispano communities. Subsequently, the Brotherhood of Penitentes grew from this order, and San Juan de Nepumeceno became one of its main saints. Boyd and Gavin, *Saints and Saint Makers of New Mexico*, appendix D, 94.

47. According to author Virginia McConnell Simmons, "If San Juan de Nepomuceno del Cañon was also known as Cañon, then it was located two and a half miles southwest of Mogote. Cañon was east of the mouth of Conejos Canyon and on the south side of the Conejos River." Simmons, *San Luis Valley*, 276.

48. Juan Pedro Herrera was sixty-five years old, and Vicente Sánchez was fifty. José Antonio Suaso, age seventy, was the father of José Silverio Suazo. NARA, Washington, DC, M1120, RG 393, Letters and Telegrams Received, 1860–1880, "Abstract of Military Census of District of Conejos (continued), Plaza of San Judas de Tadeo," RG 393, Fort Garland, Letterbook, C.T., part V, entry 4, box 1.

49. It appears that Major Gillespie transposed the number reported in the "Memorandum Abstract"; he wrote 357, yet in the "General Recapitulation" report his total equals 375. NARA, Washington, DC, Register of Letters Received and Letters Received by Headquarters, Department of New Mexico 1854–1865, Letters Received 1862, E–L, M1120, Roll 18, "Memorandum Abstract showing the proportion of Men in the District of Conejos above and below the Age of 45 Years," January 20, 1863; "General Recapitulation of the Military Roll of the District of Conejos, Colorado Territory," January 20, 1863.

50. The six men included Lafayette Head, John Mayes Francisco, James Bernard Woodson, Francisco Wurtz, C. B. Amitz, and H. B. Smith. Denver Public Library, Western History and Genealogy Department, Colorado 1861 Territorial Election, Districts 8 and 9, Precinct 12, Conejos.

51. Maes led an independent militia against the Navajo and may have been absent when Gillespie conducted his military census. No records of his unit exist today. See also NARA, Washington, DC, M1120, RG 393, Letters and Telegrams Received, 1860–1880, "Abstract of Military Census of District of Conejos (continued), Plaza of San Juan de Pumeceno of the Cañon, #15," RG 393, Fort Garland Letterbook, C.T., part V, entry 4, box 1.

52. Ibid.

53. NARA, Washington, DC, Register of Letters Received and Letters Received by Headquarters, Department of New Mexico 1854–1865, Letters Received 1862, E–L, Maj. Gillespie to Capt. Cutler (regarding "Graphic idea of the District of Conejos"), January 20, 1863, M1120, Roll 18.

54. NARA, Washington, DC, M1120, RG 393, Letters and Telegrams Received, 1860–1880, "Abstract of Military Census of District of Conejos, Plaza of San Juan de Pumeceno of the Cañon, #15," RG 393, Fort Garland Letterbook, C.T., 1860–1887, part V, entry 4, box 1. Also Ancestry.com, 1863 Colorado Territorial Tax Roll, Division 10, Jose Maria Jaquez, San Juan, Conejos County, Distiller, Tax = $10.42.

55. Hart Library, History Colorado Center, Denver, CWA, Paper owned by Jesus Velasquez, son of Vicente, Charles E. Gibson, Jr., 1933–1934a, 40.

56. NARA, Washington, DC, Registers of Letters Received and Letters Received by Headquarters, Department of New Mexico 1854–1865, Maj. Gillespie to Capt. Cutler, November 8, 1862, M1120, Roll 18. According to a third letter sent to Captain Cutler that same day, Gillespie named Juan José Martín as the courier

who dispatched Gillespie's reports to Santa Fe. Martín was to "go and return in six days . . . at a cost of fifteen ($15) dollars." Maj. Gillespie to Capt. Cutler (regarding courier), November 8, 1862.

57. Colville, *La Vereda*, 207.

58. NARA, Washington, DC, Registers of Letters Received and Letters Received by Headquarters, Department of New Mexico 1854–1865, Letters Received 1862, E–L, Maj. Gillespie to Capt. Cutler, November 8, 1862, M1120, Roll 18.

59. Ibid.

60. NARA, Washington, DC, Registers of Letters Received and Letters Received by Headquarters, Department of New Mexico 1854–1865, Letters Received 1862, E–L, Maj. Gillespie to Cutler, January 20, 1863.

5

Conejos Indian Agency

The US government established an Indian agency for the Southern Utes (Tabeguache and Muache) at Conejos on September 25, 1859. Prior to this time, the Utes had received their "presents" from the Indian agency at Cimarron or Abiquiú in New Mexico Territory. President James Buchanan named Lafayette Head as the agent responsible for receiving and delivering their quantities of government-supplied provisions at Conejos. By treaty, the federal government had agreed to provide the Utes with provisions for their land. Agent Head arranged for transportation of the provisions in exchange from Santa Fe to Guadalupe, as Guadalupe, later known as the town of Conejos, was more accessible from Santa Fe than it was from Denver. However, soon this would change and thus impact agent-Ute relations. Provisions stored in Denver often turned moldy due to the length of storage and transportation problems south in the winter.

Because the federal government continually had problems meeting its annuity agreements, Hispano settlers stepped in to assist. José Julián Espinosa and José Seledonio Valdez of Conejos assisted the agency by providing blankets,

DOI: 10.5876/9781607329145.c005

cattle, sheep, and wheat. For their aid, the federal government paid them in cash. For example, on August 20, 1860, Espinosa supplied the Conejos Indian Agency with 600 Mexican blankets ($1.75 each), three cows ($30 each), fifty sheep ($3.00 each), and sixty-five fanegas of wheat ($4.00 each). In error, the government paid him fifty dollars less than $1,550 for these items. Five days later, on August 25, Valdez arrived at the agency with livestock, Mexican blankets, and wheat, for which the US government paid him $1,383.[1] The government identified these blankets as Mexican because they had a seam down the middle.[2] Horizontal treadle looms produced long, narrow strips that weavers double-wove or stitched together to increase a blanket's size. This much-needed cash would come in handy when territorial and federal taxes would be due the following year. Many times the Anglo settlers falsely blamed the all indigenous bands for raids on their livestock; however, one or more indigenous bands only committed these "depredations to prevent [the band from] starvation."[3] The influx of additional Anglo settlers and miners affected their hunts of the available fish and game.

Between 1862 and 1862 bands of Utes had complained to the Fort Garland officers regarding the quality and quantity of their rations. Because several Conejos settlers corroborated the Utes' statements, Major Adolph H. Mayer notified the Commissioner of Indian Affairs and the New Mexico Military Department about their grievances. A hearing was held in Conejos in late December of 1862 to determine three major issues: whether Agent Head had "withheld goods, provisions, and commissary stores" from the Ute, sold government property; and "employed an interpreter" who could not speak Ute.[4] Witness testimony affirmed that the interpreter was not fluent in Ute. The hearing also determined that Head had withheld provisions from the Utes and speculated in government property. However, Governor Evans did not act to replace the agent. A second investigative hearing had the same result.

The distribution of goods, such as blankets, cloth, clothing, cooking utensils, beads, guns and powder, and food (sometimes including livestock), helped to cement bonds of trust and friendship between the parties to the treaties. In contrast, the receipt of goods in lesser quantities or quality than expected might foster both distrust of the government and a degree of restiveness among the indigenous peoples. Settlers who suffered the theft of livestock and other property in Indian raids often blamed their losses on the local agent, whose suspected crooked administration of the goods promised to the indigenous nations was the presumed motivation for the Indians' retaliatory forays.

Agent Head also accompanied a peace delegation of about a dozen Ute chiefs to Washington, DC, in 1863. Years later, Head's teenage nephew, Finis Downing, recorded his recollections of the trip. His report provides a vivid account of the considerable efforts involved in transporting people and provisions and the dangers of such a long trip.

A Ute treaty council was held in Conejos in 1863. There to meet the 1,500 Utes were territorial and federal officials representing the government.[5] To assure the Utes' peace throughout the conference, six companies of US cavalry and a battery of artillery had arrived from Fort Union in New Mexico Territory. To assist the Ute delegation were two Hispano interpreters. The treaty negotiation concluded with the United States having acquired Ute lands east of the Continental Divide, nearly one-third of Colorado Territory.

According to an oral history, Governor Evans had spoken about the "gewgaws and trappings" that adorned the Utes' clothing.[6] His casual comment sheds light on his opinions of the Utes. The following year in November, General John Milton Chivington led a bloody massacre of peaceful Arapahoe and Cheyenne at Sand Creek. Denver citizens praised his actions. Ultimately, both Evans and Chivington were investigated, then chastised by federal officials. Evans was replaced by Governor Alexander Cummings.

Agitation against Head's performance as Indian agent continued. Territorial Council member Celestino Domínguez headed up a petition to remove Head from office, charging him with causing troubles and difficulties in Conejos County by, among other misdeeds, buying Indian children (elsewhere reported as Navajos) with government property intended for the Utes. The petition went to Governor Evans and to the Commissioner of Indian Affairs in Washington. Again, despite a consistent accumulation of testimonial evidence against him, Agent Head continued to remain in office as agent for several more years.

Then, when Evans had Head report the instances of Indian slavery in Conejos and Costilla Counties, Head appears to use his report to embarrass his critics and political enemies while omitting evidence of slave ownership by his supporters—and himself.

Accusations against Agent Head

In 1860 President James Buchanan appointed Lafayette Head as the US Indian agent of the Tabeguache Ute at Los Conejos. The following year, Head met face to face with William Gilpin, governor of Colorado Territory and ex-officio superintendent of Indian affairs. Governor Gilpin was responsible for superintending the territory's Ute Indian Agency.[7] Nearly 2,000 Utes (Muache, Tabeguache, and some Capote bands) received their rations at the Conejos Indian Agency. Incidentally, Agent Head estimated his agency was responsible for 6,000 Utes. Because he received only $1,000 in supplies, Head likely inflated his estimate to obtain more provisions.[8]

The federal government continually had problems meeting its annuity (treaty) agreements with the nations. Ute bands were upset in 1862 that their government provisions were late. Because Governor Evans and Agent Head were worried that the Ute would retaliate, Evans asked General Edward Canby to send "at least" one regiment of cavalry and infantry, plus a section of artillery, "as an idea of . . . force."[9] Meanwhile, the settlers received the brunt of the trouble. Captain Charles Deus, who had just returned to Fort Garland from Conejos, reported that the Indians were "stealing large quantities of stock."[10] He observed that "frequent complaints were made that the Indians kill cattle belonging to various parties; at the same time, excuse is made . . . that they only commit these depredations to prevent starvation."[11]

Between 1862 and 1863 a band of Tabaguache Ute Indians made several complaints to officers at Fort Garland regarding Agent Head and the quality of the rations they had received at the agency. On August 18, 1862, they reported that the food was moldy, wormy, and too scant for their needs. By mid-November, a severe snowstorm had occurred. Regarding the Utes' request for gunpowder and lead, "to hunt game and protect themselves from their enemies," Major Adolph H. Mayer told them that only an agent was authorized to provide them with ammunition; however, he gave them "a little" powder and distributed a few provisions for their immediate needs. He distributed these items, stating that "the Government intends to treat you kindly, and . . . aid you all it reasonably can . . . In return for its kindness . . . it demands . . . that you do not violate your Treaty by killing any stock, or people, or by stealing any horse or mules." A headman then told Mayer that Agent Head's interpreter did not speak Ute. Mayer stated he would inform the Commissioner of Indian Affairs and the general commanding the military department about their grievances.

After the twenty-four Utes left Fort Garland with their provisions, the major documented the meeting, conversation, and outcome.[12]

Agent Head was in the habit of receipting for the Indian's provisions at Fort Garland and arranging for the goods to be transferred to the Conejos Agency, which was located at his residence. In New Mexico individuals caught with property belonging to the US government were ordered to return the goods to the quartermaster at the nearest military post. Anyone concealing government property or refusing to give it up was to be immediately be arrested and tried in a military court.[13] Colorado was still a new territory, and no records indicate whether Governor Gilpin dealt with such issues.

Mayer then met with "some of the most responsible persons [living] in and [about] the Conejos [settlements]" who corroborated the Utes' statements. He sent a copy of the meeting minutes to Gilpin and a letter to William P. Dole, Commissioner of Indian Affairs in Washington. Mayer suggested that Head explain to the New Mexico Military Department what he did with the provisions he was issued and recommended his removal. As further evidence, he attached Major Daniel P. Whiting's list of the "subsistence items" Head had received and the documentation of his meeting with the "Guerrilla Bands and dissatisfied Natives." "There is no doubt," Mayer concluded, "that Head has been speculating with Government property. His every action proves him to have acted dishonestly."[14]

Caleb B. Smith, secretary of the Department of New Mexico, wrote to Charles E. Mix, acting Commissioner of Indian Affairs, requesting a full investigation and to determine if the interpreter could speak Ute.[15] Three days later, on September 26, Mix advised new Colorado territorial governor Evans about the investigation. Evans responded by stating that an investigation and removal of Head were "hasty actions." He wrote, "Should I find any delinquency or malfeasance . . . [I will make] every effort to have it set right . . . and fully exposed."[16]

Evans took three months to act on the investigation and name a commissioner. On November 25, 1862, Major Archibald Gillespie, who was conducting military business in Conejos for the New Mexico Military Department, wrote Evans asking permission to take testimony in Agent Head's hearing. Instead, the governor appointed former judge William P. Bacon. The following month Bacon summoned witnesses and arranged to take their statements.

Commissioner Bacon's Hearing of Agent Head

From Monday, December 29, 1862, to Wednesday, December 31, 1862, at Juan Martín's hall in Guadalupe, Commissioner Bacon heard witness testimony—the hall did double service as the courtroom of the Third Judicial District.[17] Unfortunately, due to the military and civilian issues taking place in and around Conejos during this time, Captain Ethan Eaton of the First New Mexico Volunteers was not present for the hearing and thus could not cross-examine "on the part of the government." Also, Dr. Lewis B. McLain, a citizen physician who was one of the witnesses in support of Major Mayer's charges, could not attend the hearing in Guadalupe due to his duties as post surgeon.[18] It is not known when Bacon learned the captain, the doctor, and the major could not attend the hearing, but he did not postpone the hearing. He agreed to hear their testimony on Saturday, January 3, 1863, at Fort Garland.

Each day before taking witness testimony, Bacon explained the purpose of the hearing. Specifically, he would determine if Agent Head "withheld goods, provisions, and commissary stores" from the Utes, sold government property, or employed an interpreter who was "wholy [sic] ignorant of the Ute language." After each witness took his oath, Bacon said it was each man's duty to state "anything in reference to the truth or falsity" of the charges against Head by Major Mayer. Each witness then affirmed that he was the same person as subpoenaed and stated his age and occupation (table 5.1). After his testimony, each witness signed his name or made his mark to affirm that his statements were true. US deputy marshal George O. Austin attended the hearing. Bacon did not document why Austin was present; however, Austin was a correspondent who regularly sent news reports to the *Rocky Mountain News*. For some reason, Austin's news report about Head's hearing was not published. Bacon closed the examination of the witnesses on January 6, 1863.

During Bacon's hearing at Fort Garland, several witnesses testified about Head's personal use of government issues.[19] Quartermaster clerk Rudolph F. Cordua said Head was "anxious to get . . . candles and [soap], for which he might deduct other rations." Agency interpreter José Amador Sánchez testified that although the Utes did not use candles and soap, the Indians had not received all their provisions:

TABLE 5.1. Witnesses subpoenaed for the hearing of Indian agent Lafayette Head

Juan Martin's Hall at Conejos, December 29, 1862, to December 31, 1862, and Fort Garland, January 3, 1863, Commissioner William P. Bacon

Residence	Witness	Occupation
unknown	Jesus M. Sanches	Conejos Indian Agency Interpreter
Conejos	Teodoro Maes	Ranchman
	Jose F. Martines	Justice of Peace
	Jose M. Martinez	Constable
	Jesus M. Sanches	Conejos Indian Agency Interpreter
Guadalupe	Jose Nemecio Lucero	Conejos Indian Agency Interpreter
	Jesus M. Velasquez	Farmer, Conejos County Judge
	James B. Woodson	Ranchman
Servilleta	Miguel A. Martin	Conejos County Sheriff
	Juan B. Silva	Farmer, Merchant, Conejos County Commissioner
Culebra	Jose Nasario Gallegos	Farmer [Alcalde-Mayor]
	Jose Amador Sanches	US Army Guide, Interpreter
Fort Garland	Rudolph F. Cordua	Clerk in Quartermaster's Subsistence Department
	Henry Diagre	Employee of John Lawrence
	Hon. John M. Francisco	Territorial Council, Stock Raiser, Merchant
	Dr. Lewis B. McLain	Post Surgeon (citizen)

Source: Letters Received by the Office of Indian Affairs, 1824–1881, Colorado Superintendency, 1861–1864, M234, RG 75, Roll 197, NARA, Washington, DC.

They had received no presents of sugar or coffee, nor corn. They had not received any of the flour brought from the Fort for them, very little bacon, but little rice; and they had not had enough to eat.[20]

According to Teodoro Maes, Head obtained some bacon for his own use:

I met [Diego Marquez] about six miles from Conejos who had a piece of bacon. I asked him where he got it. He told me, "Major Head." I then went to Mr. Head and wanted to bring bacon, sugar and coffee. Mr. Head told me he had brought but little of each article and that for his own use. Mr. Head showed me a piece of bacon rolled up and [said] it was the last he had and . . . it was for the priest.[21]

When asked about Head's interpreter, Territorial Council member James Bernard Woodson testified, "I know that Head has one Nemecio Lucero employed as an interpreter who could not speak the Ute language." During the hearing, no one questioned José Nemesio Lucero about his ability to speak Ute, how he learned to speak it, or how long he had spoken it. In addition, Lucero was never asked what he knew about Head's withholding or speculating in government property. Sometime after his testimony Woodson reportedly told Bacon that there were "witnesses of importance to the Government, who could and ought to be summoned, who would testify the truth in relation to this matter." Bacon responded that "he did not consider himself authorized to summon any person, but those whose names were on his list." When Woodson asked, "Were it not necessary for the Indians to be present?" Bacon replied, "I really do not know that it is."[22]

From Pueblo on January 10, 1863, Bacon sent the transcription of witness testimonies to Governor Evans along with "their fees and mileage and a list of other incidental expenses." In his correspondence he presented no opinion or comment regarding the hearing. The following month Evans wrote the Commissioner of Indian Affairs, stating that "it will be seen that the defense is triumphant in refuting the charges." The governor then forwarded the bills incurred in the investigation to Commissioner Dole and asked if he should pay these expenses from the territory's contingent expense fund.[23] Although the hearings determined that Head had withheld government provisions from the Indians, had speculated in government property, and had used an interpreter who was not proficient at speaking Ute, Evans made no attempt to request that he be replaced.

Major Gillespie's Personal Hearing

Major Archibald Gillespie had heard unsatisfactory reports about the manner in which Bacon conducted Agent Head's hearing. In his first letter to Captain R. C. Cutler, dated February 7, 1863, Gillespie wrote, "An investigation of the Head delinquency has been made by a Judge Bacon . . . but as the manner in which it was done is quite peculiar, a narration of the facts will, we doubt, be interesting at Headquarters, as well as to the Secretary of the Interior." In a subsequent letter, Gillespie shared that he had heard that the hearing was "altogether of a partial character [and neglected] the interests of the United States and of the Indians."[24] Cutler forwarded Gillespie's report to General James Carleton, who approved Gillespie's request to obtain additional information about the hearing and about Head's misappropriation of U.S. property.

On February 23, 1863, Gillespie conducted his hearing at Middle Culebra (San Luis). Gillespie asked a few residents from Conejos and Costilla Counties to state what they knew about the hearing, what and how they knew or heard about Head's improper "appropriation and use of subsistence supplies,"[25] and how they knew that the information was true. After documenting each man's testimony, Gillespie asked each to affirm his statements. The handwritten transcription of Gillespie's hearing did not state if either Agent Head or Major Mayer was in attendance. Major Mayer was convinced that Head had been speculating with government property and wished to prove it.[26] He could not attend the hearing to cross-examine witnesses and did not receive a copy of the witnesses' transcribed responses.

During Gillespie's hearing, James Bernard Woodson, a neighbor of Agent Head, stated that, according to Juan Jáquez, Head had squandered government provisions by "buying young Indians." Jáquez was not on Bacon's witness list; however, according to Woodson, "Jáquez was present in the place [Guadalupe] and could have been brought before the Commission, but he was not summoned." Woodson also testified that had seen one man with tin pans and another with red flannel—"such as comes for the Indians"—leaving Head's house. The second man had purchased the red flannel from Head for "$1.50 per yard for six to eight yards . . . he had a shirt made of it." However, "these men were not summoned, they were at hand, but as the [manner of the] investigation was conducted, their testimony would not have been received."[27]

A member of the Colorado Territorial Council, Woodson recalled the time Head had asked him to sign his agency accounts. Perhaps Woodson was one of three sureties for Head and, as such, approved such documents. According to Woodson, Head arrived at Woodson's house in August 1862 with vouchers for Indian property. Woodson had just recently returned from Denver after attending a session of the territorial legislature. He saw that the vouchers were issued in his absence and was annoyed that Head wanted him to approve the items obtained:

> After Mr. Head had asked me to sign his accounts, I made inquiry and ascertained to my own convenience and satisfaction that the [government] property had not been properly dispensed . . . I know that the Indians, not having received what they know the Agent had obtained from the Government for them . . . were very angry . . . I firmly believe that much of the robbing and

depredations committed by the Indians in Conejos have sprung from the bad and unfaithful treatment on the part of the agent, Mr. Head.[28]

José Nasario Gallegos testified that he was the prefect of Costilla County and that he and Jesús María Velásquez, the prefect of Conejos County, had been in Denver to meet with Governor Evans.[29] Gallegos testified that, when asked, Velásquez told the governor that Head's interpreter could not speak the Ute language and that the previous year Velásquez had not been paid for interpreting for Agent Head. It is interesting that Gallegos felt compelled testify on Velásquez's behalf. Gallegos also testified that during the trip home Velásquez told him, "Head was making away with Indian goods by selling them and doing a great deal of injury otherwise, for the Indians were dissatisfied, and were committing a great many outrages in consequence of Head's bad faith." Gallegos closed his testimony by stating that Velásquez later denied making those statements. Velásquez was present during Bacon's hearing; yet he presented none of this testimony.

John Mayes Francisco testified that "none of the Utah Tribe were present at this investigation and none were summoned. They were not far away." Had the Utes been invited to participate in Commissioner Bacon's hearing, several interpreters would have been available to translate their testimonies. Agent Head used the services of four known interpreters: José Nemecio Lucero, Martín Rodriguez, José Amador Sánchez, and Captain Jesús María Velásquez.

Major Gillespie, who knew Spanish, translated the statements of the Hispano witnesses. To ensure accuracy, he read his translation before the witnesses in the presence of John Mayes Francisco, James Bernard Woodson, and merchant W. F. Posthoff, who allegedly spoke Spanish and affirmed that Gillespie's translation was accurate. Gillespie believed his narration of the facts would interest US Army headquarters as well as the secretary of the interior.[30]

With regard to the agency's twenty-one-year-old inept interpreter, witness testimony affirmed that José Nemecio Lucero was not fluent in Ute; however, he was the only interpreter available at the time. Velásquez had testified before Bacon that "there are but two or three good interpreters in the county. They are difficult to get. . . . The other, Jesús M. Sanches, your present interpreter [Lucero], and myself."[31]

On February 7, 1863, Major Gillespie sent a dispatch to Captain Cutler regarding the investigation into Head's troubling actions. "On investigation of the Head delinquency," he wrote, "a narration of the facts will, no doubt, be interesting at Head Quarters, as well as to the Secretary of the Interior."[32] Communication among the departments of the military, Indian affairs, and the Colorado superintendency were so convoluted with layers of bureaucratic red tape due to the US Civil War, the Indian Wars, protection needed along the Santa Fe Trail, and more. Ultimately, Head retained his position for many more years. He had the full support of Governor Evans, and he was a presidential appointee who could only be removed by the president. But that alone did not stop Head's problems at the agency or among the people of Conejos.

The Utes Go to Washington

About mid-January of 1863, Governor Evans and Agent Head escorted thirteen Ute chiefs to Washington, DC, as part of a peace delegation. Ouray, Shavano, and Grouley and his brother were four of these delegates.[33] Incidentally, after Head left the military district without the required pass, the commander at Fort Garland advised headquarters at Santa Fe that Head took the wrong chiefs. Although Head was not charged with any wrongdoing, the New Mexico Military Department questioned this expense, as it was during the Civil War and the Indians were in much need of their promised provisions. "Mr. Head having just started for Washington, with six Ute Indians, representing them [as] Chiefs when they are not, neither are they men (quite young) of any influence in their tribe . . . Not being over eight or ten including boys—the Ute tribe knows nothing about this visit to Washington . . . this cannot be considered a delegation from the tribe."[34]

While in Washington, federal military officials staged a demonstration of the "might of the Army of the Potomac."[35] President Lincoln appointed Ouray "head chief of the Confederated Ute Nation of Colorado" because Ouray spoke English and because his Tabeguache or Uncompahgre band was the largest of the seven Ute bands. However, because the indigenous social system prevented one man from making decisions impacting the entire Ute Nation, some Capote and Muache chiefs strongly rejected his title.[36]

The Commissioner of Indian Affairs scheduled a treaty council to be held at Conejos the following September or October. Head submitted an order for the provisions to be distributed to the Utes during the council. Additionally, because the president had already presented Ouray with a silver-tipped cane, Head submitted a handwritten request to Commissioner William P. Dole for seven silver peace medals. Head intended to present these medals himself during the upcoming treaty council: "I would present the same [medals] to the three Principal Chiefs in the name of their 'Great Father' at Washington. This token although trivial to a white man, goes far with an Indian, and might be the means of cementing their friendship and good will, which we are so anxious to retain."[37]

Before leaving Washington, Head received "a large amount of money" to cover expenses of the upcoming council. According to Head's sixteen-year-old nephew, Finis E. Downing, when Head and his secretary, William James Godfroy, arrived for a visit at the Downing home in Illinois, both men "looked humpbacked [as] thousands of dollars in greenbacks, in the original sheet form, [were] strapped around their backs."[38]

About May 16, 1863, Head and his large group of travelers, which included his sister, Eliza Jane Head Downing, her son Finis, and a female Irish cook from New York, joined the Utes and a large contingent of military troops at St. Joseph, Missouri, for the return trip to Colorado. The unidentified woman would be responsible for cooking meals for the Anglo dignitaries attending the October council. Many years later, Finis Downing documented what he saw there. At that time, while the Civil War raged, "Missouri was a hot-bed of Rebel guerrilla warfare, and the whole country was practically under martial law and news of raids and small battles was common." But young Finis recalled that "among the sights was a big Mississippi steamboat loaded with a tribe of Indians, from some of the southern states, which the U.S. Government was taking to the Indian Territory in an effort to civilize them." Onboard the boat he saw "Indians aplenty, some strutting around in feathers, and on one deck there were a lot lying around with blankets and appeared to be sick."[39]

Head's caravan "outfit" consisted of about 500 travelers, five companies of troops plus 200 civilians. Major Jacob Downing (no relation to Finis Downing), from New York, commanded three companies of the 1st Colorado Cavalry. Major Downing named Captains Bonesteel and Sanborn as two company commanders. Finis Downing noted that he saw "several notches on [the] guns" of some troopers of the 1st Colorado, "indicating the number of Indian scalps they had taken in battles with Indians." Ten days later the outfit started to cross the plains. The thirteen Ute chiefs

who had been taken to Washington, D.C., for treaty negotiations had to be constantly guarded, as they were at war with all the prairie tribes known as

Blackfeet, Cheyenne, Arapahoe and other tribes[,] and danger seemed to be just around the corner everywhere. The cavalry soldiers rode single file on each side of the [wagon train], making a "V" shape at front and behind. That was to guard against surprise attacks from all sides against the Indian chiefs and the rich stores of provisions carried for food, as well as a large amount of money, for in those days all carried their fortune with them.[40]

Downing had occasion to ride beside several of the chiefs in one of the wagons and was able to communicate with those who could speak a little English; he also learned some of their sign language. He credited them with being "quick to learn and understand." They were, he noted, "grateful and kind to those they reposed confidence in, but as sullen and hard as flint when they were suspicious or felt that someone was wronging them."[41]

Downing also recalled that during the trip the Irish cook prepared biscuits and gravy and some of the Utes hunted antelope and buffalo. That June the caravan was miles away from Julesburg, Colorado, when they learned that the "Prairie Indians" had gathered to take revenge because some northern Utes had raided them several months earlier. According to Downing, these Utes had "licked them badly [and] had captured a lot for servants and killed others by the wholesale." Downing then recorded that "there were Indians by the thousands, thick as bees in a hive."[42] For protection against the Prairie Indians, "three companies of Cavalry formed two abreast in close formation on each side of the [wagons] before and behind." The Ute chiefs in the party "were stripped of every sort of arms" to ensure that they did not trigger a conflict. "Every soldier and civilian was armed to the teeth." Young Downing himself carried a double-barreled shotgun and two Colt revolvers.[43]

According to Downing, the caravan had to push its way through "bold, jeering and taunting Indians, who seemed anxious for a fight." As they approached the principal chief, he "sprang forward and grasped the ring of the bridle bit of [our] key soldier's horse and stopped him." The soldier raised his saber to cut down the chief, but Major Downing barked out an order to halt. Lafayette Head arrived suddenly at the chief's side and "began to talk in a language that the chief understood." Head then threw a fresh bearskin under the chief's horses, rendering the horses panic-stricken, plunging, and unmanageable, and confusing the Indians, a disruption that cleared enough room for the caravan to proceed forward. The cavalry "kept the way clear and for twelve miles we went as fast as possible." The wagon train then made camp for the night in a horseshoe bend, protected by the river on three sides, and sent a scout for reinforcements.[44]

About 3:00 a.m., close to 150 reinforcements arrived and the Indians began to scatter. The cavalry remained with the caravan until it reached Camp Weld, a few miles from Denver. Head and his travelers remained there for ten days before entering the city of Denver, then in its infancy, where "a wild and wooly west prevailed in the very atmosphere." Downing wrote that "gambling houses and saloons were thick and ran wide open." When the travelers arrived at Pueblo, he noted that "some of our fellows got drunk and nearly tore up the town."[45] They finally reached Fort Garland, where the families of the Ute chiefs were there to meet them. Head and his travelers later continued on to Conejos; it was July 1863.[46]

Freighting Provisions

Sometime that fall, Finis Downing traveled to Denver with William James Godfroy to receive and transport the requisitioned provisions for the Utes that arrived from the East. Once the goods finally arrived, Godfroy supervised as the Mexican fleteros loaded the "big government wagons." Three yoke of oxen pulled each wagon. One yoke of inexperienced oxen spooked and ran a wagon into a drug store, knocking the frame structure off its foundation. "The U.S. Government was to pay the damages and we soon got matters quieted down and started out for home."[47]

An empty freight wagon used in the San Juan Mountains weighed about 3,000 pounds. The bed was about eleven feet long by three feet wide, and each of its four wheels was only two and a half to three inches wide. The main sideboard was nineteen inches high; additional sideboards could be attached to raise the height to about three and a half feet.[48] If needed, two or more wagons were coupled and pulled by multiple yokes. Freighters doubled their teams to assist each other when climbing steep mountainous terrain and in managing the animals and load during difficult descents.

Just outside of Denver, the party got trapped in a terrible thunderstorm. According to Downing, continual lightening bolts "ran around the wagon tires, up and down gun barrels and O my God it was terrible . . . The

Mexicans screamed and prayed, and crossed themselves and I was nearly scared to death."[49]

Most of the freighting was handled by "picturesque Mexican hands in wagons drawn by ox teams."[50] In some cases, families pooled what money they had to purchase a team and wagon.[51] Freighting was hard and dangerous work. Many fleteros lost their lives due to injury and illness, including pneumonia. Fleteros were responsible for the contents they transported and the care of their wagons and animals. Animals needed to be rested, fed, and shod, and wagon hubs had to be greased when they ran hot. Larger freighting companies provided way stations for their fleteros. There they slept indoors on a bunk while their animals were attended to and their wagons serviced. Self-employed fleteros often slept under their wagons or tarps, took care of their own animals, and serviced their own wagons. On longer trips fleteros often traveled in family caravans for protection and assistance.

In 1870, P. G. Scott, from Canada, wrote about his trip with a Mexican freight outfit from Kit Carson to Trinidad. The caravan had over a hundred oxen; he witnessed fourteen yokes hauling one wagon.[52] He wrote that he did not enjoy the trip, the company, or the food. Rather than paying "exorbitant" railroad freight rates once the railroad started making its way south from Denver in 1873, Mexican fleteros—"using mule or bull"—were employed at lower wages.[53]

Downing described how the fleteros prepared the teams to haul up a mountain. They readied the teams by facing the lead team downhill. After all the teams were hitched and lined up, the fletero yelled out and turned the lead uphill. As they were carrying a heavy load of barrel sugar up the hill, a fletero on the lower side broke his whip. Unfortunately, the driver on the uphill side was unable to see the trouble through the thick-falling snow, and he kept lashing the oxen on his side. That caused the lead team to turn downhill, upsetting the wagon. "Barrels of sugar rolled down the mountain side, struck rock and bursted [sic] the staves and sugar flew high in the air, a total loss."[54]

According to Downing, due to the accident and snowfall, the travelers made camp. But Downing bedded too close to the campfire and when he woke, he found his robes and blanket ruined by fire. He deeply regretted the loss of the buffalo robe, especially, as it had been a present to him from Chief Ouray and was the "largest and best" Downing had ever seen.[55]

Meanwhile at Conejos, Agent Head directed his interpreter, José Amador Sánchez from Culebra (San Luis), to "ride out to Ute territory" to inform the Utes that he would soon be distributing their provisions. Head directed Sánchez to instruct the Utes to come to the Indian agency to receive the issue of their supplies, but not to pass through settlements on the way.[56] Along with the provisions, Agent Head also received the Lincoln peace medals he had requested of Commissioner Dole.

"Gew-Gaws and Trappings": The 1863 Treaty Council

On September 28, 1863, Governor Evans arrived at Fort Garland with John George Nicolay, presidential secretary; Simeon Whitely, Ute agent for western bands; and Dr. Michael Steck, New Mexico Indian agent.[57] After two days, they departed for Conejos, escorted by Colonel Samuel F. Tappan. The Tabeguache Utes, numbering 1,500, arrived at Conejos. Some of the band's key headmen had refused to attend. According to Downing, "All of the Indians of the Ute tribe assembled at Conejos, at Uncle's home, to receive their share" of the provisions. "They sat, or stood, in rows around the goods and each received his allotment. Nicolay bossed the distribution."[58]

Newspaper reports indicate that the Utes encamped on the creeks and in the canyons not many miles away. Because they were in great number, they began arriving at the fort with large quantities of blankets and buckskins or other trade items. One correspondent reported they numbered no fewer than 5,000 or 6,000. He also wrote that Agent Head had estimated 25,000 would attend.[59] Six companies of cavalry and a battery of artillery also arrived from Fort Union in New Mexico. Many military forces were there to meet them should the treaty negotiations fail and the Utes go to war.[60] "One regiment of cavalry guarded against any trouble [and] there were never less than 500 soldiers to preserve peace . . . There were about three hundred Mexicans, 500 soldiers and some Jew merchant traders."[61]

The two Hispano interpreters who attended the council were Juan V. Valdez and Bernardo Sánchez.[62] No historical documentation reported that key Hispanos, such as Representative José Victor García or Captain Jesús María Velásquez, had been invited to attend. Velásquez, the Conejos prefect, had served as Head's former interpreter.

As the Utes passed the time waiting, they raced horses. For protection, the horses were secured in the post corral under guard by the officer of the day. Sergeant Nicholas Hodt provided an account of a Navajo horse race:

> Large bets, larger than on either of the other races, were made on both sides. The Indians flocked in by hundreds, women and children; some of them mounted on fine ponies, richly dressed, and all appeared to be there to see the race, and not with any hostile intentions . . . The Indian's horse did not run a hundred yards before it ran off the track. I being at the upper end of the track, could not see the cause of it, but the report was that the Indian's bridle broke.[63]

On the first day of the council, the Utes marched toward the agency in military formation. Governor Evans and several unidentified men climbed onto the agency's roof for a better view of the parade. He thought that because some headmen had "seen the armed might of the U.S. Army" during their recent trip to Washington, the Utes had "staged a military show of their own for the edification of the treaty commissioners." He observed that they "rode as hard as they could" around each platoon, "with their feathers and gew-gaws and trappings making a grand show." It was "one of the finest Indian performances you ever saw."[64]

The gew-gaws and trappings Evans referred to were the shell casings, buttons, fringes, and Mexican coins that likely adorned the Utes' heavily beaded ceremonial clothing.[65] Unfortunately, existing historical documents do not provide details about the council proceedings or the horse races, trades, and other events that likely took place.[66] The treaty negotiation concluded with the United States having acquired Ute lands east of the Continental Divide, nearly one-third of Colorado Territory.

The following day, after Chief Ouray accepted the ratified the treaty on behalf of those Utes in attendance, Secretary Nicolay presented a Lincoln peace medal to each of the seven headmen he "considered more cooperative." Ouray received one of these medals as he had encouraged cooperation with the government as a means to retain Ute lands.[67] Interestingly, about ten years later, an unidentified Ute sold his medal because he considered it "heap bad medicine." His medal had a bullet lodged in it. During a "skirmish with another tribe," a warrior fired a bullet at the Ute and the bullet became lodged in his medal (figure 5.1). One might say the medal had

FIGURE 5.1. Front (a) and back (b) of Abraham Lincoln peace medal with embedded bullet, minted 1862. (In (b), the Indian on the left prepares to scalp the one on the right and the center image shows Indians farming.) American Numismatic Society, New York, 1917.161.1.obv.600, rev.600.

saved the Ute's life; however, the unidentified Ute believed that the medal had attracted the bullet.[68]

Chief Ouray never received copies of the original and ultimately revised versions to the 1863 treaty, and it was not the last one the government would force onto the Utes during the 1860s and 1870s. Additional treaties continued to alter the Ute way of life and jeopardize the traditional ways in which they provided for their families. Now corralled domestic livestock replaced the hunt, and rations and merchandise would be distributed only as quickly as transportation, weather, roads, and federal funds allowed.

Hispanos Petition for Agent Head's Removal

On January 18, 1864, twenty-two Hispanos from Conejos petitioned the territory's attorney general, Samuel E. Brown, to replace Agent Head (table 5.2). Among the petitioners were Territorial Council member Celestino Domínguez, Representative José Víctor García, county coroner Pedro Salazar, and probate judge Antonio G. Gálvez. They considered Agent Head the "cause of all the troubles and difficulties . . . the people [had] been subject to for these last two years."[69] These troubles and difficulties included raids by some hungry indigenous bands in Head's jurisdiction who had either not

TABLE 5.2. Petition of Celestino Dominguez to Remove Agent Head, January 18, 1864

Transcribed Petition of Celestino Dominguez, et al. to Samuel E. Brown, January 18, 1864, Requesting the Removal of Lafayette Head as Indian Agent

To General Samuel E. Brown
US Attorney, for Colorado Territory

Sir,

We the undersigned Public Officers are other loyal citizen residents in this County, would respectfully, represent to you as the legal agent of the U S in this Territory, in order that you may bring, the matter before the Government:

That we consider Lafayette Head the Indian Agent as having been the cause of all the troubles and difficulties which the people of this County has been subject to for these last two years, and that we do also consider him totally unfit for the office he occupies and undeserving of the confidence of the Government for the following reasons:

> 1st: Because the charges made against him of malfeasance in office and of having bought indian children with government property, contrary to the laws of the United States can be fully substantiated.
>
> 2nd: Because his loyalty to the Government is very doubtfull to us, as he has on a certain occasion expressed himself in the most disrespectful terms of our worthy President and all the partisans of the present administration and as a regular subscriber to the Ohio Crisis.
>
> 3rd: Because by false and malicious representations he has induced Gov. Evans to establish a military post in our mist [sic], for which there has never been any occasion and three of our good and peaceable citizens have met with a premature and violent death at the hands of the soldiers.
>
> 4th: Because all those persons who have known him for years pronounce him to be a bad and dangerous man of a mean and revengeful disposition and public opinion points him out as the cause of the deaths that have lately been committed.

Therefore we earnestly believe that his removal from the office he occupies as indian Agent wants (sic) not only promote the best interest of the Government but would restore quietness and harmony of feeling in this community of which it has been deprived since he is in office.

Conejos—19th January 1864
Very Respectfully,

Petitioner	Title
Celestino Dominguez	Member of the Council
[Jose] Vitor Garcia	Representante
[Jose] Pablo [Antonio de Jesus] Ortega	Representante
Visente Atencio	Solo Alguacil
Antonio Montoya	Solo Alguacil
Juan Jose Gallegos	Juez de Paz
Pedro Ortega	Jues de Paz
Antonio G. Galvis	Judge of Probate

continued on next page

Petitioner	Title
Jose Maria Xaques	Terosiso
Juan Ysidro Lucero	County Clerk
Pedro [Ignacio Nabor] Salasar	Coronario
Juan Jose Mascarenas	Comisionado
Bautista Silba	Comisionado
Feliz de J. Romero	Commissioner
[Francisco] Esteban Aragon	
Manuel Aragon	
Francisco Antonio Atencio	
Miguel Casias	
Jesus Cordoba	
Manuel [Antonio] Gallegos	
Jesus Maria Galves	
Juan Garcia	
Manuel Gonzales	
Jose Policarpio Lobato	
Jose Bonifacio Lopes	
Jose Maria Lucero	
Consision Lusero	
Jesus Maria Maes	
Antonio Abad Marques	
Juan Pedro Martines	
Miguel Montoya	
Tomas Ribera	
Jose Gregorio Ruis	
Jose Ygnacio Salasar	
Reymundo Salasar	
Bicente Sanches	
Pedro Sanches	
Ygnacio Silva	
Roman Sisneros	
Jose Lino Trugillo	
Seledonio Valdes	
Jose Maria Vigil	
Juan Bautista Vigil	

Source: Samuel E. Brown, M91, Denver Public Library, Western History and Genealogy Department.

received their government distributions or had received food that was old and moldy.

The petitioners considered Head "unfit for his office as Indian Agent . . . and undeserving of the confidence of the Government." Head's removal from office, they thought, would "restore [a] feeling of quietness and harmony in this community." For example, in 1862 Agent Head had met with some "Americans" in southern Colorado to advise them about steps they might take were the "Mexicans" to rebel.[70] About June 9, 1863, Head testified that brothers Felipe and José Vivián Espinosa and a presumed cousin, Vicente Espinosa, of Conejos ambushed and killed William Smith at Conejos, although no court records exist to determine how Head could have known the Espinosas were the killers.[71] Posses made up of Anglo miners, accompanied by Fort Garland soldiers, searched the area, which created intense conditions. Perhaps escalating paranoia led Agent Head to believe that several Hispanos had abetted them.[72] Due to the newspaper accounts, rumors, and allegations of their horrific attacks, the Hispano petitioners likely thought it best not to specifically name the Espinosas in their petition. As discussed in chapter 6, there were four men who had in fact met with their "premature and violent" deaths.[73]

The petition cited four specific areas of concern. First was Head's malfeasance in that he bought Indian children with government property. The territorial hearing conducted by Commissioner Bacon during the latter part of 1862 and the military hearing conducted by Major Gillespie at the beginning of 1863 found that Agent Head had withheld goods from the Utes, sold government property, and relied on an interpreter who could not speak Ute.[74] In 1863 rumors circulated in southern Colorado that much of Head's wealth came from selling captive indigenous persons.[75] On November 30 Head was charged with purchasing Navajo captives from the Utes; however, nothing more came from this charge.[76]

The second area of concern was the question of Head's loyalty to the national government. He was either known to subscribe or suspected of subscribing (it is not clear which) to *Crisis*, an Ohio publication that promoted the politics of Northerners who supported the positions and opinions of the Confederacy, and he was accused as well of expressing his opinion of President Lincoln in disrespectful terms.

Third, it was suggested that certain of Head's "false and malicious representations" needlessly induced Governor Evans to establish a military presence in the area, with the result that three local Hispano citizens had been killed by soldiers. The settlers claimed that some Fort Garland soldiers had been in and near the Conejos settlements by the order of Agent Head, although no extant records of Head, Evans, or Fort Garland support this claim.

Fourth, longtime acquaintances of Head admitted that he was "bad and dangerous" and "revengeful," and public opinion held him responsible for recent Hispano deaths: Representative Francisco Gallegos, for example, had been found dead on the plaza with a rope around his neck, and other Hispanos had also met their deaths. Many Fort Garland soldiers had been stationed in and around Conejos for a number of reasons, including claims of "secret" meetings and suspected abetment during the search for the Espinosas as well as the anxieties and suspicions aroused by a military census and the Ute council.

In January of the past year, Major Gillespie had conducted a military census in Conejos by order of the New Mexico Military District. Gillespie arrived in each settlement on horseback to interview the occupants of each home. Accompanying him were a sergeant and nine armed soldiers who conducted a house-to-house search for arms, food stores, and livestock. The Hispanos feared forced conscription into the US Army and confiscation of their stores and livestock. Further, they worried about being arrested for nonpayment of taxes due the prior year.

After Attorney General Samuel E. Brown reviewed the petition, he wrote to Governor Evans and recommended a hearing. No records indicate that Evans responded to Brown's request. The following month, on February 4, Brown wrote to the Commissioner of Indian Affairs, stating that "in justice to both parties the charges [against Head] should be investigated."[77] However, nothing was done.

Domínguez's Charges against Head

On March 11, 1864, Territorial Council member Celestino Domínguez wrote to Governor Evans, citing specific examples of Agent Head's inappropriate actions, questionable character, and vengeful nature. Domínguez hoped the governor would investigate the charges and remove Head from the office of Indian agent for the public good.[78]

Interestingly, the first example of Agent Head's misconduct that Domínguez cited was actually about the problematic actions of Head's wife, Maria

Juana de la Cruz Martinez, also known as Martina Martin(ez).[79] Evidence found in a letter from Lafayette Head to Kit Carson suggests that both Head and his wife were accustomed to whipping others into action, literally. According to the letter of May 2, 1861, Head gave Carson (and Chepeta, Chief Ouray's wife) permission to whip his fifteen-year-old stepson, Crecencio Cisneros: "Whip him when ever he needs it. Martina says she wants Dna. [Doña] Chapita [sic] to whip him also and not allow him to idle his time away on the street."[80]

Head had also sent Carson forty-five dollars "to pay for Cracencio's [sic] schooling" and to cover the amount "owed on [Crecencio's] account."[81] Crecencio died six years later at age twenty-one. His obituary, published in the Rocky Mountain News, named him as Head's "adopted and only son."[82]

Also, according to Domínguez, on an unspecified date Head "led a mob who took a man forcibly out of jail and strung him up to a tree, and then gave him two lashes each." Domínguez did not state the reason for the lashing nor did he provide any names. No further information about this incident is available. However, "to save himself from criminal prosecution," Head then accused his "informers of disloyalty and of having held a revolutionary meeting," which was, at the time, punishable by law.[83]

Domínguez wrote that to further Head's private interests or to secure some personal revenge, Head had at different times misrepresented and deceived county officers. The charge is not specific, but perhaps Head had claimed superior knowledge of the laws, or new laws, and had in some manner intentionally misled the Spanish-speaking officers of Conejos and Costilla Counties.

Domínguez also charged that Head did not want Americans to settle in his county. This claim is difficult to comprehend and may be related to the territory's desire for statehood or the fact that a number of Hispanos were in peonage because they owed money to one or two Anglo patrónes (contractors or bosses).[84] Perhaps Head did not want anyone who might challenge his authority in the region.

On March 12, 1864, Governor Evans forwarded the Domínguez letter to Commissioner James MacDonald, who scheduled a hearing to examine the charges on April 18, 1864, at the Conejos Indian Agency.[85] Unfortunately, the full testimony of Head's hearing no longer exists. The existing one-page fragment shows scant notes, such as: "Witness not sworn. Slave of Head's step-son? Kept one-third of his old store thence had goods of his own." From these notations, it can be presumed that Agent Head kept a third of his old store and sold goods from that store to his neighbors and that the slave, perhaps indigenous, was owned by Head's stepson, José Crescencio Head.[86]

It appears that Commissioner MacDonald transcribed testimonies from 575 questions and submitted them to Governor Evans. Unfortunately, that transcription no longer exists. Evans waited two months, until June 10, 1864, to forward the testimony to Commissioner William P. Dole in Washington. In his letter to Commissioner Dole, Evans wrote that MacDonald's "explanations leave my mind still in doubt on some points. This testimony is so conflicting that I have judged it expedient to get further information before expressing an opinion."[87] The comptroller of the US Treasury ultimately presented the official bond of Lafayette Head as Indian agent on December 6, 1864.[88]

Two years later, on January 27, 1866, Lieutenant Colonel Samuel F. Tappan wrote to the new Indian commissioner, Dennis N. Cooley, stating that he felt satisfied of the "complicity of Lafayette Head . . . in the kidnapping and enslaving of Navajoe [*sic*] Indian women and children."[89] Both Tappan and Cooley were aware of the previous petitions asking for Head's removal. Tappan, of the 1st Colorado Cavalry, felt civil officers and Indian agents often took advantage of the Indians and their annuities and had written to Senator Charles Sumner about the issue a year earlier:

> The officials are induced to retain the favor and support of their friends and
> have the monetary resources to assist in their elections. But military officers
> are independent of all local authorities and local influences, sure of their posi-
> tion as long as they do their duty.[90]

Tappan recommended Head be moved to another agency. His recommendation had no effect as Agent Head was a presidential appointee. Agent Head retained his position until 1875, when he served as the delegate to the Constitutional Convention from Conejos County. The following year Congress conferred statehood on Colorado and Lafayette Head was elected Colorado's first lieutenant governor.

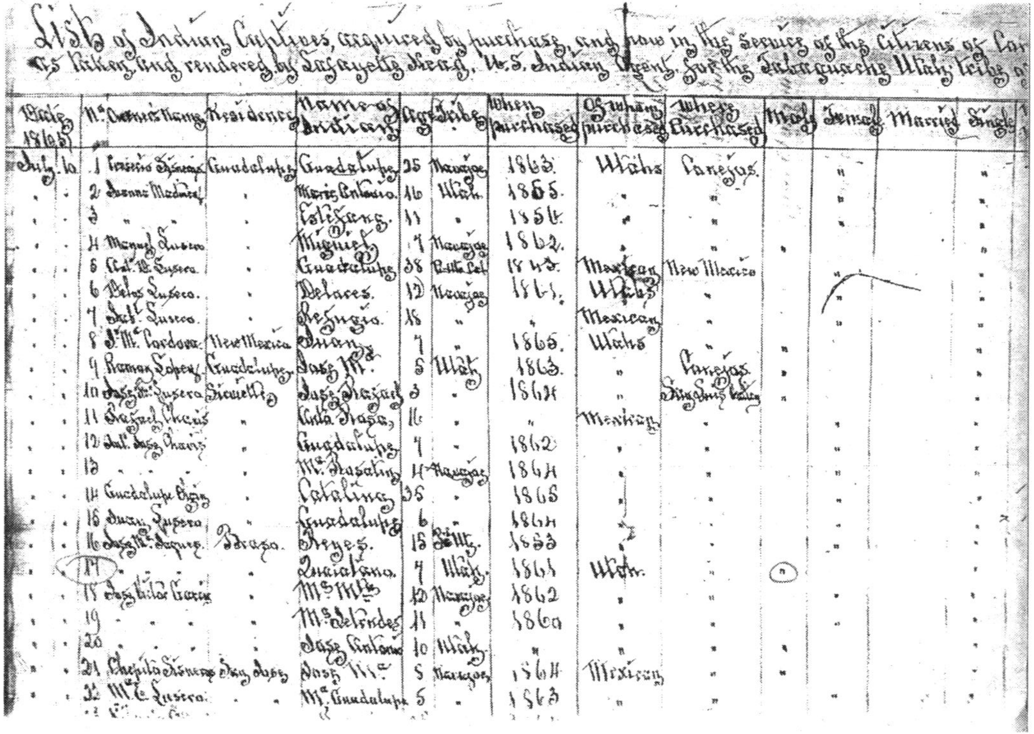

FIGURE 5.2. Captive Indians report for Conejos County, Colorado, 1865. NARA, Washington DC, Letters Received by the Office of Indian Affairs, 1824–1880, Roll 198, Frame 127, Colorado Superintendency, 1865–1866.

Agent Head Retaliates

In light of the Civil War, Congress discussed the issue of slavery and the Emancipation Proclamation. As instructed, on June 28, 1865, Governor Evans asked his four agents to report instances of slavery of American Indians (figure 5.2). The following month, between July 10 and July 13, Agent Head interviewed the enslaved indigenous laborers of eighty-eight owners living in thirteen settlements in Conejos County. Two days later, US marshal Edward R. Harris reportedly interviewed the enslaved workers of sixty owners who resided in settlements along the Culebra and Costilla Rivers of Costilla County. Why Harris prepared that county's report is not known. Also, it is not known if Marshal Harris accompanied Agent Head during his Conejos interviews. If he had, was he there to impose the law or as a show of force?

When Head submitted the Conejos and Costilla County reports to the governor, he wrote that within his knowledge the reports were complete and accurate. Head needed only to report to the governor the total number of instances of enslavement, but he chose to itemize the slaveholders by name, with details about their indigenous laborers. Some of the owners he listed included those men who had earlier petitioned for his removal. Although Head reported about servitude only within the two counties, it is important to note that his lists were in fact incomplete. For some reason, he and the marshal failed to include some well-known, prominent neighbors and merchants.[91] More important, Head did not report himself or his wife as owners of enslaved indigenous persons. Certainly, the owners whom Head had named felt Head had acted in retaliation to disparage them.

Notes

1. NARA, Washington, DC, Records of the New Mexico Superintendency of Indian Affairs 1840–1880, M574, T21, Roll 4, United States to Julian Espinosa August 20, 1860; and United States to Seledonio Valdes, August 25, 1860.

2. The term "Mexican" refers to style and not the point of origin. Meketa, *Legacy of Honor*, 371n17.

3. NARA, Washington, DC, Maj. Mayer to AAA General, July 27, 1862, M1120, RG393, Fort Garland Letterbook, CT, Box 1, 166.

4. NARA, Letters Received by the Office of Indian Affairs, 1824–1881, Colorado Superintendency, 1861–1864, Major Mayer to Commissioner of Indian Affairs,

August 28, 1862, M234, RG 75, Roll 197; and Registers of Letters Received and Letters Received by Headquarters, Department of New Mexico, Maj. Mayer to AAA General, August 25, 1862, M1120, RG 393, Fort Garland Letterbook, 1860–1887, box 1, p. 180.

5. Price, *Season of Terror*, 213.

6. Pettit, *Utes*, 59.

7. Simmons, *Ute Indians of Utah*, 112.

8. Ibid.

9. NARA, Washington, DC, Registers of Letters Received and Letters Received by Headquarters, Department of New Mexico, John Evans to Gen. Canby, August 16, 1862, M1120, RG 393, Roll 18.

10. Ibid., Maj. Mayer to Capt. Cutler, November 16, 1862, M1120, RG 393, Roll 17.

11. Ibid., Maj. Mayer to AAA General, July 27, 1862, M1120, RG 393.

12. NARA, Washington, DC, Letters Received by the Office of Indian Affairs, 1824–1881, "Notes of Interview between Maj. Mayer and Headmen of Ute Indians," August 25, 1862, Roll 197; Letters Regarding the Superintendent of Indian Affairs, Gov. Evans to W. P. Bacon, December 16, 1862, and "Hearing Testimony," December 29, 1862–January 15, 1863, Roll 197; Letters Received by Headquarters, Department of New Mexico 1854–1865, Maj. Gillespie to Capt. Cutler, March 4, 1863, Roll 19.

13. Thompson, *Civil War History*, 204.

14. NARA, Washington, DC, Letters Received by the Office of Indian Affairs, 1824–1881, Colorado Superintendency, 1861–1864, Major Mayer to Commissioner of Indian Affairs, August 28, 1862, M234, RG 75, Roll 197; Registers of Letters Received and Letters Received by Headquarters, Department of New Mexico, Maj. Mayer to AAA General, August 25, 1862, M1120, RG 393.

15. NARA, Washington, DC, Letters Received by the Office of Indian Affairs, 1824–1881, Colorado Superintendency, 1861–1864, Smith to Mix, September 23, 1862, M234, RG 75, Roll 197.

16. Ibid., Evans to Dole, September 16, 1862, M234, RG 75, Roll 197.

17. NARA, Washington, DC, Registers of Letters Received and Letters Received by Headquarters, Department of New Mexico, W. P. Bacon to Witnesses (fragment), December 24, 1862; W. P. Bacon to Lafayette Head, December 25, 1862; Maj. A. H. Gillespie to Capt. R. C. Cutler, March 4, 1863, M234, RG 75, Roll 197.

18. Dr. L. B. McLain was considered "competent and attentive to his duties." NARA, Washington, DC, Registers of Letters Received and Letters Received by Headquarters, Department of New Mexico, Dr. McNulty to Dr. Bailey, October 29, 1862, M1120, RG 393, Roll 17. See also Charles E. Gibson Jr., *Entries Picked at Random from the Journal of F. W. Posthoff Store* (Denver: Civil Works Administration, 1934), CWA Pioneer Interviews Collection, Hart Library, History Colorado Center,

Denver, PAM 349/5, 14. On September 1, 1864, he made several purchases from the F.W. Posthoff store at Fort Garland: two looking glasses for $22; an unspecified number of cigars for $1.50; and a pint of black whiskey for $0.65. On September 17, 1864, he purchased three pounds of crackers, size 50, at $1.50; one can of peaches for $1.25; two cans of chicken for $2.50; and a box of Wake Up for $3.00.

19. NARA, Washington, DC, Executive Department of Colorado Territory, "Papers Containing Charges against Lafayette Head," January 10, 1863, RG 75, Roll 197.

20. NARA, Washington, DC, Register of Letters Received and Letters Received by Headquarters, Department of New Mexico 1854–1865, Major A. H. Gillespie to Capt. R. C. Cutler, "Witness Interview by Maj. Gillespie," March 4, 1863, M234, RG 75, Roll 198, Frame 220.

21. NARA, Washington, DC, Letters Received by the Office of Indian Affairs 1824–1881, M234, RG 75, Roll 197, Letters of the Colorado Superintendency, 1861–1864, Roll 197, Frames 196–97.

22. NARA, Washington, DC, Register of Letters Received and Letters Received by Headquarters, Department of New Mexico 1854–1865, Major A. H. Gillespie to Capt. R. C. Cutler, "Witness Interview by Maj. Gillespie," March 4, 1863, M234, RG 75, Roll 198, Frames 217–218.

23. NARA, Washington, DC, Letters Received by the Office of Indian Affairs 1824–1881, Colorado Superintendency, 1861–1864, M234, RG 75, Roll 197.

24. NARA, Washington, DC, Headquarters, Department of New Mexico, Major A. H. Gillespie to Capt. R. C. Cutler, Fort Garland, C.T., February 7, 1863, M234, RG 75, Roll 198.

25. Ibid., Major A. H. Gillespie to Capt. R. C. Cutler, March 4, 1863, M234, RG 75, Roll 198, Frame 214.

26. NARA, Washington, DC, Letters Received by the Office of Indian Affairs, 1824–1881, Colorado Superintendency, 1861–1864, Major Mayer to Commissioner of Indian Affairs, August 28, 1862, M234, RG 75, Roll 197; Registers of Letters Received and Letters Received by Headquarters, Department of New Mexico, Maj. Mayer to AAA General, August 25, 1862, M1120, RG 393.

27. NARA, Washington, DC, Register of Letters Received and Letters Received by Headquarters, Department of New Mexico 1854–1865, Major A. H. Gillespie to Capt. R. C. Cutler, "Witness Interview by Maj. Gillespie," March 4, 1863, M234, RG 75, Roll 198, Frames 216–19.

28. NARA, Washington, DC, Register of Letters Received and Letters Received by Headquarters, Department of New Mexico 1854–1865, Major A. H. Gillespie to Capt. R. C. Cutler, Santa Fe, "Witness Interview by Maj. Gillespie," March 4, 1863, M234, RG 75, Roll 198, Frames 218–19.

29. No record of this meeting exists today.

30. NARA, Washington, DC, Letters Received by the Office of Indian Affairs 1824–1881, Colorado Superintendency, 1861–1864, M234, RG 75, Roll 197.

31. Ibid., "Testimony in the Charges against Lafayette Head," December 29, 1862–December 31, 1862, M234, RG 75, Roll 197.

32. NARA, Washington, DC, Register of Letters Received and Letters Received by Headquarters, Department of New Mexico 1854–1865, Major A. H. Gillespie to Capt. R. C. Cutler, February 7, 1863, M1120, RG 393, Roll 19.

33. Downing, "With the Ute Peace Delegation of 1863," 200. In his article, Downing described how he and Shavano slipped out of camp, near Julesburg, to hunt antelope; and, the "bawling out" they received when found by a search squad. Shavano made "signs" to borrow Capt. Sandborn's horse "to run down" the antelope he had wounded. "The horse was stripped of all but its bridle and the chief leaped upon it with his bow and arrows . . . It was quite a sight to see the Indian on that horse running at full speed . . . In a short time we were back at camp [with the dead antelope and] getting a lot of scolding." According to New Mexico governor Arny, Grouley and his brother belonged to his superintendency. Grouley spoke Spanish. NARA, Washington, DC, Gov. Arny to Com. Dole, February 21, 1863, M234, RG 75, Roll 197.

34. NARA, Washington, DC, Maj. Gillespie to AAA C. Cutler, February 7, 1863, M1120, RG 393, Roll 19. See also Capt. Eaton to AAA Cutler, February 8, 1863, M1120, RG 393, Roll 19. According to acting New Mexico governor Arny, chief Grouley and his brother traveled with Agent Head to Washington, DC; they "belong[ed] to [the] Band of Utahs in New Mexico." NARA, Washington, DC, Gov. Arny to Com. Dole, February 21, 1863, Records of the New Mexico Superintendency of Indian Affairs, 1840–1880, M574, T21, Roll 4.

35. He refers to the Potomac River, which separates the District of Columbia from the Commonwealth of Virginia. Kelsey, *Frontier Capitalist*, 132.

36. Decker, *Utes Must Go*, 29–30.

37. NARA, Washington, DC, Letters Received by the Office of Indian Affairs, 1824–1881, Colorado Superintendency, 1861–1864, Receipt of Lafayette Head, March 6, 1862, M234, Roll 197.

38. Downing, "With the Ute Peace Delegation of 1863," 194.

39. Ibid., 195.

40. Ibid.

41. Ibid., 196–97.

42. Ibid., 197.

43. Ibid., 198.

44. Ibid., 199. This is the only document that states that Agent Head spoke an indigenous language. Most agents never learned the language of the indigenous nation they represented.

45. Ibid., 203.

46. Ibid., 200, 201. Virginia Simmons, "Rabbitbrush Rambler: Uncle Lafe, Part III," *Valley Courier*, January 29, 2013. See also NARA, Washington, DC, Letters Received by the Office of Indian Affairs 1824–1881, Lafayette Head to Commissioner Dole, July 20, 1863, RG 98, Roll 197.

47. Downing, "With the Ute Peace Delegation of 1863," 202.

48. Crawford, "Leadville Muleskinner," 185.

49. Downing, "With the Ute Peace Delegation of 1863," 202.

50. Wilson, *Denver and Rio Grande Project*, 11.

51. Michael L. Olsen, *Las Vegas and the Santa Fe Trail* (Fort Union, NM; pamphlet), 9.

52. Scott, "Diary of a Freighting Trip," 146–53.

53. Wilson, *Denver and Rio Grande Project*, 26.

54. Downing, "With the Ute Peace Delegation of 1863," 203.

55. Ibid., 202–3.

56. NARA, Washington, DC, Letters Received by the Office of Indian Affairs, 1824–1881, Colorado Superintendency, 1861–1864, Gov. Evans to Com. Dole, September 16, 1862, M234, RG 75, Roll 197.

57. Steck was named to the New Mexico Superintendency in 1864. Fort Garland Museum Library, Post Return, September 30, 1863, Microfilm 0118. See also Price, *Season of Terror*, 213.

58. Downing, "With the Ute Peace Delegation of 1863," 203.

59. According to Price, 15,000 attended. Price, *Season of Terror*, 214.

60. *Rocky Mountain News Weekly*, October 21, 1863; and "More about Espinosa," *Weekly Commonwealth and Republican*, October 28, 1863, 4, col. 2. See also Price, *Season of Terror*, 213.

61. Downing, "With the Ute Peace Delegation of 1863," 203.

62. Price, *Season of Terror*, 214.

63. Thompson, *Civil War History*, 85.

64. The Oxford Dictionary defines "gew-gaw" as "a showy thing, especially one that is useless or worthless." "Trappings" refers to the beaded indigenous dress. Kelsey, *Frontier Capitalist*, 132. Also, Pettit, *Utes*, 59.

65. Pettit, *Utes*, 59.

66. In *Empire of the Summer Moon*, author S. C. Gwynne writes a vivid description of the 1867 Comanche Treaty Council proceedings and the military displays of force demonstrated by both groups.

67. Simmons, *Ute Indians of Utah*, 38. NARA, Washington, DC, Letters Received by the Office of Indian Affairs, 1824–1881, Colorado Superintendency, 1861–1864, Receipt of Lafayette Head, April 22, 1863, M234, Roll 197.

68. Proceeding of the American Numismatic Society, 60th Annual Meeting, 1918. *Proceedings of the American Numismatic Society for the Sixtieth Annual Meeting* (New York: American Numismatic Society, 1918). Also correspondence from Dr. Elena Stolyarik, Collections Manager, American Numismatic Society, October 10, 2014.

69. Denver Public Library, Western History and Genealogy Department, Samuel E. Brown, M91.

70. NARA, Washington, DC, Registers of Letters Received and Letters Received by Headquarters, Department of New Mexico, 1854–1865, Posthoff to Maj. Mayer, August 4, 1862, M1120, RG 393, Roll 19.

71. Parkhill, *Law Goes West*, 53.

72. Carrigan and Webb, *Forgotten Dead*, 113.

73. Denver Public Library, Western History and Genealogy Department, Samuel E. Brown, M91, item 3.

74. NARA, Washington, DC, Letters Received by the Office of Indian Affairs 1824–1881, Colorado Superintendency, 1861–1864, M234, RG 75, Roll 197; Letters Received by the Office of Indian Affairs 1824–1881, Colorado Superintendency, 1861–1864, Major A. H. Gillespie to Capt. R. C. Cutler, M234, RG 75, Roll 198.

75. Quintana, *Pobladores*, 79.

76. NARA, Washington, DC, Office of Indian Affairs, Hon. Charles Sumner, Form 80 (7-45), Cross Reference Sheet, file no. 1863, col. S208. Other than this form, no further information exists.

77. NARA, Washington, DC, Letters Received by the Office of Indian Affairs 1824–1881, Colorado Superintendency, 1861–1864, S. E. Brown to Commissioner of Indian Affairs, February 4, 1864, M234, RG 75, Roll 197.

78. Ibid., C. Dominguez to Gov. Evans, March 11, 1864 (copy), M234, RG 75, Roll 197.

79. Stoller and Steele, *Diary of the Jesuit Residence*, 121. On July 21, 1874, the parishioners were working on the church cemetery. According to a diary entry, Head's wife contracted out her Indian servants as laborers. "All of Doña Martina's laborers have come to work on the cemetery."

80. University of California at Berkley, Bancroft Library, Kit Carson Papers, BANC MSS P-E 64, Reel 9, FF Bonds of Traders, 1855–1860, Lafayette Head to C. Carson, May 2, 1861, Conejos, Colorado Territory.

81. University of California at Berkley, Bancroft Library, Kit Carson Papers, BANC MSS P-E 64, Reel 9, FF Bonds of Traders, 1855–1860, Lafayette Head to C. Carson, May 2, 1861, Conejos, Colorado Territory.

82. *Rocky Mountain News*, July 26, 1867, 4, col. 3. According to the obituary, "Jose Crecincio [*sic*] Cisneros . . . drowned the morning of July 12, 1867, while attempting to cross the Rio Grande. This unexpected circumstance cast a gloom over the

entire community here, as he was a young man in the bloom of life, and cherished and esteemed by all who knew him." Crecencio Sisneros was enumerated in the household of Lafayette Head. 1860 US Census, Taos County, New Mexico, Conejos Precinct 16, 185, Schedule 1, line 27, ancestry.com.

83. NARA, Washington, DC, Letters Received by the Office of Indian Affairs 1824–1881, Colorado Superintendency, 1861–1864, C. Dominguez to Gov. Evans, March 11, 1864 (copy), M234, RG 75, Roll 197.

84. *Rocky Mountain News*, "From Conejos and Costilla," Wm. J. Godfroy to editor, February 1, 1865, 2. Some Hispanos entered into peonage, a form of sharecropping, to provide certain labor in payment of a loan, fine, or service. A peon was a laborer of any working age. Peons were not considered property or capital, as distinct from the southern practice of black slavery.

85. NARA, Washington, DC, Letters Received by the Office of Indian Affairs 1824–1881, Colorado Superintendency, 1861–1864, Macdonald to Gov. Evans, March 12, 1864 (copy), M234, RG 75, Roll 197.

86. NARA, Washington, DC, Letters Received by the Office of Indian Affairs 1824–1881, Colorado Superintendency, 1861–1864, "Sec Tues 189" (fragment), n.d., 1864, M234, RG 75, Roll 197. Salazar and Yost, *Our Lady of Guadalupe Church*, Deaths: 38, July 15, 1867; Reference to Church Burial Register, 50. Also *Rocky Mountain News*, obituary, July 26, 1867, 4, col 3.

87. NARA, Washington, DC, Letters Received by the Office of Indian Affairs 1824–1881, Colorado Superintendency, 1861–1864, Gov. Evans to Commissioner Dole, June 10, 1864, M234, RG 75, Roll 197.

88. NARA, Washington, DC, Colorado Territory Treasury Department, Second Comptroller's Office, December 6, 1864, M234, RG 75, Roll 197. See also Gov. Evans to Commissioner Dole, December 12, 1864.

89. Rogers Library, University of New Mexico at Highlands, RG 98, Department of New Mexico Letters, Vol. 1, p. 428, Tappan to Cooley, January 27, 1866, M234, RG 75, Roll 198.

90. NARA, Washington, DC, Office of Indian Affairs, Letters Received by the Office of Indian Affairs 1824–1881, Lt. Col. Tappan to Senator Sumner, March 24, 1865.

91. Head failed to report several members of the Gallegos family—for example, brothers José Narsico, Juan Gabriel, and Diego Antonio Gallegos and their nephew Dario Gallegos.

6

Manifestations of Intimidation

With the formation of Colorado as an organized territory in 1861, the United States set about establishing a more systematic and formal court system amid the propensities for violence and lawlessness that sometimes accompanied the population explosion. President Lincoln appointed a three-person supreme court, whose justices also rode circuit and presided over district and appellate courts. At the local level, justice of the peace courts and probate courts operated while miner's courts laid down the rules for arbitrating claims and conflicts.

Hispanos had long been accustomed to administration of justice by alcaldes. In that court system an alcalde relied less on legal precedent than on his personal judgment of the facts of a case and his own sense of justice within established codes. English (or common) law, on the other hand, brought to the region by the Anglos, adhered more closely to legal precedent as codified in statutes and law books. Miners' "claim clubs" frequently ignored alcalde law and established rules and meted out justice for themselves. The miners' position found official sanction when territorial law in late 1861 accorded

DOI: 10.5876/9781607329145.c006

precedential authority to the previous judgments of such quasi-judicial miners' courts.

Hispanos were the victims of racial and cultural discrimination in a frontier society still struggling to define itself in Colorado. Whether through miners' courts or vigilante groups, Hispanos—and Indians, Chinese, other "off-whites,"[1] and suspected Confederate sympathizers—were also vulnerable to summary trials and execution, commonly by hanging at the hands of lynch mobs, and commonly following various forms of torture, with or without the pretence of a fair trial.

The Espinosa brothers, Vivián and Felipe, and a presumed cousin, Vicente Espinosa, are together a vivid example of the reach of arbitrary Anglo justice into the lives of Hispano settlers. Accused of numerous murders, the Espinosas escaped from a squad of soldiers that had been sent to arrest them at home at night. When they escaped arrest, though they were not informed about the reason for the arrest, their home was plundered by the troops and then burned, and their livestock and family possessions were confiscated. The story rapidly spread that the fugitives were heavily armed and dangerous. However, archival documents show they had few firearms of any kind and little ammunition. Victims of crimes widely spaced around the territory, or those who were reporting the crimes for newspapers or in official capacities, attributed the attacks to the Espinosas with little or no plausibility to their assertions. The brothers were soon wanted, dead or alive. The three Espinosas were eventually tracked down and in two separate incidents were shot and killed from ambush, without the opportunity to surrender, much less to stand trial and defend themselves. Their bodies were desecrated, and the heads of Felipe and Vicente became grisly objects of display. The review of information about the Espinosas discussed in this chapter presents new sources that may help readers examine their guilt or innocence based on a different context.

Courts in the New Territory

Now that the executive and legislative branches of government were in place in Colorado Territory, it was time to establish its judicial branch. In 1861 President Abraham Lincoln appointed three justices to the Colorado Territorial Supreme Court. The two-tiered court system consisted of the chief justice, Benjamin F. Hall, hearing cases under the laws of the federal government, and two associate justices, S. Newton Pettis and Charles Lee Armour, hearing cases under territorial law.[2] When all three justices heard the same case, they became the supreme court of the territory. All three men were from eastern states and knew very little about the frontier West. They performed duties similar to those associated with the attorney general, and they offered opinions on bills either pending before the territorial assembly or already enacted.[3] Between sessions of the supreme court, they filled the roles of trial judges, who rode a circuit from one town to another presiding over the district courts within their jurisdictions.[4] For their service, each earned an annual salary of $1,800 for a four-year term, paid by the US Treasury.

In contrast, the nuevomexicanos were accustomed to the two-tiered federal court system in which one court heard cases under the laws of New Mexico Territory and the other heard cases under federal laws. The same judge filled the role of both trial judge riding circuit and sitting *en banc* (on the bench) as an appellate court.[5] Judges were also accustomed to the canon law in the Catholic Church, which handled cases such as adoption and divorce.

By authority of the territory's organic act, Governor William Gilpin established three judicial districts on July 11, 1861. Denver became the headquarters of the First Judicial District under Chief Justice Hall.[6] Justice Charles Lee Armour served the Third District, headquartered at Cañon City. His district encompassed Conejos, Costilla, Huerfano, Fremont, Lake, and Pueblo Counties. By November, Gilpin had accused Justice Armour of indulging in vices and associating with the Confederates.[7]

While serving in the Third District, Justice Armour recommended the territorial assembly create the office of inspector of weights and measures. Because Spanish and Mexican weights and measures were so much a part of Hispano agricultural culture and custom,[8] Hispano vendors and traders continued using the weights and measures in the language they knew and understood. Effective February 8, 1864, the assembly authorized the county commissioners of each county to select an inspector of weights and measures. His responsibilities included livestock inspections for identifying livestock brands or marks and "weighing or measuring any goods, wares, vendor merchandise, gold dust, or other articles of traffic."[9] This 1864 statute approved the use of Spanish weights and measures used by the Hispanos in southern Colorado.[10]

The commissioners of Costilla County appointed Spanish-speaking Ventura (Buenaventura) Pacheco as its inspector. In 1865 Pacheco received fifty cents from the county for inspecting measurement of each half fanega, twenty-five cents for each *almud* (one quart), and twenty-five cents for each *vara* (about 33.3 inches).[11] (The *cuartilla* and *cuartillo* were equal to one pint; the *frasco* was a liquid measure equal to 2.5 quarts; and the *pulgada* was a measure for one inch.[12]) Pacheco allowed vendors and traders to use the Spanish weights and measures.

Unfortunately, three years later, in 1867 the territorial assembly restricted the use of the Spanish language and customary order when it repealed the law allowing vendors and traders to use the Spanish weights and measures.[13] This statute placed English-speaking traders and vendors at an unfair advantage over those who spoke only Spanish and thus used Spanish terms in their weights and measurements. Unfortunately, as discussed later, there would be additional English-only sentiments raised among officials at both the territorial and federal levels.

Colorado's Second Judicial District, under Associate Justice Pettis, included the northwestern mining area headquartered at Central City. Justice Pettis soon left the territory because he did not appreciate Central City's "crude miner living conditions." He also did not care for the practice of drinking and gambling during court and thought Denver suffered from "the effects of mob law and violence."[14] One June 2, 1862, President Lincoln replaced Justice Pettis with Justice Allen Alexander Bradford.[15] Gilpin then assigned Bradford to the Third District and moved Justice Armour to the Second District.

Anglo miners and lawyers considered Justice Armour incompetent and "ungentlemanly," a cigar-smoking, "cranky, inscrutable, many-sided tyrant."[16] Although they petitioned the US Justice Department for his removal, he remained in the Second District.[17] In 1864 the members of the Territorial House addressed the grievances of the miners and lawyers and passed a resolution demanding Armour's removal.

The resolution, which was sent to President Lincoln, listed several charges of malfeasance and was supported by eight pages of sworn testimony. Some of the charges were politically motivated, while others attacked Armour's personal conduct. In the end, the president's administration supported the judge.[18] In response, the territorial assembly attempted to gerrymander judicial districts to force Justice Armour either to resign or to switch the justices of the Second and Third Districts, with Armour hearing cases only in Conejos and Costilla Counties. In defiance, Justice Armour ceased hearing court cases, yet continued drawing a salary.

Justice Bradford, who had been moved to the Third District, "spoke in a high-pitched falsetto" and he often "wore a vari-colored Mexican blanket" as his judicial robe. Historian Forbes Parkhill described him as "fat, gross, slovenly, [and] ungainly." The Mexican residents of the Third District called him *el juez gordo* (the fat judge).[19]

Parkhill also provides a vivid description about traveling to hear court at Pueblo:

> Lawyers, with the judge, other court officials, litigants, witnesses, interpreters and prisoners, traveled from court to court in a motley caravan of wagons, ambulances, primitive buggies, horseback and mule, over . . . mesas[,] mountain ranges [and] rivers, in heat, snow, wind and . . . dust. [They camped] out [at] nights . . . sleeping in blankets on the ground, smoking pipes round the campfires, singing songs, [and] swapping lies[;] then holding courts within rude adobe walls.[20]

Inside the courtroom the judge sat on a small box and used a larger, sheepskin-covered box as a table. "The lawyers sat on boards supported by boxes or chunks of wood. The others squatted on the dirt floor and leaned against the adobe walls . . . Everybody smoked during the proceedings."[21]

Because the attempted change in the justices was unfair to citizens of the Third District, the representatives of Conejos, Costilla, and Huerfano Counties stepped forward. In the House Representative Norton W. Welton (Costilla and Huerfano) moved to place Conejos and Costilla Counties in the Second District with Huerfano, Fremont, El Paso, Pueblo, and Summit Counties. When Welton's motion lost, Representative José Víctor García (Conejos), through an interpreter, moved to retain Justice Bradford in the Third District. Again, the motion lost. García then attempted to get the bill moved into committee, following which the Speaker of the House would appoint three legislators to determine a solution and recommend action. This motion also lost. During the final vote on March 5, Representatives Welton, García, and Jesús María Barela (Costilla) were the only three assemblymen to vote against the bill to move Justice Armour to the Third District, headquartered at Servilleta, Conejos County's largest plaza.[22]

Therefore, between 1861 and 1864, southern Colorado's Third Judicial District went through several justices, which left its citizens vulnerable to violence and corruption. As a further indicator of instability, the assembly moved the headquarters of the Third Judicial District from Servilleta to Middle Culebra (San Luis) in Costilla County, then to Cañon City in Fremont County, and finally to Pueblo in Pueblo County.

Due to the decline in the population of the itinerant miners, on February 10, 1865, the territorial assembly changed the judicial district boundaries and placed El Paso, Fremont, Huerfano, Lake, and Pueblo Counties into the Third Judicial District with Conejos and Costilla Counties. This was a lot of terrain to cover. The assembly moved Associate Justice Stephen S. Harding of the First Judicial District to the Third. No historical documents prove Justice Harding ever heard court in his new district.

The following year, when voters elected Justice Bradford as the territory's delegate to Congress, President Andrew Johnson appointed Moses Hallet as Harding's replacement. Hallet, an Illinois attorney, was among the twenty-seven Anglo attorneys who in 1861 were legally authorized to practice law in Colorado. The people of southern Colorado referred to Chief Justice Hallett as the "gunman's terror" or *el juez severo* (the severe or harsh judge). Citizens could no longer "squat on the dirt floor, [play] Spanish monte [or] smok [*sic*] cornshuck cigarettes."[23] Males were required to remove their hats and revolvers during court.[24] Court sessions were held in whatever space was available.[25]

Alcalde Courts and Common Law

At the local level of US judicial rule, the justice of the peace, probate, and district courts were elected by popular vote and usually had no legal training. Each justice had jurisdiction to hear cases involving sums of less than $100, but not those cases concerned with land titles or boundaries.[26] Appeals from the justice of the peace courts were taken first to the district court and then to the supreme court. Appeals from the probate and district courts were taken directly to the supreme court.

In the far northern frontier, the nuevomexicanos were accustomed to Spanish and Mexican law, and they used the alcalde court system. Spanish and Mexican law, or civil law, is less formal; whereas the Anglo miners and settlers were accustomed to English law, also known as common law, which is based on precedent and relies on established laws according to the provisions of applicable code.[27] For example, under English law, the owner of livestock was responsible for his cattle and should fence them in. Spanish law assumed that rangeland was communal property available to all. Thus, the owner of cropland was himself responsible for the protection of his crops.

The office of alcalde evolved in Spain and was introduced into its colonies. The alcalde acted as a justice of the peace and probate judge. In Mexico the governmental act of May 23, 1837, gave the alcaldes and justices of the peace a general civil jurisdiction over complaints that did not exceed one hundred pesos and over criminal cases involving only "slight injuries and other similar faults" that warranted only "light rebuke or correction."[28] Further, by a decree of March 2, 1843, the alcalde system recognized alcaldes and justices of the peace—located in the underpopulated frontiers of New Mexico, Alta California, Baja California, and Tabasco, Mexico—"to act in the capacity of judges of the First Instance," when proceedings have just begun.[29]

In frontier areas like northern territorial New Mexico and Alta California, the alcalde was elected by his district or community to serve as both mayor and judge.[30] In this type of local government, his authority was limited to lesser civil and criminal issues occurring within the limits of his jurisdiction. He often represented the only justice on the frontier. Although most alcaldes lacked any formal legal training, law books, or written statutes, they relied on local tradition to resolve disputes.

The alcalde was a locally elected community official and often was a respected figure in the community. Quite likely he obtained his leadership experience as a mayordomo or an officer of the militia or military.[31] His administration of law was typically an informal verbal process that was designed to avoid formal litigation.[32] To contribute to tranquil relations in the community, he incorporated conciliation, propriety, and justice in handling disputes rather than the formal rules of law.[33] He also used local custom and ethical or practical judgment as the basis for his decisions. He was confined only by the cultural and religious mores of the local plazas in which he served.[34] In municipal matters and local disputes, the alcalde's word was literally "the law." Some alcaldes on the northern frontier recorded their court decisions into a "book of decisions."[35] Although his decision could be appealed, in New Mexico the appeal resulted in a trip to Taos or Santa Fe or even to Mexico City, depending on the civil or criminal matter (table 3.2).

In southern Colorado the Hispanos were well accustomed to the alcalde system, a less formal system based on local custom and conciliation. Because the Third Judicial District had a problem keeping its associate justices, the alcaldes stepped in to keep the peace. Miners who created hostile situations went before the local alcaldes but rejected the system and failed to acknowledge the local alcaldes. They thought the locally elected Hispano judges could not be depended on for Anglo justice. Miners viewed the alcalde system as inadequate; they refused to abide by it because they considered it inapplicable to them as "Americans."[36] The lack of a "clear and precise legal code" bothered most Anglos: "[They] could not understand how the system operated with no enforcement . . . by a sheriff, to levy against assets, or to have that possibility realistically available to as to induce compliance with judicial judgments."[37] Likewise, the alcalde found he had very little power over the Anglo miners, who dismissed the Hispano legal system, culture, religion, and language.

By Colorado territorial law enacted on November 7, 1861, all trials for criminal offenses were in accordance with common law. Likewise, the Hispanos in California and New Mexico found the new territorial laws (regarding inheritance, family and spousal relations, and administration of estates), which were based on English law, difficult to understand and its court proceedings foreign. This territorial law allowed precedential authority to prior miners' court decisions. It mandated that all adjudication, decision, or judgments given or pronounced by any miners' court judge within Colorado Territory, or the decision of its jury, had the same "force, validity, and effect" as a territorial judge or jury.[38] This law validated the decisions of the miners' court, but it failed to recognize the authority of alcaldes or the decisions made in the alcalde courts. Because some alcalde decisions affected or were directed toward certain miners, those "cases" appear to have been automatically dismissed.

Similarly, in 1850, Anglo miners in California lobbied against the use of conciliation as a required legal procedure used by alcaldes. Thus, the first term of the California State Supreme Court rejected alcalde conciliation as a required legal procedure. Conciliation may have been suitable for the Mexicans, the court noted, but "amongst American people it can be looked upon in no other light than as a useless and dilatory formality."[39]

The alcalde system was in use in southern Colorado from early settlement in the 1850s, during the brief Jefferson period, and after the US Congress established Colorado Territory in 1861. The alcalde system was known to have operated in the towns of Conejos, Costilla, and Saguache (table 4.2).[40]

"Hanged on Circumstantial Evidence"

Although justices heard cases in district courts on a scheduled basis, namely every six months, having to wait six months, or until the justice's next term, tested many men's patience. Additionally, there were no funds for a well-constructed and guarded territorial prison, let alone county jails. Because the Colorado territorial justice system was still being established, Anglo miners continued using the code of the miners' courts to handle legal affairs.

The discovery of gold in 1859 transformed the region into a lawless area where Hispanos were more likely to be killed by mob violence. One Jefferson Territory delegate said, "Due to the rapidity with which cities and towns have sprung up . . . citizens were exposed to the attack of . . . men, who have but little care or thought for the . . . rights of others."[41] In the absence of any legal authority or direction, these control-oriented miners developed miners' or people's courts and vigilance committees. Such courts were also known as "kangaroo courts." Under the influence of alcohol and acting as a group, some men got caught up in the excitement in "meting out informal justice."[42] Alleged Hispano offenders received no legal protection against the injustice handed down by these miners' courts.[43] The swiftness of miners' courts usually translated into mob action. According to historian LeRoy Hafen, "The rules were simple and clear;"[44] defendants found guilty were whipped or, worse, hanged by the neck until dead. Many of the accused escaped prosecution by fleeing to other states or territories, so US marshals signed many arrest warrants with "can't find him" and stopped the search.[45] Hafen has written that these "simple democratic methods . . . resulted in a fair trial and speedy justice." Many trials using such methods were speedy, but for many Hispanos they were not fair.

In the spring of 1860, a vigilance committee formed a miners' court at Colorado City (Colorado Springs) to try an unnamed Hispano accused of horse theft. The committee denied the accused due process by immediately selecting three judges and naming two "bystanders" as prosecutor and defense attorney. The attorneys presumed to present each case before a crowd that then immediately issued a convenient verdict. In this particular case, the crowd voted to hang the Hispano. When two ministers objected to the verdict, members of the crowd prevented them from performing "any type of [religious] service." The mob then led the Hispano to a tree near an arroyo and lynched him.[46]

Mobs executing Hispanos preferred to hang their victims because hanging implied that, due to racial and cultural inferiority, the Hispano was a dishonorable and guilty person who deserved such a death.[47] According to oral history, in Trinidad "shootings were frequent and hangings occasional. 'Court' was held on the bridge which spanned the arroyo."[48]

Mobs often bragged about their heroic efforts. John Lawrence named one vigilante group the Saguache Rifle Company. Another vigilante group, composed of miners in the California Gulch district in southern Colorado, was the California Gulch Boys.[49] The Downer Guards was another group "called out and stationed" on the Upper Saguache.[50]

William Newton Byers, the opinionated editor of the *Rocky Mountain News*, successfully promoted and galvanized public support, influenced and helped spread attacks on rival newspaper editors,[51] and promoted anti-indigenous and anti-Mexican sentiment. He once spoke about vigilante acts:

> We never hanged on circumstantial evidence. I have known a great many such executions, but I don't believe one of them was ever unjust. But when they proved guilty, they were always hanged. There was no getting out of it. No, there were no appeals in those days; no writs of errors; no attorneys' fees; no pardon in six months. Punishment was swift, sure and certain. Murderers almost always confessed their crimes.[52]

In 1860 Alexander Cameron Hunt served as a judge in the people's (miners') court at Denver. The following year, Governor Gilpin supported him as US marshal for Colorado because Hunt had "sanctioned a number of hangings to rid the territory of its early criminal element."[53] He became Colorado's third territorial governor and served as land agent for the Denver and Río Grande Railroad.[54]

By 1860, John McCannon was among the 10,000 miners in the California Gulch district.[55] He became quite an effective leader. On May 14, 1863, the *Rocky Mountain News* reported that he and his posse had caught two suspicious-looking Anglos.[56] The posse strung two ropes over a sturdy branch of a nearby tree and placed the nooses around the men's necks. They hanged each man for a few seconds, then let him down and threatened to hang him again. They continued the process about three or four times to force their confessions. Ultimately, McCannon ordered one of the men to get out of town and had the other transported to Fairplay to address the California Gulch miners' court. There army soldiers hanged the man.[57] After the posse left Fairplay, McCannon and his men came upon another suspicious man whom they forced into disclosing his gang's hiding place.[58]

By territorial law, juvenile prisoners were to be "treated with humanity and in a manner [that would] promote their reformation." Jailers were supposed to keep juvenile prisoners in a separate area "from those more experienced and hardened criminals." Furthermore, visits from parents and friends of good moral influence were permitted at all "reasonable" times.[59] On November 5, 1861, the legislature passed a law that convicted horse thieves were either condemned to death or imprisoned for no less than twenty years.[60] For some impatient men, this wait was too long. Prisoners met their deaths illegally at the hands of an angry group of men who acted under the pretext of service to justice, race, language, religion, custom, and tradition. Forbes Parkhill wrote that those who got off with a warning "didn't linger" around long. "They just got up and got," leaving no forwarding address.[61]

The country was in civil war from 1861 to 1865. Colorado Territory's loyal Union citizens, territorial officials, and the military actively searched for Confederate sympathizers. Miners and citizens with itchy trigger fingers and lynch fever became suspicious of every stranger and neighbor. Due to the limited number of documented accounts, the number of murders committed on the Hispanos, indigenous, Chinese, and other off-white groups are unknown (table 6.1). In 1866, Kit Carson wrote that the "advancing tide of American progressive civilization [produced] a clash of language, laws, and customs, [and] a diversity of mistrust and influence." These factors, according to Carson, rendered the "necessary and judicious . . . presence of [continued] military surveillance and police."[62]

According to authors John Boessenecker, William Carrigan, and Clive Webb, Anglo miners forced the californios out of mining districts during the California gold rush and threatened to shoot or hang those who remained. Carrigan and Webb, who researched "extralegal violence" against Mexicans in the Southwest, located twenty-three known areas where Spanish-surnamed miners were expulsed from California mines.[63] By means of the

TABLE 6.1. Recorded Hispano lynchings in Colorado Territory, 1860–75

Date	Name	Location	Crime	Cause of Death
1860	Unidentified	Colorado City (Colorado Springs)	Theft	Hanged by vigilance committee
Oct. 1863	Felipe Nerio Espinosa		Theft	Beheaded
Oct. 1863	Vivian Espinosa		Theft	Beheaded
June 1866	Unidentified	Golden	Attempted murder	Hanged
1870	Serafino Pino	Saguache	Murder of Pete Evertt	unknown
Oct. 1870	2 unidentified	Iron Springs	Murder	Hanged
May 1870	Jose Rodriguez	Conejos	Livestock theft	Taken from jail and shot in head
Jan. 1871	Donaciano Sanchez	Saguache	Horse theft	Taken from sheriff and hanged
July 1871	Unidentified	Jimmy's Camp	Horse theft	Hanged
June 19, 1873	Merijildo Martinez	Las Animas	Murder	Taken from jail and hanged
Aug. 1873	Unidentified female	Trinidad	Knew Merijildo Martinez	Hanged
Aug. 1873	2 unidentified	Trinidad	Murder	Taken from officers and hanged
Aug. 1873	3 unidentified	Hole in the Rock	Theft	Hanged
Oct. 1873	Julian Espinosa		Theft	Shot
Jan. 1874	"Indian Charley"	Frankstown	Murder	Hanged

Source: Data compiled from Carrigan and Webb, *Forgotten Dead*; Leonard, *Lynching in Colorado*; Martin, *Frontier Eyewitness*; and various other sources.

US war against Mexico, Anglos believed they were entitled to control all the newly discovered riches in all recently acquired land. Anglo miners resented Hispano miners, especially when unable to find any gold of their own. In Colorado between 1859 and 1876, Anglo mobs carried out 102 lynchings, 74 of which occurred after 1865.[64] No doubt these numbers are quite understated. Many newspaper editors and their correspondents failed to report the deaths and murders of Hispanos, whom they identified only by nationality rather than by name and residence.

Anglo military and civil law enforcers also participated in meting out informal justice. In Colorado Colonel John Chivington was known as the "Fighting Parson," as he cleaned up frontier towns "in the name of the Lord."[65] When his company captured five Confederates and placed them in leg irons, Colonel Chivington bragged, "I told the guards when they left that if they did not kill those fellows, I would play thunder with them." After leaving Denver, the five were shot to death. Although shackled and under military guard, reportedly they had attempted to escape.[66]

Led by a charismatic leader and armed with a rope and beliefs about frontier justice, many men allowed prejudice, anger, and suspicion to drive vigilante acts. Before they shot, beheaded, hanged, or even burned their prisoners to death, some mobs performed "nonlethal collective violence," such as whipping, branding, dragging, harassment, or ripping clumps of hair from their scalps.[67] Leaders often allowed the use of torture to coerce alleged thieves into a confession.

Regarding immigration from the East, historian Lamar wrote, "Missouri badmen, many leaving behind a record of trouble in Kansas, also came out to drink and fight over their cut of the gold."[68] On July 2, 1863, Chief Justice Hall wrote about the issues caused by the "heavy tide of immigration from Missouri, Indiana, and Iowa." Justice Hall believed these immigrants were avoiding Civil War conscription, were disloyal to the Union, and were the cause of many problems in the new territory: "this emigration brings a mass of people into these mountains amongst whom there are many disorderly men to tamper more or less with the Indians and find ways to provoke the latter to retaliate indiscriminately upon the settlers."[69] According to Lamar, Justice Hall "successfully persuaded the miners . . . to respect [the earlier] decisions" made during and prior to the Jefferson period. This action led to the "continuity and precedent" of the court system used throughout Colorado's gold rush.[70]

Hispanos and other off-whites in Colorado became frequent targets of Anglo violence against property and lives during the gold rush and the Civil War years. Carrigan and Webb's research concluded that "the explicit goal of much mob violence against Mexicans was to initiate an exodus of Spanish speakers, leaving their mining claims and their lands behind for

Anglos." Mobs hoped to frighten them to leave and to "discourage more from coming":

> Most Anglos in the American Southwest . . . made no effort whatsoever to
> protect Mexicans from mob violence, to investigate the actions of lynchers, or
> to hold mob leaders accountable. Instead, they willfully ignored or cruelly cele-
> brated the mob violence that led Mexicans to be expelled from their own lands,
> to be stripped of their property, and to be killed without trial or legal process.[71]

Alleged Hispano offenders received no legal protection against the injustice handed down by Anglo miners' courts and vigilance committees. Hispanos were punished more severely than Anglo offenders. The minimum sentence imposed on Hispanos convicted of rape, for example, was two to three years; the maximum sentence was life imprisonment.[72] In contrast, an Anglo convicted of the same offense received a one-year sentence. The judicial system, administered by Anglo lawmakers and judges, worked against Hispanos.

According to historian Berwanger, Hispanos repeatedly complained that they were "punished more severely than Anglo offenders" (table 6.2). He also wrote that the *Colorado Chieftain*, a newspaper that typically had "no great sympathy for Hispanos," considered their complaint a valid one.[73] In 1866 a Mexican was accused of assaulting an Anglo women in Golden. After he was quickly hanged, the other Mexicans in town were ordered to leave or risk being hanged. In Huerfano County in 1872 José Gonzales graciously gave *posada* (room/board) to a Texan named Baker and his cowboys. When Gonzales protected his wife from being raped by Baker, Baker shot Gonzales. Gonzales was not severely injured; however, Baker and his party fled and escaped justice as they were not apprehended by Anglo authorities. The following year near Trinidad, an Anglo and two Mexicans were accused of murdering a rancher and his wife. Anglo vigilantes lynched the Mexicans but allowed the accused Anglo to escape. Trinidad's Hispano males became enraged, and they seized and hanged an unidentified woman who named the accused Mexicans. Her ethnicity was not reported.[74]

With every new mining district came trouble in terms of prejudice, greed, and want. In October 1870 two Hispanos were accused of murdering "two Americans." The men were caught, transported by unknown parties, and shot without trial somewhere between the mining districts of Temp and Iron Springs.[75] In August 1873 the *Rocky Mountain News* reported on a new mining

TABLE 6.2. Offenses and punishments

Offense	Punishment
Theft of any domesticated animal valued more than $10	20-year jail sentence or death
Altering a brand or cattle rustling	1- to 5-year prison sentence
Kidnapping	1- to 7-year prison sentence
Permanent disfigurement of an opponent, such as "putting out" an eye or slitting an ear or lip	1- to 3-year jail sentence
Counterfeit of coin or gold dust	1 to 14 years
Counterfeit by mixing gold dust with base metals	10-year jail sentence or $1,000 fine
Use of false scales to weigh gold dust	6-month jail sentence or $500 fine
Perjury to secure conviction and execution of any innocent person	Death
Aid in escape of a convicted prisoner	Same penalty imposed on the rescued prisoner
Gambling; betting on Three Card Monte, Strap Game, Thimble, Patent Safe Game, or other similar games	5-year jail sentence or $1,000 fine
Disturbing the peace of private families on the Sabbath, such as "Noise, rout, amusement, or work"	$30 fine
Swearing or using vulgar language that disturbs Sabbath worship	$100 fine (ministers excluded)
Dueling (a fight by consent)	1- to 5-year jail sentence of each dueler and their aides and abettors and
	Disbarment from public office if one dueler dies within a year as a result of the contest

Source: Data compiled from various sources, including territorial newspapers and books such as Carrigan and Webb, *Forgotten Dead*, Leonard, *Lynching in Colorado*, and Parkhill, *The Law Goes West*.

district on the southwestern side of Wet Mountain Valley, where an Anglo couple had been murdered along the Apishipa River. According to the newspaper, "after a severe search," the murderers were "apprehended and taken in charge by a guard." While being transported to the Trinidad jail, the guard was fired upon by a gang of masked men. To circumvent the possibility of a majority Hispano jury, the vigilantes found other ways to dole out justice: "After a hard struggle on the part of the guard, the prisoners were taken from them and hung. The coroner having been notified he left for the place of the scene, and took them to town, with the ropes [still] on their necks. They are Mexicans and their names are unknown."[76]

Although the inequities of physical oppression and racism appeared insurmountable, no memory of mob violence in southern Colorado was recalled in the form of a *corrido* (ballad), an important form of southern Colorado's Hispano oral culture. Stories, mentioned in this and other chapters about the deaths of the Espinosa brothers, Representative Francisco Gallegos, Juan Pedro Baca, Felipe Nerio de Herrera, and the unnamed man whipped by Lafayette Head, were never retold in any ballads, skits (*actos*), or songs (*cantares*).[77] We find none perhaps because at the time they would have been interpreted by Anglos as treasonous acts.

Alleged Hispano offenders received no legal protection against the injustice handed down by people's or miners' courts and vigilance committees led by Anglos.[78] Unfortunately, due to the indifference and hostility of Anglo officials, Hispanos recognized the futility of relying on conventional legal channels. In the hunting and killings of the Espinosas, no attempts were made to bring them in alive so that they could be tried according to the laws of the federal government. Their premature and violent deaths were intended to suppress any future Hispano insurgent activities, whether due to issues of taxation, legislation, peonage, religion, land use, or access to natural resources, including valuable ores. Anglos saw the Espinosas as worthless villains. To the Hispano community, however, the Espinosas were *vecinos* (neighbors) and fellow nuevomexicanos who settled and worked the land. It is also important to note that no oral histories have been found that document these deaths from the point of view of the Hispano troopers stationed at Fort Garland.

By 1870, the town of Saguache, then in Saguache County, had fewer than 325 residents and served as a mining supply area.[79] It had not yet constructed a jail. The afternoon of Christmas Day, Charles Heartman told James Bernard Woodson, John Lawrence, and Sheriff James Fullerton about a meeting to be held that night at his house to discuss the November 23 theft of two horses, a saddle and bridle, "and other things."[80] The accused, a thirteen-year-old named Donaciano Sánchez,[81] allegedly stole these items from merchant partners Otto Mears, a Russian immigrant who rose from rags to riches building Colorado's mountain roads, and Isaac L. Gotthelf, a major sheep raiser. Author Virginia McConnel Simmon wrote about the character of Mears: "Mears missed no opportunity to advance his enterprises and ambitions, even giving voters groceries from his store to influence county elections, and he quickly became closely involved with Utes as a trader, interpreter, and special commissioner and through any other means of profit that came his way."[82]

When Woodson, Lawrence, and the sheriff arrived at Heartman's, they found waiting for them Mears, Gotthelf, Ben Tuttles, Samuel Ashley and his son W. Thomas Ashley,[83] Nathan Russell, Dr. W. A. Settle, a Mr. Schneider, and a number of other Anglo men. Many of them would become members of a posse set on finding Sánchez. John Lawrence did not write that any Hispanos were invited to attend this meeting, and Heartman likely served alcohol. The group decided they would "hunt Sanches [sic] down." The next day they found Sánchez hiding in the home of William James Godfroy. When Sánchez broke free, some men shot at him as he fled.

> We concluded to go and get him and bring him to [the Mears] house to see
> if we could not make him confess whether he had taken them or not. Five
> of us went after him & we found him [hiding under the bed] in the house
> of Godfrey [sic]. We got [Sánchez] out and as we started out the door . . . he
> broak [sic] away . . . & ran for the brush. Some of the men shot about 5 times
> at him but he got away.[84]

On December 26, Sheriff Fullerton and Lawrence found Sánchez at José Antonio Morán's home and transported him to the Mears home. Probate Judge David Goff scheduled a hearing for December 29 at 10:00 a.m. and subpoenaed witnesses. Sheriff Fullerton then had blacksmith Ben Tuttles put Sánchez "in irons." Sánchez was transferred to the Lawrence home, with guards posted around the house. The sheriff periodically moved Sánchez from one home to another for his protection. On December 27 the sheriff and a Mr. Brewer transported Sánchez by wagon to the sheriff's home.

On January 3, 1871, Donaciano's brothers, their uncle, and José Gabriel Martínez arrived from Conejos to attend Donaciano's trial.[85] Lawrence's diary does not provide the date the jury found Sánchez guilty of theft; however, sentencing was scheduled for the next court term, presumably six months later. The evening of January 8, 1871, Tuttles and one of the Ashleys guarded Sánchez at the sheriff's home. At midnight Lawrence learned from George Brewer and José Antonio Morán that vigilantes had seized Sánchez. Just before 10:00 a.m. on January 9, Sheriff Fullerton, Trinidád Tafoya, and Gabriel Woodson found Sánchez "lynched and hung" on a tree by the river, about 200 yards from Woodson's home.[86] They released his dangling body and took him to the home of a Mr. Moreno.

The following day, Lawrence and "a lot of the Mexicans [selected] a burrying [*sic*] place . . . out on the south side of the valley." Lawrence had the Mexican laborers dig the grave. Donaciano Sánchez was "desently intered" [*sic*] in the Mexican portion of the Saguache cemetery at 3:00 p.m. on January 9, 1871.[87] In his diary Lawrence wrote, "A coroner's inquest on the body [determined] that [Sánchez] had been taken by persons unknown and hung." The trial and sheriff's expenses amounted to $167.75.[88]

When Texas longhorn cattle began arriving in southern Colorado,[89] trouble often ensued when sheepherders encountered racist Anglo cowboys who attacked Hispano and indigenous herders and mutilated, poisoned, or killed their sheep.[90] One letter written in 1871 by Father Salvatore M. Personé, pastor of the Nuestra Señora de Guadalupe church, also attests to the violence experienced during this period: "The enmities among the principal families were such that nobody dared to go twenty steps unarmed . . . There was nobody who could rest secure in his own house, because through nocturnal attacks various persons had lost their lives in their own beds, and about four months before our arrival three men were found . . . hanged from three different branches of the same tree."[91]

In 1874 Representative José Anastacio de Jesús Valdez (Huerfano) introduced a bill in the Territorial House prohibiting the malicious injury or death of livestock or malicious interference with the work of any herders.[92] This bill was desperately needed, at least in southern Colorado, as verified in the following two accounts of intimidation and violence against Hispano sheepmen.

Juan Vallejos had about a thousand sheep in the lower Huerfano Valley. According to the oral history of his nephew, he "had to change his sheepherders several times on account of they even [dragged] one."[93] One time three boys from the Lewis family arrived on horseback and whipped his sheepherders with lariats "till they were raw." Vallejos told a herder to return to the area where the whipping had occurred and assured him he would be "looking out for him." As he predicted, the Lewis "boys arrived waving their lariats." Just as they approached the herder, Vallejos jumped out from behind some bushes of soapweed "with his .30-.30 [Winchester rifle] blazing." Vallejos, "a little guy, but a good shot," stopped the boys at gunpoint and made them drop their lariats and weapons. After he forced them to dismount, he tied them up and had them remove their boots. He then sent them home with no boots, lariats, or weapons. "That was the last . . . whippin' [by] them Lewis [sic]."

This historical account is also the only record of an act of retaliation taken by a Hispano. Although neither party seems to have taken any legal action, the story lacks important details about any subsequent or continued cycle of violence and retribution as a result of Vallejos's heroics.[94]

The case of Teófilo Trujillo and his property is probably the best-documented account of intimidation and violence in southern Colorado (figure 6.1). Unlike other Hispano settlers, Trujillo had not settled on granted land. The history of violence against him began during the territorial period in 1865, when Texas cattlemen who had migrated into the San Luis Valley began intimidating Trujillo to make him sell his land.[95] Violence against Trujillo and his property continued well into the statehood period. In 1866 he moved his family to Medano Springs, twenty-seven miles northwest of the fort where he raised spring wheat, tobacco, peas, and potatoes. By 1870, the estimated value of his real estate was $3,000. His personal estate, valued at $5,715, included ten horses, three mules or asses, a hundred milk cows, ten oxen, and three swine.[96] His livestock was valued not only the highest of any Hispano in Costilla County but also second-highest of all ranchers in the county.[97]

Within four years, Trujillo built a "remarkably fine" five-room log home, sixty-two feet by fifty-five feet, that featured many stained-glass windows. He also constructed a four-room adobe home and a house for a laborer.[98] With help from his sons, peones, and enslaved indigenous laborers,[99] he hand-dug a half-mile-long acequia, known as the Trujillo Ditch. By appropriation of the territorial court, this ditch still receives water and is second in priority only to the People's Ditch in San Luis.[100]

By 1885, Trujillo's fertile land produced 450 tons of hay; he raised 600 sheep and 500 lambs, making him the largest sheepraiser in the San Luis Valley.[101] In 1897 the *Aspen Times* reported that Trujillo, "The Big Mexican," lost 500 head of sheep during the winter storms. By 1900, his livestock was valued at $6,000, and the value of his farm had risen from $1,300 in 1880 to $4,000.[102]

According to the *Alamosa Courier*, in January of 1902 employees of a farmer named George Dorris "killed about ninety head of Trujillo's sheep and drove additional sheep away."[103] Dorris reportedly warned Trujillo's herders to move the flock, saying, "failure to do so would result seriously." Dorris, his brothers, and his hired hand, Burt Davis, were accused of malicious mischief

FIGURE 6.1. Teófilo Trujillo. Courtesy Deborah Quintana.

resulting in the killing of twenty-three sheep, three burros, and two dogs. They reportedly burned the herders' tents and bedding, so the band was also accused of attempted murder. The trial was moved to the town of Mosca (a *mosca* is a housefly). According to the *Monte Vista Journal*, "The evidence failed to identify either of the accused as parties to the sheep killing and they were consequently discharged."[104] Three Colorado newspapers reported that men rode over, killed, or dispersed the sheep. The *Alamosa Courier* reported that when the Trujillo family was away for the day, four men "proceeded to enforce their injunction by the shooting process, killing a number of sheep and driving away many others in plain sight of the herders."[105] According to oral history, while the Trujillos attended the day-long trial, arsonists started a fire in a workman's cabin. The fire spread to the larger buildings on the ranch. Then the violent mob traveled to Trujillo's sheep camp and shot or maimed half of the herd.[106] At night the mob fired their guns into the house, "narrowly missing the occupants."[107] The *Fort Collins Weekly Courier* reported that Trujillo's barn had been burned to the ground.[108] Most Hispanos living in the San Luis Valley believed that Teófilo Trujillo's ranch house was burned to the ground because he refused to sell his land.[109]

The land in Los Conejos owned by José Seledonio Valdez became known as La Isla de don Seledonio (the island of don Seledonio).[110] According to a reconnaissance report for the US secretary of war, La Isla was a "long point of land" that lay between the San Antonio and Conejos Rivers. Lieutenant C. C. Morrison referred to it as "the best watered and most fertile land" in the area: "It is, without doubt, the garden-spot of the entire valleys of the two rivers, and would be literally 'flowing with milk and honey,' were it in the hands of eastern farmers instead of those of Mexican descent, whose ambition is generally satisfied with cigarettes and a [cheer] 'ouile' [*olé* in Spanish]."[111]

The Colorado Territorial Assembly legalized the operation of ferryboats in 1875 and set the toll rates. The prior spring, José Seledonio Valdez had purchased a ferry on the Rio Grande from Ferdinand Meyer for $450. José María Jáquez and Territorial Council member José Víctor García helped Valdez obtain a permit to operate his ferry. In his military report Morrison described the ferry as a "dilapidated affair."

> The ferry crossed the Conejos River at la Plaza of Los Cerritos [but] sank the following fall. Last spring [in 1875, Valdez] replaced [it with] the present one, [which is] very serviceable and greatly superior to Stewart's [ferry]. It is about 45 feet long and 12 [feet] in width and strongly constructed of stout timbers. A strong side railing . . . and a small row-boat is in tow for a possible necessity, certainly a nice precaution . . . The cable is firmly held upon strong piles about a foot in diameter, with heavy triangular braces, thence passing over a windlass to the rear . . . In its location this ferry has, furthermore, an advantage over its rival.[112]

Morrison reported that there was no small pier or any type of plank in use when Valdez ferried the cavalry and equipment across the Conejos River. Due to the size of the lieutenant's party, Valdez did not charge to ferry the cavalry's wagons but charged him twenty-five cents per riding and team animal: "[Eight] horses were led on the boat, heads alternating up and down stream, to equalize the load. [The trip lasted] eight minutes, four six-mule wagons, including the teams. [All] were ferried over safely in one and a quarter hours."[113]

The Valdez ferry crossed south of today's old state bridge toward San Luis. Morrison also reported that a loaded ferry could cross the river in four minutes and that the fees were similar to Stewart's fees.[114] As ferryman, Valdez transported travelers at any hour of the day. He told Morrison that, at a single crossing, he had carried 400 sheep for a cost of five dollars.[115]

Father Personé blessed Valdez's ferryboat on May 3, 1875.[116] Unfortunately, shortly thereafter someone intentionally cut the cable during the night, "sending the large boat floating through the Rio Grande Gorge." Reportedly, the boat became lodged and abandoned on a sand bar about sixty miles downriver.[117] Archaeological evidence recorded in 1996 verified the location of the pediments securing the cable, the adobe building for the ferry man, and the narrow path on which animals pulled the ferry across the river.[118] Unfortunately, the motive and the culprit remain unknown.

Violent deaths of Hispanos continued, whether through vigilante action or armed disputes. After a hanging of two Hispanos in 1876, for example, the Pueblo newspaper wrote that "only the Mexican population of Cañon City was not pleased with the action of the vigilantes."[119] In 1880 in Las Animas County Juan Pedro Baca died while attempting to recover sheep that had strayed onto a neighboring rancher's land. Once he entered to reclaim his property, a gunfight ensued with cowboys at El Moro, located four miles east of Trinidad. Reportedly, the Sparks brothers were charged in his murder but were acquitted during a trial in Pueblo.[120] Juan Pedro was the son of territorial representative Felipe de Jesús Baca.[121]

Spanish-language newspapers would have been wonderful resources of the types of news reported to Hispanos; regrettably, no back issues of these newspapers exist today. And rather than printing reports to try to end these violent actions, Anglo news correspondents and editors of English-language newspapers chose to advertise the availability of irrigated land for sale at cheap prices. For example, on May 12, 1872, the *Daily Chieftain* advertised that Mexicans are "willing to sell" their irrigated lands; "Americans" are "anxious to have whites as neighbors."

The Espinosas: Wanted Dead or Alive

At the parish church in Conejos on April 27, 1862, María Gertrudis Chávez and her twenty-nine-year-old son served as godparents to the infant daughter of

José Manuel Gálvez.[122] By Hispano custom, relationships between *compadres* (parents and godparents) were based on honor, principle, and trust. The spiritual ties of *compadrazgo* (co-parenthood) was and still is an important indication of respect, affection, and familial bonding. Historian Frances Leon Quintana wrote that the compadrazgo was "the chief cohesive and integrating force in a community [that channeled] reciprocal behavior."[123] Hispano parents would never select an immoral person to act as a godparent to their child.[124] The godfather was José Vivián Espinosa. The following year Vivián and his brother, Felipe de Nerio Espinosa, were accused of a large number of murders that occurred in southern Colorado, and they were hunted down and violently killed.

At Fort Garland on January 9, 1863, Captain Ethan Wayne Eaton received orders from Brigadier General James Carleton of the Military District of New Mexico to arrest Felipe and Vivián Espinosa and a third unknown party.[125] In response, General Carleton purportedly sent military orders to Fort Garland for the arrest of the Espinosas. Perhaps Carleton had heard about the various murders occurring within his district; however, this military order has not been located in local or national archives.

Sometime after January 9, 1863, Captain Eaton ordered Second Lieutenant Nicholas Hodt to San Rafael in Conejos County to make the arrests of the Espinosa brothers. Hodt and his First New Mexico Cavalry, Company D, were stationed at Fort Garland during this time. From a review of historical records, it is not certain whether the captain was acting on Carleton's purported order or reacting to the mysterious murders taking place and the uneasiness of the Anglo miners, merchants and settlers.

About the end of January, Deputy Marshal George O. Austin rode with Hodt and a detachment of ten soldiers to San Rafael.[126] According to a military census of 1863, the Espinosas lived in the small settlement of San Judas de Tadeo within the San Rafael district.[127] San Rafael was the main settlement within this district.

José Vicente Velásquez, one of the original settlers of the Guadalupe settlement, personally knew the Espinosas and retold stories about them to his children. He told them the brothers "were not outlaws . . . they were good, law-abiding citizens."[128] As a respected citizen and elder, Velásquez was a credible character witness. He had participated in a punitive expedition against the Utes[129] and had served under Captain Jesús María Velásquez as a soldier in the 1860 Conejos Militia against the Navajo.[130]

The newspapers reported the events in a manner that sold newspapers, while information provided by Velásquez helps readers understand the story from another point of view. Lieutenant Hodt reportedly wanted to arrest the Espinosas without confrontation. Once he was at the door, he falsely represented himself as an army recruiter and told the brothers he was on a military recruiting trip for the US Army. According to the plan hatched by Hodt and Austin, each would grab a brother and the troopers would rush in to assist. However, when Hodt arrived at the door, Vivián told him he would get back to Hodt in the morning.

Hodt's plan B went into effect five days later when Hodt and his troopers again appeared at the Espinosas' door. According to a news correspondent known as "A," Austin and Hodt had partially succeeded in holding them in a room and placing a sergeant "at the door." Correspondent "A" was in fact Deputy Marshal Austin.

Velásquez told his children he was at the Espinosas' home the night Hodt arrived. Velásquez was asleep "in one room with one of the brothers [and] the other [brother slept] in an adjoining room." According to Velásquez, as the soldiers surrounded the house, the Espinosas "jumped out of the doors [of the other] rooms and ran towards the woods along the Conejos river."[131]

But according to an 1895 interview of Thomas Tate Tobin, Vivián had stepped out to greet Hodt.[132] When Hodt asked about enlisting the brothers, Vivián answered that they would not. Hodt then attempted to grab Vivián, but Vivián ducked back into the house.[133] According to Austin again, Hodt then attempted to gather the remaining soldiers, and when he returned, the two Espinosas "had broken through the partition and procured arms, guns, pistols and bows and arrows, and commenced firing the arrows from the doors and windows." Neighbors started to gather outside to see what was happening. As Austin reported, Hodt was as "liable to be attacked from those outside as those inside."

However, reportedly Hodt ordered the house set on fire to compel the brothers to come out, but "while the latter order was being executed, the [brothers] made a rush out of the door, discharging a shower of arrows."[134]

What happened next appeared to be a comedy of errors. Hodt fired "all the charges from one pistol without any apparent effect." He drew his second pistol but found it would not stay in the cocked position. The frustrated Hodt then threw the pistol. When it hit the ground, the pistol discharged and a ball struck Hodt on the forehead, severely wounding him. As soon as the soldiers arrived, he ordered an immediate pursuit and had Deputy Austin assist them. In crossing the river, Austin's horse fell on the ice and broke Austin's leg just above the ankle. Some of Hodt's men returned Austin to the San Rafael area, while the others pursued the Espinosas into the mountains. Then Hodt sent an express man to Fort Garland to fetch Dr. Lewis B. McLain, a citizen physician in charge of the Fort Garland post hospital.[135]

It is difficult to understand from Austin's report how the Espinosas could "discharge a shower of arrows" while holding on to arms, guns, and pistols. Also, it is important to note that Thomas Tate Tobin later recalled that the Espinosas "had no weapons with them."[136] Interestingly, Velásquez does not mention any gunfire returned by the Espinosas on the night in question. It is the gunfire and commotion that he would have likely remembered most.

Major Gillespie's 1863 census of the San Judas de Tadeo settlement, where the Espinosa family lived, lies within the San Rafael district. This census provides valuable information about the armaments he found (figure 6.2). By October 1862 Felipe Espinosa owned one carbine (rifle) and had a half pound of ammunition; Vivián Espinosa, however, owned no weapons and had no ammunition.[137] Their neighbors, the Durán and Sánchez families, were also in the same economic condition. Regarding their weapons, Gillespie reported that José Manuel Durán owned a shotgun but had no bullets. Luís Durán owned a rifle and had a pound of bullets. Jesús María Sánchez owned two pistols but had no bullets. Vicente Sánchez owned one rifle and had a pound of bullets. Gillespie recorded no arms or ammunition for the next eight San Judas households on his census.[138] Gillespie also reported that "the people [there were] notoriously bad and lawless,"[139] though he did not state how he knew this. For the whole San Rafael District, Gillespie reported two rifles, two pistols, a shotgun, and a carbine along with two and one-half pounds of ammunition owned by five men; however, the owners of the pistols had no bullets.[140] The families lacked sufficient armaments or ammunition to protect themselves from raiding indigenous bands, dangerous animals, or drunk and angry miners.

Gillespie would have found it beneath his rank to record the number of bows and arrows in the plazas. Also, there was a shortage of firearms in southern Colorado, even as late as the mid-1800s.[141] Guns and rifles required ammunition, and ammunition cost money—all of which were also lacking there at the time.[142] Due to the lack of firearms, Hispanos used lances and

No.	Name	Age	Women	Children	Arms	Ammo	Horses	Mares	Mules	Oxen	Cows	Calves	Sheep	Land	Corn	Wheat	Potatoes	Hay	Wagons	Houses	Mills	Misc	Land Cult
1	Jose Manuel Duran	35	1		shotgun															1			
2	Luis Duran	48	1		rifle	1 lb														1			
3	Felipe Espinosa	38	1		carbine	.5 lb														1			
4	Vivian Espinosa	30	1																	1			
5	Santiago Giron	30	1																	1			
6	Francisco Gomez	40	1																	1			
7	Jo Anto Gonzales	40	1	17 males between the ages of 1 month to 12 years; 7 females between the ages of 2 to 7 years; 15 females between the ages of 7 to 15 years			Seven	Five	One	Five	Seven	Four			10.5 bushels	208 bushels	75 bushels			1		20 Goats 3 Jacks	
8	Juan Pedro Herrera	65																		1			
9	Nesario Herrera	21																		1			
10	Jose Lobato	44	1																				
11	Teodoro Maes	36	1																	1			
12	Juan Luis Martin	25	1																	1			
13	Jesus Maria Sanchez	38	1		2 pistols															1			
14	Vicente Sanchez	50	1		rifle	1 lb														1			
15	Jose Antonio Suaso	70	2																	1			
16	Silverio Suaso	21	1																	1			
17	Alejandro Valdez	26	1																	1			
18	Nesario Valdez	30	1																	1			
19	Gatusa Chaves	30	widow																	1			
20	Agapita Duran	28	widow																	1			
21	Juana Maria Medina	32	widow																	1			
			22	Total 39	2 rifles, 2 pistols, shotgun, 1 carbine	2.5 lbs	7	5	1	4	7	4			10.5	208	75		20	20		20 & 3	
			20 families																				

FIGURE 6.2. Abstract of Major Gillespie's military census for San San Judas de Tadeo Plaza, 1863. Felipe and Viviàn Espinosa are both listed. NARA, Washington, DC, M1120, RG 393, Letters and Telegrams Received, 1860–1880, "Abstract of Military Census of District of Conejos, Plaza of San Judas de Tadeo Plaza," Fort Garland Letterbook, C.T., Letterbook, Part V, Entry 4, Box 1.

bows and arrows for hunting and protection.[143] In 1854 the Costilla settlement had only one gun and one musket.[144] For their mutual protection, one group of settlers watched over the crops, while another group watched over the livestock. A third group was responsible for making bows and arrows.[145] Frank Hall, an early Colorado historian and friend of Wilbur Fisk Stone, wrote that only the more "refined residents" owned a Colt army revolver and a good horse with saddle and bridle.[146] Clearly, the Espinosas were not men of this class. By May 2, the *News* had reported that the Espinosas had two pistols and a double-barreled shotgun.[147]

The Espinosa family was not rich in money or possessions. According to author Charles F. Price, the Espinosa family lived in a jacal and had only one trunk, four beds with bedding, four fanegas of wheat, two water buckets, a beaver trap, and some livestock.[148] Before setting the house on fire, Hodt confiscated the Espinosas' household goods and a steer, ox, and two cows. Marshal Alexander Cameron Hunt took possession of eight more cows and oxen and corraled them at Fort Garland. Now the Espinosa family had no home, household items, food, or livestock. Interestingly, those newspaper correspondents who had meticulously documented information about the numerous murder sprees failed to mention with whom the displaced family members stayed; they also and overlooked the fact that the soldiers or possemen would have observed every move made by family members and their caring neighbors.

Deputy Austin also reported another mysterious shooting between Fort Garland and Culebra (San Luis). An express man had been shot at but not injured. This was opposite from the direction in which the Espinosas had headed when they ran from their home. Austin also reported that Kiowas were at Mosca Pass to retaliate against the Utes. Austin completed his report by stating that Marshal Hunt and Deputy Marshal Olmsted recently left Fort Garland for Pueblo with several Confederate prisoners.[149] Clearly, many events were taking place at this time. Everyone became a suspect, whether Hispano, Indio, Confederate, or newcomer. In *Tom Tobin and the Bloody Espinosas*, author Bob Scott wrote about a visitor from California was "promptly hanged from [a] tree": "Mr. Valdez[,] who had the misfortune to be of Hispanic descent[, was] visiting old friends in [the mining town of] Fairplay, when someone assumed Valdez was a killer."[150]

The *Denver Post* reported that after being shot in the chest, one Anglo male later reported seeing "two dark-skinned Mexicans standing in the bushes."[151]

Hispano settlers were farmers and thus all tended their subsistence crops under the strong rays of the bright sun, and many men, including Anglos, had dark hair and grew bushy beards. Author James E. Perkins considered that although an Anglo who was shot near Fairplay had claimed to have recognized his assailants, the town "was many miles away," too far for the Espinosas to have committed the assault.[152] Nonetheless, in the excitement of the times, many Anglos quickly attributed the shooting to the Espinosa brothers. It is important to note that Fairplay was formerly known as the California Gulch. Because this mining town comes up again and again in this chapter, perhaps the events relating to the Espinosas begin there.

Governor John Evans wanted the Espinosas found dead or alive. In response, Hunt posted a notice in a newspaper about a fifty-dollar reward for the arrest and delivery of the Espinosa brothers and a man named Jesús M. Sánchez. None of the newspaper correspondents reported any real physical or helpful description of the Espinosas,[153] and Hunt's description of the Espinosa brothers was no different: "BROBAN and PHILIP OSPENACIA, one of them 5 feet 6 inches in height and slender built; the other a little shorter and heavier."[154] Hunt's notice did not usefully identify or describe Sánchez or indicate how he was involved with the Espinosas, but only stated that he was from Upper Conejos.

According to an oral history of George W. Griffin, a California Gulch miner, "It was hard to believe that two men could cover so great a territory[, for] the widely scattered locations of these killings gave every indication that there were several bands of desperadoes at work."[155] In fact, no records prove the posse or soldiers had a description or drawing of the Espinosas. In a lengthy report submitted to the *Rocky Mountain News*, Wilbur Fisk Stone, as correspondent "Dornick," simply described Vivián as the larger of the two Mexicans, about twenty-five years old.[156] Authorities appeared to solely be looking for two Mexicans.

The Manhunt

Sometime in April 1863, George W. Griffin's relative, Benjamin Griffin, and a Mr. Martindale started out and tracked the Espinosas past Hartsell, where they were "overtaken by a party" of the California Gulch miners headed by John McCannon. McCannon and his posse of the California Gulch Boys from Fairplay soon came upon the Espinosa's camp in a canyon about eighteen miles from Cañon City. There they found a team and wagon the Espinosas had allegedly obtained at Oil Spring. At one point members of McCannon's posse mistook one of their men for Felipe Espinosa because the two wore similar shirts.[157] Joseph Lamb recalled, "[John Endleman] of our party unexpectedly became insane from excitement and exertion." Because Endleman began to sing and yell, John McCannon ordered his men to "gag him when he became too noisy." Another man, named Egeton, also "lost his mind and become very noisy . . . he was not a fit man to have along."[158] Such deliriums were known as Gold Fever.

When four of McCannon's men spotted two horses presumably used by the Espinosas, McCannon ordered Lamb, the best shooter of the four men, to fire. "The shot struck the Mexican in the back and he pitched forward. The four started running toward him. Joe Carter from the group of four was the one who aimed his rifle at the heart of the Mexican but the bullet struck him at the top of his nose and blew his head to pieces."[159]

After the California Gulch Boys hunted, ambushed, and shot Vivián, they reportedly "buried his torso." According to another report, the posse left Vivian's body where they shot him, leaving him "where he fell as food for wild animals."[160] Felipe Espinosa escaped.

At Cañon City the posse displayed the wagon's contents "to a large and excited crowd." The posse identified the clothing and personal effects as those belonging to men the Espinosas had allegedly murdered. Because they could not associate "two or three" items of clothing, "besides those of four or five others," the posse assumed that the Espinosas had "murdered at least twelve persons." As reported, also found among the items in the wagon were a coat, hat, boots, and horses belonging to Frederick Lehman, a miner who had earlier been shot and tomahawked.

After John McCannon's posse killed Vivián, they returned to Fairplay. At various auctions, they displayed and sold the plunder as souvenirs. Such souvenirs include two pistols that were later donated to the History Colorado Center.[161] One of the pistols was an 1858 .36 caliber Remington Navy percussion revolver, a six-shot, single-action gun. Its barrel was seven and three-eighths inches long. The other was a .44 caliber 1860 Colt Army revolver.[162] Because Joe Carter's successful rifle shot blew Vivián Espinosa's head to pieces, how, from that distance, were any of the members of the posse able to precisely confirm that he was an Espinosa? Remember, as stated earlier, the descriptions they had were useless.

Joseph Lamb took Vivián's spurs as a souvenir; he later sold them to a judge named Castello.[163] Writing as "Dornick" in the *Weekly Commonwealth and Republican*, Wilbur Fisk Stone alleged that Vivián stole from the California Gulch miners: "A party of the California Gulch boys [said] they had at last overtaken the outlaws [on May 9] and meted out a just reward to one of them . . . upon the one who was killed was found $123.75 in [California] gulch gold dust. These murderers being thus found to be Mexicans, accounts for many hitherto mysterious things."[164]

John McCannon also found a small, red-beaded buckskin bag around Vivián's neck. Inside the bag was an oval-shaped gold medal commemorating the miracle of La Virgen de Guadalupe (the Virgin of Guadalupe). The medal is of historical and religious significance. In Mexico in 1531 Juan Diego received several visions of the Virgin Mary. These visions resulted in the Miracle of Tepeyac, a rose-petal-laden *tilma* (cloak) in the Virgin's image. This same tilma can still be seen today at the Basilica of Our Lady of Guadalupe in Mexico City. Incidentally, the early towns of Guadalupe and Guadalupita near Conejos and the Conejos Catholic church were named in honor of this saint.

McCannon kept the medal as a souvenir. In 1964 presumed descendants of McCannon donated the medal to the Colorado State Historical Society. Unfortunately, while on exhibit in January 1965, it was stolen.[165] No one knows what became of the red-beaded buckskin bag in which Vivián stored the medal. The fact that it had red beads sewn into it indicates it was made by indigenous hands. This was Ute country. Many Hispanos, and some Anglos like Lafayette Head, regularly traded with them for goods, including captives. Vivián may likewise have traded for this bag.

Stone considered McCannon's ambush of Vivián and the vigilante actions of his mob justifiable in light of the alleged malicious "bloody crimes" that the Espinosas had committed.[166] The hunt continued for Felipe Espinosa.

There are no written accounts regarding who determined the value of the dust, where or how it was found, and who ended up with the gold. The notion that Vivián had it on his body raises additional unanswered questions. Did Vivián or Felipe mine for gold? Had the Espinosas had earlier encounters with the California Gulch miners in the mining districts, which then resulted in their being hunted down and killed by the miners' posse?

Typically, to collect the reward for capturing or killing a wanted man, someone delivered a body to show proof of the capture. McCannon and his posse either did not know about or were not interested in the reward, for they did not return the corpse to Fort Garland officials or to the US marshal. On Vivián Espinosa's arrest warrant, Marshal Hunt simply wrote, "Can't find. Dead."[167]

Felipe's Letters and an Ode

Felipe Espinosa reportedly composed several letters and an ode during his time in hiding. According to the oral history of elder José Vicente Velásquez, Felipe arrived at the office of Indian agent Lafayette Head and delivered five handwritten letters addressed to Head, First Lieutenant William B. Moore of Fort Garland, Colonel John Milton Chivington, Governor John Evans, and the Conejos County judge. An unidentified correspondent wrote that Felipe had arrived in Conejos and acted like a *zorro* (fox), darting in and out, while visiting his two sisters,[168] and firing off six shots from his revolver.[169] But why would he waste his much-need bullets and risk capture? Another unidentified correspondent wrote that Felipe Espinosa "should be immediately hunted down and hung on the highest limb in the Sangre de Cristo ranges."[170]

Lafayette Head's letter from Felipe was written in Spanish as a bit of rhyme. According to José Vicente Velásquez, the elder Hispano who told his children stories about the Espinosas, it read:

Felipe le dice a Nerio,	Felipe tells Nerio,
Vamos matando este gringo.	Let us kill this gringo.[171]

Two men named Felipe Nerio lived in San Rafael. One was Felipe de Nerio Espinosa, the alleged murderer, and the other was Felipe Nerio de Herrera, a poblador. Needless to say, the similar names caused some confusion among the Anglo community. According to Velásquez, Head misinterpreted Felipe Espinosa's poem as Espinosa calling upon Nerio de Herrera to join him in killing *"este gringo"* Lafayette Head, when Espinosa was actually referring to himself as Felipe Nerio.[172] Unfortunately, we will never know how much Agent Head, who knew Spanish, relied on the literal expression to exaggerate or dramatize the meaning or the emotional spirit of the verse. Simply said, too many pieces are missing from the full Espinosa story. However, it appears that Head clearly felt there was a threat against his life. Perhaps rightly so. Some Hispanos were upset with him and had submitted various petitions to have him replaced as Indian agent.

According to Velásquez, Agent Head implicated de Herrera in the murder of an Anglo fisherman and sent for some Fort Garland soldiers to execute de Herrera "in his own house."[173] Unfortunately, no additional information appeared in newspapers and Head left no personal or agency records. However, according to the 1864 petition submitted to Attorney General Samuel E. Brown, Agent Head was "the cause of all the troubles and difficulties which the people of this County [have] been subject to for these last two years."[174] Had escalating paranoia, triggered by Felipe's threat, led Agent Head to turn on an innocent Hispano who had no known connection with the Espinosas? Did Head believe de Herrera was abetting the Espinosa brothers? As reported by Celestino Domínguez in the previous chapter, was de Herrera the man that a mob, led by Head, took from jail, strung up to a tree, and then lashed?[175] Unfortunately, Domínguez did not, or could not, provide us with more details.

Felipe Nerio de Herrera died and was buried at Guadalupe on September 9, 1863. His widow, María Deluvina Sánchez, was pregnant with their fifth child. The baby girl was born that December. At her christening the priest recorded "Rafael Cabeza" (that is, Lafayette Head) and his wife as her godparents.[176] By Hispano custom, as godfather, Lafayette Head would have sponsored and aided in his godchild's welfare until her marriage.[177]

The trail stops here, although many factors may have compromised the way Head interpreted Felipe's verse. No surviving military records for Fort Garland prove Agent Head sent for the military and had the soldiers execute de Herrera. As an official of the US government, he would have had the authority to order soldiers to action; however, soldiers are trained to follow orders from the military chain of command and not civilian officials. Also, Head could have hired them to kill de Herrera. If he had de Herrera executed in error, Head was in a financial position to provide welfare to the family and aid in the child's well-being until her marriage. By this action, he attempted to redeem himself to the grieving family and community.

Dolores Sánchez: Fact or Fiction

The following account adds another dimension of mystery and possible conspiracy. In October 1863 a woman named Dolores Sánchez had traveled "north" from Trinidad on an overnight trip by horse and wagon to Fort

Garland. Why she traveled north rather than directly west is unknown. Her driver was identified as Leander D. Philbrook. Reportedly, Felipe and his nephew Vicente Espinosa stopped and robbed them. Philbrook escaped on foot.[178] Sánchez was reportedly raped and left to die.

According to military documents, Philbrook was known to suffer "severe" mental and physical attacks that rendered him "unable to undertake any form of labor." In fact, his request for a medical discharge was due to "broken health" (mental incapacitation). Colonel Chivington authorized his discharge from the First Colorado Volunteer Infantry Regiment on June 24, 1862.[179] A news correspondent known only as "Battery" wrote that Sánchez was "a very intelligent Mexican lady,"[180] yet no one in the county seemed to know her. By Hispano custom, a "lady" would never travel unchaperoned on such a long trip, especially if led by a mentally unstable escort. Another correspondent, known as "Typo," wrote that Sánchez was not raped and that she sat talking to the Espinosas for some time.[181] No post records include any entries about Dolores Sánchez and Philbrook and their presumed altercation with the Espinosas. In addition, the name Dolores, Spanish for "sorrows," was commonly used by both genders. A woman might be named María Dolores or María de los Dolores; likewise, a man could be named José de los Dolores or José Dolores. Due to the many convoluted stories and misinformation about the whole Espinosa affair, this Dolores may have been the Jesús M. Sánchez wanted by the authorities as an accomplice to the Espinosas;[182] his name could have been Jesús María de los Dolores Sánchez. Unfortunately, we will never know whether she was molested and beaten or just spent time in conversation. Although the reports submitted by both "Battery" and "Typo" make for an intriguing tale, their accounts cannot be verified.

Deaths by Decapitation

Thomas Tate Tobin, an experienced scout who was not a member of the posse of either Marshal Hunt or John McCannon, tracked down Felipe Espinosa and his presumed nephew Vicente Espinosa. On September 7, 1863, Tobin left Fort Garland with a "Mexican boy" named Juan Montoya, a man known as Loren Jenks, Lieutenant Horace W. Baldwin, and fifteen soldiers. Tobin obtained permission to take Juan Montoya, who worked for the quartermaster at Fort Garland,[183] on the manhunt "so he could lead [Tobin's] horse while [Tobin] tracked the assissins [*sic*]."[184] Jesús María Manzanares, who granted historian Leroy Hafen an interview in 1930, said Tobin had offered the boy a hundred dollars to tell him where the Espinosas were hiding, but Tobin "never paid it."[185]

An oral history of George W. Griffin stated that Tobin located Felipe's camp by sighting "the birds flying around" and the "smoke from his fire in the pines."[186] Lieutenant Baldwin's report made no mention of the smoke, and according to his "imperfect and hurried report" to Lieutenant Colonel Samuel F. Tappan, the area was almost impassable due to the amount of dead timber lying on the ground.[187] Due to Felipe's experience living in the region, he would have known how large a fire and what type of foliage to burn so as not to generate much smoke. He would have known how to withstand hardship, exposure, cold, and hunger. Felipe Espinosa was in hiding, so why would he start a smoking fire or do any activity that would attract attention? However, without making any noise on the "almost impassable . . . dead timber," Tobin and four soldiers ascended on the camp. The Espinosas appeared to be totally unaware that they were being hunted.

According to Baldwin, Tobin saw Felipe Espinosa through the pine trees and fired his rifle, sending Felipe into the campfire.[188] Though shot and badly burned, Felipe supported his back against a tree. Baldwin saw a boy, presumably Vicente Espinosa, "run from a spot" where Felipe sat, until someone shot him in the lower back, killing him.[189] As Tobin approached, Felipe fired a misdirected shot at him. Baldwin's soldiers rushed forward and "pierced him" with as many as nine shots, killing him instantly. Tobin then "caught him by the hair, drew his head back over a fallen tree and cut off his head."[190] Tobin also decapitated thirteen-year-old Vicente.[191]

Tobin and Baldwin's company arrived at the fort with Felipe's and Vicente's bloodied heads on October 16, 1863.[192] Fort Garland surgeon F. Rice Waggoner placed each head in a jar filled with alcohol, where they remained in the post adjutant's office for several days. According to Manzanares, "Tobin brought in the heads of the two Espinosas to Fort Garland. Settlers arrived at the fort to view the heads . . . [he] saw them."[193] Correspondent Stone wrote, "Too much praise cannot be awarded to the citizens of the mountains who have so persistently followed them up and taken so active a part in the ridding the Territory of these demon foes."[194]

Sometime later, Tobin reportedly returned to the death site to transport the headless bodies of Felipe and Vicente and bury them somewhere near San

Rafael. No historical accounts record where Tobin buried the bodies, leaving no closure for the grieving family. As another example of purchased redemption, after Tobin buried the beheaded bodies, he "was so concerned over the [Espinosa family's] poverty, he regularly contributed to their welfare."[195]

The Plunder and Spanish Scribbles in a Notebook

Correspondent "Dornick" (Stone) reported that the posse found Frederick Lehman's manuscript book at Vivián's camp. In it Vivián had written several pages in Spanish. Tom Tobin's grandson, Christopher Kit Carson III, thought Tobin had given Felipe's so-called diary or memo book to Colonel Tappan in October 1863. Apparently, George Hinsdale, Stone's partner, also attempted to translate Felipe's diary.[196] Reportedly, Vivián's diary was later in territorial secretary Frank Hall's possession for an unknown number of years. In an article written for the *Denver Post* in 1901, Hall described it as "an old memorandum book . . . covered with pencil scrawls in Spanish." According to a letter Stone later wrote to John McCannon, Captain Charles Kerber delivered the memorandum book to Stone because, there and at that time, Stone and Hinsdale were the only men who "knew any Spanish." Stone made a copy of the manuscript, but he later stated he did not know what became of the original.[197] Stone and unnamed members of the posse attempted to translate those pages "without the aid of Spanish books,"[198] and no records indicate any native Spanish speakers ever saw the original manuscript or Stone's copy of Vivian's pages. Stone's "translation" included such vague phrases as "so far as we have been able to translate" and "seems to be" and "alludes to." The translation was pure conjecture and speculation at best.[199] Author Price wrote, "Though [Battery's] translation falters . . . Espinosa seemed to acknowledge burning the Philbrook carriage and killing the mules"; he also called Americans "*gringos* and cowards . . . and ridiculed the idea of their [arresting] him." However, Stone wrote, the Espinosas were "sworn to exterminate Americans [and would] kill Americans while they live."[200] Stone, as "Dornick," instilled fear and incited his readers to take action. His comments and unique selection of words made readers, near and far, look forward to his reports.

Those who attempted to translate the Espinosa manuscripts were not suited to translate the language the Espinosas used. Even Anglos who spoke

Spanish did not necessarily understand the type of Spanish spoken in northern New Mexico and southern Colorado. These settlements were unique in that they were "isolated from other Spanish-speaking centers" and used an archaic sixteenth- and seventeenth-century vocabulary mixed with indigenous and local words. These Hispanos spoke and wrote in Castilian Spanish, using the letters *b* for *v*, *c* for *s* (and vice versa), *da* for *dad*, *i* for *y*, *ll* for *i*, and *s* for *z*. Their distinct dialect also incorporated words and expressions derived from Arabic and American Indian contexts.[201] Although we have Stone's loose translation, the diary is lost. Unless the diary resurfaces, we will never know how much the translators ignorantly or even maliciously changed its intended meaning.

They Were Not Penitentes

Due to a shortage of Catholic priests that continued into the first half of the following century, Hispano settlers of northern New Mexico and southern Colorado maintained their Christian faith under difficult conditions. Recent authors Charles Price and Jerry Thompson incorrectly suggested that, as a *penitente*, Felipe Espinosa murdered Anglos as an offering to the Virgin Mary.[202] Penitentes, or members of La Fraternidad de Nuestro Padre Jesús Nazareno (the Fraternity of Our Father Jesus the Nazarene), aided their communities by acting as lay ministers in a priest's absence by providing aid to widows and the ill.[203]

Upon a man's admission to the fraternidad, he received three four-inch vertical cuts on each shoulder. When a penitente was banished from the fraternidad, he received three horizontal cuts over his three vertical scars.[204] Additionally, had Felipe been a penitente and self-flagellated, Thomas Tobin, who later returned to bury the severed body, would likely have mentioned any such visible scars on Espinosa's back, and "Dornick" and other correspondents also would have made much of the fact. However, absolutely no evidence supports the notion that either Felipe or his brother was a penitente. As members of a close-knit group, penitentes took care of each other, in both life and death. Had Felipe Espinosa been a penitente, his fellow members would have brought his remains back to their *morada* (meetinghouse), where they would have respectfully prepared his remains for burial.

The Mighty Heroes

As for John McCannon and Thomas Tate Tobin, both earned acclaim and respect. The following year, Lake County citizens elected McCannon to represent them in the Territorial House. Yet McCannon had sought to mete out death over providing legal justice. McCannon could have ordered possemen to capture Vivián, then turn him over to military officials at Fort Garland or to the US marshal, but, he did not. Instead, once the posse had Vicente Espinosa secretly in view, McCannon ordered Lamb to shoot, initiating the gun battle in which Vivián was killed. Like McCannon, Tobin might have brought Felipe and Vicente Espinosa in alive, but he chose not to.

The severed heads of the Espinosas were treated with marked disrespect. On October 16, 1863, to prove he had killed the Espinosas and to make a statement about his prowess as a tracker, Tobin rolled out the bloodied heads of Felipe and Vicente Espinosa at Colonel Tappan's feet.[205] As mentioned earlier, the new Fort Garland surgeon, Dr. F. Rice Waggoner, placed each head in a jar filled with alcohol[206] and put them on display at the fort.[207] Reportedly the doctor took one jar back east.[208] An unidentified southern Colorado physician is supposed to have kept Vicente Espinosa's skull for several years, although its whereabouts is unknown today.[209] As a continued practice of ritual sadism, the severed heads were displayed throughout the territory.

Over the years various rumors surfaced that Felipe Espinosa's skull was returned to Colorado for burial at Pueblo, that both heads were buried at Fort Garland, that the heads were stored in the basement of the state capitol, and so on. It is extremely curious that no skulls or heads or written diaries have surfaced. Why all the mystery and deception? Why were there so many fabricated tales? If the Espinosas were scapegoats for some reason, why were the Espinosas chosen and not some other family? Did their malicious deeds have anything to do with a gold mine, the secret meetings at Conejos, or the wrath of Agent Lafayette Head? No church burial records exist for these three Espinosas because, at that time, a priest could perform a burial sacrament only on an intact body. Thus, the Espinosa family was left with no home and no closure. The convoluted stories written about their family members caused the Espinosa family and their descendants much shame and trauma.

During this time the air was rife with suspicion, blame, mistaken identity, and alcohol. In southern Colorado there were many unfortunate and intolerant miners, angry Confederate sympathizers, unhappy Hispanos, eager US soldiers, and hungry Utes. There were simply too many events taking place that had everyone on edge. So were the Espinosas responsible for any or all of the thirty-two murders taking place in southern Colorado?[210] Obviously, we will never know.

Regarding the written accounts about the Espinosa brothers, the new research discussed here strongly suggests that the Espinosas were not penitentes and that they did not have enough weapons and ammunition to pull off the alleged numerous murders. Colorado author Stephen J. Leonard wrote that, whether the number they killed was "thirty or seven, lynched or murdered . . . Anglos triggered a hunt for the Espinosas."[211] The deaths of the Espinosas by McCannon's posse and by tracker Tom Tobin were a type of vigilante action similar to lynch fever.[212] Further, the Anglo, nonnative translators of the Espinosas' penned documents deceived others into believing all these murders had been conducted and planned out by the Espinosas, when in fact the Espinosas were violently killed by Anglo men intent on having their names remembered as conquering heroes.

Notes

1. Term coined by Gómez, "Off-White in an Age of White Supremacy," 20.

2. President Lincoln appointed Pettis an associate justice of the Supreme Court of Colorado Territory on March 25, 1861.

3. Guice, *Rocky Mountain Bench*, 104.

4. The first term of the Supreme Court of Colorado Territory was held in January of 1864. Parkhill, *Law Goes West*, 16. See also Gómez, "Off-White in an Age of White Supremacy," 20.

5. Gómez, "Off-White in an Age of White Supremacy," 20.

6. Court files of the First Judicial District contain a limited number of mining lawsuits. Parkhill, *Law Goes West*, 77.

7. NARA, College Park, MD, Gov. Gilpin to William H. Seward, November 1, 1861, RG 60, entry 9, box 1, folder 5.

8. The weights and measures established by Congress were published as part of an act of January 12, 1852. In 1850 Colonel Monroe of New Mexico Territory authorized the use of the *cuartilla, almud,* and *fanega* as legal weights and measures.

9. *General Laws of the Territory of Colorado, 1864,* sec. 4, 149 (relating to an act concerning weights and measures).

10. Ibid., sec. 4, 149–150.

11. Costilla County Commissioners, meeting minutes, October 1865, Costilla County Records, San Luis, Colorado.

12. Campa, *Hispanic Culture in the Southwest*, 223.

13. *General Laws, Joint Resolution, Memorials, and Private Acts, Passed at the Sixth Session of the Legislative Assembly of the Territory of Colorado, Convened at Golden City on December 3, 1866* (Central City: David C. Collier, Miners' Register Office, 1867), 88–89. Hereafter cited as *General Laws of the Territory of Colorado, 1866*.

14. Giddens, "Letters of S. Newton Pettis," 7.

15. According to Parkhill, Bradford was one of the early miners of the Gregory diggings. Parkhill, *Law Goes West*, 21–22.

16. Parkhill, *Law Goes West*, 20.

17. Guice, *Rocky Mountain Bench*, 64. See also unidentified newspaper clipping, Dawson Scrapbooks, 35: 7, Hart Library, History Colorado Center.

18. Appended committee report to the memorial, August 14, 1862. Also see Guice, *Rocky Mountain Bench*, 64; unidentified newspaper clipping, Dawson Scrapbooks, 35, 7, Hart Library, History Colorado Center.

19. Parkhill, *Law Goes West*, 22.

20. Ibid., 22–23. See also Bohning, "Wilbur Fisk Stone," 23; Wilbur Fisk Stone, "Pioneer Bench and Bar of Colorado," *Report of Regular and Special Meeting of the Colorado Bar Association*, vol. 11 (Denver, Colorado Bar Association, 1908), 110. Authors Bohning and Parkhill cite different historians for the quotation. Bohning cites Stone, and Parkhill writes that the quote is attributed to the editor of the *Denver Times*, Jerome C. Smiley, in 1901.

21. Bohning, "Wilbur Fisk Stone," 23.

22. *House Journal of the Territory of Colorado, 1864*, February 11, 1864, 71–75 (relating to sec. 7).

23. Monte was a Spanish and later Mexican card game.

24. Kane and Elfenbein, "Colorado," chap. 3, 42.

25. Parkhill, *Law Goes West*, 22–26. President Ulysses S. Grant reappointed Judge Hallet in 1870 and again in 1874. See also Guice, *Rocky Mountain Bench*, 97, 101–4.

26. In 1863 this amount was raised to $300, with probate courts having jurisdiction to hear cases up to and including sums of $2,000 and with no limited amount in handling decedents' estates.

27. University of California at Berkeley, School of Law, Robbins Collection website, https://www.law.berkeley.edu/library/robbins/CommonLawCivilLaw Traditions.html, accessed December 12, 2016.

28. Langum, *Law and Community*, 38, 40.

29. Ibid.

30. Ibid., 30. Ebright, "Introduction," 4.

31. No records have been found in which a female served in this capacity; however, in the absence of the menfolk serving in militias on expeditions against warring indigenous nations or in Union companies during the Civil War, women stepped up to the task when they were asked by their community to help resolve a local dispute. Also, by civil law, married or single women could petition the alcaldes.

32. Langum, *Law and Community*, 38, 272.

33. Ebright, *Land Grants and Lawsuits*, 133; Langum, *Law and Community*, 99, 135, 274.

34. Langum, *Law and Community*, 276.

35. See entries in J. Richard Salazar and Kenneth D. Sender, *Calendar to the Microfilm Edition of the Sender Collection, 1697–1884* (Santa Fe, New Mexico State Records Center and Archives, 1988), Roll 2, 31.

36. Lamar, *Far Southwest*, 27.

37. Langum, *Law and Community*, 135.

38. *General Laws of the Territory of Colorado, 1864*, November 7, 1861, 321, sec. 145 (relating to common law), and 382 (relating to practice of law).

39. Langum, *Law and Community*, 144n36.

40. Lecompte, "John Lawrence of Saguache," 151.

41. Hafen, "Letters of George M. Willing," 188.

42. Leonard, *Lynching in Colorado*, 55.

43. Carrigan and Webb, *Forgotten Dead*, 30–32.

44. Hafen, *Colorado and Its People*: 248.

45. Parkhill, *Law Goes West*, 51–60.

46. Carrigan and Webb, *Forgotten Dead*, 42.

47. Ibid., 78–89, 114.

48. Hart Library, History Colorado Center, CWA, Conejos County, Charles E. Gibson, Jr., 1933–1934a, 239.

49. *Weekly Commonwealth and Republican*, May 21, 1863. Parkhill, *Law Goes West*, 55. Lake County citizens elected McCannon to represent them in the 1864 Colorado Territorial House. 1870 US Census, Lake County, Colorado, 10: Schedule 1, lines 33–34, Household 199, Dwelling 135, ancestry.com.

50. Saguache's Anglo residents established a separate cemetery for Hispanos. "Diary of John Lawrence," January 9, 1871, microfilm, Hart Library, History Colorado Center; Lecompte, "John Lawrence of Saguache," 143. See also Martin, *Frontier Eyewitness*, 57–58. On January 23, 1871, José Antonio Morán was elected judge in Precinct 1, and David Goff judge in Precinct 2.

51. Armstrong, "Clothed with the Authority," 369–70.

52. Smiley, *History of Denver*, 349.

53. Berwanger, *Rise of the Centennial State*, 56.

54. Lamar, *Far Southwest*, 242.

55. Price, *Season of Terror*, 87. Referring to Dill, "History of Lake County," 213. The number was 8,000 according to Chang, "Leading the Way," 33.

56. Price, *Season of Terror*, 217n17.

57. "Reminiscences of G. W. Griffin," 1862, Royal Gorge Regional Museum and History Center, Cañon City, CO, R2015.054.001, February 18, 1931, 1.

58. Perkins, *Tom Tobin Frontiersman*, 147.

59. Laws of the Territory of Colorado, November 6, 1861, 109. See also Hafen, "Colorado's First Legislative Assembly," 47.

60. Laws of the Territory of Colorado, November 5, 1861, 300; and Colorado Territory Laws, August 15, 1862, 56. In 1862 the assembly abolished the death penalty "in certain cases." See also Leonard, *Lynching in Colorado*, 192n11.

61. Parkhill, *Law Goes West*, 15.

62. Vandenbusche, "Life at a Frontier Post," 142. Reference to Colorado State Archives, Carson to Maj. C. H. de Forrest, October 3, 1866, copy in the Fort Garland Workbook.

63. Boessenecker, *Bandido*, 31. See also Carrigan and Webb, *Forgotten Dead*, 6, 34–38, 180–218.

64. Berwanger, *Rise of the Centennial State*, 101.

65. Thompson, *Civil War History*, 153.

66. Leonard, *Lynching in Colorado*, 33.

67. Carrigan and Webb, *Forgotten Dead*, 100.

68. Lamar, *Far Southwest*, 219–21; Everett, *Creating the American West*, 184.

69. NARA, College Park, MD, Chief Justice Hall to Attorney General Edward Bates, July 2, 1863, RG 60, entry 9, box 1, folder 6.

70. Lamar, *Far Southwest*, 257–58.

71. Carrigan and Webb, *Forgotten Dead*, 78, 96.

72. Ibid., 162.

73. Berwanger, *Rise of the Centennial State*, 113.

74. Ibid., 114. *Colorado Chieftain*, July 10 and 17, 1873; August 3 and 29, 1873.

75. *Rocky Mountain News*, October 25, 1870.

76. Ibid., August 30, 1873.

77. Delgado, "Law of the Noose," 304nn49,50.

78. Carrigan and Webb, *Forgotten Dead*, 12, 30–32.

79. Colorado Preservation, Inc., Town of Saguache, 2009 nomination form, http://scseed.org/wb/media/CPINominationFinal.pdf, accessed March 18, 2015.

80. "Diary of John Lawrence," December 25-26, 1870, Hart Library, History Colorado Center.

81. He was the son of Jesús María Sanches and María Antonia Mestas. Rau, *Conejos Land Grant*, 153–54.

82. Simmons, *Ute Indians of Utah*, 134. Godfroy was Head's secretary in 1862.

83. 1870 US Census, Saguache County, Colorado, p. 6, Schedule 1, lines 36, 38, Household 67, Dwelling 58, ancestry.com.

84. Martin, *Frontier Eyewitness*, 22. William James Godfroy was married to Juana Nepomucena Sánchez. Donaciano had sought refuge in her home. Her relationship to Donaciano is not known.

85. These brothers likely included Donaciano's two older brothers, José Victor Norberto Sanchez and Jose Ramon Sanchez. 1880 US Census, Conejos County, Colorado, Conejos Village, p. 47C, ED 29, Schedule 1, lines 37, 41, Household 257, Dwellings 331 and 332, ancestry.com,

86. Gabriel Woodson, a Navajo, was twelve years old when James B. Woodson purchased him in 1860 from Utes trading in Colorado Territory. NARA, Washington, DC, Letters Received by the Office of Indian Affairs, 1824–1880, Roll 198, Colorado Superintendency, 1865–1866, Conejos Report, line 84.

87. "Diary of John Lawrence," December 25–26 and December 29, 1870; January 3 and January 8–9, 1871, Hart Library, History Colorado Center.

88. Leonard, *Lynching in Colorado*, 56; see also "Diary of John Lawrence," microfilm, January 23, 1871, frame 100.

89. Louis B. Sporleder Collection, Denver Public Library, Western History and Genealogy Department, WH916, box 2, File Folder 22:265.

90. Steinel and Working, *History of Agriculture*, 147.

91. Stoller and Steele, *Diary of the Jesuit Residence*, 184. Unfortunately, Father Personé did not identify the deceased by name, nor did he provide information about their burials.

92. *General Laws, Private Acts, Joint Resolutions, and Memorials, Passed at the Tenth Session of the Legislative Assembly of the Territory of Colorado, Convened at Denver, on the Fifth day of January, 1874 at Central City*, Register Printing House, 1874, February 11, 1874, 97–98. Hereafter cited as *General Laws of the Territory of Colorado, 1874*.

93. "Oral History of Frank [José Francisco] Córdova," July 10, 1979, Huerfano County Oral History Project, Colorado Humanities, José Francisco Córdova was a nephew of Juan Vallejos and grandson of Miguel Antonio Vallejos. See also Sánchez, *Forgotten Cucharenos of the Lower Valley*, 23–24.

94. Carrigan and Webb, *Forgotten Dead*, 97.

95. Simmons, *San Luis Valley*, 294.

96. 1870 US Census, Costilla County, Colorado, Precinct 4, 10: Schedule 1, lines 10–23, Household 98, Dwelling 55, ancestry.com.

97. National Park Service, "Trujillo Homesteads," 26.

98. Ibid., 10–11.

99. NARA, Washington, DC, Letters Received by the Office of Indian Affairs, 1824–1880, Roll 198, Colorado Superintendency, 1865–1866, Costilla Report, Frame 42, lines 32–33.

100. National Park Service, "Trujillo Homesteads," 26.

101. Ibid.; National Park Service, "Trujillo Homestead, Alamosa County, CO," sec. 8, 5. Within the collection of the Museum of International Folk Art in Santa Fe is a textile woven of Trujillo's wool. National Park Service, "Trujillo Homesteads," 30.

102. National Park Service, "Trujillo Homesteads," 30.

103. Ibid.; National Park Service, "Trujillo Homestead, Alamosa County, CO," sec. 8, 6.

104. National Park Service, "Trujillo Homestead, Alamosa County, CO," sec. 8, 6; National Park Service, "Trujillo Homesteads," 32.

105. National Park Service, "Trujillo Homesteads," 31. *Alamosa Courier*, February 8, 1902, 1.

106. Hart Library, History Colorado Center, CWA, Settlement of the San Luis Valley, Charles E. Gibson, Jr., 1933–1934a, 95.

107. National Park Service, "Trujillo Homesteads," 31. See also *Alamosa Courier*, February 8, 1902, 1.

108. The cattle and sheep ranch Trujillo expanded with his son operated for nearly forty years and encompassed nearly 1,500 acres. In March 1902, Teófilo, his wife Andrea Lucero, and son Pedro sold the Trujillo Homestead and water rights to cattlemen Loren B. Sylvester and Richard W. Hossford [*sic*], owners of the Medano Ranch, for $30,000. Teófilo Trujillo moved to San Luis, where he lived until his death in 1915. His large tombstone in the Old San Luis Cemetery stands in tribute to his life. Today the Trujillo Homestead is listed in the National Register. National Park Service, "Trujillo Homestead, Alamosa County, CO," sec. 8, 6–7; and National Park Service, "Trujillo Homesteads," 14. Also *Fort Collins Weekly Courier*, February 20, 1902.

109. National Park Service, "Trujillo Homestead, Alamosa County, CO," sec. 8, 7. Referring to Sargent Centennial Bicentennial Committee, *Sargent Stanley Community Reflections* (Sargent, CO: Sargent Centennial Bicentennial Committee, 1977), 209.

110. Charles E. Gibson Jr., *Settlements and Roads in the San Luis Valley with Maps* (Denver: Civil Works Administration, 1934), CWA Interviews Collection, Hart Library, History Colorado Center, PAM 349/18, 68.

111. House of Representatives, "Lines of Communication between Colorado and New Mexico: Letter from the Secretary of War," March 9, 1878, 45th Cong., 2nd Sess., Exec. Doc. No. 66, 17 (reference to the Committee on Appropriations).

112. Colville, *La Vereda*, 197.

113. House of Representatives, "Lines of Communication between Colorado and New Mexico," 17. Lieutenant Morrison reported that in June the river was 10 feet deep and about 250 feet wide.

114. According to the lieutenant's report, Valdez's ferry was larger than Stewart's ferry.

115. House of Representatives, "Lines of Communication between Colorado and New Mexico," 17.

116. Parkhill, *Law Goes West*, 62–64; see also Stoller and Steele, *Diary of the Jesuit Residence*, 45, 153.

117. The crossing at the Rio Grande was located near the Badito crossing south of the main bridge toward San Luis. Stoller and Steele, *Diary of the Jesuit Residence*, 45, 153. See also Maestas, "Jose Seledon Valdez Family," 49.

118. Colville, *La Vereda*, 198–99.

119. "Vigilantes Hang Two Men at Canon City," *Colorado Weekly Chieftain*, July 27, 1876, 3.

120. Andrews and Humphry, "El Patrón de Trinidad," *Colorado Magazine* 21, no. 1 (January 1944): 15.

121. Convery, "Reckless Men of Both Races," 31.

122. Gálvez, of San Juan de Pumeceno del Cañon, appeared on Major Gillespie's military census. NARA, Washington, DC, RG 393, Letters and Telegrams Received, 1860–1880, RG 393, Fort Garland, CO, Box 1, "Abstract of Military Census of District of Conejos (continued), Plaza of San Juan de Pumeceno of the Cañon." Also Nuestra Señora de Guadalupe, Parish Book of Baptisms, Conejos, CO, 28.

123. Quintana, *Pobladores*, 207–8.

124. Adams and Deluzio, *On the Borders of Love and Power*, 129–30.

125. Price, *Season of Terror*, 121.

126. "The Recent Difficulties in Conejos," *Rocky Mountain News Weekly*, February 12, 1863.

127. NARA, Washington, DC, Registers of Letters Received and Letters Received by Headquarters, Department of New Mexico, 1854–1865, M1120, RG 393; Roll 19; "Abstract of Military Census for Plaza of San Judas de Tadeo, No. 14, District of Conejos," January 31, 1863. Fort Garland, C.T., part V, entry 4, box 1.

128. Hart Library, History Colorado Center, Espinosa Collection, *Ledger News*, "Vendetta," February 14, 1963, 3.

129. Stoller and Steele, *Diary of the Jesuit Residence*, 37n65.

130. "Lista de Personas que Forman la Compania de Milicianos de los Conejos," January 17, 1860, Territorial Archives of New Mexico, New Mexico Archives and Records Center, Roll 85, Frame 107.

131. Hart Library, History Colorado Center, Espinosa Collection, *Ledger News*, "Vendetta," February 14, 1963, 3.

132. Tobin, "Capture of the Espinosas," 59–60.

133. Ibid.

134. "The Recent Difficulties in Conejos," *Rocky Mountain News Weekly*, February 12, 1863, 4, cols. 5 and 6. The house was not adobe but a log house (jacal). Price, *Season of Terror*, 126, 139. Referring to Tobin, "Capture of the Espinosas," 59–60.

135. NARA, Washington, DC, Registers of Letters Received and Letters Received by Headquarters, Department of New Mexico, Dr. McNulty to Dr. Bailey, October 29, 1862, M1120, RG 393, Roll 17. See also Charles E. Gibson Jr., *Settlements and Roads in the San Luis Valley with Maps* (Denver: Civil Works Administration, 1934), CWA Interviews Collection, Hart Library, History Colorado Center, PAM 349/5, 14.

136. Tobin, "Capture of the Espinosas," 59–60.

137. NARA, Washington, DC, M1120, RG 393, Letters and Telegrams Received, 1860–1880, "Abstract of Military Census of District of Conejos (continued), San Judas de Tadeo Plaza," RG 393, Fort Garland, C.T., part V, entry 4, box 1.

138. Ibid.

139. NARA, Washington, DC, Registers of Letters Received and Letters Received by Headquarters, Department of New Mexico, 1854–1865, "Military Census Final Report," January 31, 1863, M1120, RG 393, Roll 19.

140. NARA, Washington, DC, M1120, RG 393, Letters and Telegrams Received, 1860–1880, "Abstract of Military Census of District of Conejos (continued), Plaza of San Judas de Tadeo," RG 393, Fort Garland, C.T., part V, entry 4, box 1.

141. National Park Service, "Trujillo Homesteads," 21.

142. Hall, *History of the State of Colorado*, 4:494.

143. Campa, *Hispanic Culture in the Southwest*, 193. Reyes Medina knew how to use the bow and arrow. Louis B. Sporleder Collection, Denver Public Library, Western History and Genealogy Department, WH916, box 2, File Folder 7, People: Reyes Medina, 89.

144. Van Diest, "Early History of Costilla County," 142. Also López-Tushar, *People of El Valle*, 63.

145. López-Tushar, "Spanish Heritage in the San Luis Valley," 20.

146. Hall, *History of Colorado*, Chicago: Blackely Printing Company, 1891: 494.

147. "Glorious News: The Mysterious Murders Unraveled at Last," *Rocky Mountain News*, May 1863, 1, col. 2.

148. Price, *Season of Terror*, 139.

149. "The Recent Difficulties in Conejos," *Rocky Mountain News Weekly*, February 12, 1863, 4, cols. 5 and 6.

150. Scott, *Tom Tobin and the Bloody Espinosas*, 104–5.

151. *Denver Post*, October 20, 1901.

152. "Glorious News: The Mysterious Murders Unraveled at Last," *Rocky Mountain News*, May 1863, 1, col. 2; Perkins, *Tom Tobin Frontiersman*.

153. "Reminiscences of G. W. Griffin," Royal Gorge Regional Museum and History Center, Canon City, CO, R2015.054.001, 6.

154. "The Recent Difficulties in Conejos," *Rocky Mountain News Weekly*, February 12, 1863, 4, cols 5 and 6. See also Price, *Season of Terror*, 111.

155. "Reminiscences of G. W. Griffin," Royal Gorge Regional Museum and History Center, Canon City, CO, R2015.054.001, 6.

156. *Weekly Commonwealth and Republican*, May 21, 1863, 1, col. 1.

157. Perkins, *Tom Tobin Frontiersman*, 99.

158. Price, *Season of Terror*, 93, 96: citing *Denver Daily News*, February 24, 1894; McCannon, "An Account by a Participant," 577.

159. "Reminiscences of G. W. Griffin," Royal Gorge Regional Museum and History Center, Canon City, CO, R2015.054.001, 6.

160. Price, *Season of Terror*, 100: citing *Denver Daily News*, February 24, 1894. Correspondent Wilbur Fisk Stone provided a detailed description of the head and its expression.

161. Because the New Mexico Military Department census had reported no pistols owned by the Espinosas, this author requested a review by the Acquisitions Department of the History Colorado Center to determine how the pistols in its holding are attributed to the Espinosas. As of February 14, 2018, no information had been received.

162. Hart Library, History Colorado Center, Espinosa Collection, BPF-Espinosa Brothers: Guns.

163. Perkins, *Tom Tobin Frontiersman*, 174n37. Today the spurs are housed in the Colorado Springs Pioneers Museum.

164. *Weekly Commonwealth and Republican*, May 21, 1863, 1, col. 1.

165. Perkins, *Tom Tobin Frontiersman*, 174n37.

166. *Weekly Commonwealth and Republican*, May 21, 1863, 1, col. 1.

167. Parkhill, *Law Goes West*, 55.

168. Price, *Season of Terror*, 199. According to Price, the obituary of Eugenia H. Lucero appeared in the *Colorado Springs Telegraph*, March 18, 1938. This author was unable to locate this obituary.

169. "Interesting from Conejos," *Rocky Mountain Daily*, September 5, 1862, 3, col. 6.

170. Ibid.

171. Hart Library, History Colorado Center, Espinosa Collection, *Ledger News*, "Vendetta," February 14, 1963, 3; "The Recent Difficulties in Conejos," *Rocky Mountain News*, February 12, 1863, 4, cols. 5–6.

172. Hart Library, History Colorado Center, Espinosa Collection, *Ledger News*, "Vendetta," February 14, 1963, 3.

173. Ibid.

174. Denver Public Library, Western History and Genealogy Department, Samuel E. Brown (Browne), M91, January 18, 1864, item 3.

175. NARA, Washington, DC, Letters Received by the Office of Indian Affairs, 1824–1881, Colorado Superintendency, 1861–1864, C. Dominguez to Gov. John Evans, March 11, 1864, M234, RG 75, Roll 197.

176. Nuestra Señora de Guadalupe, Parish Book of Baptisms, Conejos, CO, 87.

177. David H. Salazar and Hope Yost, *Our Lady of Guadalupe Church*, Deaths, 15. Felipe Nerio Herrera, age thirty-five, spouse of Maria Deluvina Sanches. Guadalupe, sec. 1. Reference to Church Burial Registry, 4. See also David H. Salazar, *Nuestra Senora de Guadalupe Book of Baptisms, Conejos, CO*, 27–28. Maria Viviana, seven-day-old daughter of Felipe Nerio Herrera and Maria Deluvina Sanchez. Padrinos: Rafael Cabeza (Lafayette Head) and his wife, Juana de la Cruz Martinez. Reference to Church Baptismal Registry, 87.

178. Safford, "Three Brothers in Arms," 332, 338n45.

179. Ibid., 327–34.

180. *Weekly Commonwealth*, October 28, 1863. See also Price, *Season of Terror*, 234n30; Safford, "Three Brothers in Arms," 338n45.

181. Price, *Season of Terror*, 229.

182. "The Recent Difficulties in Conejos," *Rocky Mountain News Weekly*, February 12, 1863, 4, cols. 5–6. See also Price, *Season of Terror*, 111.

183. Tobin, "Capture of the Espinosas," 59–66. See also Price, *Season of Terror*, 246.

184. Parkhill, *Law Goes West*, 52.

185. Hart Library, History Colorado Center, July 1930 interview cards, Jesus Maria Manzanares by Leroy Hafen.

186. "Reminiscences of G. W. Griffin," Royal Gorge Regional Museum and History Center, Canon City, CO, R2015.054.001, 7.

187. US War Department, *Official Records of the War of the Rebellion*, vol. 22, part 1, 704.

188. Ibid.

189. Ibid.

190. Secrest, "Bloody Espinosas," 13, 14. Thompson, *Civil War History*, 262.

191. "More about Espinosa," *Weekly Commonwealth and Republican*, October 28, 1863, 4, col. 2. In another account, Vicente was supposedly sixteen years old. Thompson, *Civil War History*, 262.

192. Secrest, "Bloody Espinosas," 13, 14.

193. Hart Library, History Colorado Center, July 1930 interview cards, Jesus Maria Manzanares by Leroy Hafen.

194. "Glorious News," *Rocky Mountain News*, May 21, 1863, 1, col. 2.

195. Secrest, "Bloody Espinosas," 16.

196. Secrest, "Bloody Espinosas," 15. See also Kenneth Jessen, John Lamb, and David Sandoval, "Colorado's Worst Serial Murders: The Espinosa Story," *San Luis Valley Historian* 27, no. 4 (1995).

197. Price, *Season of Terror*, 305–6.

198. *Weekly Commonwealth and Republican*, May 21, 1863, 1, col. 1.

199. "Dornick" wrote his correspondence from Cañon City on May 10, 1863, one day after the California Gulch Boys "had at last overtaken the outlaws and meted out a just reward to one of them." *Rocky Mountain News Weekly*, May 1863, 1, col. 2.

200. Price, *Season of Terror*, 272.

201. Cobos, *Dictionary*, viii.

202. Thompson, *Civil War History*, 260. See also Price, *Season of Terror*, 142.

203. Penitentes were members of a religious society or brotherhood that supported and aided the community. Male members practiced self-flagellation during the Lenten season.

204. Vallmar, "Religious Processions and Penitente Activities," 179.

205. Secrest, "Bloody Espinosas," 13–14.

206. Thompson, *Civil War History*, 263.

207. "More about Espinosa," *Weekly Commonwealth and Republican*, October 28, 1863, 4, col. 2.

208. Thompson, *Civil War History*, 263.

209. Perkins, *Tom Tobin Frontiersman*, 174n37.

210. "More about Espinosa," *Weekly Commonwealth and Republican*, October 28, 1863, 4, col. 2.

211. Leonard, *Lynching in Colorado*, 152.

212. Although Tobin was married to a Hispana, very few historical documents record ways in which Tobin supported his Hispano neighbors. Tobin was one of Governor Charles Bent's supporters in the 1847 Taos Revolt.

7

Pleas and Petitions

Colorado became an organized territory in 1861, which is when it absorbed the New Mexico "notch." Hispanos who were incorporated into southern Colorado Territory experienced culture shock, confusion, and unease due to their unfamiliarity with the Anglo language and laws. New federal income taxes were levied on the citizenry to support the Union's war effort, but as the laws had not been translated into Spanish, Hispanos often were inadequately informed about the tax itself and about the fines for nonpayment.

As early as 1862, unhappy Hispanos on the Colorado side of the new territorial border began petitioning New Mexico's territorial delegates to encourage the Congress to restore the notch to New Mexico. In support and with the approval of the New Mexico Territorial Legislature, New Mexico delegate José Francisco Perea sent a lengthy letter to the chairman of the US House Committee on Territories. Perea pleaded their case that the community of nuevomexicanos now straddling the border should not be sent "asunder" due to an arbitrary boundary line. In Colorado, Hispanos from Costilla, Conejos, and Saguache Counties likewise petitioned Congress for reannexation. Portions of

DOI: 10.5876/9781607329145.c007

the congressional discussions included in this chapter should enlighten and disturb readers, as ultimately Congress took no action to help these citizens.

Becaise it was still a time of Civil War, there were occasions in which Hispanos gathered in groups to discuss their situations and exchange information; they were at risk of being interpreted by Anglos as being disloyal to America and of secretly plotting insurrection. Even those Hispanos serving in the US Army were distrusted, for fear that they would not respond faithfully when called upon to quell any Hispano and indigenous insurrection of the kind New Mexico had experienced in the Taos Revolt of 1847.

Meanwhile, the Homestead Act had been signed into law in 1862, providing land at low cost to settlers able and willing to move into the western territories. In principle, the act supported the small-scale family farmer by providing him (or her) with 160 acres on which to farm or ranch and to build a home. However, many abuses of the law took place by richer and politically connected individuals and companies.

Although fencing of rangeland was treated differently under English common law, many cattlemen illegally fenced government land for their own private use. Anglo settlements and cattle corporations competed for rangeland and water sources with sheep herders, who commonly were Hispano. Injuries occurred to the Hispanos and their sheep. Because they were unable to compete, some had no recourse but to sell their land to the large cattle enterprises.

The Stirrings of Reannexation

By the end of their first year of incorporation into Colorado Territory, Hispanos living in the notch (chiefly Conejos and Costilla Counties) wanted to be reattached to New Mexico Territory due to their "ancestry, nativity, and association."[1] In 1861 Representative José Víctor García recommended to Governor William Gilpin that the boundary line between Colorado and New Mexico be surveyed.[2] Likely the purpose of his request centered on the concerned Hispanos who wished to be returned, along with their "notch," to New Mexico. However, the survey did not take place for several years. As a result of the Darling survey, conducted in 1869, only the town of Costilla was placed back in New Mexico Territory by the US Congress.

Because the Hispano settlers did not feel the Colorado officials would attend to their pleas and petitions to return, in 1861 and again in 1862 they turned to New Mexico. The New Mexico Assembly found their concerns "convincing and worthy of serious attention" and prepared a joint resolution (see figures 7.2 and 7.3). The resolution to Congress requested a resurvey of the border with Colorado. New Mexico believed Colorado had been exercising jurisdiction "on a considerable territory south of their true boundary." The memorial also stated that no formal marker had been made to determine the boundary separating the two territories "upon the face of the earth." The US House of Representatives referred the memorial to its Committee on Territories three months later.[3]

While in Washington, John Sebrie Watts, the congressional delegate from New Mexico to the House of Representatives, informed US senator James S. Green (Missouri) about the Hispanos' desire to be returned to New Mexico. He felt the preceding Congress had taken an area 60 miles wide, 250 miles in length, and with a population of 7,000 people from the Territory of New Mexico, and combined those nuevomexicanos "with a people alien in laws, alien in language, alien in association, and simply for the purpose of beautifying the lines of the new Territory of Colorado."[4]

Countering Watts, Colorado's nonvoting delegate to the House, Hiram Pitt Bennet, claimed Colorado had taken better care of the people in the notch than New Mexico ever had: "We are giving them post offices and post roads. We have given them many benefits and privileges which they did not have under the Territory of New Mexico."[5]

During this time, Congress was also discussing the notion of splitting New Mexico vertically in half to create a Confederate territory to be named Arizona. Watts warned that if Congress took "too much time in . . . the making of the Arizona Territory," it would "interrupt . . . the business and association" of the nuevomexicanos. They, too, would want to be returned to New Mexico.[6] The US Congress divided New Mexico Territory and created Arizona Territory in 1863 At that time, most of the Tucson area was more nuevomexicano than Anglo in appearance, language, and custom and remained so until the late 1870s.[7]

Secret Meetings

The Civil War was in its second year, and the US Congress had enacted the Internal Revenue Act on July 1, 1862. Back in southern Colorado, the Hispanos had not received any information in Spanish about the tax. Although many supported the Union, they were not well informed about the tax and its due date. New laws were being imposed upon them; yet the statutes were not translated to inform them about the taxes themselves or the fines assessed for noncompliance or nonpayment. A number of Hispanos of the various settlements in the notch met in *juntas de indignación* (grassroots efforts or meetings of "indignation") to discuss the territorial laws, the government tax, and the violence taking place around them.[8] Some Anglos worried about these gatherings and, based primarily on prejudice and fear, went so far as to prepare for an insurrection.

Major Adolph H. Mayer, the new commander of Fort Garland in Costilla County, received several letters of grave concern. On July 30, 1862, Costilla County clerk John L. Gaspar wrote to advise the major that he and county assessor Cornelius D. Hendren truly believed a "revolt among these people" was imminent. Based on remarks Gaspar had heard from Antonio Vigil and other Hispanos from La Culebra Plaza (San Luis), "only a sufficient force stationed at Fort Garland would prevent such an occurence [sic]." According to Gaspar, because the people were "not disposed to recognize the laws of this territory," he and Hendren would not be able to perform their duties as officers of the territory: "There can be no justice done here, and [it] places the american [sic] portion of the population in a precarious situation."[9]

Lieutenant Thomas James Durnin of the Sixteenth Infantry Regiment of the US Army did not believe such a threat was imminent. He called the reports "largely bogus" and tried to remind Major Mayer that the same "old story" had been around for the last thirteen years. Durnin was referring to the 1847 Taos Revolt in which Hispanos and Pueblo Indians revolted against the US forces attempting to install a new order of government.[10] Letters from concerned Anglo citizens, whose content was published in the *News*, added fuel to the fire of a speculative insurrection. This "news" reached all areas of the territory and alarmed Anglo readers.

Gaspar's letter was followed by three letters from San Luis merchant Frederick William Posthoff. Two of his letters, dated August 4, discussed the "general dissatisfaction among the mex. [sic] population." In his letters Posthoff took his lead from Lafayette Head:

I have never before apprehended any danger from such a source, but the fact that Mr. H [Head] whom I have known for years . . . gives evidence to the matter and having the opportunity which he has had to judge for himself, makes me inclined to believe in the report . . . P.S. Please keep this private so it can be made use of for a political purpose at the next election.[11]

According to Posthoff, Agent Head had consulted "with the americans [*sic*] of this place in regard to the steps to be taken by us in case of a rebellion of the Mexicans." Posthoff considered Head's comments credible because he had "lived among them for years" and had "always been their friend [and] defender." Head's statement, Posthoff admitted, "makes me afraid that a hostile movement of some kind is in contemplation by the mex [*sic*]."[12]

In the second letter sent to the major that day, Posthoff reported that "the tax law and the law relating to the peons are the laws which are most obnoxious" to the Hispanos. Head had "secretly consulted with the americans [regarding steps to take] in case of a rebellion . . . which from all accounts appear to be imminent," but Posthoff feared that the nuevomexicano troopers ("the Mex. Company") stationed at Fort Garland would not act against the insurgents when ordered to do so. Posthoff, who resided in the Costilla settlement south of San Luis, mentioned that he had not yet had a chance to gauge "the feeling of the people" in Costilla, but promised to "make it [his] duty to obtain all reliable information."[13]

Gaspar and Posthoff chose to notify the military of the actions by the Hispanos because they felt it was their duty as good, faithful, and patriotic citizens. They failed to acknowledge that the Hispano settlers had been citizens of the United States since 1848. In fact, Posthoff, from Prussia, was not naturalized until 1872.[14] Additionally, when some Anglos met as a group with Agent Head, no one viewed their meeting as seditious and un-American.

Four days later, on August 8, Posthoff sent a third letter to Major Mayer. To Posthoff, any Confederate action taking place in the territory during this time of civil war was less a concern than a Mexican rebellion:

Mighty happy to learn that a company of Americans is going to your post, not so much on account of the Texans, of whom I believe there is little fear, than the Mexicans who are no doubt, inclined to be troublesome.

I have ascertained, beyond a doubt that they hold secret meetings for some purpose and from their ignorance and the way they talk I have little doubt that their object is inimical to our government.

The company of americans going up will settle their plotting, as they have a proper respect for us if they see that they are not thirty to one.[15]

When word of problems reached military headquarters in New Mexico, Captain Ethan Wayne Eaton wrote to headquarters defending his company of Hispano troopers:

> They are as true to the government as any soldier in the Territory. They will most certainly not be influenced by any revolutionary party if there is such a party in existence in this part of the country and will maintain order to the extent of their power. I and my company will obey orders and do our duty when and where we are wanted or can be of most service and we do not want to be suspected of any other intentions.[16]

On August 17 several unidentified leading Hispano men from the Costilla and Culebra plazas met with Mayer to explain the problems with "certain Acts passed by the . . . Legislature." Mayer's unfamiliarity of the Spanish language must have made it difficult for him to fully understand their concerns. Mayer reported that although their meeting was "amicable," he did not believe them: "They [gave] me every assurance—in words—that they were loyal citizens, and anxious to render every aid in their power for the Union cause . . . All of which I do not believe. The great trouble seems to be certain Acts passed by the Colorado Legislature, viz: 'Territorial Tax,' 'The abolition of the right of servitude by Peons.'"[17]

He assured the men, stating that "except by Order, there would not be any military interference to enforce these Laws"; however, Congress's law "To Levy a War Tax on all States and Territories" would be rigidly enforced. Mayer did not report whether he had an interpreter present or if he had requested their translated written statements, as he had of Gaspar and Hendren when they met with the major in person at the fort.[18] Mayer also advised a "moderate and conciliatory course of action" and intended to invite some members of the legislature to meet with a few prominent Mexicans to discuss their grievances. Mayer also recommended that the commander of the military department prepare a "Printed Circular" explaining to the people of Conejos and Costilla Counties "the necessity of having the War Tax levied by the General Government."[19] Unfortunately, we do not know whom Mayer intended to invite to his meeting or if such a meeting occurred. However, the military and the territorial government did nothing further to help the Hispano settlers understand the many changes forced upon them.

In Mayer's letter to headquarters dated August 18, he mentioned two items of interest. One item indicated that he had the Mexican soldiers making adobes for the fort. These were trained soldiers, not manual laborers. Furthermore, a soldier does not have to be Mexican to make adobes. The second item relates to a one-hundred-dollar payment to an unnamed spy for "look[ing] out" for some unspecified person and reason.[20] Were Postoff or even Gaspar spies informing the government about the Mexicans' activities? From the information in their letters, this may have been the case.

The major also reported to military headquarters in New Mexico about the "uneasy feeling in the Mexican population." For this reason he kept Company J of the Second Cavalry at Fort Garland and advised the Anglo soldiers to enforce federal law, specifically the war tax law.[21] Clearly, southern Colorado was "in a state of excitement."[22]

Servitude and peonage were two very different forms of labor in the Southwest. In New Mexico and southern Colorado servitude involved the enslavement of indigenous persons, and peonage was a form of payment for an amount of money loaned by a merchant or wealthy neighbor. According to the 1860 Taos County census for the Northern District, which included Conejos, Costilla, and Culebra, forty-three men listed their occupation as "peon." The two youngest men were fifteen years old; the oldest was sixty. By reviewing the census for names of those persons who reported any real and personal property of substance and those persons who lived close to their rich neighbors, thirteen presumed contractors can be identified. These likely contractors, living in Conejos and Costilla Counties, included Harvey E. Easterday, James Bernard Woodson, Agent Lafayette Head, and Conejos settler José Francisco Gallegos.[23]

On September 3 the *News* reported that an unidentified person had found Representative José Francisco Gallegos (not to be confused with the Conejos settler) dead on the Conejos plaza with "a rope around his neck."[24] Many unanswered questions remain: Was his body left as warning that Anglos would not tolerate an insurrection? Was Representative Gallegos the elected official Posthoff wanted replaced in the next election? Had the vigilantes confused the two Gallegos men and hanged the wrong one? What was Agent Head's role in this affair? These questions remain unanswered.

On September 4 the *News* published a report from a Fort Garland cor-respondent about the impending insurgent activities in southern Colorado. The mysterious correspondent, who used the pen name "A," was, in fact, deputy marshal George O. Austin.[25] Using Gaspar's words, Austin wrote that "low threatening murmurs still continue to be heard from the Mexicans." Austin also wrote that a company of soldiers had been ordered to the fort to quell any "emergency occurring in this part of the country" and that the Anglos, plus the three companies at the fort, would level the battlefield.[26] Austin's correspondence and the *News* continued to promote fear against the Hispano settlers and rally the support of the territory's Anglos.

The following day the *News* reported that the insurrection Posthoff had warned the Fort Garland commander about had "at last made its appear-ance."[27] Editor William Byers printed an interview with territorial represen-tative Daniel Witter (Park County), who had just returned to Denver from southern Colorado. Although it is difficult to determine how much of the news was from Witter and which views Byers interjected, it explains that the Hispanos were subjected to military scrutiny and that some troops from the fort had been stationed in the Conejos plaza, such that "great excitement prevailed in that part of the country."[28]

Second Lieutenant Nicolas Hodt had traveled to Conejos and found the people "holding secret meetings with armed sentinels before the doors." Presumably Hodt and his men had stormed into a meeting just as José Francisco Gallegos, a settler of the same name as the recently deceased assemblyman, exclaimed, "The laws ought not to be enforced, and shall not be!"[29] Regrettably, the newspaper did not identify who translated the sedi-tious cry into English.

Per the First Amendment of the US Constitution, Gallegos was within his legal right to express his sentiments. However, the military and civil author-ities perceived his words as treasonous. The arrival of the military and any arrests they made created intense situations. According to the newspaper, three men—Aniceto Martínez, Antonio Gálvez, and José Nasario Gallegos—readied their weapons in support of Gallegos.

Two months later, on November 6, 1862, the military at Fort Garland seized two muskets from a Mr. Gallegos. The following day, it seized two more mus-kets and a Halls carbine rifle from two more men identified only as "Mexicans."[30] Then on December 27, 1862, Deputy Marshal Austin was in Conejos attempting to "forestall what he and other Anglos construed as an insurrection among the people." While attempting to make arrests, Austin presumably called for the assistance of Sheriffs Cornelio Lucero and José María Martínez.[31] Apparently, they refused to assist, so Austin traveled to Fort Garland to enlist military aid.

Captain Ethan Eaton, now commanding Fort Garland, dispatched Hodt and twenty-five troopers to Conejos Plaza to "compel obedience." Eaton served under the jurisdiction of the new Colorado Military District, headed by Colonel John Milton Chivington, while Hodt served under the New Mexico District. Hodt arrested "Francisco Gallegos, Aneseto [sic] Martínez, Antonio Gálvez, and [José] Nasario Gallegos [for] treason or resisting law by the force of arms" and transported them to Fort Garland. There, under guard, all four escaped. Because alcohol was a big problem, especially at isolated posts like Fort Garland, the guard may have been drunk or perhaps bribed.[32] Interestingly, no existing military records for Fort Garland exist today about these arrests or the identification of the guards. Any actions that Colonel Chivington took regarding the escape were also not recorded. Gallegos was later indicted as a disloyal citizen by the Third Judicial District Court.[33] He was about fifty-two and lived on land within the Conejos Land Grant.[34] His father-in-law, Felipe de Jesús Jáquez, was a grantee. The court decreed confiscation of his 220 acres and any improvements on his land, including homes and other structures.[35] The court later dropped the charges. No historical records exist to explain why the court dropped his indictment; and none of the other arrested men were indicted.[36]

During the following spring, news of the unrest continued to circulate. Denver newspaper editor William Newton Byers became involved and reported on the Utes and "Greasers":

> The Utes have been growling considerable about their annuity, and the Greasers a great deal more about the taxes. There will be a good and gay time . . . here for assessors and collectors. It is said, that some of them . . . Greasers . . . have sworn to pay their taxes with the rifle [and] there is no chance of [military] reinforcement till navigation opens [as] the "Sangre de Cristo Pass" is closed [due to the amount of spring snow], not even for travel by caballo [horse].[37]

It was true that the Ute Nation had not been receiving its government-issued food and supplies, but Byers incorrectly attributed Hispano discontent solely to taxation. Rights of property had been controlled and settled by a variety of sometimes conflicting territorial laws. Many of these laws created discord within communities because persons who informed on neighbors, who might have been out of strict compliance with the law, stood to receive half of any resulting fine.

During these secret meetings, the Hispanos discussed ways to be reannexed to New Mexico along with their land. Less than two years had passed since the federal government changed the territorial border and had them living in Colorado Territory, but they were already tired of the treatment and laws and of not having their voices heard. News about the dissension in southern Colorado between the Hispanos and Anglos would continue to be publicized throughout the territorial period. So, they turned to the New Mexico Territorial Assembly for assistance.

Returning Her People to New Mexico

In 1861 Congress had taken an area sixty miles wide and 250 miles in length, and with a population of 7,000 people from the Territory of New Mexico, it combined those nuevomexicanos "with a people alien in laws, alien in language, alien in association . . . simply for the purpose of beautifying the lines of the new Territory of Colorado."[38] Just as former New Mexico delegate Miguel Antonio Otero had predicted back in 1861, the Hispanos began submitting two petitions to the New Mexico Territorial Assembly, asking to be returned with their land to New Mexico. One such petition was reportedly signed by all present, and before forwarding it to New Mexico's new delegate Francisco Perea, leaders reached out to Conejos County, where they garnered another 380 signatures.[39]

In opposition, Colorado's nonvoting delegate to the House, Hiram Pitt Bennet, claimed Colorado had taken better care of the people in the notch than New Mexico ever had: "We are giving them post offices and post roads. We have given them many benefits and privileges which they did not have under the Territory of New Mexico."[40]

The New Mexico Assembly found the concerns of the people from the notch "convincing and worthy of serious attention,"[41] and on January 24, 1863, approved a joint memorial authorizing Perea to lobby Congress to survey the boundary line between New Mexico and Colorado (figures 7.2 and

FIGURE 7.1. Hon. Francisco
Perea, New Mexico delegate
to the US Congress, 1863–
1865. Palace of the Governors
Photo Archives, New Mexico
History Museum.

7.3). It is important to note here that this memorial only addressed the land in
the notch; it did not include Huerfano and Saguache Counties.

The Santa Fe *Weekly Gazette* praised Delegate Perea for his support of the
people in the notch, saying his work aligned with "every consideration of justice and humanity . . . a prompt restitution to New Mexico of that unjustly dis-
membered portion of her territory"[42] Sadly, the congressional session ended, so
the reannexation effort had to wait until the next year's congressional session.

Boundary Line between Colorado and New Mexico

As no formal marker had been made to determine and mark the boundary
separating the two territories, New Mexico believed Colorado had been exercising jurisdiction "on a considerable territory south of their true boundary."
The 37° parallel north divided the two territories and separated several settlements in the Rio Grande valley. Thus, many citizens were uncertain as to
which territory had legal jurisdiction over them.

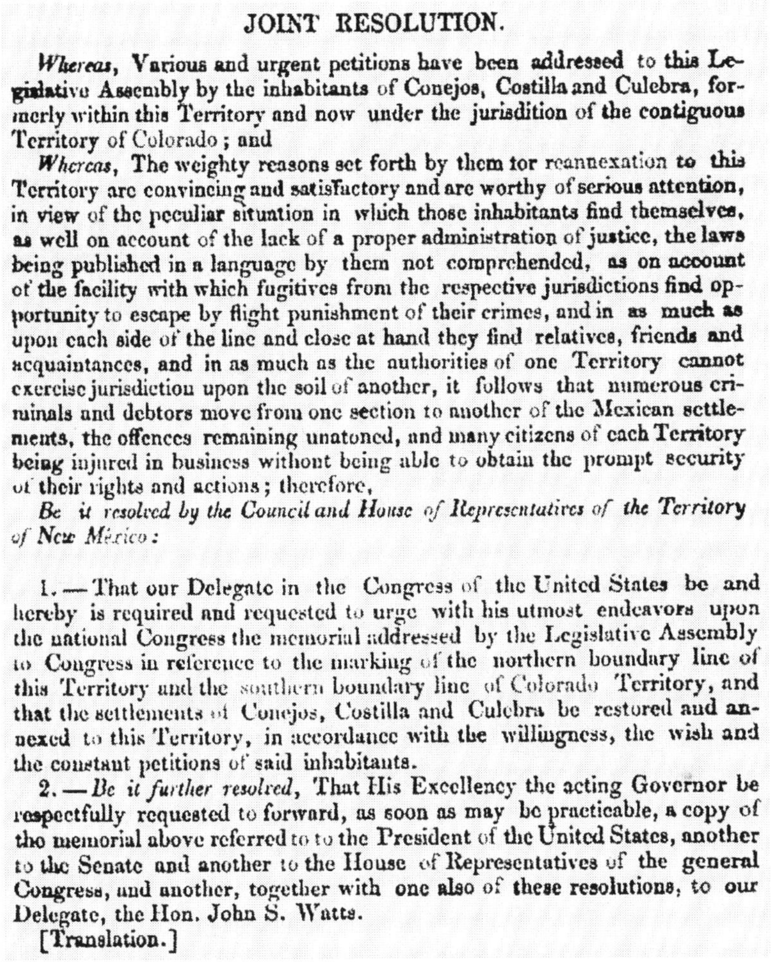

JOINT RESOLUTION.

Whereas, Various and urgent petitions have been addressed to this Legislative Assembly by the inhabitants of Conejos, Costilla and Culebra, formerly within this Territory and now under the jurisdition of the contiguous Territory of Colorado ; and

Whereas, The weighty reasons set forth by them tor reannexation to this Territory are convincing and satisfactory and are worthy of serious attention, in view of the peculiar situation in which those inhabitants find themselves, as well on account of the lack of a proper administration of justice, the laws being published in a language by them not comprehended, as on account of the facility with which fugitives from the respective jurisdictions find opportunity to escape by flight punishment of their crimes, and in as much as upon each side of the line and close at hand they find relatives, friends and acquaintances, and in as much as the authorities of one Territory cannot exercise jurisdiction upon the soil of another, it follows that numerous criminals and debtors move from one section to another of the Mexican settlements, the offences remaining unatoned, and many citizens of each Territory being injured in business without being able to obtain the prompt security of their rights and actions ; therefore,

Be it resolved by the Council and House of Representatives of the Territory of New Mexico :

1. — That our Delegate in the Congress of the United States be and hereby is required and requested to urge with his utmost endeavors upon the national Congress the memorial addressed by the Legislative Assembly to Congress in reference to the marking of the northern boundary line of this Territory and the southern boundary line of Colorado Territory, and that the settlements of Conejos, Costilla and Culebra be restored and annexed to this Territory, in accordance with the willingness, the wish and the constant petitions of said inhabitants.

2. — *Be it further resolved*, That His Excellency the acting Governor be respectfully requested to forward, as soon as may be practicable, a copy of the memorial above referred to to the President of the United States, another to the Senate and another to the House of Representatives of the general Congress, and another, together with one also of these resolutions, to our Delegate, the Hon. John S. Watts.

[Translation.]

FIGURE 7.2. New Mexico Legislative Assembly, joint resolution (English) regarding reannexation of Conejos, Costilla, and Culebra Counties, January 24, 1863. New Mexico Territorial Joint Legislature, 1863 Session, Joint Resolutions, Page 104.

On January 24, 1863, leaders of the New Mexico legislature T. M. Gallegos and Francisco Salazar and acting governor of New Mexico W.F.M. Arny addressed a memorial directly to the members of both chambers of the US Congress, requesting renewed attention to the Colorado–New Mexico boundary (figure 7.4). The memorial requested a resurvey of the border with

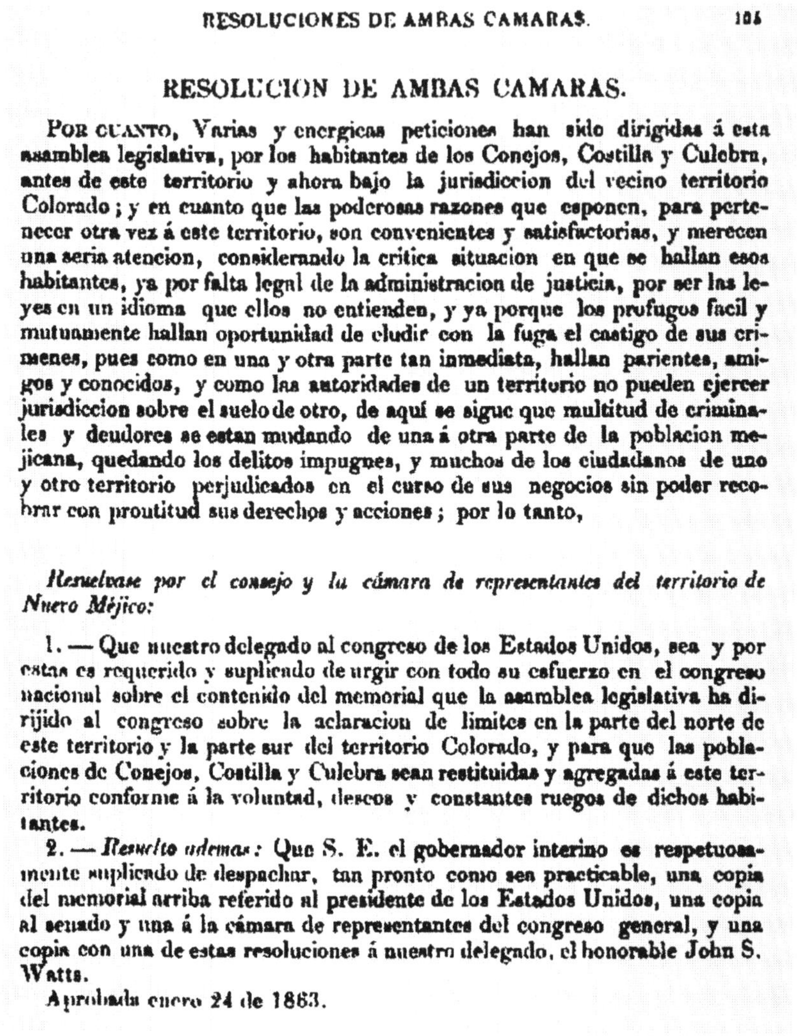

RESOLUCION DE AMBAS CAMARAS.

Por cuanto, Varias y energicas peticiones han sido dirigidas á esta asamblea legislativa, por los habitantes de los Conejos, Costilla y Culebra, antes de este territorio y ahora bajo la jurisdiccion del vecino territorio Colorado ; y en cuanto que las poderosas razones que esponen, para pertenecer otra vez á este territorio, son convenientes y satisfactorias, y merecen una seria atencion, considerando la critica situacion en que se hallan esos habitantes, ya por falta legal de la administracion de justicia, por ser las leyes en un idioma que ellos no entienden, y ya porque los prufugos facil y mutuamente hallan oportunidad de eludir con la fuga el castigo de sus crimenes, pues como en una y otra parte tan inmediata, hallan parientes, amigos y conocidos, y como las autoridades de un territorio no pueden ejercer jurisdiccion sobre el suelo de otro, de aquí se sigue que multitud de criminales y deudores se estan mudando de una á otra parte de la poblacion mejicana, quedando los delitos impugnes, y muchos de los ciudadanos de uno y otro territorio perjudicados en el curso de sus negocios sin poder recobrar con proutitud sus derechos y acciones ; por lo tanto,

Resuelvase por el consejo y la cámara de representantes del territorio de Nuevo Méjico:

1. — Que nuestro delegado al congreso de los Estados Unidos, sea y por estas es requerido y supliendo de urgir con todo su esfuerzo en el congreso nacional sobre el contenido del memorial que la asamblea legislativa ha dirijido al congreso sobre la aclaracion de limites en la parte del norte de este territorio y la parte sur del territorio Colorado, y para que las poblaciones de Conejos, Costilla y Culebra sean restituidas y agregadas á este territorio conforme á la voluntad, descos y constantes ruegos de dichos habitantes.

2. — *Resuelto ademas :* Que S. E. el gobernador interino es respetuosamente suplicando de despachar, tan pronto como sea practicable, una copia del memorial arriba referido al presidente de los Estados Unidos, una copia al senado y una á la cámara de representantes del congreso general, y una copia con una de estas resoluciones á nuestro delegado, el honorable John S. Watts.

Aprobada enero 24 de 1863.

FIGURE 7.3. New Mexico Legislative Assembly, joint resolution (Spanish) regarding reannexation of Conejos, Costilla, and Culebra Counties, January 24, 1863. *Ambas Camaras* del Territorio de Nuevo Mexico, Seccion de 1863, *Resolucion de Ambas Camaras, Pagina 104.*

Colorado and also stated that no formal marker had been made to determine the boundary separating the two territories "upon the face of the earth." The US House of Representatives referred the memorial to its committee on the

38TH CONGRESS, } HOUSE OF REPRESENTATIVES. { MIS. DOC. No. 73.
1st Session. }

BOUNDARY LINE OF NEW MEXICO AND COLORADO.

MEMORIAL

OF THE

LEGISLATU·RE OF NEW MEXICO,

IN RELATION TO

The boundary line between that Territory and Colorado.

APRIL 11, 1864.—Referred to the Committee on the Territories and ordered to be printed.

Memorial of the legislative assembly of the Territory of New Mexico to the Senate and House of Representatives of the United States in Congress assembled:

Your memorialists, the council and house of representatives of the Territory of New Mexico, respectfully represent, that by an act of Congress, entitled "An act to provide a temporary government for the Territory of "Colorado," approved February 28, 1861, all that district, then constituting a part of New Mexico, lying east of the Sierra Madre, and between the 37th and 38th parallels of latitude, is included in and made part of the Territory of Colorado; that no provision has been made by law for ascertaining and marking upon the face of the earth the boundary line between said Territory of Colorado and this Territory; that the 37th parallel of north latitude, constituted by the above act the boundary line between the two Territories, it is believed, divides the settlements in the valley of the Rio Grande, rendering it uncertain which Territory is entitled to jurisdiction over them; that much inconvenience to the inhabitants has arisen in consequence of this uncertainty; that your memorialists are informed, and have good reason to believe, that the Territory of Colorado is now exercising jurisdiction on a considerable territory south of their true boundary, and within the limits of this Territory.

Your memorialists, desirous of avoiding all controversy with the Territory of Colorado upon the question of boundary, respectfully ask that Congress will, at its present session, provide by law for the running and marking the boundary line between this Territory and the Territory of Colorado.

T. M. GALLIGOS,
P. de la C. de Representantes.
FRANCISCO SALAZAR,
Vice-Presidente del Consejo Leg.

Approved January 24, 1863.

W. F. M. ARNY,
Acting Governor.

FIGURE 7.4. Memorial of the Legislature of New Mexico to the US Congress, regarding the Colorado–New Mexico Boundary Line, January 24, 1863. US House of Representatives, 38th Congress, 1st Session, Mis. Doc. No 73, April 11, 1864; Keleher Papers, Box 8, Fd28 1.

territories three months later.[43] This action started the expensive, long, and tedious task of measuring and marking the boundary.

Protesting New Mexico's memorial as "detrimental to Colorado's attempts for statehood," Colorado's pro-statehood assemblymen passed a joint resolution on February 24, 1864, instructing Delegate Bennet to "be especially watchful . . . and oppose all attempts to reduce [the] limits" of Colorado's land.[44] Colorado wanted the area retained for its rich minerals and fertile land; in addition, any loss in the state's population might postpone its statehood efforts.

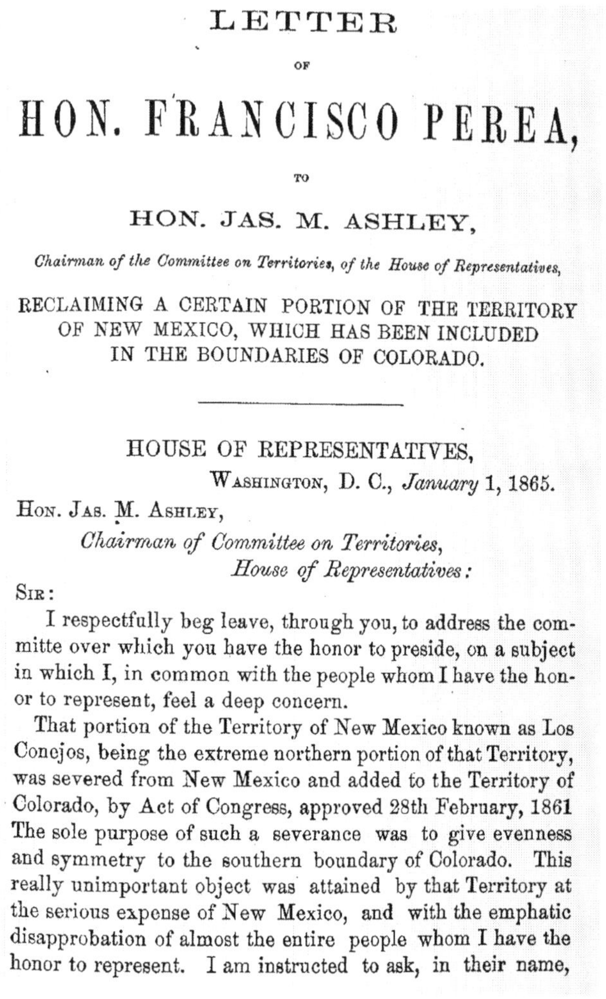

LETTER

OF

HON. FRANCISCO PEREA,

TO

HON. JAS. M. ASHLEY,

Chairman of the Committee on Territories, of the House of Representatives,

RECLAIMING A CERTAIN PORTION OF THE TERRITORY
OF NEW MEXICO, WHICH HAS BEEN INCLUDED
IN THE BOUNDARIES OF COLORADO.

HOUSE OF REPRESENTATIVES,
Washington, D. C., *January* 1, 1865.

Hon. Jas. M. Ashley,
Chairman of Committee on Territories,
House of Representatives:

Sir:

I respectfully beg leave, through you, to address the committe over which you have the honor to preside, on a subject in which I, in common with the people whom I have the honor to represent, feel a deep concern.

That portion of the Territory of New Mexico known as Los Conejos, being the extreme northern portion of that Territory, was severed from New Mexico and added to the Territory of Colorado, by Act of Congress, approved 28th February, 1861 The sole purpose of such a severance was to give evenness and symmetry to the southern boundary of Colorado. This really unimportant object was attained by that Territory at the serious expense of New Mexico, and with the emphatic disapprobation of almost the entire people whom I have the honor to represent. I am instructed to ask, in their name,

FIGURE 7.5. Letter of Hon. Francisco Perea to Hon. Jas. M. Ashley (page 1). Yale Collection of Western Americana, Beinecke Rare Book and Manuscript Library, Yale University

After Perea reportedly received the petitions from the notch settlers, he sent a lengthy letter to James Ashley (Ohio), the chair of the US House Committee on Territories, describing the condition of the Hispanos living in Colorado Territory (figure 7.5). According to Perea's letter—in light of their history, their struggle against the incessant "aggressions" by warring indigenous nations, their generations of tilling the land, their affection for the mountains that surrounded them, their "harmonious, fraternal [peoplehood], bound together by the ties of ancestry, a common language, a common system of law and a common religion—it [would be] ungenerous for this Government to rend them asunder."[45]

During congressional discussion about Colorado's essential bid for statehood, Perea did not express objection but did allege that the "sole purpose" of severing the New Mexico portion from its rightful territory—which was to "give evenness and symmetry to the southern boundary of Colorado"— implied a serious loss of fertile land and people at the expense of New Mexico. Perea emphasized the foreignness of the Hispanos now in Colorado, their affinity for Spanish institutions, and their incompatibility with Colorado's Anglos and its American jurisprudence. This situation, said Perea, was "utterly repugnant to the true principles of liberty," for "the laws of that Territory are enacted and published only in the English language, which they do not understand and the legislative discussions and deliberations are conducted in the same language."[46]

A member of the US House Committee on Territories, Ebon C. Ingersoll (Illinois), informed Perea that a majority of the committee was in favor of the proposition to return the lost portion of New Mexico. This was good news for Perea, southern Colorado, and New Mexico. However, Ingersoll stated that the congressional session had run out and the reannexation effort would have to wait until Congress reconvened nine months later, on December 4. The congressional session ended on March 4, 1865, exactly one month before the end of the Civil War.

The *Santa Fe Weekly Gazette* expressed its confidence that Perea would be successful in restoring the limits of New Mexico to their original status during the session to follow.

> It is pleasant to the eye see State boundaries running with parallels of latitude and longitude, and intersecting each other at right angles, but to secure this symmetry of appearance the Government is scarcely justifiable in doing a great wrong to a large population . . . attaching it to Colorado, for no other purpose than to straighten the Southern boundary line of the latter Territory. No complaint was ever made by New Mexico because her northern boundary was not straight, and did not run directly East and West from beginning to end.
>
> No interest demanded this change . . . They [the Hispanos] constitute a population of a homogeneous people, whose habits, customs, language, laws, and religion were to every respect different from those to whom they

were attached . . . they were thrown into a strange land, among a strange people, with whom they had no sympathy, and to whom they were bound by no tie except that of being citizens of the general Government. It is natural, therefore, that they should want to come back to us, and that we should wish them to come back and join their old associates and enjoy their old habits and customs.[47]

In Colorado, news correspondent William James Godfroy reported on December 27, 1864, that someone erroneously and perhaps maliciously had told Colorado Territorial Council member-elect Celestino Domínguez that the people from Costilla County "had seceded," no longer wished to be represented in the Colorado legislature, and had asked its territorial assemblyman to remain at home during the next session. As reported by Godfroy, Domínguez had stopped in San Luis on his way from Conejos County to Denver when the citizens of Costilla County met *en junta* (as a group) and voted to support the reannexation of Conejos, Saguache, and Costilla Counties.

According to Godfroy, "all this [confusion] was brought about by the [actions] of two Americans [from] Costilla County." He implied that Lafayette Head did not want more settlers from the east and stated that many of those in peonage owed money to an Anglo *patrón* (boss) or two. He also claimed that the majority of the Hispanos wanted to remain in Colorado[48] and pointed out that the Hispanos in his county were a "peaceful and law-abiding class of people," but they simply wished to be returned to New Mexico. "[The laws and customs differ] so much from those of New Mexico, they find it very difficult to comprehend and conform with those laws and customs, particularly the former, as they are obliged to be told those laws through the medium of an Interpreter."[49] Two months later, in a separate correspondence to the *Rocky Mountain News* Costilla county clerk John L. Gaspar also commented about the Hispano discontent saying, "Give the citizens . . . the laws in the Spanish language." He continued, "[A]nd they will not be surpassed for order, tranquility, and conformity to those laws . . . for which, their past conduct most substantially proves."[50]

On January 22, 1866, New Mexico's new delegate to Congress, José Francisco Chávez, submitted a bill to restore Los Conejos to New Mexico Territory. Chávez asked committee chair James Ashley for permission to introduce an amendment to the statehood bill, an adjustment to the south Colorado border such as to return the notch to New Mexico. "I cannot yield for that amendment," Ashley declared, closing off any more discussion on the Mexicans of southern Colorado.[51]

Beginning in early 1868, a great deal of contentious activity around the status of the notch kicked up in southern Colorado. Saguache County residents John Lawrence and William Godfroy had initially shared the return–to–New Mexico sentiment and had reportedly submitted a petition to change the southern boundary to the 37.5° parallel north, thus moving the Hispano communities back to New Mexico.[52] Although their petition has not been located, it raises an interesting question. If the region south of the 37.5° parallel had been reannexed to New Mexico as proposed, how would the nuevomexicanos been affected? Moving Colorado's southern boundary approximately thirty-five miles north would have made the territory even less nearly square than it was. This action would have placed four towns in New Mexico: Conejos, San Luis, La Veta, and Trinidad.

Lawrence and Godfroy later changed their minds as perhaps, like some other men, they had learned about the coal deposits discovered in Huerfano and Las Animas Counties. In 1870, they were among the thirty-one Anglo men from Saguache County who petitioned directly to the Colorado Territorial Legislature against reannexation. Their petition sadly implied that those Hispanos wanting reannexation were not citizens, nor were they loyal to the United States, and it framed the issue in terms of the threatened dismemberment of "loyal American citizens," as opposed to any injustice to the Mexican population.

> Because they [Anglo settlers] are fully identified with Colorado and its interests, it was a manifest injustice of their rights to attempt to force them back with a race for whom they can entertain no common sympathy whatever. They came here as American Citizens, and in good faith to settle in this Valley, and have passed through all the dangers and privation attached to pioneers, yet attempting by our energy and perseverance to help develop the inexhaustible resources of our common country and now that we have succeeded in bringing this heretofor unknown region into notice and these non valuable lands into market shall reannexation be our reward? It cannot, it must not be as loyal American citizens, we honestly feel, that the authorities

at Washington cannot, will not, give its sanction in trying without cause or justice, to forcibly separate us from our own race.[53]

Other known petitioners who signed the Saguache County petition included Otto Mears, Samuel and W. J. Ashley, Edward R. Harris, Andrew Settle, Robert A. Morrison, Nathan Russel, and James Bernard Woodson.

Two years later, on January 10, 1870, Colorado delegate Allen Alexander Bradford introduced a resolution from the citizens of "Guadalupe"[54] (Conejos) County against any change in the boundary line between Colorado and New Mexico. The resolution was forwarded to the US House Committee on the Territories. To thwart Bradford's resolution, New Mexico delegate Chaves immediately asked Taos probate judges Pedro Sánchez and Juan Santistevan to write to "a few citizens . . . urging them to obtain all the signatures possible to petition Congress to cut these three counties—Costilla, Conejos, and Saguache—from Colorado, thus annexing them to New Mexico."[55] The Chaves request resulted in two community meetings.

In Conejos sometime before January 27, 1870, county probate judge José Arcario Velásquez called the community meeting to order and read the letter from Hon. Sánchez and Santistevan. Lafayette Head was selected chairman and Juan Bautista Jáquez secretary. José Seledonio Valdez and Manuel Sabino Salazar spoke in favor of changing the Colorado–New Mexico boundary. Valdez and Salazar reminded the attendees that New Mexico had a "fairer justice [sic] [system and] less taxation," its laws were in Spanish, and they would be with a "similarity of race."[56] According to the Rocky Mountain News their "persuasive eloquence [cited] the immense advantages to be gained by annexation."

The memorial submitted to the US Senate and House of Representatives expressed that they—"of Mexican descent," natives to the area, and "ignorant of the English language, and of American laws and customs"—were "separated from New Mexico without their knowledge and against their wishes." Further, they protested against the fraudulent petition drawn up in 1861 that claimed to represent their preference for the new territory, and they challenged the notion that they were better off in Colorado.[57] They described the community from which they had been separated as one to which they "naturally" belonged, for it reinforced their sense of peoplehood "by reason of its geographical position and identity of language and customs, business relations, ties of consanguinity, and ancient associations." They had been compelled "to a forced and unnatural union with a community which looks upon them as strangers, and whose laws are published in a language which they do not understand, have been and are productive of much evil without, as they have experienced, any compensating benefits or advantages, either to them or to the country." The people had never been adequately advised of the changes of the laws that the territorial assembly had codified two years ago. Moreover, their counties were situated in a valley "excluded" from the rest of Colorado "by high and rugged mountains, nearly impassable during a portion of the year by reason of the snows, and are also a long distance from the capital of the Territory, while the capital of New Mexico is always accessible at all seasons by fair roads, and is not more than half the distance." In view of the "hardship and injustice of keeping them in [Colorado] Territory against their will, solely for the enlargement of that at the expense of a neighboring Territory," the Hispanos humbly prayed that their counties be reannexed to New Mexico, "to which your memorialists believe that they naturally belong, and ought to belong by law and right."[58]

The citizens of Costilla County met at the county courthouse in San Luis on February 14 to discuss the proposed change in the border. Jesús M. Silva "condemned" Delegate Chaves's meddling in Colorado. Both José Victor García and José Pablo Antonio de Jesús Ortega spoke in a "plain, straightforward and forceable language."[59] After a "spirited discussion," the majority of the participants voted to support the proposal against any change in the boundary and submitted two main resolutions: (1) the best interest of Conejos and Costilla counties would be "irrevocably sacrificed" by annexation; and (2) those attending the meeting would "oppose by all . . . means such annexation." The gathering opposed being annexed to New Mexico—a movement they called "obnoxious," because it would "sacrifice the best interests of the people of this valley." The participants pledged to oppose, by all honorable means, "such an unjust movement in derogation of [their] rights . . . and inflicting irreparable injury upon the people, as well as an unwarranted declination of the Territory of Colorado."[60] Other known attendees included Harvey E. Easterday,[61] Fred Walsen,[62] José Ignacio Ortega, Dario Gallegos, José Nasario Gallegos, and Territorial Representative Juan Miguel Vigil (Costilla).[63] Dario Gallegos served as meeting chairman. Walsen, who served as secretary, likely submitted information about the remonstrance to the newspapers. Both he and Easterday actively promoted statehood, were politically well connected, and had successful financial interests in southern Colorado. Clearly, they did not want their personal and financial interests jeopardized by a change to the Colorado–New Mexico border. The proceedings of the meeting were forwarded to Colorado delegate Bradford, along with a plea that he "use his utmost exertions to thwart this attempt of annexation."[64] Bradford introduced the proceedings to Congress on March 4, 1870; it was then forwarded to the Committee on the Territories.

The *Rocky Mountain News* claimed to speak for "the people" of San Luis who stood opposed to the boundary change, stating, they would "fight against it to the bitter end." The editor of the *Weekly Chieftain* claimed to know that the people of Conejos stood against the annexation scheme and that the "enterprising citizens" of Saguache County "would reject with scorn and indignation any proposition to place them in a country so far behind in the path of progress and prosperity as is the Territory of New Mexico."[65]

Unfortunately, the Conejos memorial for annexation to New Mexico did not convince Congress. With the final nail pounded into the annexation and boundary coffin, all Coloradans now focused on statehood.

Fraudulent Homestead Claims

Although a legal procedure was in place for acquiring low-fee land through the Homestead Act, much land was acquired through unfair advantage and fraudulent claims. By law, a claimant could not acquire more than 160 acres of federal land except through purchase from a private seller. However, there were any number of ways around the letter and certainly the spirit of the law, especially for those with liquid capital. For example, during the 1870s, wealthy Anglos, with key information about the railroad coming into the southern counties, were involved in land schemes to fraudulently enter into a "pretended proof of right in pre-emption,"[66] taking advantage of "preemption," a settler's right to buy public land at low cost from the government, rather than at sale or auction (and at a higher price) from a private seller. Monied individuals or companies might arrange for people who had no intention of settling the land to apply for land patents (deeds of title) nonetheless and then to turn around and sell the property to their patrons, who might wish to develop the land for themselves—as along railroad rights-of-way, for example—or, as speculators, to resell the land at a profit. Or, for another, less fraudulent example, the offspring of an original settler might, on coming of age, acquire homesteads of their own adjacent to the original parcel, contributing to the accumulation of a large and contiguous family estate.

In some notable cases, Jerome Bunty Chaffee, David H. Moffat Jr., and Samuel H. Elbert reportedly "seized certain public lands in southern Colorado [by recording] their claims in a midnight session with the . . . county clerk."[67] In Saguache John Lawrence helped Gabriel Woodson file a claim on some land that Lawrence was interested in acquiring. Lawrence even provided Gabriel, a former enslaved Navajo of Lawrence's partner, with the money for miscellaneous required fees.[68] In addition to the three-dollar filing fee on a 160-acre tract, there was a ten-dollar patent fee, a one-dollar recording fee, and survey costs. By law, Lawrence himself could not acquire more federal land except through purchase from a private seller. Woodson never settled on or made improvements to the land; however, Lawrence testified that Woodson had done so. Lawrence purchased Woodson's land on March 1, 1873, and thus acquired more than the allotted 160 acres.[69]

The USFLEC used a fictitious person to claim homestead land, then "fabricated a legal challenge to its own [title] to perfect the deed and resurvey the boundary."[70] And, in a separate case on December 10, 1874, grand juries at Pueblo and Del Norte submitted a report to Judge James B. Belford of the Third Judicial District regarding indictments of pretended proof of right in preemption on homestead land filings. In July 1874 at Del Norte the grand jury foreman wrote that "although large sums of money [between $50 and $400] were collected from defendants, we have yet to learn of a single dollar which has ever found its way into the public treasury." Apparently, when a defendant was arrested for perjury, D. C. Russell, the US commissioner of the Third Judicial District, together with the US marshal and the prosecuting officer, advised the defendant to retain Del Norte attorney G. M. Clay as his counsel. After retaining Clay's services, "the defendants were immediately discharged after a pretended hearing" before Justice Russell. The commissioners of judicial districts were appointed by and were responsible for duties assigned by the district judge. On November 27, 1874, in Rio Grande County, Antonio E. Montoya appeared before Russell, who requested $500 to fix the perjury charge. Although the legal case before Russell lingered in the courts for several years, existing historical judicial records do not verify Montoya's final disposition. Forbes Parkhill wrote that Russell was "an absolute terror to the community."[71]

A land-grab case of the so-called Denver Ring—prominent and politically connected men who included Alexander Cameron Hunt, Jerome Bunty Chaffee, and David H. Moffat—was brought to trial under Colorado chief justice Moses Hallet in 1875. The case involved Hunt, Chaffee, and Moffat as well as several other statehood proponents. Justice Hallet was said to have been "politically independent" and not "sympathetic" to the ring, which led its members to attempt to remove him as chief justice.[72]

Land frauds that occurred on the Mexican land grants of Las Animas and St. Vrain–Vigil became known as the "Animas Land Grab." A grand jury in Pueblo found many frauds of "pretended proof of right in pre-emption." Although land was preempted, no settlement or improvement had been made as mandated by law; in many cases "both the pre-emptor and witnesses were fictitious persons."

> We learned that portions of the school section in Huerfano County were fraudulently pre-empted and that United States patents were obtain (sic) by fraud, at the site of a small lake, probably the most valuable tract in the [six-mile-square] township, adjoining a townsite along the line of a prospective [Denver & Rio Grande] railroad.[73]

The land located at this site was that of Walter V. Stevens. He had constructed a lake on his property located near what would become the railroad town Cuchara Junction.

As the D&RG made its way through southern Colorado, its subsidiary companies began acquiring much land. The following year, General William Jackson Palmer and his associates purchased land along projected rights of way for their D&RG railway. Through often ruthless means, subsidiary companies purchased 2,640 acres for the rail yard, 1,000 acres for the railroad town, and additional mineral land.[74]

To protect their holdings, Hispanos found that they had to file homestead claims quickly, attached with cash fees. As the D&RG made its way through Huerfano County, probate judge and Cucharas postmaster John Foster Read was busy processing "homestead claims from Mexican settlers." Read and his partner, Charles D. Hayt, were in business to survey real estate and file land claims, and they procured titles under the homestead, preemption, and mining laws.

On August 20, 1874, Read and Hayt purchased 160 acres at $3.46 an acre from Juan José de Aguero, whose application for his homestead was still in process. The following day, Read and Hayt sold 120 acres of this land to Fred Walsen, a Read associate. Shortly after, Walsen leased the land along the right of way to the D&RG. It is quite doubtful that Read and Hayt advised de Aguero that his valuable piece of land was near the proposed D&RG depot and right of way.[75]

Like de Aguero, many Hispanos lost their homes, properties, crops, grazing land, and positions of economic and political power due to land grabs. In connection with land frauds associated with the Las Animas Land Grant, fifteen charges of conspiracy at three counts each were filed against Philip and Mike Quinlan of Huerfano County, Alexander Cameron Hunt, Jerome Bunty Chaffee, David H. Moffat Jr., Irving W. Stanton, and Charles A. Cook. The Quinlans were "supposedly induced to make the fraudulent filings." Stanton was the land office register at Pueblo, and Cook was an employee at this land office. Cook had previously been a partner of Moffat and Chaffee.[76] The case was brought to trial under Judge Hallet in 1875. When called as a witness, Delegate Chaffee was in Washington, DC, and thus failed to appear. He was cited for contempt by Hallet. The trial took place in June and resulted in a hung jury.[77]

Another land grab occurred along the Arkansas River in Pueblo County. Land claimed by D. W. Hughes lay along the projected route of the Atchison, Topeka and Santa Fe Railway. Hughes knew this land would significantly increase in value when the railroad was completed. The land claims were filed under aliases: "Residents learned that no one had ever seen or heard of the new claimants and that they had transferred their titles, through a third party, to David H. Moffat and Robert E. Carr." According to historian Eugene H. Berwanger, Moffat and Carr were "political cohorts" of territorial governor Samuel H. Elbert in a land-grab scheme. These men were also trustees for the Arkansas Railroad Company.[78]

An investigation ordered by the US General Land Office determined that an employee or other person connected with the land office in Pueblo knew "the character of these transactions and aided and abetted the fraud." The US Department of Justice started criminal proceedings, and the attorney general for Colorado called for a grand jury investigation. Moffat, Carr, and Cook were indicted for fraud. The case was heard by the US District Court in 1878; it could not prove that the three men were aware that the transaction constituted fraud, so the case was dismissed.[79]

Fence Law and the Open Range

Hispano settlers constructed fences from natural materials such as tree limbs, stone, or adobe, which prevented wandering livestock from damaging acequia embankments, gardens, and crops.[80] In fact, settlers erected sturdy fences around cemeteries to prevent animals from entering and grazing there. When Charles (Carlos) Beaubien issued a deed to all the settlers on his Sangre de Cristo Land Grant in 1863, the deed stipulated that the inhabitants had to "immediately erect a fence sufficiently good to prevent animals from entering the cemetery, etc."[81] English law held that the owner of livestock was responsible for his cattle and should fence them in. Spanish law assumed that rangeland was open to all and the owner of cropland was himself responsible for the protection of his crops.[82] The thinking was that, by nature, animals ran free; thus the crops should be fenced in, not the animals. However, according to researcher and author Joanna L. Stratton, "Homesteaders had no effective defenses or recourse against the intruding animals [and] fencing off their fields and pastures was not an easy solution, either."[83] Not until the widespread marketing of barbed wire in the early 1880s were farmers finally able to cordon off their lands and protect their crops. However, the cost for one hundred pounds of barbed wire in 1874 was twenty dollars.[84]

On February 12, 1874, the territorial assembly enacted a rigid-fence law that applied to Conejos County. By law, post-and-plank fences had to be of "sound" wood, and stand "four feet, six inches high, made of sound posts five inches in diameter . . . not more than eight feet apart, with three planks not less than one inch thick and six inches wide, securely fastened by nails or other [fastener]." For any animal that trespassed from its fenced area and caused damage, the county could hold that animal as security for payment by the owner. In addition, the assembly established specific regulations on the right to petition against the law. The citizens could petition against the law only if 100 voters of legal age—at least half of whom had to be farmers—signed a petition and presented it before the Conejos County commissioners.[85] This law created much hardship and discord in the county. Men now had to travel by horse and wagon into the mountains and cut down trees for the posts or travel to Anglo-owned mills to purchase milled lumber.[86]

Anglo settlement and their cattle corporations absorbed much of the available open-range land. Hispanos now had to pay for national forest grazing permits or to lease privately held land. During the summer months, cattlemen turned their cattle out to graze on the open range, but in winter months many cattlemen illegally fenced government land to reserve grass for their exclusive use or to lease out to other cattlemen, whom they charged by the head. Legal and illegal fencing continued to keep sheep out and reduce the open lands. Judge Hallet issued a decree that if the fences were not removed within the time allotted, the marshal would remove them "with the cost reverting to the cattle company."[87]

Due to the different environmental impacts of the grazing characteristics of sheep and cattle, herders and cattlemen competed for rangeland. Flocks of sheep congregated more closely on the land than did the wider-ranging cattle and tended to compact soil and crop vegetation in ways that made it harder for pastures to recover quickly. There was also an ethnic component to many of the conflicts that arose between sheep herders and cattlemen, for the shepherds often were Hispanos or Indians, whereas the cattlemen commonly were Anglos. Hispano farmers and ranchers unable to compete with the Anglo ranchers sometimes had no recourse other than to sell their land to big cattle companies at low prices.[88]

By 1869, the entire region of Las Animas County was open range. Cattlemen and their range cattle arrived from Texas. Trinidad became headquarters for a number of large and well-known cattle companies, such as the Cleveland, the Jones, and the Prairie cattle companies. Each of these had "numbers of thousands of cattle."[89] Anglo settlement and cattle corporations absorbed much of the available rangeland. They attempted to control key water sources, occupy large tracts of the public domain, and prevent settlement on their land.

By 1870, the territorial legislature regulated grazing as a means to demonstrate to the US Congress that Colorado was an established and vital center of activity deserving of statehood. Territorial officials wanted legislation authorizing justices of the peace to have animals kept under control in Conejos, Costilla, Huerfano, and Las Animas Counties.[90] By their customs and traditions, Hispanos tried at all costs to keep their stock away from crops and acequias, and they guarded their stock so as not to damage canal embankments, which then might cause the acequia to lose water.

The relationship between the cattlemen and the D&RG Railway proved to be a long and profitable venture that stimulated growth in both industries. Cattlemen were on hand to supply beef for railroad workers, and the D&RG was available to transport cattle. Because the acreage allowed by government land laws was not enough to meet their needs, some cattlemen used fraudulent means and made false claims to obtain additional land and to fence in large tracts of public domain lands along a river or stream. Some had their employees "put up a few boards" in lieu of true housing on a quarter section of land and file a homestead claim. When the required time passed, these employees swore they had lived on the claim as required by law. After obtaining the land patent, they deeded the land to their employer, either directly or through a third party.[91]

Notes

1. Hon. Francisco Perea to Hon. Jas. M. Ashley, January 1, 1865, Yale Collection of Western Americana, Beinecke Rare Book and Manuscript Library, Yale University.

2. Hart Library, History Colorado Center, CWA, Conejos County, Charles E. Gibson, Jr., 1933–1934a, 142.

3. "Joint Resolution in Relation to the Marking of the Boundary Lines," January 24, 1863, *Laws of the Territory of New Mexico, Passed by the Legislative Assembly, Session of 1862–63* (Santa Fe: C. Leib, 1863), 104. "Memorial of the Legislature of New Mexico, in Relation to the Boundary Line between That Territory and Colorado," January 24, 1863, US House of Representatives, 38th Cong., 1st Sess., *Miscellaneous Documents of the House of Representatives*, Vol. 3 (Washington, DC: GPO, 1864), Misc. Doc. No. 73; Keleher Papers, Zimmerman Library, University of New Mexico, box 8, Fd28, 1; see also Everett, *Creating the American West*, 174.

4. *Cong. Globe*, 36th Cong., 2nd Sess., 728–29 (1861). Lamar, *Far Southwest*, 189–90. Stein, *How the States Got Their Shapes Too*, 54, 183. "Joint Resolution in Relation to the Marking of the Boundary Lines," January 24, 1863, *Laws of the Territory of New Mexico, Passed by the Legislative Assembly, Session of 1862–63*, 104.

5. *Cong. Globe*, 37th Cong., 2nd Sess., 2024 (1862); cf. Everett, *Creating the American West*, 174.

6. *Cong. Globe*, 37th Cong., 2nd Sess., 2024 (1862); cf. Everett, *Creating the American West*, 174.

7. Paul, "The Spanish Americans in the Southwest, 1848–1900," 40.

8. Deutsch, *No Separate Refuge*, 19.

9. NARA, Washington, DC, Letters and Telegrams Received, 1860–1880, Fort Garland, C.T., 1860–1888, J. L. Gaspar to Maj. Mayer, July 30, 1862, M1120, RG 393, Roll 17; Maj. Mayer to AAA General, August 18, 1862, M1120, RG 393, 179–80.

10. NARA, Washington, DC, Letters Received, Department of New Mexico, Lt. Durnin to Capt. Chapin, July 31, 1862, M1120, RG 393, Roll 15.

11. NARA, Washington, DC, Registers of Letters Received and Letters Received by Headquarters, Department of New Mexico, 1854–1865, Posthoff to Maj. Mayer, August 4, 1862, M1120, RG 393, Roll 19.

12. Ibid.

13. Ibid.

14. US Naturalization Record for Frederick W. Posthoff, October 15, 1872, US Naturalization Record Indexes, 1791–1992 (Indexed in World Archives Project), ancestry.com, accessed June 11, 2018.

15. NARA, Washington, DC, Registers of Letters Received and Letters Received by Headquarters, Department of New Mexico, 1854–1865, Posthoff to Maj. Mayer, August 8, 1862, M1120, RG 393, Roll 19.

16. NARA, Washington, DC, Registers of Letters Received and Letters Received by Headquarters, Department of New Mexico 1854–1865, Capt. Eaton to Capt. Chapin, August 18, 1862, M1120, RG 393, Roll 18.

17. NARA, Washington, DC, Registers of Letters Received and Letters Received by Headquarters, Department of New Mexico, 1854–1865, Maj. Mayer to AAA General, August 18, 1862, M1120, RG 393, Roll 17.

18. NARA Washington, DC, Registers of Letters Received and Letters Received by Headquarters, Department of New Mexico, Maj. Mayer to AAA General, July 31, 1862, M1120, RG 393. The following men could have taken written statements if requested: Thomas Tate Tobin, Lafayette Head, John Mays Francisco, James B. Woodson, Cornelius D. Hendren, Archibald H. Gillespie, Charles Deus, and Ethan Eaton.

19. NARA Washington, DC, Registers of Letters Received and Letters Received by Headquarters, Department of New Mexico, Maj. Mayer to AAA General, August 11, 1862, and August 18, 1862, M1120, RG 393, Roll 17.

20. Ibid.

21. Ibid.

22. Ibid.

23. "1863 Colorado Tax Schedule, Annual Assessment," St. Vrain and Easterday, ancestry.com, accessed July 4, 2015.

24. "Interesting from Conejos," *Rocky Mountain News*, September 5, 1862, 3, col. 6.

25. Alexander Cameron Hunt was appointed on June 18, 1862. Copeland Townsend was appointed the first US marshal in Colorado Territory on March 25, 1861. US Marshals Service, History of District of Colorado, http://www.us marshals.gov/district/co/general/history.htm, accessed October 8, 2014.

26. "From Fort Garland," *Rocky Mountain News Weekly*, September 4, 1862, 1, col. 8.

27. *Rocky Mountain News Daily*, September 5, 1862, 3, col. 6.

28. Ibid.

29. Ibid.

30. NARA, Washington, DC, "Records of the Provost Marshal, 1862–64," Department of New Mexico, RG 393, part 1, entries 3180, 3214, vol. 121, 298, 299.

31. NARA, Washington, DC, Maj. Gillespie to Cap. Cutler, "Conejos Alcaldes and Constables Reported by Maj. Gillespie in 1862," Letters Received, Department of New Mexico, M1120, RG 393, Roll 18.

32. Thompson, *Civil War History*, 377: citing NARA, Washington, DC, General Order No. 41, May 1, 1862, *General Orders, 1862*, DMN, RG 393, AGO; and Letters Received, Col. Paul to Capt. Nicodenus, May 6, 1862, M1120, RG 393, Roll 17.

33. Parkhill, *Law Goes West*, 43. Unnumbered indictment.

34. Spanish Archives of New Mexico, Conejos Land Grant, PLC No. 109, Roll 45. See also Esquibel, "Rio de los Conejos Grantees," 13.

35. Parkhill, *Law Goes West*, 43.

36. Price, *Season of Terror*, 123.

37. Editorial, *Rocky Mountain News*, March 19, 1863, 3, col. 3.

38. *Cong. Globe*, 36th Congress, 2nd Session (February 4, 1861), 728–729. Hereafter cited as *Cong. Globe*. Lamar, *Far Southwest*, 189–190. Stein, *How the States Got Their Shapes Too*, 54, 183. *Laws of the Territory of New Mexico, Passed by the Legislative Assembly, Session of 1862–63* (available on Google Books), Joint Resolution, in relation to the marking of the boundary lines, 24 January 1863, 104.

39. Yale University, Yale Collection of Western Americana, Beinecke Rare Book and Manuscript Library, "Hon. Francisco Perea, Letter to Chairman of the Committee on Territories, of the House of Representatives," February 18, 1865. Gonzales and Sánchez, "Displaced in Place," 285.

40. *Cong. Globe*, 37th Cong., 2nd sess. (May 8, 1862, 2024); cf. Everett, *Creating the American West*, 174.

41. *Laws of the Territory of New Mexico, Passed by the Legislative Assembly, Session of 1862–63* (available on Google Books), Joint Resolution, in relation to the marking of the boundary lines, 24 January 1863, 104. Attempts to locate these petitions in various state and federal archives were unsuccessful.

42. *Cong. Globe*, 38th Cong., 1st sess. (January 11, 1864, 150); A Friend of the Country ("From Washington City"), *Santa Fe Weekly Gazette*, July 23, 1864.

43. *Laws of the Territory of New Mexico, Passed by the Legislative Assembly, Session of 1862–63,* Joint Resolution (available on Google Books), in relation to the marking of the boundary lines, 24 January 1863, 104. T. M. Gallegos and Francisco Salazar, "Memorial of the Legislature of New Mexico, in Relation to the Boundary Line between that Territory and Colorado," January 24, 1863, US House of Representatives, 38th Congress, 1st Session, Mis. Doc. No 73, April 11, 1864; Keleher Papers, Zimmerman Library, University of New Mexico, box 8, Fd28 1; see also Everett, *Creating the American West,* 174.

44. *General Laws and Joint Resolutions, Memorials and Private Acts, Passed at the Third Session of the Legislative Assembly of the Territory of Colorado* (available on Google Books), begun at Golden City, on February 1, 1864, adjourned to Denver on February 4, Joint Resolution, February 24, 1864, 256. Hereafter cited as *General Laws of the Territory of Colorado, 1864.*

45. Yale University, Yale Collection of Western Americana, Beinecke Rare Book and Manuscript Library, "Hon. Francisco Perea, Letter to Chairman of the Committee on Territories, of the House of Representatives," February 18, 1865. Gonzales and Sánchez, "Displaced in Place," 285.

46. Ibid.

47. *Santa Fe Weekly Gazette,* July 1, 1865, Image 2.

48. "From Conejos and Costilla," *Santa Fe Weekly Gazette,* Wm. J. Godfroy to editor, February 1, 1865, 2.

49. Ibid.; "From Conejos and Costilla," J. L. Gaspar to editor, March 21, 1865, 2.

50. J. L. Gaspar to editor, February 21, 1865, *Rocky Mountain News,* March 21, 1865, 2. Gaspar response to Wm. J. Godfroy to editor, December 27, 1864, *Rocky Mountain News,* February 1, 1865, 2.

51. *Cong. Globe,* 39th Congress, 1st session, (Jan. 22, March 12, April 24, April 25, 1866), 350, 1328, 2135–2140, 2166; and (May 3, 1866), 2373.

52. Martin, *Frontier Eyewitness,* 44.

53. NARA, Washington, DC, "Petition of Citizens of Colorado to the Senate and House of Representatives," February 27, 1868, "Senate Miscellaneous Document," 40th Congress, 2nd Session, Territorial Papers of the United States Senate, 1789–1873, Colorado, 1860–1868, M200, Roll 17.

54. Interestingly, Bradford had referred to Conejos County by its original name, "Guadalupe County," which had been changed to "Conejos County" in 1861, during the first session of the Colorado Territorial Assembly.

55. "More about Annexation," *Colorado Weekly Chieftain,* February 17, 1870, 2.

56. "From Guadalupe," *Rocky Mountain News,* February 4, 1870, 2, col. 1.

57. *Cong. Globe*, Memorial of Voters of the Counties of Costilla and Conejos in the Territory of Colorado, February 25, 1870, 41st Congress, 2nd Session, House of Representatives, Miscellaneous Doc. No. 67.

58. Ibid.

59. "From Guadalupe," *Rocky Mountain News*, February 4, 1870, 2, col. 1.

60. "More about Annexation," *Colorado Weekly Chieftain*, February 17, 1870, 2.

61. Easterday, from Virginia, had wealthy connections who were associated with the Ceran St. Vrain and the Cornelio Vigil–St. Vrain Land Grant located in Huerfano County. In 1870, Easterday reported the value of his real estate as $15,000 and personal property at $800. 1870 Costilla County Census, Precinct 3, San Luis, Costilla County, Colorado, 7, Lines 13–15, Household 49, Dwelling 46.

62. When Walsen served as a San Luis postmaster in 1868, he was not yet a US citizen. With the arrival of the D&RG into Huerfano County, he constructed a large warehouse where sheep growers paid him to store their wool. Hart Library of the History Colorado Center, Fred Walsen Collection, "Walsen and Levy: Traders, Merchants, Stock Growers, and Rail Road Builders."

63. "More about Annexation," *Colorado Weekly Chieftain*, February 17, 1870, 2.

64. "Costilla County Against Annexation," *Colorado Chieftain*, March 3, 1870, p. 1, col. 5.

65. *Colorado Weekly Chieftain*, February 17, 1870, 2.

66. David H. Moffat was a banker and railroad builder. Parkhill, *Law Goes West*, 139–40.

67. Lamar, *Far Southwest*, 248.

68. NARA, Washington, DC, Letters Received by the Office of Indian Affairs, 1824–1880, Roll 198, Colorado Superintendency, 1865–1866, Conejos Report, line 84.

69. Martin, *Frontier Eyewitness*, 76.

70. National Park Service, National Register of Historic Places, "The Culebra River Villages of Costilla County, Colorado," sec. E, 23.

71. Parkhill, *Law Goes West*, 101–2. P. G. Goodman served as the US grand jury foreman. The indictment (458) records Montoya as "Montoyo."

72. Berwanger, *Rise of the Centennial State*, 133.

73. Parkhill, *Law Goes West*, 139.

74. Lamar, *Far Southwest*, 244. See also Brayer, *William Blackmore*, 1: 195.

75. Sánchez, *Forgotten Cuchareños of the Lower Valley*, 85, 88, 104, 105.

76. Berwanger, *Rise of the Centennial State*, 132.

77. Parkhill, *Law Goes West*, 140.

78. Berwanger, *Rise of the Centennial State*, 132.

79. Ibid., 131–33.

80. Steinel and Working, *History of Agriculture in Colorado*, xx.

81. Ron Sandoval, "The San Luis Vega," in Teeuwen, *La Cultura Constante de San Luis*, 20.

82. De Oñis, *Hispanic Contribution to the State of Colorado*, xx.

83. Stratton, *Pioneer Women*, 212: "Whipping wind made fencing all the more difficult."

84. By 1885, the price was $4.20. The Colorado Fuel and Iron Company at Pueblo began producing barbed wire in 1888. "Giant of the West," in Colorado Cattlemen's Centennial Commission, *Co-Operative Century*, 55.

85. *General Laws of the Territory of Colorado, 1874*, 142–43.

86. "Giant of the West," in Colorado Cattlemen's Centennial Commission, *Co-Operative Century*, 55.

87. White, "Illegal Fencing on the Colorado Range," 109.

88. President Grover Cleveland ordered all illegal fences removed in 1885. White, "Illegal Fencing on the Colorado Range," 101, 109.

89. Ibid.; McHendrie, "Trinidad and Its Environs," 169.

90. *House Journal of the Legislative Assembly of the Territory of Colorado, Eighth Session, Convened at Denver, January 3rd, 1870* (Central City: David C. Collier, 1870), January 25, 1870, 85 (relating to justices of the peace).

91. White, "Illegal Fencing on the Colorado Range," 97.

8

Continued Obstacles

English-only sentiments continued to hinder efforts to have statutes published in Spanish. Territorial auditor Nathaniel Cheeseman urged the Colorado Council to forgo the "great" cost of translating and printing statutes for the benefit of the territory's Hispano citizens and their assemblymen.

Effective communication through a trusted interpreter and translator works best when communication is seamless; this requires a level of trust and a mutual connection. But what happens when the personalities clash between the legislator and the interpreter, or when the interpreter is incompetent? The matter of translation pushed over into disagreements in the Colorado House about whether the Spanish-speaking representatives should be allowed to choose their own interpreter.

Through its parliamentary tactics, the House majority party used partisan politics to allow Albert W. Archibald to present his comments about the chamber seat occupied by representative-elect Lorenzo Antonio Abeyta (Las Animas). Abeyta had served one month in office when Archibald, a Republican attorney, contested the election, although Archibald was not the candidate

DOI: 10.5876/9781607329145.c008

who had run against Abeyta.[1] The speaker permitted Archibald, a private citizen, to speak on the House floor, which is quite rare. The speaker also allowed the attorneys representing the two men to speak; however, it does not appear that Abeyta was given the same opportunity and time. Ultimately, Abeyta lost his seat to a citizen and not a candidate. Additionally, the House denied the county's voters the right to elect its party's replacement.

Editor Byers promoted negative feelings toward the Hispano community and criticized it for not adopting his language, politics, and culture. He considered the Hispanos more loyal to Mexico than to the United States, when, in fact, by 1870 the United States was their country of origin. To Anglo readers, the Hispanos were not assimilated citizens, with proper civic mindedness, and in consequence were frequently suspected of being deviously un-American.

When Conejos County officials held an election to name a new county seat, they found out only later that the current session of the territorial legislature, whose approval was necessary to make the change, had been canceled and the county election was therefore meaningless. They did not receive the laws in their language, so how would they have known that the session had been canceled and that a statute determined the selection of county seats and not the citizens?

Relative to the new road tax, those people who were too poor to pay a road tax in cash and who lived outside of incorporated towns—a definition that included a great majority of Hispanos in the southern counties of Colorado—were required to pay their taxes in the form of labor on the roads, even at the expense of removing needed workers from family farms. Simply stated, they were being punished for their poverty.

Questioning the Need for Translations

Colorado's Anglo lawyers, justices, and assemblymen became increasingly frustrated over the need for translators in the courts and in legislative chambers. Because the majority of the territorial population in southern Colorado was Spanish-speaking, juries for trials held in these court districts would be composed mainly of Hispano men. Some Anglos worried that in cases pitting an Anglo against a Hispano, such juries would find in favor of the Hispano due to ethnic bias. When the Anglo population increased, Anglo judges and attorneys sought to limit juror qualifications and lobbied for laws that limited non-English speakers from serving on juries.

In 1868 in Las Animas County a probate case was heard in Spanish. Apparently, the defendant, probate judge, and jury members all spoke or understood Spanish. The plaintiff, Señor Montoya, attempted to sue an Anglo, Mr. Dunton, for an amount of money Montoya believed Dunton owed him. When Montoya won his case, Dunton appealed to the Colorado Territorial Supreme Court. This case, *Dunton v. Montoyo* [*sic*], was heard by Chief Justice Moses Hallet and Associate Justices Christian S. Eyster and William R. Gorsline. The territory's Supreme Court reversed the judgment "because the case was argued in Spanish" and not according to Anglo rules of practice. Justice Eyster rendered the following opinion on behalf of the court: "It is not to be tolerated in this country that judicial proceedings should be in any other than the adopted language of the nation."[2]

Between 1870 and 1890, Colorado's "language restrictionist legislation" prohibited the use of the Spanish language in public schools and eliminated any instruction in Mexican history.[3] In succeeding years, Anglo lawmakers continued their attempts to limit voter rights and restrict the selection of jurors based on language, creed, and color. In 1883 the Colorado Assembly again moved to establish voter limits by disenfranchising the state's Spanish-speaking citizens from their constitutional right to vote. Such moves to limit access to the vote by the use of language continued to be a constant threat.[4]

By 1870, the territory had finally translated the statutes of the first six assembly sessions into Spanish. That achievement brought the translation current only up to 1867. Now, however, the territory would question the need for any translation. Territorial auditor Nathaniel F. Cheeseman introduced the English-only conversation in Colorado in 1870 when he analyzed the cost to translate and print the statutes in Spanish. Cheeseman reported that the two printed volumes of translated statutes were "now but little better than old lumber." The need for statutes in Spanish became a political and emotional issue. Cheeseman's audit created a stir with Anglo Coloradoans, and the Republican-led assembly again began questioning the need for translated statutes: "the cost of a translation is very great, while the benefits of such translations are temporary and partial."[5]

Cheeseman caught the attention of his like-minded assemblymen when he stated that "the laws of the United States, and of the several States, are printed in the English language, and no other." However, Cheeseman was wrong. During the early periods of statehood in California, Indiana, Louisiana, New Mexico, Ohio, and Pennsylvania, the laws were printed in English and one other language. Indiana sought to publish its laws in English, German, and French; however, the amendment to include the French language was rejected. In some of its state courts, jury deliberations were in German. Pennsylvania established a state printer for printing laws in both English and German. In the case of Ohio, only selected laws were printed in German, which led to questionable politics. Louisiana's laws were printed in English and French.[6]

Further, in his audit report to the Colorado Territorial Council, Cheeseman marginalized all "citizens of Spanish extraction" because they could not read in English. Cheeseman not only questioned their patriotism; he criticized the literacy of their own foreign language. Even though they could not read the English versions, they should still obey the laws: "If the laws are what they ought to be, 'rules of action, commanding what is right, and prohibiting what is wrong,' no well-intentioned person need be at all apprehensive of violating them unwittingly, even though they were written in Sanscrit."[7]

Cheeseman failed to grasp how the Hispanos were deceived by not having access to the laws in a language that they knew. Like many others, he had failed to realize that non-English laws "were not only useful but necessary for a better administration of justice."[8] He promoted English and deprecated Spanish, which doomed Spanish in territorial Colorado to a minority-language status.

Immediately, Byers editorialized in the *Rocky Mountain News* that appropriations for translations of statutes were an unnecessary expense, and he raised issues about patriotism, racism, language loyalty, and assimilation:

> Not more than a dozen or twenty officials require copies of the laws in Spanish, and they ought to be able to understand the laws in English. There is no demand for them by Spanish residents generally, any more than for the laws in English by other citizens. It seems to us to be bad policy to perpetuate separate nationalities among our citizens. It is for the interest of adopted citizens of all classes to become Americanized as rapidly as possible.[9]

A much worse expression of opposition to the Spanish provisions appeared in Byers's paper the following month, on March 16, 1870. Among other

The Southern Counties – The Oher Side

SAN LUIS RIVER
SAGUACHE COUNTY, CT
March 1, 1870

EDITORS NEWS: No public or enthusiastic demonstration was made on the arrival of the "colored members" from the territorial legislature! No joyful welcome greeted their return! And like degenerate curs they are writhing and squirming over their melancholy defeat, occasional by Gov. McCook's veto messages, and appropriately selected (like assassins) the hour of midnight to reach their ignominious dens! Why should the citizens of Colorado longer detain this mongrel race within their borders? What actual benefit are they to this territory? What actual benefit are they to this territory? We have no traffic and but little intercourse with them, their language is dissimilar as well as their religion. The translation of the laws entails heavy expense on the territory, and by referring to the territorial auditor's report (page 48) for the year ending December 31, 1869, you will find that the translation of the laws made in 1864, was at the enormous expense of $3,840; and the revenue contributed at that time by the counties of Huerfano, Costilla, and Conejos was only $3,792.92, just $2,046.08 less than the actual cost of said transaction. Again, the same report, (page 5), under the head of "delinquent taxes," you will find, that both, Costilla and Conejos counties do not occupy very envious positions! And as Gov. McCook justly states, in one of his message, they "do not in any way improve the condition of the territorial finances! Brought up in ignorance, they are destitute of all manly principles of honor and justice; their marketable votes will always prove a source of corruption in our legislation. Under the now ponding "Chaves bill," – lately introduced in congress – let us quietly permit them to take their exit from our borders! and return back to their first love, in New Mexico, where they properly belong! Inured to habits of indolence, there is no life, or energy among these people, which fact seriously retards the advancement and progress of this section of our territory. Who among us will mourn or deplore their departure? Adios! Conejos and Costilla.

Baden Weiler

FIGURE 8.1. Editorial of "Baden Weiler" against the inhabitants of the southern counties, *Rocky Mountain News*, March 16, 1870. This version was rekeyed for clarity.

comments, an author from Saguache County, using the German pen name of Baden Weiler, degraded the economic status of the Hispanos, their continued requests for the laws printed in Spanish, and the "enormous expense" for the territory to translate the laws. Weiler would just as soon have given the notch area of Conejos and Costilla Counties back to New Mexico. Editor Byers chose to publish Weiler's piece (figure 8.1).

The following paraphrases Weiler's comments: no one in Saguache County noticed "the return of the 'colored members' from the territorial legislature! No joyful welcome greeted their return!" Why should Colorado any longer "detain this mongrel race within [its] borders? What actual benefit are they to this territory?" We have little interaction with them, for "their language is dissimilar as well as their religion." Their taxes are delinquent,[10] and Governor McCook reports that Costilla and Conejos Counties "'do not in any way improve the condition of the territorial finances!' Brought up in ignorance, they are destitute of all manly principles of honor and justice; their marketable votes will always prove a source of corruption in our legislation." We should quietly allow them to leave Colorado "and return back to their first love, in New Mexico, where they properly belong! Inured to habits of indolence, there is no life, or energy among these people, which fact seriously retards the advancement and progress of this section of our territory. Who among us will mourn or deplore their departure? Adios! Conejos and Costilla."[11]

Weiler brings up the hotly contested issues of color, language, religion, and taxation. Regarding his reference to the issue of purchasing votes, Otto Mears of Saguache was known to have used dirty politics and questionable methods to gain votes. In 1866 Mears offered John Lawrence $500 to secure the Hispano vote to win the seat for the newly created Saguache County. Lawrence held out for $700. During another election, Mears distributed hams, bacon, and sacks of flour in exchange for votes.[12] His circle of friends included Fred Walsen, John Mayes Francisco, Lafayette Head, Nathan Russell, and Isaac Gotthelf.

Although Weiler promoted the Hispanos' return to New Mexico, he said nothing about returning their land by changing the territory's boundary line. Byers, a strong proponent of statehood, wrote that the boundary of the territory should remain as it is. Commenting on Weiler's letter, Byers wrote that his newspaper did not endorse the opinions or spirit of the correspondent, but that the United States would be united legally and socially under one language, the English language. Weiler exaggerated the evils of the Hispanos, Byers observed. In any case, his Anglo readers would in time see them improved and assimilated due to the population increase of the "Yankee element." The boundary of the territory as it was should therefore remain, Byers recommended, "and let us treat our Spanish citizens in a fair and friendly way, but without petting them for the sake of their votes. This is the policy of the republicans [*sic*] of the territory, as we understand it, and it is right and will bring success."[13]

During Colorado's first ten years as a territory, there were several reasons why its statutes had never been translated into Spanish: the territorial treasury had no funds, the territorial secretary refused the appropriation because he needed "direction" from the federal government, and the US treasurer erroneously believed that the Hispanos of southern Colorado were "foreign born."

In 1872, however, the territorial treasurer hired Spanish-national José Domínguez de Soto to translate the codified (indexed) laws of the first through ninth sessions.[14] The secretary hired the Denver printing company Dailey and Smart to publish 200 copies. A total of 860 pages were published in one hardbound, three-volume collection. The territorial librarian received the books in April 1873, when he sent the copies to "officers in the Spanish counties."[15] Unfortunately, someone discovered that two of the three volumes of statutes printed in Spanish omitted some statutes or parts of them. Historical records do not provide the volume number or indicate whether the problem was due to the clerk, territorial secretary, the translator, or the printing company. The Territorial House continued with its business and approved no additional funds to correct the volume.

During the 1874 legislature southern Colorado voters elected seven Hispanos to represent them in the Territorial House; only one was a member of the Republican Party. That session, the Territorial Assembly approved a resolution to translate and print fifty copies of the statutes. Secretary Hall refused the request in his letter to the Territorial Council, saying, "I am not authorized to print any part of your proceedings in the Spanish language."[16] No historical documents exist to tell how the Hispanos felt and what, if anything, they did in response to the territorial auditor's report, the Weiler letter, and the territorial secretary's decision. Certainly, the Hispanos would have considered their words and actions hurtful and insulting to their culture, language, and heritage.

TABLE 8.1. Interpreters in the Territorial Assembly

Name	Year	Interpreter	Council	House
E. B. Smith	1861	x		x
Charles A. Brassler	1861, 1862	x		x
Mr. Dubreuille	1862	x		x
Celestino Dominguez	1861	x		x
	1862		x	x
	1864		x	x
	1872	x	x	
	1876		x	x
E. P. Parker	1864	x		x
John Lawrence	1865	x	x	
	1874	x	x	
Henry Bell	1868	x	x	
Mariano Larragoite	1870	x	x	
Henry Vidal	1870	x		x
	1872	x		x
Jose Dominguez de Soto	1872		x	x
Silas Hawes	1874	x	x	
Albert R. Dyer	1874		x	x
	1876		x	x

Information compiled from legislative statutes, session laws, and journals and newspapers

The Right to Select the Interpreter

In 1874 the House hired Silas Hawes to interpret for the Spanish-speaking representatives from southern Colorado. Nine days into the session, Colorado Council member Juan Bautista Jáquez (Huerfano) sought to have Hawes replaced by Celestino Domínguez because Hawes was "not competent in Spanish and did not keep him posted on the proceedings." In return, Council president George Miles Chilcott (Pueblo) suggested that former Indian agent Lafayette Head (Conejos) interpret "any remarks Jaques [*sic*] might make."[17]

Hispano representatives trusted Celestino Domínguez to interpret for them, for Domínguez respected them, understood their language and customs, and helped them understand and communicate more effectively. He was inseparable from the Hispano representatives during discussion and debate in the legislature. Because Domínguez likely took on additional interpreting duties during informal conversations and in restaurants, Anglos likely became suspicious of his actions or motives. They may have questioned if Domínguez was, in effect, lobbying for his own personal interests and if he would maintain confidentiality and recuse himself from discussions that might create conflicts of interest.

As reported in the January 15, 1874, issue of the *Rocky Mountain News*, the following discussion took place in the Council Chamber to determine who might replace Silas Hawes as interpreter:

Hugh Butler (Gilpin) stated he did not want to "thrust the appointment upon the Mexican member"; however, he believed that "the Council had the right to exercise its judgment in selecting an interpreter."[18]

Then Rufus H. Clark (Arapahoe, Douglas) stated that "although Mr. Hawes understood Spanish he might not be qualified to act as interpreter."

Juan Bautista Jáquez then addressed the Council in Spanish. (The clerk did not identify who interpreted for him.)

> Mr. President: The opposition I manifest to the gentlemen is not because
> I have anything against him personally. I only consider that I come here as
> member of this honorable representative body to look after the welfare
> and interests of the whole territory as well as the county to which I belong.
> Inasmuch as none of the proceedings of this body have been properly
> explained to me, I hope you will take this reason into consideration and give
> me . . . an interpreter who will keep me well posted in regard to the bills and
> other matters going on in the Council.

Henry Pelham Holmes Bromwell (Arapahoe) added, "As Mr. Jaquez was a descendant of the oldest settlers of this country, and we were the newcomers . . . I believe the honorable member should have the right to decide who should interpret the proceedings for him."

Butler objected to the "spirit" of the resolution as it "assailed the character and skills of Silas Hawes." He continued, "Citizens down south should learn that they were citizens of Colorado and that the English language was the prevailing language of the country." He concluded by saying that in every session of the legislature, there had been "some difficulty about the interpreter."

Chilcott replied to Butler, saying, "The Mexicans were entitled to be represented and heard. They were here before we were." To which Butler quickly replied, "So were the Indians."

After the initial vote that ended in a tie, Butler verbally attacked Chilcott, stating that he knew of Chilcott's political aspirations to Congress and that Chilcott "needed the Mexican vote." Butler quickly retorted, "The sooner the Mexicans learn our language the better." Lafayette Head then moved to table the discussion to the following day "so as to require the committee to report on the matter."[19]

Unfortunately, the newspaper did not print a subsequent report about the interpreter issue. However, on January 19, 1874, by a ballot vote of eight to five, the Council selected John Lawrence (Conejos, Costilla) as its interpreter.[20] No doubt, between the time Councilman Head tabled the discussion and the session the following day, the Lawrence faction got together that evening to lobby for its selection and to secure the vote of a previously absent Council member.

Remarks by Jáquez, Butler, and Cheeseman are very important. Representative Jáquez wanted an effective and honest interpreter to alleviate future problems of miscommunication and misinterpretation. He wanted to work with a competent, loyal, and trustworthy interpreter and felt that he and other Hispano assemblymen had a right to select the interpreter. With regard to Hispanos learning English, they very well understood the importance of learning English, as it was the language of commerce, industry, politics, and education. The comments made in chamber by Hugh Butler and Nathaniel F. Cheeseman publicly ridiculed the intelligence and principles of all Hispano legislators and their constituents.

In addition to not being familiar with the needs of Hispano citizens, most nonnative Anglos who spoke Spanish did not understand the type of Spanish spoken in northern New Mexico and southern Colorado.[21] In June 1864 Samuel E. Brown, the attorney general for the territory, described San Luis as "an old Mexican Plaza [where we] live[d] on sheep and *chile colorau*" (red chile).[22] Here, Brown used the vernacular pronunciation of *colorado*. According to author Rubén Cobos, the fact that the Spanish spoken in the area has continued to use the archaic local Spanish dialect speaks to the strength of the language as an important and distinctive part of Hispano culture.[23]

To be effective, the interpreter had to be bilingual and have a working knowledge of public policy as exercised in the legislature. No records exist to document the interpreters' or translators' levels of experience in verbal and written communication. Sadly, only few translated documents have survived. In addition, surviving records do not prove that Hawes used any translation aids, such as a Spanish dictionary. Additionally, it is unknown if any Spanish dictionaries appeared in Colorado during the early period. At the time, the territory had not yet established a complete legislative library or any public libraries, and there was a scarcity of law books in general. During this time, the librarian also served as the territorial superintendent of common schools.[24]

Hugh Butler stated the Council had the right to exercise judgment in selecting an interpreter and that Jáquez had attacked the character and skills of Silas Hawes. Jáquez simply stated that Hawes did not properly explain the proceedings. Hawes was not doing the work the legislature had hired him to perform. Butler was correct when he asserted that there had been "some difficulty about the interpreter" in every session of the legislature, but for a different reason than he was suggesting: the assembly had not appropriated funds for or hired qualified interpreters.

The Contested Seat

In 1872 representative-elect Lorenzo Antonio Abeyta, a Democrat from Las Animas County, took his seat in the chamber. According to Major José Rafael Sotero Chacón, who had run against Abeyta on the Republican ticket, the election was filled with "fraud, bribery, and double voting." Chacón proposed that the county's Democratic Party had altered the election results and certified only its candidates.[25] Abeyta had served one month in office when Albert W. Archibald, a Republican attorney from Trinidad, met with his party's members in the House to contest the election.[26] Why Archibald contested, rather than Chacón the candidate, is not known. However, Abeyta and Archibald hired attorneys to present their cases before the House members. Abeyta hired a judge named Miller, and Archibald hired Judge Henry Pelham Holmes Bromwell.

On January 18, 1872, the chamber approved Abeyta's request to present certain papers relating to his contested seat.[27] House Speaker Alvin Marsh (Gilpin) then gave these papers and appointed Pedro Rafael Trujillo (Costilla), a Republican, to the Elections Committee. This committee, made up of members of the majority party, was asked to review the information and make its recommendations to the House at a later date. After learning that there would be a majority report, on January 27, J. M. Givins (El Paso, Pueblo) announced that the House Democrats would prepare its (minority party) report with its recommendation regarding the contested seat.[28] Givins presented the minority report on January 29. Then the speaker allowed Archibald, a private citizen, to speak on the floor on his behalf.[29]

The following day, the speaker permitted the judges for Abeyta and Archibald to speak before the House members. Judge Miller spoke for Abeyta's case; Judge Bromwell followed "in argument" for Archibald.[30] After the House clerk read both the majority and minority reports to the membership, George Engs Randolph (Gilpin), a Republican, stated that he thought Abeyta was entitled to the seat. He continued, emphasizing that if the members did not agree with his statement, "the house [*sic*] could . . . order a new election in Las Animas County."[31] Mariano Sísto Larragoite, who spoke English, and Casimiro Barela, both Las Animas County Democrats, presented their statements in support of Abeyta. Unfortunately, the editor of the *Rocky Mountain News* failed to publish any of Larragoite's and Barela's comments in either language.

On January 31 Archibald was again given the "privilege of translating his address in Spanish for the benefit of the representatives of the Latin race."[32] According to the *Rocky Mountain News*, Archibald spoke for two hours, sometimes in Spanish for "the benefit of the Mexican members."[33] Neither the House Journal or any newspapers reported whether Abeyta was offered or allowed equal time to speak either in Spanish or in English through an interpreter. Abeyta, however, then followed with a request that a commission issue subpoenas to testify about the election; the request, presumably through the interpreter, was refused.[34] In a House vote that same day Abeyta lost his seat to Archibald by four votes.[35]

The majority party seems to have changed the House rules in their favor by allowing three citizens (Archibald, Judge Miller, and Judge Bromwell) to speak in the chamber. It allowed Archibald, a private citizen, to speak on the floor of its chamber in both languages. Presumably he spoke just enough Spanish to prove to members of both parties that he was proficiently bilingual. (Interestingly, two years later the House would be discussing an English-only issue.)

This incident is an excellent example of the tactics the majority party used to assure political inequality and inequity. The majority party willingly took the seat from the Hispano Democrat and gave it to an Anglo Republican.

It did not allow Abeyta to represent himself adequately through his attorney or his translator. The House did not need the extra Republican seat, as that party's majority status was never in question. Was the seat offered to former candidate Chacón before considering Archibald's candidacy? How did Trujillo, the only Hispano Republican, feel about how his party handled the situation? Unfortunately, we do not know.

However through its parliamentary tactics, the House used partisan politics to punish the Las Animas Democratic election judges for allowing "fraud, deceit, and abuse" in an election.[36] Although Randolph advocated for voter rights, his party ignored his suggestion and denied Las Animas County voters the right to elect its party's replacement. This power play clearly disenfranchised Las Animas County voters. The decision in the House had been made by men who did not represent them and had no concern for their needs. These voters had no voice in the decision the majority party made. And, for Abeyta, as if the contested seat state of affairs was not distressing enough, seven years later he and Archibald became brothers-in-law once they married daughters of Reprepresentative Felipe de Jesús Baca (Las Animas).

Shaping Views via News Reporting

Editors solicited letters and reports about information from all parts of the territory.[37] Some men used pen names to protect their identities: "A" was US deputy marshal George O. Austin, "Dornick" was Wilbur Fisk Stone, "Baden Weiler" was a German from Saguache County, and "TENDO" was a correspondent to the *Pueblo Daily Chieftain* in 1873. William James Godfroy, who served as Lafayette Head's secretary at Conejos, also sent letters containing newsworthy items to newspapers. William D. Dawson, who wrote about his trip from Santa Fe north through the San Luis Valley to Fort Garland and Denver, used the pen name "WDD." John Lawrence submitted letters to newspapers in which he passed "local gossip."[38] Their "embellished and manufactured facts" were edited by newspapers to sell papers.[39]

During the early part of the territorial period, many events took place in southern Colorado that newspapers and their correspondents attributed solely to the issue of taxation. However, they failed to write about other key issues of the time. They were not concerned that the Spanish-speaking citizens did not have access to the laws of the territory, that they did not understand what the tax money was for, that several Hispanos had been mysteriously killed, that their land was systematically being taken from them, or that the US Army was interested in confiscating their harvests and livestock for the war effort. They simply did not care about these citizens, nor did they care why these citizens were unhappy being in Colorado. The Hispanos wanted to be back under the jurisdiction of New Mexico, where they understood the laws, where their representatives were treated with respect, where their religion was not ridiculed, and where their customs were not questioned. Instead, these correspondents reported that the Hispanos met in secrecy and were planning an insurrection because they did not want to pay taxes. To Anglo readers, the Hispanos were not assimilated citizens, with proper civic mindedness, and in consequence were frequently suspected of being deviously un-American.

Due to the legislation passed during Colorado's first territorial session, Hispanos in Conejos and Costilla Counties held meetings to voice their concern about the enacted statutes. Despite their petitions to be reannexed to New Mexico Territory, Congress unjustly kept them in Colorado at the expense of their Hispano "ancestry, nativity, and association" to New Mexico. Curiously, Hispanos in Costilla County were just as unhappy about taxation and prejudice and met to discuss similar issues, including the return to New Mexico. So why did these newspaper correspondents only concentrate on issues in Conejos County? Unfortunately, we will never know.

Anglo newspaper editors in Denver, Pueblo, Colorado Springs, Del Norte, and Walsenburg continued to berate Hispanos for retaining their language, customs, traditions, and religion. Many correspondents and editors wrote disparaging comments, referring to Hispanos as "greasers and mongrels of little worth, honor and intelligence."[40] Men like Byers and Stone wrote pejorative and bigoted racist reports about the Hispanos. Both men devalued Hispano culture, religion, and language; they promoted anti-Hispano and anti-indigenous attitudes, and they openly endorsed mob vigilante action. Yet many of this type of citizen became noted men in Colorado history.

On March 19, 1863, Byers published a report from an anonymous correspondent from Fort Garland that suggested "the Greasers" were sworn to pay their taxes "with the rifle."[41] Byers suggested that these "Greasers" failed in their civic duty to pay their taxes and therefore were not "good Americans." It is perhaps a mitigating circumstance, however, that at this time the territorial statutes had not been translated into Spanish. Because the Hispanos were not properly informed in a language they understood, they were being taxed without proper representation. When Anglo miners had refused to pay taxes imposed by the Jefferson Territorial Assembly, they were viewed as citizens exercising their rights. Yet when Hispanos questioned equitable taxation as citizens of the Territory of Colorado, they were branded as disloyal citizens who refused to assimilate in language and norms.

By continuing to publicize the foreignness of the Hispano people, newspaper editors effectively promoted laws that created obstacles to political participation based on language, culture, and religion. Editors and their correspondents directed their articles to potential Anglo immigrants, feeding a nativist sentiment that gave rise to many restrictive laws to maintain a national identity based on Anglo language and culture. Ironically, of course, the attitudes of the Anglo immigrants against those who were "foreign born" were directed against the indigenous peoples who were truly the natives of the region. This nativism, the practice of opposition to the indigenous and Hispanos on the grounds of their foreignness, encouraged a society in territorial Colorado that treated non-English speakers as second-class citizens.

Issues over Sheep, a County Seat, and a Road Tax

In 1861 the territorial legislature passed a law preventing imported stock from grazing in Colorado, more specifically in Conejos and Costilla Counties. The law was intended to keep Colorado's grasses for Colorado livestock. Further, the residents of Conejos and Costilla Counties could not contract for the grazing of any stock. This law did not apply to ranchers with larger holdings or to persons lawfully engaged in driving or selling stock in Colorado Territory, none of whom were Hispano at the time.

The Hispanos in Conejos, Costilla, and Huerfano Counties were predominantly sheep raisers by custom and necessity. Sheep became an exchange commodity for their meat as well as their wool; in a no-cash economy sheep were a means of money.[42] According to a military report submitted by Colonel Archibald Gillespie in 1863, approximately 35,000 sheep grazed on "fine grasses in the mountain parks and valleys" in Conejos County.[43] The Hispano settlers continued to disregard the grazing law and moved livestock from New Mexico into Conejos for pasturage and protection. Within their small settlements, they occasionally pastured their herds nearby to protect them from theft, inclement weather, and wolves and coyotes.

In 1864 an unidentified US military officer reported that "Mexican shepherds have for years driven their numerous flocks . . . to and from . . . [this] favorite range."[44] This grazing law targeted the tradition and custom used by the Hispanos settlers in the movement and grazing of their livestock in the far northern frontier. Although the law was needed to protect livestock from disease and infection, many Hispanos could not afford to pay the fine imposed on them and, if incarcerated, could not provide for their family's welfare. By law, the justice of the peace issued a warrant to the county sheriff, whereupon the sheriff arrested the alleged lawbreakers and brought them before the district judge.[45] The penalty for violation was a fine between one and five dollars for each head of contracted stock. Owners or herders found in violation of the law faced a twenty-five-dollar fine for each day in violation; further, the county impounded the livestock until the owner paid the fine. Little cash was available in the far northern frontier. To pay their taxes or fines in hard cash, settlers faced three alternatives: they could sell some of their livestock or land, obtain a loan from a merchant or wealthy neighbor, or enter a son or daughter into a contract for labor or debt peonage.

Laws such as those regulating imported stock and grazing created discord within the communities in the New Mexico and Colorado Territories. Neighbors could report to county officials the infractions of neighbors and, by so doing, earn some badly needed cash. By law, informants were to receive half the amount of the fines levied against the violators of the law.[46] This action of informing on neighbors undermined sentiments of *comunidád*, positive actions for the benefit of community.

In 1864 the Territorial Council discussed and passed a bill regarding the pasturing of sheep within certain towns and villages. According to the new law, to protect their sheep, owners could not keep or pasture more than twenty sheep for more than one week within two miles of Denver, Golden, or any town or village in Costilla or Huerfano Counties. As with the previous law, owners or herders found in violation of the law faced a twenty-five-dollar fine for each day in violation; further, the county impounded the sheep until the owner paid the fine.[47] Legislators favoring this bill failed to realize that, in the southern frontier counties, the reason for owners to keep their flocks nearby would be to protect them from danger or theft. While it is difficult to imagine more than twenty sheep within the city limits of Denver or Golden, just ten years earlier settlers of the Guadalupe plaza periodically herded their livestock inside the protective circular plaza to protect their animals.[48] Any loss of livestock due to weather, raids, and predators could force many sheep raisers into debt.

During the lambing season in April 1865, some Costilla County settlers grew fearful about anticipated raids by indigenous bands. Pedro Durán and several other men petitioned their county commissioners "to pasture their herds near the settlements . . . due to anticipated Indian troubles." The commissioners supported the citizens' request and allowed them to break the territorial law—a law that was unsuited to the realities of sheep herding in the southern counties.[49] In sharp contrast to the territorial legislators, the southern county officials acted on the clear priority to protect the livelihoods of the local Hispano residents.

Due to limited funds resulting from expenditures under the former administration of Governor William Gilpin, the 1863 legislative session was canceled. Information about this cancellation appeared in English-language newspapers; however, it is not certain that the voters and county officials clearly understood the impact of the decision. During a Conejos County election in 1863, voters elected to change the county seat from the town of Conejos to the town of Servilleta.[50] At the time, Servilleta, located northwest of the town of Conejos, was the county's largest settlement. County officials and citizens rejoiced when it received the majority vote. To the voters, this location as county seat made sense as, effective in 1864, the Third Judicial District would hold court in Servilleta. The Conejos County officials had held this election based on the benefit it would provide to the county and its community. They were acting in accordance with what they thought was best for their community.

The voters soon learned that their election was not sanctioned by the territorial assembly, which had the only authority to select a county's seat of government; territorial officials therefore refused to recognize the county's selection of Servilleta as the new county seat. Unknowingly, county clerk Manuel Lucero, who presumably received no instructions in Spanish, failed to keep a register of voters.[51]

The Roads and Highways Act, passed by the Colorado Assembly in 1864, authorized county commissioners to levy a property tax (fifty cents on each one hundred dollars) for the maintenance of county roads and the construction and maintenance of county bridges.[52] Businesses and the military alike needed better roads to move goods and people throughout the new territory, and better roads in the mountains also provided miners better access to precious ores. By this law, each able-bodied man between the ages of eighteen and fifty paid an annual five-dollar tax. In lieu of payment, a man could provide two days' labor on his county's public highways.[53] The tax did not apply to incorporated cities or towns, but at this time Conejos and Costilla Counties had no incorporated towns, so their residents were not exempt from the tax, although residents of Denver, for example, were exempted. The law considered any person delinquent in his tax if he neglected to pay or refused to work. After ten days of nonpayment, the overseer could levy a fine and auction any property owned by the delinquent taxpayer.

The law provided each road overseer with a list of the men in his district who were subject to the road tax. He was responsible for collecting each man's road tax or calling for laborers. Those men scheduled to work on roads or bridges had to supply their own tools. On February 24, 1864, Representative José Víctor García (Conejos, Costilla) sought to exempt Conejos and Costilla Counties from the Roads and Highways Act. For generations, the Hispanos had participated in a barter society, in which there was a chronic lack of cash. The scarcity of cash meant they were unlikely to pay the road tax in cash; they would have to pay with their labor. The majority of these road and bridge laborers would have been Hispano men, whose labor was needed at home during the planting and growing seasons, which were so important to them and their family's well-being. In effect, because they could not pay their taxes in cash, they would be performing manual labor to build roads intended mainly for the miners instead of working their family farms. Unfortunately, García's only support came from southern Colorado's territorial representatives, José Pablo Antonio de Jesús Ortega (Conejos) and Norton W. Welton (Costilla).[54]

Notes

1. *House Journal of the Legislative Assembly of the Territory of Colorado, Ninth Session, Convened at Denver, on the 1st Day of January, 1872* (Central City: D. C. Collier, 1872), January 29 and 30, 1872, 120, 127 (relating to Abeyta). Hereafter cited as *General Laws of the Territory of Colorado, 1872*.

2. Murray, "Supreme Court of Colorado Territory," 28.

3. Galindo and Vigil, "Language Restrictionism Revisited," 41, 43.

4. Fernandez, *Biography of Casimiro Barela*, xxxiv.

5. *Council Journal of the Legislative Assembly of the Territory of Colorado, Eighth Session, Convened at Denver, January 3, 1870*, January 4, 1870, 69–70 (relating to Cheeseman audit). Hereafter cited as *Council Journal of the Territory of Colorado, 1870*.

6. Fedynskyj, "State Session Laws in Non-English Languages." 473–74.

7. *Council Journal of the Territory of Colorado, Eighth Session, 1870*, January 4, 1870, 70 (relating to Cheeseman audit).

8. Fedynskyj, "State Session Laws in Non-English Languages," 477 (referring to *Proceedings of the Constitutional Convention of Colorado of 1875–1876*).

9. Baden Weiler, "The Southern Counties—The Other Side," *Rocky Mountain News*, February 7, 1870, 1–2.

10. "The translation of the laws entails heavy expense on the territory, and by referring to the territorial auditor's report (page 48) for the year ending December 31, 1869, you will find that the translation of the laws made in 1864, was at the enormous expense of $5,840; and the revenue contributed at that time by the counties of Huérfano, Costilla, and Conejos was only $3,792.92, just $2,046.08 less than the actual cost of said transaction." Weiler, "The Southern Counties—The Other Side," "Daily News," *Rocky Mountain News*, March 16, 1870.

11. Ibid.

12. Martin, *Frontier Eyewitness*, 83; Tucker, *Otto Mears and the San Juans*, 14; Ellis, *Life of an Ordinary Woman*, 17.

13. Weiler, "The Southern Counties—The Other Side," *Rocky Mountain News*, March 16, 1870 (regarding Byers' response to Weiler's editorial).

14. In 1868 José Domínguez de Soto advertised that he was starting a Spanish-language class. *Rocky Mountain News*, April 3, 1868, 4. De Soto was also known as Joseph H. de Soto. Erickson, *Early Justice and the Formation of the Colorado Bar*, 50. Although he was a trained lawyer, de Soto was not admitted to practice in Colorado because he did not have a license. According to Erickson, de Soto lived in Peru before coming to Denver; his son Emilio D. de Soto became a prominent Colorado lawyer.

15. *Rocky Mountain News Weekly*, April 23, 1873, 2.

16. *Council Journal of the Legislative Assembly of the Territory of Colorado, Tenth Session, Convened at Denver on the 5th Day of January 1874* (Central City: Register Printing

House, 1874), January 7, 1874, 39–41 (relating to Hall's refusal to print any part of the proceedings in Spanish).

17. Ibid., January 19, 1874, 76–78 (relating to selection of interpreter). Hereafter cited as *Council Journal of the Territory of Colorado, 1874*.

18. Butler, from Scotland, immigrated to the United States in 1853 and became a wealthy Gilpin County attorney. 1870 Gilpin County Census, p. 6, Schedule 1, Central City, Colorado, line 2, Household/Dwelling 63, ancestry.com.

19. "Warm Discussion on the Interpreter Question in the Colorado Council," *Rocky Mountain News*, January 15, 1874.

20. *Council Journal of the Territory of Colorado, Tenth Session, 1874*, January 19, 1874, 76–78, and January 20, 1874, 79–80 (relating to selection of interpreter).

21. Cobos, *Dictionary*, viii.

22. NARA, College Park, MD, "Conflict between Civil and Military," S. E. Brown, US Attorney, June 8, 1864, Colorado Territory, RG 60, entry 9, box 1, folder 2.

23. Cobos, *Dictionary*, xvi.

24. *General Laws of the Territory of Colorado, 1861*, November 6, 1861, 110–13. Denver's first public library was established in a wing of Denver High School in June 1889. Denver Public Library website, https://www.denverlibrary.org/content/dpl-history, accessed April 10, 2016.

25. Meketa, *Legacy of Honor*, 322–23.

26. *House Journal of the Territory of Colorado, Ninth Session, 1872*, January 29 and 30, 1872, 120, 127.

27. Ibid., January 18, 1872, 65–66.

28. Ibid., January 27, 1872, 117.

29. Ibid., January 29 and 30, 1872, 120, 127.

30. Ibid., January 30, 1872, 126, 134.

31. *Rocky Mountain News*, February 1, 1872.

32. *House Journal of the Territory of Colorado, Ninth Session, 1872*, January 31, 1872, 139–40.

33. *Rocky Mountain News*, February 1, 1872.

34. *House Journal of the Territory of Colorado, Ninth Session, 1872*, January 29, 1872, 134.

35. *Rocky Mountain News*, February 1, 1872. See also *House Journal of the Legislative Assembly of the Territory of Colorado, Ninth Session, . . . 1872*, January 29–31, 1872, 140.

36. *General Laws of the Territory of Colorado, 1861*, November 6, 1861, sec. 19, 76–77 (regarding oath of judges and clerks). The subject of their punishment is outside the scope of this discussion.

37. Price, *Season of Terror*, 42.

38. Simmons, *Ute Indians of Utah*, 134. Other correspondents included R. Berry and Hugh Murdock. Price, *Season of Terror*, 39.

39. According to Janet Lecompte, many of Byers's stories were "pure fabrication." Lecompte, "Sand Creek," 320.

40. "The Copperhead Organization," *Daily Rocky Mountain News*, November 7, 1866, 1.

41. *Rocky Mountain News*, March 19, 1863, 3, col. 3.

42. Lambert, *Wooden Canvas*, 7. No agricultural records exist regarding the number of pure Churro sheep introduced into southern Colorado during the territorial period.

43. NARA, Washington, DC, Adjutant General's Office, Letters Received, Department of New Mexico, Major A. H. Gillespie to Captain B. C. Cutler, January 20, 1863, M1120, Roll 19. See also House of Representatives, "Lines of Communication between Colorado and New Mexico," 20 (reference to the Committee on Appropriations).

44. House of Representatives, "Lines of Communication between Colorado and New Mexico," 20.

45. Of the few surviving records from the Third District, none is associated with this law.

46. *General Laws of the Territory of Colorado, 1861*, November 6, 1861, 133.

47. In 1864 the Territorial House passed a law "prohibiting the pasturing of animals within limits of Denver or Golden, or any Town or Village in Costilla or Huerfano Counties." "Memorandum from Council Chamber to House," February 25, 1864, *House Journal of the Territory of Colorado, 1864*, 132 (Act for the Protection of Sheep and to Prohibit Pasturing the Same in Certain Localities).

48. Hart Library, History Colorado Center, Colorado Writers Project, PAM 349/10, 40.

49. Commissioner Meeting Minutes, April 3, 1865, Costilla County Courthouse, San Luis, Colorado.

50. Hispanos settled Servilleta as the first of the summer settlements. Colville, *La Vereda*, 241.

51. Hall, *History of the State of Colorado*, 4:95, 99.

52. *General Laws of the Territory of Colorado, 1870*, March 11, 1864, 127–29 (act concerning roads and highways).

53. Ibid.

54. House of Representatives, "Lines of Communication between Colorado and New Mexico," 18 (referring to the Committee on Appropriations).

9

Statehood Initiatives

A number of applications for statehood were proposed for Colorado Territory. Some initiatives were defeated in elections by the citizens of the territory, whereas others were approved in Colorado but then defeated either initially by the vote of Congress or subsequently by presidential veto.

National politics played strongly into the question of Colorado statehood. During the Civil War, Colorado statehood was advanced by Republicans who sought to create new states in the West, hoping thereby to gain electoral votes in the 1864 elections and support for legislation from the new western senators and representatives in Congress. After the war, there was less urgency for promoting Colorado to statehood. A major objection raised repeatedly was that Colorado lacked the requisite population to qualify for statehood.

Petitions for statehood that were initiated in 1864, 1865, and 1867 failed in Washington, but President Ulysses S. Grant signed a bill in 1876 admitting Colorado to the Union.

DOI: 10.5876/9781607329145.c009

Colorado Statehood and the Hispano Vote

In 1863, during the Thirty-Seventh Congress, the Senate discussed admission of Colorado to the Union. It killed the bill for two main reasons. First, Colorado's population had not sufficiently increased since its 1861 census. For a territory to be nominated for statehood, its population had to have reached 60,000 free residents. Second, its citizens had not expressed an interest in statehood, as they had not petitioned for statehood.

The following year, in June, Coloradoans elected delegates to create a state constitution. The territory was only three years old and had had its share of internal, military, and congressional issues. Many of the delegates who met in convention in Golden a month later were concerned that statehood would introduce higher taxes. To address the argument, the convention's presiding officer introduced a lower salary schedule for the territory's officials. As proposed, the territorial secretary would earn $1,000 a year, the attorney general $400 a year, and legislators would earn $3.00 each day while in session.[1] Territorial legislative sessions did not exceed forty days, except for the first one, which lasted sixty days. For those legislators who had to rely on their farm earnings to cover the exorbitant living expenses in towns like Denver and Golden, statehood was not that important. During the 1864 territorial election that September, voters and "political dissidents, including Democrats and cost-conscious leaders," defeated the initiative for a state constitution. The Hispanos' vote was a political force; collectively they defeated the statehood attempt due to their discontent at being retained within Colorado.[2]

Counting on the Congress to confer statehood upon Colorado in 1865, territorial officials prepared for an election of several offices. Fifty-five delegates from eleven of the territory's seventeen counties attended the constitutional convention held in Denver; no delegates were from Conejos County or Costilla County.[3]

Almost immediately, news editors began endorsing candidates. The editor of an unidentified paper printed an endorsement in Spanish. He promoted the reelection of President Abraham Lincoln (figure 9.1).[4] Like many other editors, he backed a state constitution for Colorado, then he listed his endorsements of candidates for office, including Colonel John Milton Chivington for delegate to Congress. Interestingly, this editor printed Chivington's endorsement above that of the governor and then again at the bottom of the list.

In his letter to Governor John Evans in June 1864, Samuel E. Brown, the attorney general for the territory, discussed Chivington's use of force. Brown hoped the governor would "adopt" measures to keep Chivington's "assumption of power" in check: "If the Military of Colorado Territory is to be superior to the Civil [authority], if men's lives are to be wantonly destroyed and [prisoners are] to be forcibly taken from the civil authorities that state of society in this region will soon become dangerous to loyal citizens and to government."[5]

Brown's prediction came true on November 29, when Chivington led his forces against the peaceful Arapaho and Cheyenne at Sand Creek. Indigenous women and children were murdered at the hands of the Third Colorado Volunteers, whose specific mission was to kill Indians. This regiment returned to Denver with ears, fingers, scalps, and body parts as trophies. Territorial secretary Samuel H. Elbert publicly supported Chivington's actions at Sand Creek as "a deserved chastisement."[6] Nonetheless, both Chivington and Evans were investigated and then chastised by the government and the territory. But Chivington had already left the service and was immune from punishment. For his part in the massacre and for then lying about it, Evans resigned the governorship on July 18, 1865, at the request of President Andrew Johnson.[7]

John McCannon, leader of the California Gulch posse, commanded Company I of the Third Colorado Regiment. He and his

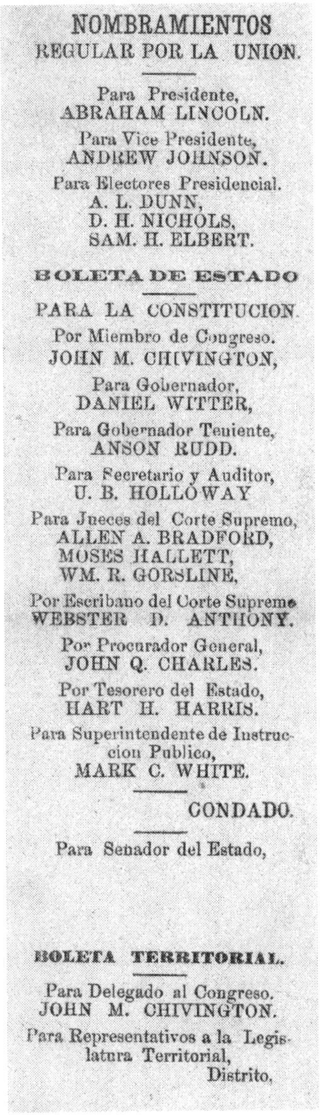

NOMBRAMIENTOS
REGULAR POR LA UNION.

Para Presidente,
ABRAHAM LINCOLN.
Para Vice Presidente,
ANDREW JOHNSON.
Para Electores Presidencial.
A. L. DUNN,
D. H. NICHOLS,
SAM. H. ELBERT.

BOLETA DE ESTADO

PARA LA CONSTITUCION.
Por Miembro de Congreso.
JOHN M. CHIVINGTON,
Para Gobernador,
DANIEL WITTER,
Para Gobernador Teniente,
ANSON RUDD.
Para Secretario y Auditor,
U. B. HOLLOWAY
Para Jueces del Corte Supremo,
ALLEN A. BRADFORD,
MOSES HALLETT,
WM. R. GORSLINE,
Por Escribano del Corte Supremo
WEBSTER D. ANTHONY.
Por Procurador General,
JOHN Q. CHARLES.
Por Tesorero del Estado,
HART H. HARRIS.
Para Superintendente de Instruccion Publica,
MARK C. WHITE.

CONDADO.

Para Senador del Estado,

BOLETA TERRITORIAL.

Para Delegado al Congreso.
JOHN M. CHIVINGTON,
Para Representativos a la Legislatura Territorial,
Distrito,

FIGURE 9.1. Newspaper endorsement of Union candidates, 1864. Denver Public Library, Western History and Genealogy Department, C324.609788 N728 1864.

company participated in the Sand Creek Massacre "with great celerity and success." Years later McCannon still defended the massacre and insisted that "600 or 700 hostiles were justifiably killed."[8]

Territorial governors were appointed by the president, but state governors were elected by a state's citizens. On the hope that in the coming election Colorado Territory citizens would vote for statehood, gubernatorial candidates ran for office to become the first governor of the state of Colorado. Among the candidates vying for governor was William Gilpin. Although President Lincoln had removed him from office in 1862, Gilpin continued residing in Colorado to promote his land-speculating scheme in the San Luis Valley.[9] On Election Day, November 14, 1865, Costilla County voters supported Gilpin, while voters in Conejos and Huerfano Counties selected other candidates. Gilpin's majority vote in this county was likely due to promises he had made about investment returns and growth of his Costilla Estates. However, because voters, including Hispanos from the southern counties, rejected statehood, the votes cast for governor were of no consequence. For the office of territorial delegate Chivington received only four votes![10] When the votes were tallied, George Miles Chilcott was named delegate, although Costilla County was the only Hispano-populated county that Chilcott won.

The abstract of voters for the 1865 election shows a Mr. Velásquez as one of six candidates for a justice vacancy on the territorial supreme court. Information about him and his candidacy does not appear in any historical records; however, the majority of his voters lived in Arapahoe and Boulder Counties. He received 880 votes in Arapahoe County, 122 votes in Boulder County, and 86 votes in Huerfano County. For both Conejos and Costilla Counties, he received a total of 14 votes![11] The number of votes Velásquez received is interesting because there was not any sizeable population of Hispanos living in Arapahoe and Boulder Counties. How did those voters know about him? Who was he and did the Hispanos in the southern counties know about his candidacy and his stands on issues important to them?

During the Thirty-Ninth Congress in 1866, the Senate voted against Colorado statehood by three votes. Senator George Franklin Edmunds (Vermont) cast a "no" vote based on his regard for the title of indigenous land and his opinion that the United States had no right to enter Indian Territory; he felt no "white man had a right to live west of the Mississippi."[12] In April, when a motion was made to have that vote reconsidered, Senator Charles Sumner

(Massachusetts) questioned the statehood bill on several counts: Colorado's population was small, its miners were transient, its proposed constitution disfranchised black voters, and the territory displayed little evident enthusiasm for statehood.

Two years later, in 1867, some Anglo citizens of the territory reactivated the notion of statehood and submitted petitions to Congress. According to Lafayette Head, "In some of the [southern] counties these petitions were signed by nearly every citizen." However, none of the signatures included the citizens of Conejos and Costilla Counties.[13] Although the Thirty-Ninth Congress passed the bill approving statehood for Colorado, President Andrew Johnson vetoed it for a number of reasons—including, this time, the fact that it *did* provide for negro suffrage and its population was too small. Johnson was also facing an impeachment trial and did not trust John Evans or Jerome Chaffee, who would have become US senators sitting in judgment of him had Colorado achieved statehood. A congressional attempt at overriding the veto failed.[14]

For a host of reasons, most centrally a high degree of factionalism among leading businessmen, the cause for Colorado statehood went into a stall; no bills for the proposition were introduced from the Fortieth to the Forty-Third Congresses.[15] By this time, Colorado's population had increased to 39,868 persons. The Colorado–New Mexico border continued to be an issue.

In 1867, the Colorado Territorial Legislature provoked New Mexico by petitioning for authority to annex the Moreno Mine diggings in its Cimarron area. New Mexico's assemblymen asked Congress not to give "any attention" to the bid and suggested in response that Congress instead reconsider restoring "that portion of the Territory of Colorado which formerly belonged to her [New Mexico]."[16] Neither proposal went anywhere.

The following year Henry Moore Teller of Weld County traveled to Washington, DC, to address the Senate to lobby against Colorado's admission into the Union under Senate Bill No. 11. On February 20, 1868, Teller's resolution "against the admission of Colorado as a State into the Union" was read before the Senate. Here Teller cited the territory's limited population and stated that that people of Colorado did not "renew their application for admission" as proposed to the Committee on Territories by Governor Evans and Delegate Chaffee. Teller mentioned that in 1865, during a convention held to ratify a constitution, none of the sixty-two delegates was from the counties of Conejos, Costilla, El Paso, Huerfano, or Pueblo.[17] Not one Spanish-surnamed delegate was selected to represent the Hispanos at this important and historic convention, leaving the Hispanos unrepresented.

Back home in Colorado, a dozen infuriated men, which included William James Godfroy and Indian agents Lafayette Head and D. C. Oaks, immediately sent a ten-page petition to the US Senate denouncing Teller for misrepresenting himself as chair of the Republican Central Committee and for including exaggerated, unreliable, and erroneous information in his resolution.[18] Teller further angered his opponents when he told the Senate that the production of gold in the territory had steadily decreased and was now less than half that reported in 1864. He also stated that Evans and Chaffee had included "certain resolutions" associated with the railroad and an annexation of a portion of Dakota Territory to add to Colorado's population and thus "secure admission of Colorado with its present boundary."[19] Ultimately, Colorado's population was "still too amorphous and its resources too underdeveloped to make its [political] parties and [quest for] statehood feasible." Additionally, the Senate was concerned about the suffrage question in that the territory denied the vote to African Americans.[20]

In 1872 leaders in the northern half of Colorado Territory "allowed their imaginations to have full swing" with ideas about how to attain the requisite population. Chaffee explored the idea of getting the northern boundary of Colorado moved north to include land south of the present Interstate 80 corridor. This area would have included the areas such as Cheyenne, Fort Laramie, and the Union Pacific east-west railways in present-day Wyoming. His idea would have solved the Colorado population issue; additionally, Colorado would have had a solid tax base in the Union Pacific Railway.[21] The remaining part of Wyoming Territory could be "distributed piece meal" among Utah, Montana, Idaho, and Dakota. "This plan would work to a charm, the people of Wyoming could not fail to be satisfied, the requisite population would be secured, the balance of power would be retained by the Denver men in the northern part of Colorado Territory."[22]

News about Colorado looking for ways to increase its population got New Mexico's attention. In New Mexico on May 12, 1872, Colonel José Francisco Chaves led a meeting in Albuquerque held by New Mexico statehood advocates. The attendees "resolved to do all in their power, by all honorable means, to defeat the alarming scheme set on foot by . . . Colorado to annex six of [New Mexico's] most populous counties . . . so as to secure [Colorado's] admission as a State." According to the resolution, New Mexico hoped to "prevent [its] people, relations, and interests from becoming separated, divided and made tributary to a neighboring Territory."[23] Nine days later the *Denver Daily Times* reported that New Mexico had no need to be alarmed: no Coloradoan "hanker[ed] after a slice of New Mexico, even to insure admission as a State."[24]

Chafee failed to interest the House Committee on Territories in adopting a statehood bill in 1872; however, he lobbied for the issue while Colorado newspapers popularized the need for statehood. Business and political leaders also lobbied President Ulysses S. Grant. While the House supported an enabling act in 1874, the Senate tabled it. Ultimately, Chafee got an enabling act passed through Congress, which the president signed, in 1875.[25]

Due to racism and many obstacles to the political process, Hispanos in the southern counties rejected statehood attempts initiated in 1864, 1865, and 1867. Although statehood would result in increased taxes, taxation was not their sole reason for rejecting statehood. Hispanos voted to reject statehood initiatives and to inform the governor and his Anglo-dominated assembly that they were not pleased with laws that penalized and degraded them.[26]

The 1875 Constitutional Convention

On October 25, 1875, members of a Constitutional Convention were elected. These thirty-nine delegates assembled at Denver for a fourth attempt at statehood with petitions from citizens who wanted to keep religion out of territorial government. The petition called for a tax on all ecclesiastical property, only public money would be used to pay prison chaplains or assist sectarian charities, and public schools could not use the Bible. Specifically, the petitioners asked for an end to any Sabbath and Christian morality laws. The ideals in this petition were in contrast to the manner in which Hispanos had lived under Spanish and Mexican rule for over 277 years in which the Catholic Church dealt with laws of morality. Part of the heated debate centered on the financing of parochial schools.[27] As in the territorial assembly's chambers, Catholic Hispano convention delegates were outnumbered by non-Catholics. The constitution included prohibitions against religious education and integrated schools for African Americans.

President Grant in 1875 called attention to the rapid increase in church property and raised the question whether it was a church or a corporation. Among the number of petitions presented to the convention delegates was a "strongly anti-clerical petition. It supported taxation of church property but thought no chaplains should be employed in state institutions; that the Bible not be read in the public schools; and the enactment of no laws enforcing the observance of the Sabbath."[28]

Feeling statehood near, in the Colorado Territorial Assembly on January 18, 1876, the Hispano assemblymen introduced a resolution providing for the publication of the constitution and laws in Spanish. After the failure of the statehood initiatives of 1864, 1865, and 1867, territorial officials began to understand that the Hispanos would not support any statehood initiative until they received the territorial statutes in Spanish. Territorial Council member Casimiro Barela (Las Animas) said:

> If Colorado is made a state, its progress will be undeniable. This is good, so be it, but it [the statehood vote] needs the residents of southern Colorado to succeed. These inhabitants need the publication of the laws in Spanish for a sufficient amount of time so that, if not they themselves, their children will know the English language. If more cannot be had, then we must ask that the laws be published in Spanish for a period of twenty-five years, and, in return, the people of southern Colorado will lend their support so that the Territory might be made a state.[29]

During the Constitution Convention meeting held in Denver on January 10, 1876, Delegate Hough offered a resolution "that all laws, decrees, regulations and provisions which from their nature require publication shall be published in English and Spanish." Delegate Samuel H. Elbert amended the resolution to include German. Seven days later, Delegates Adam D. Cooper (Fremont) and Willard B. Felton (Saguache) introduced an amendment that placed a time limit on publication in Spanish "until the year 1900."[30]

Most historians credit Barela for the translation of the Colorado Constitution into Spanish and later into German. Although Barela presented the historic legislation for the translation of the state constitution, the translations of territorial statutes were not the result of one man but of the combined efforts of those Hispano territorial assemblymen who preceded him.

A Colorado Constitutional Convention was finally held in Denver on February 29, 1876. The selected male delegates convened in the Odd Fellows' Hall of the First National Bank building, located on the northeast corner of Fifteenth and Blake Streets. There the delegates constructed a constitution modeled after the Illinois state constitution and the US Constitution and Bill of Rights.[31] The three Hispano delegates, all Democrats from Las Animas County, were Casimiro Barela, Jesús María García, and Agapito Vigil.[32] Although many Hispanos had learned the English language, no records for this period discuss their level of proficiency. There was still a need for translators; former Territorial Council member Celestino Domínguez served as the convention translator. For his services, he received seven dollars a day from the territorial treasury.[33]

Working together, these Hispanos helped to ensure that the state constitution protected their constituents' civil liberties. The entire delegation to the Constitutional Convention completed the Colorado constitution eighty-seven days later, on March 15, 1876. Celestino Domínguez and Albert R. Dyer proofread the Spanish-language version of the constitution (figure 9.2). For this service, Domínguez had estimated the cost of two dollars per page.[34] Due to the time needed to translate the information, a handwritten copy of their Spanish translation of the constitution was delivered to the printer days after the English version. Sadly, no handwritten copies of this version exist today. The Colorado citizens voted in favor of statehood on Saturday, July 1, 1876.

When President Grant issued a proclamation on August 1, 1876, declaring Colorado the thirty-eighth state of the Union, towns and cities celebrated in various ways. Citizens in Cañon City celebrated statehood by challenging South Pueblo to a game of baseball. In Pueblo citizens listened to the "historical reminiscences" of Wilbur Fisk Stone. Citizens in Black Hawk fired salvos and unintentionally lit a powder keg that exploded, thus destroying the hotel known as the Black Hawk House.[35]

The grandest celebration occurred in Denver. Its citizens held an elaborate parade that included several bands and militia units, decorated floats, pioneers, members of patriotic and fraternal orders, and city and territorial officials carrying flags and banners through the business streets. Cheers filled the air as several teams of white horses led a wagon up Larimer Street to the Denver Grove, a cottonwood grove located on the "banks of the Platte River (just north of the present Colfax viaduct)." At the time, the Grove was

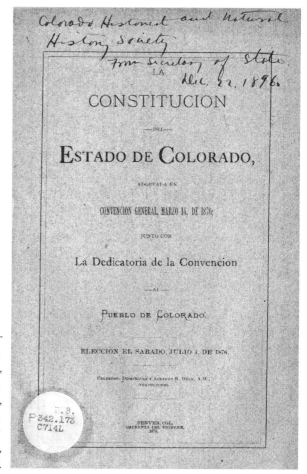

CONSTITUCION

—DEL—

ESTADO DE COLORADO,

ADOPTADA EN

CONVENCIÓN GENERAL, MARZO 14, DE 1876;

JUNTO CON

La Dedicatoria de la Convencion

—AL—

PUEBLO DE COLORADO.

ELECCION EL SABADO, JULIO 1, DE 1876.

CELESTINO DOMINGUEZ Y ALBERTO R. DYER, A.M.,
TRADUCTORES.

DENVER, COL.
IMPRENTA DEL TRIBUNE,
1876.

FIGURE 9.2. Spanish-language edition of the Colorado Constitution, 1876. *La Constitucion del Estado de Colorado,* RB342.173 C714L, Scan 30002118, History Colorado Center, Denver.

the only place in Denver "that resembled a public park." After the officials and citizens congregated at the grove, Governor John L. Routt gave a welcome address, then Denver mayor R. G. Buckingham read the Declaration of Independence. Several dignitaries, including former Colorado territorial delegate Hiram Pitt Bennet, gave speeches and toasts. Unfortunately, no historical information exists regarding celebrations in the southern counties.

Members of the Republican and Democratic Parties scheduled conventions to determine candidates to state and federal offices. Delegates to the Republican state convention met in Pueblo on August 23. Six days later delegates to the Democratic state convention met in Manitou Springs. Colorado's first statewide general election followed on October 3, 1876. With this election, the office of lieutenant governor was created; the secretary was no longer the second-ranking executive to the governor.[36] Voters in the southern counties elected thirteen Hispanos to represent them in the Colorado State Assembly; the majority of these members came from Las Animas County. In the Colorado State House of Representatives, eight newly elected Hispanos joined incumbents Jesús María García and Mariano Larragoite, both from Las Animas County. Incumbent Casimiro Barela joined newly elected Juan Francisco Chacón (Conejos) in the Colorado State Senate.

Notes

1. Ellis, "Colorado's First Fight for Statehood," 24.

2. Berwanger, *Rise of the Centennial State*, 41–43; Lamar, *Far Southwest*, 221–22.

3. *Rocky Mountain News*, July 14, 1865, 1, col. 1.

4. The title of the endorsement of Lincoln and the other candidates, *Nombramientos Regular por la Union*, can be translated as "Named (Candidates) for the Union (Party)." For purposes of trying to attract votes from Democrats who opposed secession, the Republican Party called itself the National Union Party in the 1864 election. Sweig, "Civil Administration of Governor William Gilpin," 187. Sweig wrote that the Republican and Union Parties were the same.

5. NARA, College Park, MD, "Conflict between Civil and Military," S. E. Brown, US Attorney, June 8, 1864, Colorado Territory, RG 60, entry 9, box 1, folder 2.

6. Collins, "Colorado's Territorial Secretaries," 198.

7. According to Jim Trotter, Rocky Mountain Public Broadcasting Service, Denver University and Northwestern University in Chicago released a study assessing Governor John Evans's culpability for the Sand Creek Massacre. *La Sierra*, November 28, 2014, 1.

8. Men in McCannon's posse who also participated in the Sand Creek Massacre: George L. Shoup, Luther Wilson, John McCannon, and Joseph Lamb. *Rocky Mountain News*, January 26, 1881. See also Price, *Season of Terror*, 107n44.

9. Lamar, *Far Southwest*, 230–231. Gilpin's business partner, William Blackmore, handled the sale of the Sangre de Cristo land in Europe. He was also involved in the sale of land on the still-unconfirmed Conejos Land Grant.

10. Most of Chivington's votes came from Lake County. (That election year, Lake County voters elected John McCannon, a known vigilante, to represent them in the Colorado Territorial House.)

11. NARA, Washington, DC, Territorial Papers of the US Senate, 1789–1873, Colorado 1860–1868, "Admission of Colorado into the Union," September 5, 1865, M200, Roll 17, 32–34.

12. Ibid., 226–27. *Rocky Mountain News*, January 30, 1867.

13. NARA, Washington, DC, Territorial Papers of the US Senate, 1789–1873, Colorado 1860–1868, "Petition for Statehood, 1868," M200, Roll 17.

14. *Cong. Globe*, 39th Cong., 1st Sess., House of Representatives, 2609 (1866), part III. See also Everett, *Creating the American West*, 175.

15. Berwanger, *Rise of the Centennial State*, 56, 140; Lamar, *Far Southwest*, 222–50.

16. "Memorial of the Legislature of the Territory of New Mexico, Relative to the Annexation of a Part of Said Territory to the Territory of Colorado, and Protesting against the Same," *Index to Miscellaneous Document of the House of Representatives for the Second Session of the Fortieth Congress, 1867–1868*, vol. 2 (Washington, DC: Government Printing Office, 1868), Misc. Doc. No. 96, March 6, 1868, 712; Convery, "Reckless Men of Both Races," 26.

17. Kelsley, *Frontier Capitalist*, 164.

18. NARA, Washington, DC, "Memorial of Citizens of Colorado in Reply to Remonstrance of H. M. Teller," February 20, 1868, M200, Roll 17.

19. *Cong. Globe*, 40th Cong., 2nd Sess., US Senate, Misc. Doc., No. 39, "Memorial of H. M. Teller," February 20, 1868.

20. Lamar, *Far Southwest*, 228.

21. "The State Question," *Colorado Weekly Chieftain*, January 4, 1872; Berwanger, *Rise of the Centennial State*, 140–41.

22. Ibid.

23. L. Bradford Prince, *New Mexico's Struggle for Statehood: Sixty Years of Effort to Obtain Self Government*, (Santa Fe: New Mexican Printing Co., 1910), 30. Nieto-Phillips, *Language of Blood*, 64.

24. *Denver Daily Times*, May 21, 1872.

25. Lamar, *Far Southwest*, 250–51; Berwanger, *Rise of the Centennial State*, 143–44.

26. Kelsley, *Frontier Capitalist*, 164.

27. Lamar, *Far Southwest*, 252.

28. Hafen, *Colorado and Its People*, 347–48. This policy of blocking public taxation from supporting religious institutions became known as the Blaine Amendment. It was named for James G. Blaine, who proposed such an amendment to the US Constitution in 1875. Most states have some version of a Blaine amendment in their state constitutions.

29. Fernandez, *Biography of Casimiro Barela*, 38–39; Berwanger, *Rise of the Centennial State*, 148.

30. Fedynskyj, "State Session Laws in Non-English Languages," citing *Proceedings of the Constitutional Convention of Colorado of 1875–1876*, 100.

31. Erickson, *Early Justice and the Formation of the Colorado Bar*, 56; Sweig, "Civil Administration of Governor William Gilpin," 192.

32. The Hispano clout in Conejos County had lost its hold as Lafayette Head was its elected delegate. Wilbur Fisk Stone served as the delegate from Pueblo County. Although a fourth delegate was presumably nominated, A. C. Gutiérrez was not selected to serve as a Republican delegate. Fernandez, *Biography of Casimiro Barela*, 37. See also Beshoar, *All about Trinidad and Las Animas County*, 87.

33. *House Journal of the Legislative Assembly of the Territory of Colorado, Eleventh Session, Convened at Denver, Colo., on the 3d Day of January 1876* (Central City: Record Book and Job Printer, 1876), January 31, 1876, 145 (oath administered to Dominguez as interpreter). Hereafter cited as *House Journal of the Territory of Colorado, 1876*.

34. Ibid.

35. "Statehood Celebration of 1876," 146. Hafen, "Steps to Statehood in Colorado," 96.

36. Collins, "Colorado's Territorial Secretaries," 207.

Conclusion

The 1860s were a time of great change and adjustment in Colorado, especially for Hispanos who had been inhabiting the southern region for generations. The transfer of the New Mexico province from Mexico to the United States in 1848, of course, began a profound transformation, intensified by the discovery of gold and a consequent inrush of Anglos starting in 1859—miners, settlers, businessmen, ranchers and farmers, and military and government officials.

Hispanos' lack of access to timely and complete information in Spanish and their exclusion from key committees in the legislature proved disastrous because of discriminatory ways. No Hispano member of the Council was named to the powerful Finance Committee or the Ways and Means Committee until 1864; in the House, no Hispano was named to either committee until 1872. Even though mining was actively conducted in the San Juan Mountains in Conejos County during the territorial period, no Hispano representatives were named to the important Mines and Minerals Committee until 1867.

DOI: 10.5876/9781607329145.c010

This book has identified some key issues that greatly impacted the lives of the Hispano citizens who found themselves living in Colorado Territory. It discussed a historical account of the policies developed by a powerful Anglo majority party in its efforts to control discussion about legislation that benefited the northern half of Colorado Territory. Although the Hispanos constituted an important part of the population, the dominant Anglo culture frequently swamped the Hispano way of life and caused it to assume a reduced prominence and a lesser role.[1]

Language Restrictionism, Nativism, and Nationalist Sentiments

After 1848, when the United States signed the Treaty of Guadalupe, US maps no longer included diacritics in Spanish-named towns and counties. Names along with their identifying characteristics began to change from Spanish to English. In addition, the Hispanos in Colorado Territory paid a very high price for statehood in their struggle for fair and equal representation. They contributed to the creation of Colorado despite the various efforts to disenfranchise them and despite the ongoing racism in finance, representation, language, property acquisition, and access to public policy.

When the Colorado General Assembly convened on November 1, 1876, Spanish was still the primary language in southern Colorado. Unlike those immigrants who arrived into the United States from the East, the Hispanos had retained the language, culture, and religion practiced in New Mexico. Some Anglos considered Hispanos disloyal and un-American because they had failed to assimilate, and therefore thought them not entitled to all the rights of "true" citizens.[2]

By 1879, California had lost support of minority language rights. During a convention to revise the state constitution, the all-Anglo delegation voted to eliminate California's former guarantee for Spanish-language publications. None of the elected delegates were Hispano. The delegates also limited all official proceedings to English, which made California one of the first English-only states in the United States. Although in 1966 it amended its English-only statute, much damage had been done. During discussion by the delegates for and against the amendment, one delegate implied that recent immigrants [from] Mexico "pretend to be citizens . . . some of them bandits, cutthroats, and robbers . . . On election day they are corralled and [vote]." In response, another delegate made the following memorable remark:

> I do not believe, because we [the United States] are stronger, because we outnumber them and are continually increasing the ratio, that we should entirely ignore the rights that these people ought to have under a free government. It is a simple question whether we will do right because it is right, or whether we will do wrong because we have the power to do it.[3]

Californios and nuevomexicanos were the first major population of citizens to experience continued practices of prejudice and language suppression since 1848. Yet many Anglo citizens of the United States consider us, their descendants, aliens based on the Spanish language and customs we retained, and the physical features we possess.

Many Anglo territorial assemblymen incorporated the use of collusion, language restrictionism,[4] and nativism in the legislative process to control legislation that benefited their constituents in the northern part of the territory. In many cases, they passed laws to "force assimilationist ideology."[5] Language use in the United States still remains a political and emotional issue, as the discussion of it involves questions of patriotism, racism, language, loyalty, and assimilation.[6] In 1987 former Colorado state representative Richard Thomas Castro passionately worked to defeat the English-only bill that declared English to be Colorado's official language: "The English Only movement has equated language ability to loyalty to this country. They have attempted to create the impression that language minorities, Hispanics in particular, are resisting assimilation into the mainstream of the U.S. They have even [gone so far as to] suggest . . . Hispanics pose a deadly threat of disunity to this country."[7]

Ultimately, in 1988, Colorado voters amended the state's constitution to make English the state's official language, although the voters in Conejos, Costilla, La Plata, and Las Animas, with their heavy Hispano representation, rejected the measure.[8] This action diminishes the importance attached to the Spanish language and heritage of the settlers of early Colorado. In contrast, in New Mexico there was no petition of the people for such an initiative; its General Assembly defeated the English-only discussion in its chambers. Today there are about twenty-five states that have some form of language restrictionist legislation stipulating that English will be used in most or all government transactions.

Many descendants of the Spanish colonials living in California, Arizona, Texas, New Mexico, and Colorado are proud of their language and have retained it because it is a part of their heritage. This strong retention of language and custom as a part of the culture and heritage of southern Colorado is important.

The discussion in this book underscores what Hispanos have been saying to this day about the relationship to the underlying currents about language and culture in the United States. Should English, and English only, be a symbol of national identity in a melting-pot society? Some Anglo citizens do not want to accept this melting-pot vision of the country because they fear losing their position at the top of a racial pyramid. The United States today cannot seem to get past color, status, language, and religion—all that make us a melting-pot society. The fight for equal protection under the law, and the access to the opportunities that individual states and our great country provide, continues to be a never-ending battle for Hispanos and other people of color. State legislatures and the US Congress are again internally involved in divisive policy discussions about citizenship, culture, and language, while ethnic minorities face barriers and challenges due to inequities in education, healthcare, taxation, voter representation, and housing. The struggle against institutional racism, such as that built into English-only legislation, continues to be a priority for Hispano legislators.

Northern New Mexico and southern Colorado are connected by the land formations, the Spanish language, and the Hispano customs and traditions. We are a homogeneous people connected by blood, history, collective memory, community, and social change. Southern Colorado's Hispanic heritage is still attached to the land and its Spanish and Mexican heritage.[9] Despite these challenges, the Hispanos of southern Colorado continued to retain the culture, and many continue speaking the Spanish language. We are proud of our heritage and still talk about the beauty of the land and sustenance it continues to provide. It is that land itself that was "so important to those whose lives [were] tied to it."[10]

Significant progress has been made for the Hispanos in Colorado; however, cultural conflict, racism, and bias still exist. For generations we Hispanos have felt that Colorado's leaders and citizens have devalued our contributions to the territory and state, as is illustrated in museums that reflect only a small part about our contributions. The contributions of our ancestors have long been overlooked.

A Resource for All to Share

Nuevomexicano settlement patterns were already formed in the northern frontier when Anglo miners arriving from the East created the extralegal Territory of Jefferson. These miners were independent men who considered the precious metals and ores, land, and water theirs for the taking. The customs, practices, and religion the Hispano settlers brought from New Mexico connected them to the land on which they labored and to each other for protection and comunidád.

Spanish and Mexican custom had regulated not just land but water. This custom basically states that no one person could own the water; water is a benefit that all people must share. In other words, take only what you need and no more. This custom sharply differed from common laws maintaining the principle of prior appropriation of water under English land law.

During state court appropriations in the 1890s, acequia associations were required to submit an English version of their bylaws along with a claim and survey map. Members of each acequia association quickly scrambled to provide the state with their translated bylaws, claim, and map. Where the claim required the name of the acequia, some names were anglicized or determined by a clerk. For example, the Hispano settlers likely referred to their first acequia as *la acequia de la gente*, which ultimately was recorded in English as "The People's Ditch." Similarly, in Huerfano County an acequia named for a community was recorded in water district records as the Mexican Ditch. The settlers would not have named their ditches after a country or ethnic heritage. Acequias were typically named for a land formation, settlement, or the person or family cutting the ditch. Unfortunately, available water records do not include the original Spanish names.

Crop failure might induce the settlers to sell and move on, reducing the number of members available to pay dues or work on the imperative spring cleaning. By custom, *parciantes* (farmers or irrigators) could sell their individual water rights, but "not before offering it first to parciantes in the association."[11] This custom helped protect the community and the acequia system. Water in the acequia was so vital to their livelihoods that Hispano ditch associations allowed no bathing or misuse of the water and established fines for damage to the acequia and its embankments. The territorial assembly incorporated this important precedent in 1874, when it passed a law and established a fine for polluting water in any stream, acequia, or flume.[12]

To promote the newly formed town of Saguache, its trustees in 1874 offered free lots to settlers with the provision that they erect buildings "valued above a set minimum amount."[13] In other words, they did not want any adobe structures. Another ordinance stipulated that owners had to plant cottonwood trees on each of the hundred available lots. Cottonwoods provide much shade, but their roots require much water. Isaac L. Gotthelf supervised the planting of these trees, likely by Hispano laborers. Gotthelf also managed the construction of the acequias that moved water from Nathan Russell's water right. By 1800, there were 325 people in Saguache.[14] In addition to the cottonwoods and new settlers, the available water was further divided for upstream and downstream use, which caused much concern to farmers in times of drought. Any increase of water loss threatened the acequia system, which in turn caused crops to fail.

When Anglo farmers acquired water rights through the purchase of land irrigated by an acequia, they became members of an acequia association. Major issues surfaced. In addition to not knowing how to speak Spanish, they were unfamiliar with acequia terms and customary protocols. By Hispano custom and tradition, water disputes were settled within the acequia association. The reasons were simple: acting quickly to resolve the conflict fostered comunidad and ensured "tranquil relations in the community." This action also saved the association from expenses incurred through formal litigation.[15] In the face of the profound changes that Anglos brought to southern Colorado, parciantes continued to practice Hispano acequia customs and water-sharing regimes. Surviving acequia ledgers, some written in Spanish, demonstrate that Colorado's Hispanos retained their language, customs, culture, and traditions.

That assurance of access of everyone contrasted with the Anglo law of prior appropriation in Colorado Territory, in which the first person to construct a ditch could divert as much water as he wished. By Hispano custom, water was measured in units of time, not by priority number. When water was scarce, the acequia comumidád ensured that those in greatest need received access to the water and limited the amount of time each poblador could irrigate. Everyone shared in the available water; everyone received at least some water. Hispano assemblymen in the territorial legislature succeeded in establishing acequia norms as law in Conejos and Costilla Counties, and then in Huerfano and Las Animas Counties. Agricultural demands for water preceded that of manufacturing, and domestic water needs were allowed by prior right.

With regard to Colorado territorial law, the assembly passed a law in 1861 that, from a Hispano perspective, hardly protected and regulated water use. The following year the amended water law established the duties of the mayordomos, regulations for their elections, and the power to regulate compulsory labor from those who used the water. Only those persons who work the ditch and maintain it to keep the water freely flowing to the fields receive access to its water.[16] Hispano acequia norms worked for the benefit of the whole community. Many of these ideals were already in place in acequia communities.

According to Lamar, where water rights were concerned, the territory had no need for English common law and the assembly passed bills more fitting to Colorado's climate and water needs. Territorial chief justice Moses Hallett restricted the use of jurisdictional English common law when it came to the needs of the "mining industry and to the Western environment."[17] The doctrine of riparian rights, which evolved from English common law practiced in the eastern states, was inapplicable in the arid West. In 1864 Justice Hallet essentially broke away from the riparian rights system and created the doctrine of prior appropriation—first in time, first in right—which basically stated that during periods of limited water supply, the priority number of a water right determined when water could be diverted and delivered relative to other water rights. By law, the earliest water user had access to all the water needed before the next user in line. Hispano acequia ledgers show that its water users continued to use acequia rules and custom when the water was scarce.

This assurance of access of all to water contrasted with the territory's Anglo law of prior appropriation, in which the first person to construct a ditch could divert as much water as he wished. In 1864 the Colorado Territorial Assembly passed a water law that recognized the prior appropriation system used by Anglo miners. Based on this doctrine, during time of drought, the first person to have diverted water through a ditch had rights to as much water as he wanted, thus leaving the next water user "vulnerable to the possibility" of receiving little to no water.[18] During periods of limited water supply, the priority number of a court-decreed water right determined when water could be diverted and delivered relative to other water rights. By law, the earliest user had a right to access all the water needed before the next user in line could access the water.

Both the 1866 and 1872 laws normalized acequia governance, custom, and water-distribution values transferred from New Mexico. To comply with the water law, all acequia associations and ditch companies now held annual meetings and gave elected officials power to levy compulsory labor from those persons who used the water. These customs included distributing water first to those communities in greatest need, taking water only in orderly succession, and using no more than the amount needed by homes, farms, or ranches. This legislative action is a wonderful example of how the Hispano and Anglo legislators collaborated to enshrine Hispano water custom and tradition into law for the common good of southern Colorado.

By 1875 the priority number of a court-decreed water right determined when water could be diverted and delivered relative to other water rights during periods of limited water supply. By law, the earliest decreed right had access to all the water needed before the next user in line could access the water. Further, water belonged to all the people; it was the "property of the public":

> When the waters of any natural stream are not sufficient for the service of all those desiring the use of the same, those using the water for domestic purposes shall have the preference over those claiming for any other purpose, and those using the water for agricultural purposes shall have preference over those using the same for manufacturing purposes.[19]

Because the doctrine of prior appropriation contradicted the custom of water sharing used in the southern counties, Hispano legislators worked to incorporate acequia custom and governance into the territory's water law. In 1866 the assembly finally realized the important results that acequia norms had on water use, access, and conservation; however, this law applied only in Conejos and Costilla Counties. In 1872, the water law would apply to Huerfano and Las Animas Counties.[20] That same year the territorial assembly passed a law making irrigation ditches exempt from taxation.[21]

As a means to acknowledge the Hispano custom in Colorado's water history, in 2009 the Sixty-Seventh Colorado General Assembly recognized the continuing existence and use of acequias in preserving and caring for the water essential for crop growth. This historic act recognizes Colorado's acequias as ancient irrigation practices that allocate water as a community resource based upon equity rather than priority of appropriation.[22] This legislation, sponsored by Colorado state representative Val Vigil (Costilla) in 2009, helps tell a story of the culture and history of some of the New Mexico "notch" Hispanos who became a part of Colorado in 1861. Today the historic San Luis People's Ditch, the first acequia constructed by the early Hispano settlers, has continuously moved water from the Culebra River to farm fields for well over 150 years. This ditch retains its first-priority water rights in Colorado, rights that precede any mining claims in Colorado.

Was a Square State Really Necessary?

The Hispanos' petitions, pleas, and prayers to "withdraw" from Colorado and to be reunited with New Mexico went unanswered. Their sole desire was for an act of Congress to withdraw them from Colorado and reattach them to New Mexico. When New Mexico delegate José Francisco Perea lobbied on behalf of the Hispanos in the notch, he stated that New Mexico as a whole deserved the "restoration" of her people. Perea also pointed out that, had they arrived in Colorado on their own, "for purposes of protection or other benefits, it would be proper that they should conform in language and other usages, political and juridical, to the customs of the country with which they had formed a voluntary association." However, the association with Colorado had not been voluntarily sought by the residents of the notch: "Those people were brought under that sovereignty and authority of this government not by their own volition but by the fortune of war . . . and [the] conquest of New Mexico by the United States." Had they been consulted, "they would greatly have preferred remaining under the authority and protection of their native sovereign."

> This change was not a matter of their own choice; they cannot take an intelligent part in legislation, nor can they understand from their laws . . . either the rights they confer or the obligations they impose. Yet they must remain in darkness as to the character of the laws under which they live as Congress and the Territorial Assembly will not appropriate money to have those laws translated into Spanish. They are entitled to the enjoyment of their native language, and their system of law and domestic usages, so long . . . as they do not conflict with the principles of the general government.[23]

In retrospect, should the insistence on making Colorado's border appear "square" have been such an important consideration? Consider what might have happened if Congress had passed the petition to return the notch to New Mexico. The natural boundaries of the notch belonged to New Mexico; it was an "artificial line [that had] separated them from New Mexico."[24] Or consider what might have happened had Congress passed a bill to make Colorado's southern border straight, as it did, but move the whole line north by just a half degree of longitude. The nine leading towns now in southern Colorado would have been included in modern New Mexico: Cortez, Durango, Pagosa Springs, Conejos, Alamosa, San Luis, La Veta, Trinidad, and Springfield; and on its northern boarder Cheyenne, Laramie, Rawlins, and Rock Springs would be in modern Colorado. Would Congress have been willing to return at least the notch area back or some of the north by just a half degree of this area to New Mexico? Would Congress have granted Wyoming's southern boundary to Colorado? Imagine that Congress made these changes but did not give the citizens of these affected areas a vote or even a chance to lobby against the move. How would such a move promote unity and work toward the greater good? How would this move have affected the two territories and their economies and citizens? These are question we all should consider.

Divisive Laws and Barriers

The new historical information presented in this book dismisses the notions that the insurrection in Conejos occurred solely due to taxation and peonage. The review of previous research about mob violence, combined with newly found Hispano oral histories and the new historical research introduced here, provides new information about past behaviors and practices against Hispanos during the early territorial period. James L. Gaspar, Cornelius Hendren, Frederick William Posthoff, Lafayette Head, William Newton Byers, and George O. Austin, along with some Anglo citizens and Fort Garland military officials, all opposed the Hispanos on the grounds of their skin color, culture, and language. Opportunistic Anglo nativist correspondents, businessmen, and politicians such as Byers, Wilbur Fisk Stone, William Gilpin, and John Evans, promoted divisive laws and erected barriers to full and equal Hispano participation in territorial affairs. Even as they attributed Hispano discontent solely to taxes and peonage as the only two causes of discontent, they pushed conformity and assimilation and opposed the Hispanos for resisting. They made little or no effort to accommodate the needs of Spanish-speaking citizens and in fact used the language, law, religion, and custom of the Hispanos to denigrate them and fuel ethnic discrimination.

Newspapers excited nativist fears against the Hispanos, branding them disloyal citizens, or even hostile foreigners, when they questioned the laws imposed upon them. Rumors circulating about the "secret" meetings the Hispanos held to discuss their unique situation in Colorado Territory, the taxes imposed upon them, and preparation of petitions to be returned to New Mexico confirmed the Anglos' wariness about Hispano insurrections of the kind that had wracked Taos in 1847. Colorado's territorial newspapers continued to degenerate the Hispanos. These editors failed to understand that iron was not readily available in the northern New Mexican frontier. These editors chose to characterize all Hispanos as uncivilized and prejudicially questioned their ancestry.

> The greater portion of the richest valleys of Southern Colorado are owned or claimed by these degenerate descendants of the Spanish explorers . . . a more worthless, unprogressive people cannot be found anywhere on the habitable globe . . . [They are] behind the times in all matters, customs and uses pertaining to progressive civilization . . . rude implements are very generally in use . . . by this mongrel race.[25]

As the driving force, the Anglo-majority policymakers left a detailed record of their biased and unfair role in the implementation of legislation and deciding Colorado's future. The territorial assembly gave its Spanish-speaking representatives no fair conditions in the legislative process, and thus they were unable to protect their constituents from unjust laws introduced and passed by an Anglo-majority assembly. The Hispano assemblymen had no political or economic power and were forced to work through interpreters who did not have their best interests in mind. The Hispano assemblymen were never regarded as equal to the likes of such men as William Gilpin, George Miles Chilcott, Charles F. Holly, Samuel H. Elbert, Henry Moore Teller, and others, whose names appear throughout the state on street signs, city parks, and maps.

Colorado Territory was a place where violent deaths occurred without the due process of the legal system. In response to the violence and racism experienced, the Hispanos formed mutual societies. Mutual societies were essentially extensions of the penitente brotherhood in that they provided their communities with support and aid. In 1900 Hispano community leaders met at Antonito in Conejos County to unite in collective action for social change. This society soon grew to more than a thousand members. The Sociedad Protección Mutua de Trabajadores Unidos (Society for the Mutual Protection of United Workers), or the SPMDTU, still exists today and continues to support its communities in Colorado and New Mexico. Interestingly, to remember the collective violence against their ancestors, the initials SPMDTU are attributed to the phrase "Some Poor Mexican Died Tied Up."[26]

Nativist intolerance against Hispanos and other nonwhites continued into the twentieth century through ethnocentric hostility and verbal insults.[27] Protestant Americanization efforts, such as America First Societies, located in Denver and Pueblo, and the coal camps in Huerfano and Las Animas Counties, promoted English-only efforts and "American" ideas in food and custom. Junior America First Societies for school-age children were organized by company camps of the Colorado Fuel and Iron Company. In time, some Americanization efforts to restrict culture and language became more militant. The Ku Klux Klan infiltrated deep into Colorado and its politics in the 1920s. In southern Colorado KKK chapters were created in Pueblo, Walsenburg, and Trinidad.[28] Its influence was such that by 1921 there was only one Spanish-surnamed male serving in the State Assembly—Andres Lucero (Las Animas).[29]

During the 1930s, Colorado governor Edwin Carl Johnson sought to halt an "invasion of aliens and indigent persons" into his state. He considered nuevomexicanos aliens and wanted to keep these undocumented outsiders from undercutting wages and taking jobs away from Coloradoans. On April 18, 1836, Governor Johnson declared martial law and ordered the Colorado National Guard to establish checkpoints on the roads from New Mexico into Colorado. Johnson had received constituent mail in support of keeping Mexicans out of Colorado. Unfortunately, like many Americans today, he regarded New Mexicans as foreigners and not as fellow US citizens. Johnson backed off once New Mexico charged that the blockade was unconstitutional and then stated that Colorado "must not alienate the friendship of our sister states." His action, supported by Anglo politicians, business leaders, and constituents, appealed to their nativist sentiments.[30]

The Hispano assemblymen who served during the territorial period served against overwhelming odds. They were valiant advocates who continually fought for fair representation. The territorial assembly created the opportunity for future Hispano assemblymen to continue the fight for equal rights and a better life. I hope the information in this book has given a voice to the few—forgotten Hispano territorial assemblymen—to give them a rightful place in Colorado's history. Like their Hispano predecessors during the territorial period, today's Hispano men and women represent their constituents in the Colorado State Assembly. They will continue to evolve as courageous leaders in business, government, philanthropy, and education. Their battle continues for fairness, respect, equality, and achievement of the promises of life, liberty, and the pursuit of happiness.

Notes

1. Campa, *Hispanic Culture in the Southwest*, 142.

2. Galindo and Vigil, "Language Restrictionism Revisited," 28.

3. Comment made by delegate Blackmer. "Spanish Language Rights in California: Debates of the 1879 Constitution," http://www.languagepolicy.net/archives/1879con.htm, accessed May 11, 2016. The Anglo delegates attending the 1879 California Constitution voted to make English the language of the state's official proceedings.

4. Defined as "efforts to stop a linguistic or ethnic group of people from speaking, learning, or maintaining their native or home language." Josué M. González, ed, "Encyclopedia of Bilingual Education," https://sk.sagepub.com/reference/bilingual/n175.xml, accessed May 8, 2018.

5. Galindo and Vigil, "Language Restrictionism Revisited," 28.

6. Dennis Baron, "Official American English Only: The Legendary English-Only Vote of 1795," http://www.pbs.org/speak/seatosea/officialamerican/englishonly/, accessed July 21, 2017.

7. Fearing the long-range implications of the law and its impact on civil rights, in 1988 Richard T. Castro addressed the US Civil Rights Commission stating that "the English-only movement [led] to a society that treated non-English speakers as second-class citizens [with neither] a Spanish-[language] '911' emergency response line nor translation services in the Colorado court system." Richard T. Castro to US Civil Rights Commission, September 8, 1988, Baltimore Hotel, Los Angeles, California.

8. State of Colorado, *Abstract of Votes Cast, 1988* (Denver: Secretary of State, 1988), 168–69.

9. This attachment is known as *querencia*, a cherished sense of place and belonging.

10. Colville, *La Vereda*, 8.

11. Sánchez, "Linked by Water, Linked by Blood," 440.

12. General Statutes of the Territory of Colorado, February 18, 1874, 99. The fine was set between $100 and $500.

13. Town of Saguache and Cochetopa Coridor Historic Resources Survey, 2000, Front Range Research Associates, Inc., Denver, Colorado (2001):13.

14. Simmons and Simmons, *Town of Saguache and Cochetopa Corridor*, 13, 16.

15. Sánchez, "Linked by Water, Linked by Blood," 442.

16. Ebright, "Sharing the Shortages," 11, 15–17.

17. Lamar, *Far Southwest*, 207, 258.

18. Baxter, *Dividing New Mexico's Water*, 87.

19. "Article XVI—Mining and Irrigation," *Proceedings of the Constitutional Convention for the State of Colorado*, sec. 6, 700.

20. Colorado Session Laws 143, Act of 22 January 1872, Ninth Session (act to make the Act of 6 February 1866 applicable to Huerfano County); Act of 9 February 1872, 1872 Colorado Session Laws 145, Ninth Session (act to make the Act of 6 February 1866 applicable to Las Animas County).

21. Ibid., January 22, 1872, 143 (act to exempt irrigation ditches from taxation).

22. Colorado Session Laws 1990, First Regular Session, 67th General Assembly, HB 09-1233, https://leg.colorado.gov/agencies/office-legislative-legal-services/session-laws-archive.

23. Francisco Perea to Hon. Jas. M. Ashley, Chairman of the Committee on Territories of the House of Representatives, January 1, 1865, Yale Collection of Western Americana, Beinecke Rare Book and Manuscript Library, Yale University. Also *Gazette*, February 18, 1865; cf. Gonzales, *Política*, 478–79.

24. *Cong. Globe*, 39th Cong., 1st Sess., House of Representatives, 2609, part III (1866).

25. "From Trinidad," *Pueblo Chieftain*, June 7, 1874.

26. Colorado Society of Hispanic Genealogy, *Hispanic Pioneers in Colorado and New Mexico*, 216.

27. Carrigan and Webb, *Forgotten Dead*, 177.

28. Abbott, Leonard, and McComb, *Colorado*, 266.

29. Van Nuys, *Americanizing the West*, 53, 105–6, 172. Colorado Legislator Biographies website at http://www.leg.state.co.us/lcs/leghist.nsf/LegHistory.xsp?OpenDatabase, accessed October 1, 2017.

30. Andrew Oxford, "New Mexicans Once Cast as Those to be Kept Out," *Santa Fe New Mexican*, September 2, 2017, http://www.santafenewmexican.com/news/local_news/new-mexicans-once-cast-as-those-to-be-kept-out/article_59c231aa-3f7d-5acd-902f-9e9a309e2849.html, accessed September 2, 2017.

Appendix A

The Hispano Territorial Assemblymen

The biographies of some of the Hispano territorial assemblymen introduce twenty-two of the thirty-two members who served in the Colorado Territorial Assembly between 1861 and 1875. They came from similar backgrounds in that their fathers were merchants, farmers, or stockmen; they all spoke Spanish; and, at the time, most were members of the Roman Catholic faith. Some Hispanos experienced the glory of success; others did not. Unfortunately, I could not locate historical information for all of them. Despite several setbacks, including unfair disadvantage in the legislative process, they sought to dedicate their time and efforts to legislation affecting the economies and livelihoods of their Hispano constituents.

I identify and refer to the following Hispano legislators by the names recorded on ecclesiastical records. Although church and civil records used various spellings of some names, I chose the most commonly used spelling. Upon baptism into the Catholic Church, the names of saints became part of a person's name. Many first names began with or included the names Jesús, Cruz, José, Juan, Miguel, or María to honor Jesus Christ, the Holy Cross, or the Catholic saints Joseph, John, Michael, and Mary.

DOI: 10.5876/9781607329145.c011

Several generations of family groups served in the Colorado Territorial Assembly and/or the Colorado State Assembly. Territorial Representative Felipe de Jesús Baca, for example, represented Huerfano, Costilla, and Saguache Counties in 1870. His uncle, Juan Antonio Baca, served as a councilman (senator) in the New Mexico Territorial Legislature in 1870 and in the Colorado Senate in 1878. Almost one hundred years later in 1974, their descendant, Polly Baca-Barragan (Denver), became the first female elected to the Colorado State House of Representatives. She later worked in President Lyndon Johnson's administration as a public information officer for a White House agency and later as an assistant to the chair of the Democratic National Committee.[1] Four years later, she became the first woman elected to the Colorado State Senate.

In the García family, the sons of territorial representative José Víctor García, José Alejandro de Amarante García and Celestino José García, both served in the Colorado State Legislature. Amarante served in the House in 1881, representing Conejos and Costilla Counties. Celestino José García represented Conejos County in the House for twenty-four years. José Alejandro de Amarante García's son, Reginaldo, served in the House, representing Conejos County, in 1927.

Territorial representative José Seledonio Valdez represented Conejos County in 1866; his son, Crescencio, represented that county in the Colorado State House in 1889.[2] Both worked endlessly to confirm the claim of the Guadalupe (Conejos) Land Grant, issued in 1833. Territorial representative Pedro Antonio Lobato represented Conejos County in 1865; his nephew, Juan Bautista Lobato, represented Conejos and Costilla Counties the following term. And Territorial Council member Jesús María Velásquez represented Conejos County in 1865. Seven years later his son, José Arcadio, represented the same county in the Territorial House (tables A.1 and A.2).

Lorenzo Antonio Abeyta

1835–93

TERRITORIAL REPRESENTATIVE | LAS ANIMAS COUNTY | 1871

Abeyta was born about June 1835 in New Mexico Province of Mexico to Pablo Antonio Abeyta and María Concepción Suazo. Lorenzo Antonio Abeyta married María Dionisia Baca in 1866.[3] When he moved to Colorado Territory is not known.

TABLE A.1. Hispano members of the Colorado Territorial Council, 1864–75

Name	Years Served	Counties Served	Party	Committees
Celestino Dominguez	1864 1865	Conejos	?	1864: Printing (Chair), Territorial Library (Chair), Expenditures, Federal Relations 1865: Highways and Bridges (Chair), Territorial Library (Chair), Agriculture, Finance, Ways and Means, Incorporations
Jesus Maria Velasquez	1865 1866 1867 1868 1870	Conejos	U	1866–67: Agriculture, Military Affairs, Printing 1868: Counties, Indian Affairs, Printing 1870: Agriculture, Federal Relations, Highways and Bridges, Indian Affairs, Territorial Library
Francisco Sanchez	1867 1868 1870	Conejos, Costilla	D	1867: unknown 1868: Agriculture, Highways and Bridges, Territorial Affairs 1870: Counties, Finance
Jesus Maria Garcia	1872 1876	Las Animas	D	1872: Elections, Expenditures, Printing 1876: Impeachment, Federal Relations, Miscellaneous
Jose Victor Garcia	1872	Conejos, Costilla	D, R	1872: Highways and Bridges (Chair), Counties, Military Affairs
Jose Silverio Suazo	1872 1876	Huerfano	D, R	1872: Indian Affairs, Penitentiary, Territorial Library 1876: Indian Affairs, Federal Relations, Immigration, Roads and Bridges, Territorial Library
Juan Bautista Jaquez	1874	Huerfano	R	1874: Roads and Bridges (Chair), Indian Affairs, Military Affairs, Territorial Library

Note: D = Democrat; R = Republican; U = Union Ticket; ? = party unknown.

Source: Colorado Legislator Biographies, http://www.leg.state.co.us/lcs/leghist.nsf/LegHistory.xsp?OpenDatabase, accessed October 1, 2017.

In 1871 Las Animas County voters elected Abeyta, a Democrat, to represent them in the Territorial House. Major Rafael Chacón believed the election was filled with "fraud, bribery, and double voting." Chacón, a Republican, charged that the Democratic Party altered the election results and certified only its own candidates.[4] Abeyta had served one month in office when Albert W. Archibald, a Republican attorney, contested his election.[5] In the end,

TABLE A.2. Hispano members of the Colorado Territorial House, 1861–75

Name	Years Served	Counties Served	Party	Committees
Jesus Maria Barela	1861 1862 1866	Costilla Conejos, Costilla	D	1861: Agriculture, Election and Apportionment, Printing 1862: Education, Rules and Joint Rules
Jose Victor Garcia	1861 1862 1864	Conejos	D, R	1861: Roads and Bridges, Territorial Affairs 1862: Roads and Bridges, Territorial Affairs 1864: Territorial Affairs (Chair), Indian Relations, Military Affairs, Ways and Means
Jose Rafael Martinez	1862	Conejos	?	Agriculture, Printing
Jose Francisco Gallegos	1862	Costilla	D	Indian Relations (Chair), Elections and Apportionment, Territorial Affairs
Jose Pablo de Jesus Ortega	1864 1865 1867 1868	Conejos Conejos, Costilla	D	1864: Agriculture and Manufactures, Counties and County Lines, Education, Printing 1868: Counties and County Lines, Federal Relations, Incorporations
Jose Gabriel Martinez	1865 1866	Conejos Conejos, Costilla	?	1865: not on any committees 1866: Agriculture and Manufactures, Elections and Apportionment, Territorial Affairs
Pedro Antonio Lobato	1865	Costilla, Huerfano	U	
Pedro Aragon	1865–66	Conejos	U	
M. S. Mondragon	1866	Conejos, Costilla	?	
Juan Miguel Vigil	1866 1867	Costilla, Huerfano	?	Education
Jose Celedonio Valdez	1866 1867	Conejos, Costilla	?	Judiciary, Mines and Minerals, Ways and Means
Juan Bautista Lobato	1866 1867	Conejos, Costilla	R	1867: Territorial Affairs
Jose Silverio Suazo	1867–68	Huerfano	R	Federal Relations, Military Affairs
Tomas Suazo	1867–68	Huerfano	R	

continued on next page

Name	Years Served	Counties Served	Party	Committees
Jose Clemente Trujillo	1870	Conejos, Costilla, Saguache	D	Agriculture and Manufactures, Elections and Apportionment, Territorial Library, Military Affairs
Felipe de Jesus Baca	1870	Huerfano, Las Animas	R	Counties and County Lines, Education, Territorial Affairs
Manuel Lucero	1870	Conejos, Costilla, Saguache	R	Agriculture and Manufactures, Territorial Prisons, Ways and Means
Mariano Sisto Larrogoite	1872 1874	Las Animas	D	1872: County and County Lines, Judiciary 1874: Federal Relations (Chair), Rules and Joint Rules (Chair), Judiciary
Francisco Sanchez	1872	Conejos, Costilla	D	Indian Affairs, Territorial Library
Pedro Rafael Trujillo	1872	Costilla	R	Elections and Apportionment, Finance, Ways and Means, Stock
Casimiro Barela	1872 1874	Las Animas	D	1874: Agriculture and Manufactures, Elections and Apportionment, Indian Affairs
Antonio Lorenzo Abeyta	1872	Las Animas	D	County and County Lines, Territorial Prisons
Juan Andres Manzanares	1872	Huerfano	D	Railroads, Roads and Bridges, Stock
Jose A. (Arcadio) Velasquez	1872	Conejos	D	Incorporations, Military Affairs
Juan S. Esquibel	1874	Conejos, Costilla	D/R	Federal Relations, Incorporations, Printing
Manuel Sabino Salazar	1874	Conejos		Incorporations, Military Affairs
Jose Antonio de Jesus Valdez	1874	Huerfano	R	Roads and Bridges, Stock, Territorial Affairs

Note: D = Democrat, R = Republican, U = Union Ticket

Source: Colorado Legislator Biographies, http://www.leg.state.co.us/lcs/leghist.nsf/LegHistory.xsp?OpenDatabase, accessed October 1, 2017.

Abeyta lost his seat to Archibald by four votes in the House.[6] Seven years later, Abeyta and Archibald became brothers-in-law, as they married daughters of territorial representative Felipe de Jesús Baca (Las Animas).[7]

Abeyta returned to Trinidad and served several terms as a Las Animas county commissioner between 1868 and 1875.[8]

By 1869, Las Animas County was open range. Cattlemen arrived from Texas with their cattle. Trinidad instantly became headquarters for such well-known companies as the Cleveland, the Jones, and the Prairie cattle companies. Each of these had "thousands of cattle."[9] Trouble often ensued between the sheepmen and the cowboys. In 1882 armed men of the Prairie Cattle Company killed 4,000 sheep. One of the homes they burned was Abeyta's.[10]

Known birth children of Lorenzo Antonio Abeyta and María Dionisia Baca were Cecilia, Elena, Estevan, Manuel, Pedro Antonio, Pablo, Mercedes, Victoria, and Tomas. Lorenzo Antonio Abeyta was killed in Sonora, Mexico, by a Yaqui band in 1893.[11] Other details about his death are unknown.

Pedro Aragón

1820–?

TERRITORIAL REPRESENTATIVE | CONEJOS COUNTY | 1865

Aragón was born about 1820 in New Mexico Province of colonial New Spain, just before Mexican independence. In 1860, while living in the far northern frontier of Taos County, he served in the Conejos Militia under Captain Jesús María Velásquez on a campaign against the Navajo.[12] By 1863, Aragón lived in San Jose, Conejos County, Colorado Territory, where he ran a store. He also had a license to sell liquor.[13]

While in office during the fourth legislative session in 1865, he supported the Constitutional Union Party. The Union Party began around the onset of the US Civil War as an independent minority party that attracted voters who advocated saving the Union while compromising on the issue of slavery.

Pedro Aragón's daughter, Genoveva, married José Arcario Velásquez, son of territorial representative Jesús María Velásquez on October 28, 1867, in Conejos, Conejos County.[14] Other birth children of Pedro Aragón and María Guadalupe Ortíz were Abelino, Jesús, Ana María, and Manuela.[15]

Felipe de Jesús Baca

1828–79

TERRITORIAL REPRESENTATIVE | HUERFANO AND
LAS ANIMAS COUNTIES | 1870

FIGURE A.1. Felipe de Jesús Baca.
10026852, History Colorado.

Baca was born January 8, 1828, near Abiquiú, New Mexico Province of Mexico, to José Manuel Baca and María Rosa Vigil (figure A.1). Felipe married María Dolores Gonzales in March 1849. By 1855 they were living in Guadalupita, Mora County, New Mexico Territory, where he built a mill on commons land and became a wealthy farmer. About 1859 he freighted four wagonloads of flour to sell to miners arriving at Cherry Creek (Denver).

Around 1860 Felipe moved his family north to Trinidad, which, at the time, was in Mora County, New Mexico Territory. Baca built his home on the north side of the Río de Las Ánimas Perdidas en Purgatorio (Las Animas River). To stave off indigenous attacks on his herds and herders, Baca gave the Utes and Arapahos flour and cornmeal. Incoming Anglo travelers and settlers had problems pronouncing Río Purgatorio and used instead the translated name—Purgatoire—assigned to the river by French trappers.

In 1860 the unofficial Territory of Jefferson recognized the Trinidad area as part of Huerfano County. The following year, Congress officially incorporated Trinidad within Huerfano County in the Territory of Colorado.

On November 30, 1861, Felipe de Jesús Baca began constructing an acequia, the third constructed in the area. The original headgate of the Baca Ditch was located on the north bank of Las Animas River east of present-day Commercial Street.[16] It irrigated 400 acres of land.[17] Commercial property later replaced farmland irrigated by the Baca Ditch. When cropland again went under cultivation outside Trinidád, the parciantes reopened the ditch.[18]

Due to Trinidad's increased growth, the ditch went through several changes, including enlargements, diversions, and, later, ownership and control by the Baca Irrigating Ditch Company. Felipe Baca was associated with the ditch until his death in 1879.[19] Little did he realize that his acequia would direct a significant amount of water during its 158 years of continued use.

On March 5, 1865, Baca obtained rights to seventy-seven acres located within the Vigil–St. Vrain Land Grant.[20] Baca later donated all but two acres to the Town of Trinidad. This land lay on the east bank of the Las Animas River. Commercial and Main Streets became the business center of town during the days of the Mountain Branch of the Santa Fe Trail. Commercial Street ran past the north side of Baca's adobe home. By 1870, he was among the wealthiest citizens of Las Animas County.[21] Due to his ready supply of capital and connections with influential and prosperous Anglos, Baca made much money in merchandising and cattle raising.[22] Although the year 1872 signaled the end to the major use of this railroad branch, Trinidad's economic base, along with its proximity to the mighty Las Animas River, provided an impetus for attracting and maintaining businesses.

On February 6, 1866, the Colorado Territorial Assembly approved an act to incorporate the Trinidad Town Company, organized by Felipe Baca, Juan Ignacio Alires, and William A. Bransford.[23] Three days later the assembly approved an act to create Las Animas County. The southern part of Huerfano County became Las Animas County, with Trinidad as its county seat.

In 1869 voters elected Felipe Baca, a Republican, to represent Las Animas and Huerfano Counties in the Territorial House of Representatives. That same year, Felipe Baca purchased a building in one of the best business locations of Trinidad. Until the summer of 1871, Commercial Street, known as Bridge Street, ran south from the "pole-floored" bridge over the river to intersect with Main Street.[24] In 1873 he sold two lots on Main Street for $1,000. At the time, these lots were opposite the Overland House Hotel.[25] That same year he purchased the house now known as the Baca House. He paid for the house in wool, a transaction that amounted to $7,000 plus $1,500 for its furnishings.[26] The following year, Baca made his will.[27]

Baca opposed the early statehood initiatives. He worried that the political and economic rights of the Hispanos living in the southern half of the territory would be undermined by the "unequal and unjust representation" of Anglos living in the northern half.[28]

Trinidad businessmen formed the Board of Trade to promote mining and other business interests.[29] After Baca's death on April 4, 1879, the Trinidad Board of Trade published a resolution in the *Trinidad Enterprise* describing Baca as "an earnest and energetic co-worker, a genial companion, a faithful friend and an upright citizen."[30]

To honor Felipe de Jesús Baca, in 1889 the Colorado Assembly created Baca County. This county was the first in Colorado's thirteen years of existence to be named for a Hispano assemblyman.

In the 1870s Baca sent three of his sons by train to attend schools in the East. His son Luís became a civil engineer and land surveyor.[31] Son Félix earned a law degree from Northwestern University in Chicago. He was also associated with the Baca Ditch. Son José Facundo earned an undergraduate degree from Notre Dame University and a postgraduate degree from New York University and became a physician.

Felipe de Jesús Baca's daughter Dionisia married Lorenzo Antonio Abeyta in 1866.[32] Another daughter, Apolonia,[33] married territorial representative Albert W. Archibald on April 3, 1879, in Trinidad[34] Some friction likely occurred in the family when Archibald contested and won Abeyta's seat in 1869 in the Territorial House (see Lorenzo Antonio Abeyta in this appendix). Other birth children of Felipe de Jesús Baca and María Dolores Gonzales were Juan Pedro,[35] Catarina,[36] Luz,[37] and Rosa.[38]

Casimiro Barela

1847–1920

TERRITORIAL REPRESENTATIVE |

LAS ANIMAS COUNTY | 1872, 1873, 1874

Casimiro Barela was born March 4, 1847, in Embudo, Río Arriba, New Mexico Province of Mexico (figure A.2).[39] His parents were José María Barela and María de Jesús Abeyta. Barela attended school in Mora County, New Mexico Territory.[40] He also attended school taught by Archbishop Jean Baptiste Salpointe.[41] Barela and his sister, Seferina, operated a mercantile in Lucero, Mora County.

Barela freighted goods to Colorado and in 1866 moved to Trinidad at age nineteen.[42] He returned to Mora County and married Josefa Ortíz on March 4, 1867, in Sapello.[43] After her death he married Damiana Rivera on February 16,

1884, in Trinidad.[44] His ranch in Barela, about twenty miles east of Trinidád, was known as one of Colorado's finest ranches.

Barela served as justice of the peace in 1869 and as a Las Animas county assessor in 1871. From 1872 to 1875 he first served in the Colorado Territorial House of Representatives as a Democrat. He later held office as a Populist and as a Republican.

Barela was a member of the Colorado Constitutional Conventions of 1874 and 1876. He then served seven consecutive terms in the Colorado State Senate, representing Las Animas County until 1916. In all, he served for forty-four years, earning the nickname "The Perpetual Senator."

FIGURE A.2. Casimiro Barela, AA00000987. Auraria Library Digital Collections.

Once Colorado became a state in 1876, Barela successfully introduced legislation to publish the Colorado Constitution in English, Spanish, and German. He also wrote the bill, introduced by his Anglo colleague from Las Animas County, to have the Colorado state statutes published in Spanish for the next twenty-five years. This, he said, was "for the benefit of the portion of our citizens who speak that language."[45]

In 1886 he became the first Hispano from Colorado to run for the US Senate. Although he did not win, he returned to the state senate and served as president pro tem. He held this position again in 1901. Barela worked to protect Hispanos' grazing rights from the land interests of the Colorado Fuel and Iron Company. His biographer, José E. Fernandez, wrote: "Barela [was] a steadfast advocate for the Spanish-speaking community of southern Colorado, a noteworthy accomplishment considering that Colorado was a place where anti-Mexican sentiments ran high and often resulted in intimidation and open violence against the Spanish-speaking."[46]

According to the *Biographical Compendium of Colorado*, Barela was a "man of keen perception and analytical mind." Although he spoke English with some difficulty, when he rose to speak in the Senate, "his words [were] listened to with more than ordinary attention" as his ideas were those of a "close thinker."[47]

On April 6, 1887, Barela earned the rank of colonel in the Colorado National Guard.

In 1891, when Congress established the Court of Private Land Claims, Barela presented a resolution to the Colorado State Assembly asking the court to adjudicate the land grants, including the Conejos Land Grant. In forty-two years only 130 of the 1,350 claims had been determined. Barela also spoke about the numerous unconfirmed claims in New Mexico Territory and stated that the "promise [to adjudicate land grants] has not been kept, save for a few exceptional cases, and then only in a very disadvantageous way."[48]

Barela, who was five feet seven, was an energetic and engaging businessman. He became one of the largest landowners and leading entrepreneurs of southern Colorado and served as director of the Trinidad National Bank and director of the Trinidad and San Luis Railroad.[49] His commission and forwarding house, located on Barela Block, was "an imposing office building" in Trinidad.[50] He helped edit the *Trinidad Daily Democrat* newspaper and owned Trinidad's *El Progreso* newspaper; his newspaper, *Las Dos Republicas*, served the Denver Spanish-speaking community.

Due to his ready supply of capital and connections with influential and prosperous Anglos, Casimiro Barela made much money in merchandising and cattle raising.[51] Barela and territorial representatives Felipe de Jesús Baca and Jesús María García were very well acquainted and quite connected. They were friends, associates, compadres, and influential leaders of the community who arranged their children's marriages, thus keeping their lands, wealth, and holdings intact.

As a Republican National Convention delegate in 1909 in Chicago, Barela assisted in nominating William Howard Taft for US president. Barela died in Barela, Las Animas County, on December 18, 1920. Based on his contributions as a leading Colorado assemblyman, he is honored by having his likeness on one of thirteen glass-stained windows in the State Capitol Building.[52] In 2016 Barela was posthumously inducted into the Colorado Latino Hall of Fame as one of Colorado's early Latino leaders.[53]

Casimiro Barela's daughter Leonor married Eugenio Leo García, son of territorial councilman Jesús María García and María Rafaela Alires. Barela's daughter Sofia married Eusebio Chacón, son of Captain José Rafael Sotero Chacón. Leonor and Sofia attended colleges and universities of the Sisters of Charity in Denver and Trinidad. Other known birth children of Casimiro

Barela and Josefa Ortíz were Alipio, Leo Francisco, Juana Crisostoma, Cleofas, Ambrosia, and Isabel. Known birth children of Casimiro Barela and Damiana Rivera were Margarito, Viola, and Rea.

Jesús María Barela

?–?

TERRITORIAL REPRESENTATIVE | CONEJOS AND
COSTILLA COUNTIES | 1861, 1862, 1866

Jesús María Barela served a total of three terms in the Territorial House. He diligently persevered in his requests for a Spanish translation of the House rules and territorial laws of the first session.[54]

In 1861 Barela was among the fifteen-member board for a territorial university. This board selected the area in Boulder where the University of Colorado is located today.[55] Ultimately, the House killed the bill for a territorial university because the session was almost over and there was no money in the territorial treasury for its construction.[56] During the remainder of the territorial period, no other Hispanos were named as trustees of the University of Colorado.

During Barela's second term, in 1862, he represented both Conejos and Costilla Counties. He also sought to secure interpreters to help them understand resolutions and public policy debates conducted in English. During his third, nonconsecutive term, in 1866, Jesús María Barela represented both Conejos and Costilla Counties in the Territorial House.

Celestino Domínguez

CA. 1820–?

TERRITORIAL COUNCIL | CONEJOS COUNTY | 1864–66

Domínguez was born in Spain about 1820. He graduated from the Royal College of Barcelona and was proficient in English, French, and Spanish. It is not known when he immigrated to the United States; however, he was in northern New Mexico Territory by about 1860.

Domínguez became a well-known figure in the affairs of the first Colorado territorial legislative session. In 1861 he was nominated and named among the incorporators and board members who selected the area in Boulder where the University of Colorado was later constructed.[57] Ultimately, the House killed the bill for a territorial university because the session was almost over and there was no money in the territorial treasury for its construction.[58] During the remainder of the territorial period, no other Hispanos were named as trustees of the University of Colorado.

Domínguez was often requested by the Hispano assemblymen to translate legislative proceedings. He made it more possible for the Spanish-speaking assemblymen to understand and participate effectively in territorial matters affecting their Hispano constituents. The Hispano assemblymen trusted and respected his ability to help them understand and communicate more effectively than some Anglo interpreters. His translations likely also assisted them during legislative functions as well as in restaurants and casual gatherings.

On September 18, 1861, Domínguez, who was present in the chamber, "came forward and took the oath of office at the Speaker's desk, as interpreter for the House"[59] Sometime after that date Domínguez learned that the assembly had requested territorial secretary Lewis Leydard Weld to hire him to translate the 1861 statutes and resolutions. Acting on this information, Domínguez began translating the legislation, as he understood the dire need for such information by the territory's Spanish-speaking constituents and county officers. By May of the following year, he was close to completing his translation when he learned there was no money in the territorial treasury.

In 1862 Domínguez wrote a letter on behalf of territorial representatives José Víctor García and Jesús María Barela asking Colorado's territorial delegate, Hiram Pitt Bennet, for his support in obtaining federal money to print the Spanish translation of the territorial statutes. As requested, Domínguez reminded Bennet that the public officials, who were recently elected to offices in the two counties, could not "administer justice, collect taxes or perform any official duty" until they received a Spanish version of the statues. The translation made by Domínguez was not printed until three years later. The assembly then approved a joint resolution to appropriate fifty dollars from the treasury to pay for the translation services he performed in 1861.[60]

Between 1863 and 1864, Domínguez lived in the Servilleta settlement and held a Class B peddler's license for Conejos County. Because the government classified peddlers based on the number of horses used to pull wagons or carts, Domínguez presumably sold and delivered mid-sized goods such as boots, shoes, hats, and clothes not carried by local merchants.[61]

In 1864 Domínguez served as the only Hispano-elected member to the Territorial Council. He represented Conejos County; his party affiliation is not known.

On January 18, 1864, Domínguez and several Hispano territorial and county officials and citizens petitioned Samuel E. Brown, attorney general for Colorado, to remove Indian agent Lafayette Head from office. They considered Agent Head the "cause of all the troubles and difficulties . . . the people [had] been subject to for these last two years." These troubles and difficulties included raids by some hungry indigenous bands in Head's jurisdiction who had not received their government distributions or who had received food that was old and moldy. Ultimately, Head retained his position as Indian agent.[62] Three months later territorial councilman Domínguez sent a detailed letter to Governor John Evans on March 11, requesting his help in removing Agent Head from office. The letter cited four examples of the agent's inappropriate actions, questionable character, and vengeful nature.[63] In the end, Head was not removed and held the position for several more years.

During the 1864 session, Domínguez chaired the Territorial Library Committee and likely attempted to obtain copies of published session laws from other states and territories. During his brief two years on the Council, Domínguez chaired and served on more territorial committees than any other Hispano legislator. The assembly hired Domínguez to translate the annual message of Acting Governor Samuel H. Elbert. For his translation Domínguez received fifty dollars.

In 1865 territorial councilman Domínguez penned a four-page letter to territorial governor Alexander Cummings regarding Colorado's silver-mining interests and the immediate and "imperious demand [for] cheap, practical and experienced labor." Domínguez recommended recruiting experienced silver miners from Chihuahua, Mexico:

> if either the State or the General Government . . . send a suitable person to the nearest mining districts of Chihuahua . . . taking with him a quantity of good ores, a certified statement of the wages we pay to our miners, a copy of the general laws of our mining districts and the necessary means to provide transportation and provisions to those who would like to immigrate here[, we] could easily induce a large number of Mexican silver miners to locate permanently amongst us.[64]

Domínguez also wrote that his proficiency in English, French, and Spanish assisted him during a prior assignment involving international relations. No records indicate that Governor Cummings responded to Domínguez's recommendation to import experienced Mexican silver miners, and his experience in international relations went unacknowledged.

While in Colorado, Domínguez published a monthly Spanish-language commercial report; unfortunately, no report has survived. In Denver in 1872 he gave Spanish classes to local businessmen: "with Denver's central position and her commanding and growing influence on the southern trade, it will be of great advantage to our businessmen to understand the Spanish language."[65]

In 1872 he interpreted for the three Spanish-speaking members in the Territorial Council. In 1874 Councilman Juan Bautista Jáquez requested that Domínguez replace the current interpreter, Silas Hawes, because Hawes was "not competent in Spanish and did not keep him posted on the proceedings." Jáquez felt he and the other Hispano assemblymen had a right to select their interpreter. Hugh Butler (Gilpin) argued that the Council had the right to select its interpreter. After a vote was taken, the Council selected another Anglo, John Lawrence, as its interpreter.[66]

During the Colorado Constitutional Convention held in Denver on February 29, 1876, Domínguez translated for the only three Spanish-speaking convention delegates. For his services during the convention, the Territorial Treasury paid him seven dollars a day. He had estimated a cost of two dollars per page to proofread and correct the Spanish-language revisions of the state constitution.[67] Celestino Domínguez "provided a vital link between his monolingual Spanish-speaking brethren and the majority of the convention attendees."[68] Unfortunately, no information exists regarding his personal life or death. He departed Colorado Territory as mysteriously as he had arrived.

Jesús María García

1842–99

TERRITORIAL COUNCIL, LAS ANIMAS COUNTY | 1872

CONSTITUTIONAL CONVENTION DELEGATE | 1876

Jesús María García served in the Territorial Council representing Las Animas County as a Democrat in 1872 (figure A.3). In 1869 he was a probate judge.[69] He was a delegate to the Colorado Constitutional Conventions in 1874 and 1876

FIGURE A.3. Jesús María García. Denver Public Library, Western History and Genealogy Department.

and helped construct the state constitution. The following year he was one of five members of the first board of trustees of the Town of Trinidad.[70] García was very well acquainted with territorial representatives Casimiro Barela and Felipe de Jesús Baca. They were friends and associates who arranged their children's marriages, thus keeping their lands, wealth, and holdings intact. García was a stockholder in Baca's irrigation ditch and served as secretary-treasurer of the Baca Irrigating Ditch Company. García also became an influential leader of the Trinidad community and could afford to send his son east by train to attend the University of Notre Dame.

Jesús María García married María Rafaela Alires[71] on September 8, 1866, in Trinidad.[72] Their son Eugenio Leo married Leonor Barela, daughter of territorial assemblyman Casimiro Barela and Josefa Ortíz.[73] Other known birth children were José, Julian, Rafael, and Prudencia.[74] After the death of his first wife, García married María Manuela Cortez on August 21, 1875, in Trinidad.[75] Their two birth sons were Samuel and Daniel. After Jesús María García's death on October 24, 1899, Casimiro Barela presented three resolutions at a meeting held in the Trinidad courthouse to honor his friend. The resolutions addressed García's generous acts of charity and love of his fellow citizens. After the meeting the attendees pledged $400 to erect a monument in García's honor.[76]

José Víctor García

1832–1900
TERRITORIAL REPRESENTATIVE | CONEJOS COUNTY | 1861–65
TERRITORIAL COUNCIL | CONEJOS AND
COSTILLA COUNTIES | 1872–76

José Víctor García was born March 6, 1832, to José Serafín García and María de la Luz Aragón in San Juan de los Caballeros, New Mexico Province of

Mexico (figure A.4).[77] He left home at age fifteen and learned to hunt buffalo. He was recognized as "one of the most successful buffalo hunters in New Mexico."[78] He arrived in Los Conejos about 1855 and was known to have traded with the Apache, Navajo, and Ute Nations.

In 1859 García served in the New Mexico Territorial House of Representatives, which met in Santa Fe.[79] He represented the people living in the far northern frontier.

José Víctor García and Jesús María Barela (Costilla) were the only two Hispanos to serve in Colorado's first territorial assembly in 1861. As members of

FIGURE A.4. José Víctor García. Courtesy Francisco Gallegos.

the Territorial House, both diligently worked for their Hispano constituents by requesting translations of the territorial laws. During subsequent terms of office, García persevered in his requests for a Spanish translation of the House rules and the governor's messages. He and Barela also sought to secure interpreters to help them understand resolutions and public policy debates that were conducted in English.

According to oral history, in 1861 García requested Governor William Gilpin have the line between Colorado and New Mexico surveyed.[80]

By 1864 García was an attorney in El Brazo, Conejos County. That same year, on January 18, García and several Hispano territorial and county officials and citizens petitioned Samuel E. Brown, attorney general for Colorado, to remove Agent Lafayette Head from office. They considered Agent Head the "cause of all the troubles and difficulties . . . the people [had] been subject to for these last two years." These troubles and difficulties included raids by some hungry indigenous bands in Head's jurisdiction who had not received their government distributions or who had received old, moldy food.[81] In the end, Head retained his position as Indian agent, a post he held for several more years.

According to the *Portrait and Biographical Record*, "through the influence of George Miles Chilcott" García requested a government survey of the land.[82] It is not known when he requested the survey or whether it was requested in a legislative capacity as a member of either the New Mexico or Colorado territorial assemblies.

When García served on the Territorial Council in 1872, Governor Edward C. McCook commissioned him brigadier general of the Colorado Territorial Militia for the Second Division.[83] The office of brigadier general was established by the territorial assembly in 1865. By this act, the territory was divided into two, nonuniformed military divisions. By law, the militia could not leave the territory, nor could it engage in expeditions against the citizens or against the indigenous tribes. In this capacity García determined which men, within his jurisdiction, could enroll and muster into an organized company to perform any military duty in the territorial militia. The brigadier general appointed his aide, inspector, paymaster, and quartermaster, each having the rank of captain.[84] No surviving records provide the names of García's staff. By 1880, the rank served as an honorary post.[85] In 1874 the governor wished to reappoint García, but García declined in order to attend to new duties as a member of the Board of Centennial Exhibition Managers.[86]

On January 6, 1874, Governor Samuel H. Elbert urged the territorial assembly to participate in an upcoming centennial exhibition to be held in Philadelphia in 1876. About two weeks later, the assembly approved a concurrent resolution authorizing the governor to appoint a board to make "a thorough representation of our varied and important industrial and productive interests at the . . . exhibition."[87] In February the governor named José Víctor García, newsman William Newton Byers, two bankers, a Denver businessman, and a Boulder farmer to the board of managers for the centennial exposition. On February 11, 1876, the assembly repealed the concurrent resolution of 1874 and appropriated $10,000 for costs associated with the Colorado exhibition in Philadelphia. Governor John L. Routt appointed two men as commissioners to make the necessary arrangements to prepare and transport the exhibits, which consisted of gold, silver, iron, coal, coke, and flour. It is not known whether García attended the exposition; however, Colorado won sixteen mining awards at the exhibition; Nevada won thirty-seven.[88]

García was a man of significant influence among the Hispanos, yet Lafayette Head replaced him in the Territorial House. It is not known if these appointments were made to keep García from serving additional terms in the Colorado Territorial Assembly. In the past, he and Head had disagreed on many issues. They had resolved their issues when Head served as godfather to García's son, Lafayette, on December 7.[89]

According to the *Portrait and Biographical Record*, García took a squatter's claim to a section of government land where he farmed and raised his stock. His ranch, which became one of the most valuable in the county, encompassed 940 acres, 640 of which were along the Conejos River.[90]

José Víctor García married María Candelaria Jáquez on November 24, 1854, in Abiquiú, New Mexico Territory.[91] Presumably, it was his wife's land on which García previously settled, as her father was a grantee of the Conejos grant. García may have acquired this vast land due to *partido* (share) contracts, land grabs or preemption, political favors, or by means of his patrón status in Conejos County. According to an article published in the *San Luis Valley Historian*, during the land-grant hearings held in Santa Fe, García "opposed . . . the Mexican land grants and helped the government obtain title to several thousand acres of land."[92] Further research is needed to determine the validity of this statement and the rationale for opposing confirmation of the granted lands.

Three sons of José Víctor García served in the legislature in some capacity: José Alejandro served as a page in the first session of the Colorado State Senate in 1876;[93] José Alejandro de Amarante served as a legislator in the Colorado State Assembly in 1881–82; and Celestino José García served as a legislator in the Colorado State House of Representatives from 1893 to 1911.

José Víctor García married Plácida de la Trinidád Silva on September 10, 1862, in Conejos, Conejos County. Their known birth children were Isidora,[94] Juan Climaco,[95] Lafayette,[96] Adolfo, Fidela, Dolores, Galasancio, Ignacio, and Sevilla. José Víctor García died on September 10, 1900, at Conejos.[97]

Juan Bautista Jáquez

CA. 1833–?

TERRITORIAL COUNCIL | HUERFANO COUNTY | 1874–78

Juan Bautista Jáquez was the son of Felipe de Jesús Jáquez and María Micaela Chaves. His father was one of the Conejos land grantees. His brother, José María Jáquez, brought the first settlers into Guadalupe in 1854.[98]

On August 8, 1862, the Colorado Territorial Assembly allowed Juan Bautista Jáquez, Francisco Gallegos, Francisco Ruibal, and their associates to create a free cemetery in Conejos for use by the residents of that county and its neighboring counties.[99] Although the purpose of the new cemetery is unknown, this legislation likely provided for a non-Catholic cemetery, as Catholic churches in Hispano Colorado already had cemeteries for parishioners. By custom during this time, Catholic families of the deceased gave the church a donation for the mass and burial rite. If the family was poor, the community assisted by giving a donation so the baptized deceased could be properly buried. By 1874, it was unlawful to bury a body within the town limits of Conejos and Costilla Counties; the fine was set at $100.[100]

Juan Bautista was a lawyer from 1863 to 1866.[101]

During the 1874 session of the Territorial Council, Juan Bautista Jáquez represented Huerfano County. Nine days into the session, Councilman Jáquez, a Republican, requested to have the interpreter Silas Hawes replaced by Celestino Domínguez because Hawes was "not competent in Spanish and did not keep him posted on the proceedings." Jáquez felt that he and the other Hispano assemblymen had a right to select their interpreter. Hugh Butler (Gilpin), also a Republican, claimed the Council had the right to select its interpreter and accused Jáquez of attacking "the character and skills" of Hawes. After a vote was taken, the Council selected another Anglo, John Lawrence, as interpreter.[102]

Known birth children of Juan Bautista Jáquez and María Simona Martin were Sirilio,[103] José Renignioso, Francisco Esteban,[104] Juana,[105] Crescencia,[106] Juan Agustin, Felipe de Jesús,[107] Heraclia,[108] and Concepción.[109]

Mariano Sisto Larragoite

1847–1908

TERRITORIAL REPRESENTATIVE | LAS ANIMAS COUNTY | 1872–75

Mariano Sisto Larragoite was the son of Benito Anselmo Larrogoite and María Feliciana Valdez (figure A.5). Mariano's father was born in Spain and during the 1830s moved to Santa Fe, where he operated a store and farmed. Mariano Larragoite was baptized on April 6, 1846, in Santa Fe, Mexico. He learned to read and write in English and assisted in his father's store.

In 1870, at about age twenty-four, Mariano moved to Denver, then in Arapahoe County of Colorado Territory, and worked as a clerk in the Kastor Clothing Store.[110]

He settled in Las Animas County about 1871 and was elected to the Territorial House, where he served from 1872 to 1875. During his first term he introduced a bill to change the capital from Denver to Pueblo.[111] That session the members of the House authorized him to interpret for the Spanish-speaking legislators.[112] In 1874 he chaired the Federal Relations and the Rules and Joint Rules Committees.

By 1879, Larragoite was an attorney practicing law at Trinidad. By 1894, he had returned to New Mexico Territory where voters in Taos, Rio Arriba, and San Juan Counties elected him to represent them in the Council of the Thirty-First Territorial Assembly of New Mexico. He chaired the Irrigation Committee and served on the Agriculture and Manufactures, Public Property, Railroads, and Education Committees.[113] On January 14, 1895, he presented a joint resolution that was ultimately approved and submitted to the US House Committee on Territorial Affairs. The resolution proposed that the Jicarilla Nation be removed from their present reservation to a reservation in Indian Territory.[114] Nine days later he introduced a bill to prevent cruelty to animals and to bring alleged criminals to justice.[115]

Larragoite returned to Las Animas County about 1900. In 1902 he became a delegate to the Colorado Republican Convention; but according to the *Denver Post*, "[he] was not accorded the treatment he expected at the hands of the Republicans" and "[the] next year he became again a Democrat . . . Since that time . . . he has fluctuated between the two parties annually, with admirable impartiality."[116]

Mariano Sisto Larragoite, a Presbyterian, died of heart disease on December 16, 1908, in Santa Fe County, New Mexico Territory.

Known birth children of Larragoite and María Paula Lopez were Zulema, José Armando, José Claudio, and María.[117]

Juan Bautista Lobato

1833–1909

TERRITORIAL REPRESENTATIVE | CONEJOS AND
COSTILLA COUNTIES | 1866–67

Lobato was born to Antonio José Lobato and María Magdalena Trujillo in December 1833 in Abiquiú, New Mexico Province of Mexico. Juan Baustista fought in the US Indian wars; like his uncle Pedro Antonio Lobato, Juan Bautista served in the Colorado Territorial Assembly.

He became an express rider who rode on horseback to deliver official military messages and correspondence between Fort Garland and Cañon City.[118] Each express consisted of two men, one of whom carried official army matter from post to post, the other civilian mails, calling on postmasters along the route. Riders and horses were changed at every post. Escorts were provided when additional safety was needed.[119] The rides were difficult and long. Many times they rode through the night to keep out of sight of nearby indigenous warriors. They rode though storms and under difficult conditions to deliver correspondence and reports to military posts in Colorado and New Mexico. At Cañon City the express connected with the "Pony Line" to Denver.[120] Effective September 25, 1862, Fort Garland officers could no longer employ civilian expressmen to deliver mail or military dispatches.[121]

According to family lore, Lobato's land holdings stretched from northern New Mexico to the Arkansas Valley of Colorado.[122] He married María Francisca Martínez on March 3, 1862, in Conejos, Conejos County, Colorado Territory.[123]

Known birth children of Juan Bautista Lobato and María Francisca Martínez were María del Carmen,[124] José Anastacio,[125] Amada,[126] Juana Acenaida, Teresa,[127] Virginia,[128] Alberto,[129] Candelaria,[130] and Salvador Nieto.

Pedro Antonio Lobato

1799–1872

TERRITORIAL REPRESENTATIVE | CONEJOS COUNTY | 1865–66

Pedro Antonio Lobato, son of Santiago Lobato and María Candelaria Martínez, was born October 1, 1799, in New Mexico Province of colonial New Spain.[131]

By 1860, Lobato, a resident of San Antonio in Los Conejos, Taos County, New Mexico Territory, was "an expert in metalworking." He made the door fittings and padlock for the Nuestra Señora de Guadalupe Church.[132] He and Juan Francisco Luján cast a medium-sized bell for the church.[133]

Lobato became a man of substantial means and held several public offices. In 1862, at age sixty-three, Lobato served as chair of the Conejos County commissioners. In 1865 he served in the Colorado Territorial House under the Constitutional Union Party. The Union Party was formed around the start of the US Civil War as an independent minority party; it attracted voters who did not associate with the ideals supported by proslavery Democrats or antislavery Republicans but favored preserving the Union. Lobato's nephew, Juan

Bautista Lobato (Conejos), also served in the Colorado Territorial Assembly.

Pedro Antonio Lobato died at age seventy-two in Punche, Costilla County; he was buried on January 8, 1872, in Costilla, Costilla County, New Mexico Territory.[134] The following year, on January 21, the Conejos parish priest offered a customary Catholic mass for the repose of Lobato's soul. During the service a parishioner played the organ and accompanied the priest. Many family and friends attended this memorial service.[135]

Known birth children of Pedro Antonio Lobato and María Concepción Herrera were Francisca,[136] José Policarpio,[137] Teodora, Teodoro Antonio,[138] Paula,[139] Manuela,[140] and Jesús María.

José Gabriel Martínez

1821–91

TERRITORIAL REPRESENTATIVE | 1865–66

José Gabriel Martínez was born in September 1821 in New Mexico Province in the month that Mexico won its independence from Spain. He was the son of José Antonio Martín and María Manuela Trujillo.

On February 20, 1859, Martínez and other members of the Guadalupe church committee met to discuss the ongoing construction of their parish church and the annual prices for the services of a cantor and organist.[141] Like other parishioners, Martínez donated labor and materials and participated in annual feast day celebrations, known as *funciones*. During the función held on December 12, 1873, Martínez and three other men carried the canopy protecting the women carrying the statue of Nuestra Señora. Following them toward the church was a procession of the faithful and about 127 men on horseback.[142]

Martínez was also a member of the devotees of Nuestra Señora de Guadalupe. On November 25, 1883, this fraternal group met to raise money for the church. The members agreed that, every year, each would donate twenty-five cents. This donation was in addition to the contributions to the priest for celebrating mass and officiating at the various religious services, duties, and feast days.[143]

On January 17, 1860, José Gabriel Martínez served as second lieutenant in the Conejos Militia under Captain Jesús María Velásquez. It was a mounted company on a campaign against the Navajo. The militia roster listed Martínez as the company's bugler.[144]

In 1863 Martínez was the Conejos County treasurer. Because the settlers had no ready cash, they likely paid him in produce, buckskins, or blankets. County treasurers could then sell the goods and turn the proceeds over to the territorial treasurer to pay the county's taxes.[145]

Martínez was elected to the Fourth and Fifth Colorado Territorial Assemblies; the 1865 session lasted one week, and the 1866 session lasted forty days.

One historical account placed Martínez in Saguache in 1870, when an Anglo vigilante mob hanged young Donaciano Sánchez. Scanty information about this event appears in a diary kept by John Lawrence. Unfortunately, no historical documents explain why José Gabriel Martínez traveled to Saguache. Perhaps he was there as moral support for the Sánchez family.

A daughter of José Gabriel Martínez, María Francisca, married territorial representative Juan Bautista Lobato on March 3, 1862, in Conejos.[146] Other known birth children of José Gabriel Martínez and María Dolores Trujillo were Nicanora, Ramona,[147] Genoveva,[148] Antonia, Antonio, Jose Celestino,[149] Ramon, and Francisca.[150] José Gabriel Martínez died of pneumonia; his family buried him in the Conejos cemetery on May 22, 1891.[151]

José Pablo Antonio de Jesús Ortega

CA. 1817–?

TERRITORIAL REPRESENTATIVE | CONEJOS AND
COSTILLA COUNTIES | 1864–65, 1868–69

José Pablo Antonio Ortega was born about May 1817 in New Mexico Province of colonial New Spain. He was the son of Juan de Jesús Ortega and María Paula Chavez. He married Juana María Trujillo, the daughter of Atanacio Trujillo and María de Jesús Valdez, on February 26, 1862, in Conejos, Conejos County, Colorado Territory.[152]

By 1862 Ortega was serving as one of two known alcaldes of the San Jose Precinct in Los Conejos.[153] By 1863 he was a justice of the peace.

On August 18, 1862, a band of Tabaguache Ute Indians made a complaint to officers at Fort Garland regarding Indian agent Lafayette Head. They were upset about the quality of the rations distributed and the interpreter. Ortega participated in a hearing to determine if Agent Head had withheld and sold "subsistence supplies" intended for the Utes in his jurisdiction and acquired the services of an interpreter who did not speak the Ute language. A hearing was held, but Governor John Evans did not support the findings; thus, Agent Head retained his office.[154]

On January 18, 1864, Ortega and several Hispano territorial and county officials and citizens petitioned Samuel E. Brown, attorney general for Colorado, to remove Agent Head from office. They considered Head to be the "cause of all the troubles and difficulties . . . the people [had] been subject to for these last two years." These troubles and difficulties included raids by some hungry indigenous bands in Head's jurisdiction who had not received their government distributions or received food that was old and moldy. In the end, Head held the pose for several more years.[155]

Francisco Sánchez

1830–1917

TERRITORIAL COUNCIL | CONEJOS AND
  COSTILLA COUNTIES | 1868–70

TERRITORIAL REPRESENTATIVE | CONEJOS
  AND COSTILLA COUNTIES | 1872–73

Francisco Sánchez was born on March 15, 1830, in the New Mexico Province of Mexico to Luís Cristobal Sánchez and María Guadalupe García (figure A.5). Francisco married María Soledad Jaramillo on April 21, 1856, at Taos, Taos County, New Mexico Territory.[156] They later resided along the Rio Culebra near San Luis in Costilla County, Colorado Territory. After her death, he married María Teresa Córdova on September 30, 1907, at San Luis.[157] They resided in San Acacio, Costilla County. Francisco purchased his new wife a set of "beautiful amethyst [wine] glasses with gold inlay crystal that have survived and are still in the Sánchez family today."[158]

Sánchez served in both the Colorado territorial and state legislatures.

FIGURE A.5. Francisco Sánchez. Courtesy Connie Rodriguez.

He served a term in the Territorial Council in 1868, and two nonconsecutive terms in the State House in 1871 and 1876.

Francisco Sánchez died in San Acacio, Costilla County, on January 29, 1917.[159] Known birth children of Francisco Sánchez and Soledad Jaramillo were Cleofas, Veneranda, and Virginia.

José Silverio Suazo

1838–76

TERRITORIAL REPRESENTATIVE | CONEJOS, COSTILLA, AND HUERFANO COUNTIES | 1868–69

TERRITORIAL COUNCIL | CONEJOS, COSTILLA, AND HUERFANO COUNTIES | 1872–76

José Silverio Suazo was born in Abiquiú, New Mexico Province of Mexico, on June 25, 1838, to José Antonio Suazo and María Dolores Lujan.[160] He was married to María Salomé Durán and lived in Guadalupe in 1866.

By 1862 he lived in San Judas de Tadeo and served as alguacil (constable) of the San Rafael district.[161] By 1864 he was an attorney in El Cañon, Conejos County.

Suazo later moved to Huerfano County and became a friend of Fred Walsen, a "political boss" of the county's Republican Party. According to a local newspaper, in 1871 Suazo and Walsen denounced the means by which names were solicited and given to Congress to "grant and confirm to the heirs and legal representatives the entire tract of land of the Vigil–St. Vrain Land Grant."[162] Further research is needed to determine the validity of this statement and the rationale for opposing confirmation of granted land.

José Silverio Suazo died in 1876 at La Veta, Huerfano County. Sometime after his death, Juan Sántos Trujillo wrote a corrido titled "Las Muertes de Walsenburg" (The Deaths at Walsenburg). According to the corrido, Suazo's death occurred after a long night of drinking and gambling at cards in a saloon at La Veta in Huerfano County. According to Wilbur Fisk Stone, editor of the *Pueblo Daily Chieftain*, Suazo had just returned from a political convention held at Manitou Springs in El Paso County. About 6:00 a.m. on Sunday, September 3, 1876, Suazo, who had consumed much alcohol, became angry and waved his pistol. According to the report, the gamblers quarreled over thirty-five dollars and accused one another of cheating: "Suaso [*sic*], in liquor, a very dangerous man, got out his pistol and commenced striking all about him, clearing the room."[163]

The gamblers fled, but hours later Suazo found and threatened them. Again, when one of the gamblers approached, Suazo struck him with the butt of his pistol. As Suazo turned in search of the others, someone struck him in the head with a grubbing hoe. His friends moved him to a drugstore where he died "peacefully in the arms of his friend Fred Walsen" on September 3, 1876.

A known birth daughter of José Silverio Suazo and María Salomé Durán was María Victoria.[164]

Pedro Rafael Trujillo

CA. 1835–CA. 1925
TERRITORIAL REPRESENTATIVE | COSTILLA COUNTY | 1872–73

Pedro Rafael Trujillo was born about 1835 in New Mexico Province of Mexico (figure A.6). As a young lad, he was captured by a band of Utes, and he subsequently learned to speak their language. Another Ute band rescued him and presumably ransomed him to his family. He felt more comfortable wearing buckskin and moccasins. He was one of the original settlers of Garcia in Costilla County.[165]

On October 15, 1872, Trujillo received an agreement from the USFLEC regarding settlement of his claim on the Costilla Estates of the Sangre de Cristo grant. Settlers who had no proof and who had

FIGURE A.6. Pedro Rafael Trujillo. Courtesy Charlene Garcia Simms.

cultivated land between five and fifteen years could purchase the land for two dollars and fifty cents an acre, while those who had cultivated the land for two years could purchase it for twenty to thirty-five dollars an acre.

Trujillo and two commissioners of the Costilla plaza received a letter of agreement from the USFLEC on October 1873.[166] As one of the Hispano settlers on the Sangre de Cristo land who had constructed his home and had labored to clear the land and bring it under cultivation, he would have to purchase it from the USFLEC.

Litigation of the land on the Sangre de Cristo continued into the statehood period. On February 4, 1916, the Costilla Estates Development Company filed a map of the Plaza de los Manzanares area (Garcia) showing the occupants of tracts of land belonging to the company. By 1915, Trujillo had received a deed to two tracks of land now owned by the company.[167]

In December 28, 1872, Trujillo and the other elected assemblymen from southern Colorado arrived in Denver for the eleventh session of the territorial legislature. While in Denver, they stayed at the Broadwell Hotel. Trujillo served two terms in the Territorial House. His run for a third term in 1875 ended in a loss by twenty-one votes, but he continued to serve in other positions.[168] He served as a Costilla County commissioner in 1879, 1880, and 1895. In 1884 he served as county treasurer.[169]

By 1884, Pedro Rafael Trujillo was a parciante of both the Trujillo Ditch No. 15 and the Manzanares Ditch.[170] He donated land in García for a school.[171] By 1900, Trujillo had become the wealthiest man there.[172] His wife was María Nestora Chacón.[173]

José Anastacio de Jesús Valdez

1847–1927

TERRITORIAL REPRESENTATIVE | HUERFANO COUNTY | 1874–75

Valdez was born to Mariano de Jesús Valdez and Manuela de la Luz Archuleta on April 26, 1847, in Taos County, New Mexico Province of Mexico (figure A.7).[174] About 1861 Valdez lived in San Pablo, Costilla County, Colorado Territory, with his parents. By 1865, he lived in the Cuchara Valley of Huerfano County, herding his father's sheep.[175]

By 1867, at age twenty, he lived in La Plaza de los Leones (present-day Walsenburg) and reportedly taught at the county's first public school.[176] His brother and their father also taught school during their lifetimes.[177]

In 1869, at age twenty-two, Valdez was elected Huerfano County's first Hispano assessor. County clerk John H. Brown furnished him with legal cap paper, an inkstand and pen, and a published Spanish translation of the 1864 Colorado territorial statutes. With this form in hand, Valdez visited every household in the county to identify, evaluate, and assess taxable real estate,

FIGURE A.7. José Anastacio de Jesús Valdez. Denver Public Library, Western History and Genealogy Department, Bio FF J A J Valdes F46691.

personal property, and agricultural land.[178] Valdez refused the nomination for a third term as assessor.

In 1870 Valdez moved to Pueblo, Pueblo County, to study English in an Episcopal school led by Reverend Samuel Edwards. During his stay in Pueblo, Valdez lived at the residence of a former justice and former territorial delegate to Congress, Allen Alexander Bradford. During his free time Valdez studied law by reading Bradford's law books.[179] Valdez gained admittance to the Colorado bar about 1889[180] and began a successful law practice in his "pleasant home in the suburbs of the city of Walsenburg."[181]

In 1874 Representative Valdez (Huerfano) introduced an important bill in the Territorial House prohibiting the malicious injury or death of livestock or maliciously interfering with the work of any herders.[182]

After serving one term of office in the House, Valdez returned to Huerfano County and served in a variety of elected city and county positions. He owned a ranch near the Toltec Coal Mine, about two and a half miles north of Walsenburg.[183]

In 1884 Valdez was a census enumerator for the southern part of the county. In 1886 he was elected mayor of Walsenburg. Two years later, he served as the county clerk. In 1892 he was again elected mayor of Walsenburg. In 1897 he was elected city attorney.[184]

José Anastacio de Jesús Valdez belonged to the parish of Nuestra Señora de los Siete Dolores (Our Lady of the Seven Sorrows), today known as St. Mary's Catholic Church. He purchased one of three stained-glass windows made by the Benziger Brothers.[185] In 1894 he founded the Unión Católica (Catholic Union) to raise funds for the church.

Each year for the Feast of Corpus Christi members constructed one of four outdoor altars that were decorated with flowers. This day was the most beautiful of the celebrated feast days.[186] Valdez often served as mayordomo.

According to the *Walsenburg World*, he was a penitente, a member of the Fraternity of Jesus Christ.[187]

On February 12, 1873, José Anastacio de Jesús Valdez married María Silveria Salazar in Trinidad.[188] Their known birth children were Manuela Antonia,[189] Fidel,[190] and Jesús Ruperto.[191] He married Victoria Sánchez on July 29, 1882.[192] Their known birth children were Santiago,[193] José Eloy,[194] and Magdalena.[195] José Anastacio de Jesús Valdez died in Walsenburg on July 14, 1927.[196]

José Seledonio Valdez

1814–?

TERRITORIAL REPRESENTATIVE | CONEJOS AND

COSTILLA COUNTIES | 1867–68

FIGURE A.8. Celedonio Valdez. Denver Public Library, Western History and Genealogy Department, Bio FF Seledonia Valdez F33267.

José Seledonio Valdez, son of Francisco Antonio Valdez and María Rafaela Varela, was born February 2, 1814, at La Joya, New Mexico Province of colonial New Spain (figure A.8).[197] Valdez married Juana Nepomucena Chávez about 1842.

Valdez also went by the name Celedon Valdez. He served in the New Mexico Territorial Assembly in 1851, representing citizens living in the far northern "frontier points."[198] For his service, Governor James S. Calhoun presented him with a bowie knife. Its handle was engraved with the message "Gov. Calhoun to S. Valdez."[199] On July 9 the New Mexico Territorial Assembly approved a joint resolution to request authority from Congress to raise unpaid volunteer companies against indigenous raiding "invaders." In lieu of payment, the resolution allowed volunteers "under the direction of a leader appointed from among them [an] equal share of all the captives and other spoils . . . taken."[200]

The following year, on January 20, 1860, Valdez served in the Conejos Militia under Captain Jesús María Velásquez on a campaign against the Navajo.[201] After completing his term of service, he returned to his family and farm.

Catholic priests traveled to the Conejos settlements to offer mass, hear confessions, and give the sacraments. They often borrowed Valdez's horse and buggy and boarded in his home.[202] At his home in La Isla, Valdez had constructed a chapel dedicated to San José (Saint Joseph). The first Catholic baptism in Colorado occurred there on June 1, 1858, when Valdez and his wife served as compadres to a son of future territorial assemblyman José Víctor García.[203] The child, José Alejandro de Amarante García, would later serve in the Colorado State House of Representatives. By Hispano baptismal custom, the Valdez and García families were connected by an act of compadrazco.

Like other parishioners of the Nuestra Señora de Guadalupe Catholic Church in Conejos, José Seledonio Valdez donated labor and materials and participated in annual feast day celebrations. During the función held on December 12, 1873, Valdez and three other men carried the canopy protecting the women carrying the statue of Nuestra Señora. Following them toward the church was a procession of the faithful and about 127 men on horseback.[204] On November 25, 1883, sixty-nine-year-old José Seledonio Valdez served as president of the Devotees of the Nuestra Señora de Guadalupe. This fraternal group of men raised money for the Conejos church of the same name. The members agreed that, every year, each would donate twenty-five cents.[205] This donation was in addition to the contributions to the priest for celebrating mass and officiating at the various religious services, duties, and feast days.

On January 18, 1864, Valdez and several Hispano territorial and county officials and citizens petitioned Samuel E. Brown, attorney general for Colorado, to remove Indian agent Lafayette Head from office. They considered Agent Head to be the "cause of all the troubles and difficulties . . . the people [had] been subject to for these last two years." These troubles and difficulties included raids by some hungry indigenous bands in Head's jurisdiction who had not received their government distributions or who had received old, moldy food. In the end, Head retained his position for several more years.[206] While representing Conejos and Costilla Counties in 1867, Valdez became the first and only Hispano assemblyman named to the prestigious Mining and Minerals Committee.

Valdez diligently worked to petition for the regrant of the Conejos Land Grant. His life demonstrated a commitment to southern Colorado. He was an original settler who served in the militia, held public office, and helped in the planning and construction of Colorado's oldest Catholic church.

The birth children of Valdez and Juana Nepomucena Chávez were Josefa,[207] Crescencio, Francisco, Teófilo, Dolores, and Juana Epifania.[208] By 1859, his daughter Jesusita was attending school in South Bend, Indiana. When she returned to Conejos, she taught her family some English words and phrases.[209]

His son, Representative Crescencio Valdez (Conejos),[210] continued in his father's footsteps by serving in the Colorado State House of Representatives in 1889.[211] He also continued his father's efforts to confirm the Conejos Land Grant. In 1900 a court of five justices denied the claim and dismissed the Conejos petition due to lack of evidence that the grant had ever been made as claimed in 1833. Colorado's representative to this court was Justice Wilbur Fisk Stone.

Jesús María Velásquez

CA. 1816–72

TERRITORIAL COUNCIL | CONEJOS COUNTY | 1866–70

Jesús María Velásquez was born to José Velásquez and María Estefana Martínez about 1816 in the New Mexico Province of colonial New Spain. He married María Dolores Sánchez on March 24, 1835, at Ojo Caliente, New Mexico Province of Mexico.

In 1854 Jesús María Velásquez was one of the original settlers of Guadalupe, a settlement on the north side of the Conejos River.[212] Due to attempts by the indigenous nations to retain their land, Velásquez and the other settlers returned to Rio Arriba County, New Mexico Territory, for protection. Later they returned to Guadalupe.

By September 1857, over 300 New Mexican citizens had been killed by the raiding Navajo. Citizens grew tired of the US Army's failed attempt to "control the Navajo," so the New Mexico Territorial Assembly voted to raise volunteer battalions. It authorized independent campaigns that were under the authority of the governor and "independent of all other military authority."[213] Each militiaman supplied his own horse, equipment, arms, and provisions.

From 1858 to 1860, his fellow soldier-colonists on the northern frontier elected Jesús María Velásquez as captain to lead their punitive expeditions. On January 30, 1858, Captain Velásquez and his mounted men mustered in as Company D of the New Mexico Volunteers.[214]

On January 17, 1860, when Captain Velásquez led his mounted company of ninety-nine Hispano soldiers on a campaign against the Navajo, he was forty-six-years old. Because the Conejos Militia was a large company, it had two musicians.[215] After serving for an unknown period, Velásquez and his militiamen returned to their families and farms.

Like other parishioners of the Nuestra Señora de Guadalupe church in Conejos, Captain Velásquez donated labor, materials, time, and money. On February 20, 1859, Velásquez served on a twelve-member committee of male parishioners of the Guadalupe Catholic Church to discuss the ongoing construction of their parish church and to determine the responsibilities and annual payment for the services of a cantor and organist.[216] He was named mayordomo of the Guadalupe church on December 18.[217] As mayordomo, he was responsible for cleaning the church, preparing the altar for mass, and arranging and facilitating the host of activities necessary to celebrate the feast day celebrations. He may have resigned on March 25, 1860, possibly to serve as Indian agent Lafayette Head's interpreter or because he was still away on militia duty.[218]

Velásquez was literate in Spanish and spoke Ute. He once said he had heard Ute spoken "since the day [he] was born."[219] In 1861 Velásquez served the US government as interpreter for the Conejos Indian Agency under Lafayette Head.[220] At the time, government funds to pay agency interpreters for transportation and essential incidentals were in arrears,[221] so very likely Velásquez did not regularly receive the $250 government allotment.[222] Velásquez resigned the following year to serve as Conejos County probate judge.

On August 18, 1862, Velásquez was one of many men who participated in a hearing to determine if Agent Head had withheld and sold "subsistence supplies" intended for the Utes in his jurisdiction and to determine the qualifications of his interpreter. A hearing was held, but Governor John Evans did not support the findings, thus Agent Head retained his office.[223]

On November 3, 1863, Captain Velásquez served as the prefect, or alcalde, of the Conejos settlements.[224]

While representing Conejos County in the Colorado Territorial Council in 1865, Velásquez sponsored a bill, drafted by citizen John Lawrence, to create Saguache County out of Costilla County. The new county was established on February 11, 1867.[225]

The known birth children of Jesús María Velásquez and María Dolores Sánchez were José Arcario (Alcario),[226] Delida, Tomas Velásquez, Manuel,[227] Cleofas, and Viviana.

Jesús María Velásquez died at age fifty-eight; his family buried him in the Guadalupita Cemetery at Conejos on February 2, 1872.[228] That year his son José Arcadio (Alcario) followed in his footsteps and represented Conejos County in the Eleventh Territorial House of Representatives.

José Arcadio Velásquez

CA. 1840–?

TERRITORIAL REPRESENTATIVE | CONEJOS COUNTY | 1872–73

José Arcadio Velásquez was born about 1846 to Captain Jesús María Velásquez and María Dolores Sánchez. Like his father, José Arcario donated labor and materials for Nuestra Señora de Guadalupe Catholic Church. He was known to loan his *boggy* (buggy) and *boguecito* (small buggy) to Father Salvatore Personé.[229]

On January 2, 1872, José Arcadio followed in his father's footsteps to serve in public office and represented Conejos County in the Eleventh Territorial House of Representatives. Unfortunately, his first term of office ended the following month, as his father died and José Arcadio immediately returned to Conejos. On February 8, 1872, territorial representative Casimiro Barela made a motion in the House to excuse José Arcadio "from further attendance of the sessions of this House."[230]

By 1875, José Arcadio was a lawyer. He also went by the name Alcario Velásquez. Historical records do not provide information about his training or education; however, in 1875 his name appeared in the *Colorado Business Directory*.[231]

José Arcadio Velásquez married María Genoveva Aragón on October 28, 1867, in Conejos.[232] Their two known birth children were Irenea[233] and Jesús María.[234]

Juan Miguel Vigil

CA. 1815–87

TERRITORIAL REPRESENTATIVE | COSTILLA AND
HUERFANO COUNTIES | 1867–68

Juan Miguel Vigil was born about 1815 to Juan Cristobal Vigil and Antonia Viviana Torres in New Mexico Province of colonial New Spain. Juan Miguel married María Rosa Bargas in 1846 at Taos, New Mexico Province of Mexico.

Vigil knew how to use a horizontal treadle loom to weave wool.[235] Weavers cleaned, dyed, and spun wool to weave material for clothing, bags, carpets, and blankets. Hispano male and female weavers used horizontal treadle looms. This loom produced long narrow strips that they could double-weave or stitch together to increase its size. In contrast, the vertical loom, used by female Navajo weavers, produced a woven piece as wide as the two reinforced wooden supports.

By 1863, Vigil had a Costilla County license to sell liquor in San Luis.[236]

The following year, Vigil served as the Costilla County probate judge. That same year, he also served as one of three county commissioners. Some of his responsibilities included collecting money from the sale of various licenses and maintaining the courthouse in San Luis. County commissioner records show he collected thirteen dollars in fees for *fandangos* (dances or celebratory events). For his services the county paid him $1.38 to keep the courthouse in repair and $1.50 for providing wood for the stove.[237]

In 1870 Juan Miguel Vigil chose not to support reannexation of Conejos and Costilla Counties to New Mexico Territory. Perhaps this was because he thought the USFLEC and the Costilla Estates Company, two landholding companies formed by William Gilpin and his backers, promised investment returns and growth. On February 1870 Vigil attended a meeting in San Luis to condemn the action of the New Mexico Territorial Assembly to have the "notch" returned. According to the *Rocky Mountain News*, at the meeting 287 signatures were collected and submitted to Congress against reannexation.[238]

The known birth children of Juan Miguel Vigil and María Rosa Bargas were Manuela, José Eduvigen, Candelaria, Simona, and Teresa.

Notes

1. Author interview with Polly Baca, July 15, 2014.

2. Colorado Legislator Biographies, http://www.leg.state.co.us/lcs/leghist.nsf/LegHistory.xsp?OpenDatabase, accessed October 1, 2017.

3. Shortly after Felipe Baca completed his first adobe home in 1866 at Trinidad, his daughter Dionisia Baca married Lorenzo A. Abeyta. See Andrews and Humphry, "El Patrón de Trinidad," *Colorado Magazine* 21, no. 1 (January 1944): 15.

4. Meketa, *Legacy of Honor*, 322–23.

5. *House Journal of the Territory of Colorado, 1872*, January 29 and 30, 1872, 120, 127.

6. *Rocky Mountain News*, February 1, 1872. See also *House Journal of the Legislative Assembly of the Territory of Colorado, Ninth Session, . . . 1872*; January 29–31, 1872, 119, 120, 124, 134, 139.

7. Interestingly, Archibald, who had not been present at the Christmas Day Massacre at Trinidad in 1867, lied when he said he saw Sheriff A. C. Gutiérrez "deliberately [shoot and wound] an unarmed American who knelt before him and with uplifted hands [and] implored him to spare his life." Convery, "Reckless Men of Both Races," 29.

8. Beshoar, *All about Trinidad and Las Animas County*, 88–90.

9. President Grover Cleveland ordered all illegal fences removed in 1885. White, "Illegal Fencing on the Colorado Range," 101, 109. See also McHendrie, "Trinidad and Its Environs," 169; Louis B. Sporleder Collection, Denver Public Library, Western History and Genealogy Department, WH916, box 2, FF 22, 265.

10. Convery, "Reckless Men of Both Races," 31.

11. A. K. Richeson, *Interview with Nicolas Vigil of Buyeros, N.M.* (Denver: Civil Works Administration, 1934), CWA Pioneer Interviews Collection, Hart Library, History Colorado Center, PAM 359/12, 164.

12. "Lista de Personas que Forman la Compania de milicianos de los Conejos," January 17, 1860, Territorial Archives of New Mexico, New Mexico Archives and Records Center, Roll 85.

13. Colorado Territorial Tax, 1863, Division 10, Costilla and Conejos Counties, ancestry.com, accessed February 17, 2000.

14. Salazar and Yost, *Our Lady of Guadalupe Church*, Marriage: 16, October 28, 1867; Reference to Church Marriage Register, 76.

15. Salazar, *Our Lady of Guadalupe Baptismal Registry*, 1–2, 76 (reference to Church Baptismal Register).

16. Colorado Division of Water Resources, Division 2, Pueblo, Colorado, Structure ID 601, Water District No. 16, Water Decree, Baca Ditch, http://water.state.co.us/DataMaps/DataSearch/Pages/DataSearch.aspx, 23–24.

17. Andrews and Humphry, "El Patrón de Trinidad," *Colorado Magazine* 21, no. 1 (January 1944): 3–4, 7. Morris L. Taylor names Charles Raymond as Baca's partner in its construction. Taylor, *Trinidad, Colorado Territory*, 37.

18. Colorado Division of Water Resources, Division 2, Pueblo, Colorado, Structure ID 601, Water District No. 16, Water Decree, Baca Ditch, http://water.state.co .us/DataMaps/DataSearch/Pages/DataSearch.aspx, 23–24.

19. Ibid.

20. Andrews and Humphry, "El Patrón de Trinidad," *Colorado Magazine* 21, no. 1 (January 1944): 8.

21. Taylor, *Trinidad, Colorado Territory*, 10, 40.

22. Convery, "Reckless Men of Both Races," 31.

23. Juan Ignacio Alires suggested Santísima Trinidád as the name for the town. (His daughter married Representative Jesús María García.) Hart Library, History Colorado Center, Colorado Writers Project, PAM 359/6, p. 85.

24. Taylor, *Trinidad, Colorado Territory*, 27, 13, 90.

25. *Trinidad Enterprise*, August 15, 1873, 3. He sold the lots to Rowland and Hays.

26. Andrews and Humphry, "El Patrón de Trinidad," *Colorado Magazine* 21, no. 1 (January 1944): 10.

27. Albert W. Archibald served as one of two executors to Felipe de Jesus Baca's will. Andrews and Humphry, "El Patrón de Trinidad," *Colorado Heritage* (Winter 2004): 13.

28. Ibid., 15.

29. Beshoar, *All about Trinidad and Las Animas County*, 99.

30. *Trinidad Enterprise*, April 16, 1874, 3.

31. Andrews and Humphry, "El Patrón de Trinidad," *Colorado Magazine* 21, no. 1 (January 1944): 15. Also Al Regensberg, *New Mexico Baptisms, Saint Gertrudes Church of Mora: Archives of the Archdiocese of Santa Fe, Book One, 1855–1860* (Albuquerque: New Mexico Genealogical Society, 1994), 63.

32. Shortly after Felipe Baca completed his first adobe home in 1866 at Trinidad, his daughter Dionisia Baca married Lorenzo A. Abeyta. See also Andrews and Humphry, "El Patrón de Trinidad," *Colorado Magazine* 21, no. 1 (January 1944): 15.

33. Regensberg, *New Mexico Baptisms, Saint Gertrudes Church of Mora*, 30.

34. *Pueblo Daily Chieftain*, April 7, 1879. Felipe de Jesús Baca died a day after his daughter's marriage to Archibald.

35. Senator J. M. Madrid, interview by A. K. Richeson, Trinidad, CO, *Registro de la Familia Baca*, Hart Library, History Colorado Center, Colorado Writers Project. PAM 359/6, 87. See also William Thatcher, interview by A. K. Richeson, Trinidad, CO, Colorado Writers Project, PAM 359, p. 266. Arthur Sparks, of the Smith Ranch,

accused Baca of cutting off the earmarks identifying the owners of sheep. The Sparks brothers were tried in Pueblo and acquitted of murder.

36. Regensberg, *New Mexico Baptisms, Saint Gertrudes Church of Mora*, 129.

37. Ibid., 70. Senator J. M. Madrid, Interviewed by A. K. Richeson, Trinidad, CO, Registro de la Familia Baca, Hart Library, History Colorado Center, Colorado Writers Project. PAM 359/6, p. 87.

38. Regensberg, *New Mexico Baptisms, Saint Gertrudes Church of Mora*, 15.

39. Meketa, *Legacy of Honor*, 406.

40. His teacher, Isabel Suazo, was the wife of George S. Simpson. Charles Cragin Notebooks, Cragin Collection, Pioneers Museum, Colorado Springs, Book 1, 6.

41. Castro, "Senator Casimiro Barela," 155.

42. Fernandez, *Biography of Casimiro Barela*, 11–12.

43. New Mexico Marriages Sapello Our Lady of Guadalupe 1-31-1860-12-4-1882, Hispanic Genealogical Research Center of New Mexico, Albuquerquer 46.

44. Eugene L. Torres, Holy Trinity Church Marriage Registry, Trinidad, Colorado 1866–1884 (Denver: Colorado Society of Hispanic Genealogy Library), 3.143; reference to Church Marriage Register: vol. 1, 248, entry 1.

45. José Emilio Fernandez, *Biography of Casimiro Barela*: 38–39.

46. Ibid., xix, xxvii.

47. *Legislative, Historical, and Biographical Compendium of Colorado*, entry for Casimiro Barela, https://archive.org/details/legislativehistooocfcorich, accessed January 4, 1999.

48. Fernandez, *Biography of Casimiro Barela*, 58–59, 85.

49. Eberhart, *Ghosts of the Colorado Plains*, 79; Castro, "Senator Casimiro Barela," 155.

50. Taylor and West, "Patron Leadership at the Crossroads," 339.

51. Convery, "Reckless Men of Both Races," 31.

52. De Oñis, *The Hispanic Contribution to the State of Colorado*, 185.

53. The Latino Leadership Institute is sponsored by the University of Denver. See http://www.latinoleadershipinstitute.net.

54. *Rocky Mountain News Weekly*, September 18, 1861.

55. Fifteen territorial officials were named, including Celestino Domínguez, Representative Jesús María Barela, Governor William Gilpin, Representative Allen Alexander Bradford, Representative Jerome Bunty Chaffee, and Chief Justice Benjamin F. Hall. *General Laws of the Territory of Colorado, 1861*, 144–48.

56. Some of the others named included Governor William Gilpin, Representative Allen Alexander Bradford, Representative Jerome Bunty Chaffee, and Chief Justice Benjamin F. Hall. Ibid., 144–48. On September 20, 1875, the Grand Masonic

Lodge of Colorado laid the cornerstone for the university's first building, Old Main. Erickson, *Early Justice and the Formation of the Colorado Bar*, 115.

57. Fifteen territorial officials were named, including Representative Jesus Maria Barela, Governor William Gilpin, Representative A. A. Bradford, Representative J. B. Chaffee, and Chief Justice B. F. Hall. *General Laws of the Territory of Colorado, 1861*, 144–48.

58. On September 20, 1875, the Grand Masonic Lodge of Colorado laid the cornerstone for the university's first building, Old Main. Erickson, *Early Justice and the Formation of the Colorado Bar*, 115.

59. Domínguez replaced Charles A. Brassler as interpreter for the House. *House Journal of the Territory of Colorado, 1861*, September 18, 1861, 50 (relating to the oath of Dominguez).

60. An 1864 joint resolution recorded his name as M. C. Domínguez. *General Laws of the Territory of Colorado, 1864*, March 9, 1864, 258.

61. US IRS Tax Assessment Lists, 1862–1918, New Mexico Archives and Records Center, for C. (Celestino) Domínguez, June 6, 1863, 2nd Class Peddler, tax amount $13.75 (accessed June 4, 2013). See also US IRS Tax Assessment Lists, 1862–1918 for Crkste [sic] Dominguez, 1864, No. 21, Dominguez, C., from Sirvileta, Colorado, Peddler 2nd Class, tax amount $8.33, tax reassessed (accessed June 4, 2013).

62. Denver Public Library, Western History and Genealogy Department, Samuel E. Brown (Browne), M 91, January 18, 1864: item 3.

63. NARA, Washington, DC, Letters Recorded by the Office of Indian Affairs 1824–1881, Colorado Superintendency, 1861–1864, C. Dominguez to Gov. Evans, March 11, 1864, M234, RG 75, Roll 197.

64. Celestino Domínguez to Governor Evans, December 23, 1865, John Evans Collection, Colorado State Archives and Public Records, Denver. John Evans resigned from office on July 18, 1865, and was replaced by Alexander Cummings.

65. Celestino Dominguez, "Hispanic Legislators," Richard Castro Papers, Special Collections Department, Auraria Library, Denver.

66. *Council Journal of the Territory of Colorado, 1874*, January 19 and 20, 1874, 76–78, 79–80 (regarding selection of interpreter).

67. *House Journal of the Territory of Colorado, 1876*, January 31, 1876, 145 (Dominguez oath as interpreter).

68. The first day of the convention began on February 29, 1876. Dominguez, "Hispanic Legislators," Richard Castro Papers, Special Collections Department, Auraria Library, Denver.

69. Taylor, *Trinidad, Colorado Territory*, 95.

70. Beshoar, *All about Trinidad and Las Animas County*, 95.

71. According to oral history, her father, Juan Ignacio Alarí, was a Trinidad merchant. He is credited with recommending the name *Santísima Trinidad* for the town of Trinidad. Hart Library, History Colorado, Colorado Writers' Project, PAM 359/6, 85, 160.

72. Torres, Holy Trinity Church Marriage Registry, 3, entry 1. Reference to Church Marriage Register: vol. 1, 1, entry 2.

73. Fernandez, *Biography of Casimiro Barela*, 25.

74. 1885 US Census, Las Animas County, Colorado, p. 7C, ED 1, Schedule 1, lines 21–30, Household/Dwelling 80, ancestry.com.

75. Torres, Holy Trinity Church Marriage Registry, 3–58, reference to Church Marriage Register: vol. 1, 101, entry 2.

76. No photo of this monument is available. Fernandez, *Biography of Casimiro Barela*, 128–29.

77. Martinez, *San Juan de los Caballeros Baptisms*, 167.

78. Jose Victor Garcia, "Hispanic Legislators," Richard Castro Papers, Special Collections Department, Auraria Library, Denver.

79. Hart Library, History Colorado Center, CWA, Conejos County, Charles E. Gibson, Jr., 1933–1934a, 142. Also Shawcroft, "Biographical Sketches of Early Conejos County Settlers," 29.

80. Hart Library, History Colorado Center, CWA, Conejos County, Charles E. Gibson, Jr., 1933–1934a, 142.

81. Denver Public Library, Western History and Genealogy Department, Samuel E. Brown (Browne), M 91, January 18, 1864: item 3.

82. Hall, *Portrait and Biographical Record*, 815.

83. *Rocky Mountain News*, January 24, 1872, 2, col. 1.

84. *General Laws and Joint Resolutions, Memorials, and Private Acts Passed at the Fourth Session of the Legislative Assembly of the Territory of Colorado, Begun and Held at Golden City, Jan. 2d, 1865* (Denver: Byers & Dailey, 1865), 78–86.

85. Meketa, *Legacy of Honor*, 326.

86. *Rocky Mountain News*, March 3, 1874, 4 col. 2. In Garcia's place, Governor McCook appointed José Bonifacio Romero of Mogote. Mead, *Conejos Colorado*, 64.

87. Salazar and Yost, *Our Lady of Guadalupe Church*, Baptisms: 4. Reference to Church Baptismal Register, vol. 3, 89.

88. Maxine F. Benson, "Colorado Celebrates the Centennial, 1876," *Colorado Magazine* 50, no. 2 (1976): 132–33, 135, 152. Williams was a Denver businessman, Mahlon D. Thatcher was a Pueblo banker, Joseph A. Thatcher was a Central City banker, and Howell was a Boulder County farmer. Lamar, "Colorado," 114. Photographer William Henry Jackson went to the exposition to "show the reports and the

pictures from F. V. Hayden's western surveys." See also Shawcroft, "Biographical Sketches of Early Conejos County Settlers," 29.

89. Salazar and Yost, *Our Lady of Guadalupe Church*, Baptisms: 4. Reference to Church Baptismal Register, vol. 3, 89.

90. Hall, *Portrait and Biographical Record*, 815.

91. New Mexico Genealogical Society, *Marriages from the Church of Santo Tomas Apostol de Abiquiu, 1854–1910* (Albuquerque: New Mexico Genealogical Society, 2018), 2.

92. "Biographical Sketches of Early Conejos County Settlers," by Shawcroft, *The San Luis Valley Historian*, Winter 1870: 29.

93. He was appointed by Juan Francisco Chacón. Jose Victor Garcia, "Hispanic Legislators," Richard Castro Papers, Special Collections Department, Auraria Library, Denver.

94. Salazar, *Our Lady of Guadalupe Baptismal Registry*, 21–22. Reference to Church Baptismal Register, 174.

95. Ibid., Reference to Church Baptismal Register: 240.

96. Ibid., 4. Reference to Reference to Church Baptismal Register, vol. 3, 89. Lafayette Head and Juana de la Cruz Martin served as godparents.

97. Salazar and Yost, *Our Lady of Guadalupe Church*, Marriages, 5. Reference to Church Marriage Register, 14.

98. Steinel and Working, *History of Agriculture in Colorado*, 29. See also Quintana, *Pobladores*, 155.

99. *General Laws of the Legislative Assembly of the Territory of Colorado, Second Session, Convened at Colorado City, Colo., on the 7th of July, 1862*, August 8, 1862, 125.

100. The law also applied to cities, town, or villages in Douglas, Larimer, Weld, and El Paso Counties. *General Laws of the Territory of Colorado, 1874*, February 9, 1874, 303–4.

101. Division 10, Colorado Territory, Annual Assessment 1863 and 1866, ancestry .com.

102. *Council Journal of the Territory of Colorado, 1874*, January 19, 1874, 77.

103. Martinez, *Nuestra Señora de los Dolores*, Baptisms, 56.

104. 1860 Taos County Census, 179, Precinct 19, Conejos, Taos County, New Mexico, Schedule 1, lines 11, 12, Household/Dwelling 1597.

105. Salazar, *Nuestra Señora de Guadalupe Bautismos, Conejos, Colorado*, 27–28. Reference to Church Baptismal Register, 70.

106. Ibid., 69.

107. Ibid., 138.

108. Salazar and Yost, *Our Lady of Guadalupe Church*, Baptisms, 5. Reference to Church Baptismal Register, vol. 3, 35.

109. Nuestra Señora de los Siete Dolores Registros de Bautismos, Walsenburg, Huerfano County, Colorado Society of Hispanic Genealogy Library, Denver, 98.

110. 1870 US Census, Arapahoe County, Colorado, Denver, p. 68, Schedule 1, line 24, Household 661, Dwelling 656, ancestry.com.

111. *House Journal of the Territory of Colorado, 1872,* January 23, 1872, 87 (relating to changing the location of the capital).

112. Ibid., January 23, 1872, 88 (relating to absence of Vidal). Larragoite served as acting interpreter in the absence of Henry Vidál, who was interpreting for a House committee.

113. Journal Proceedings of the Legislative Council of the Territory of New Mexico, January 5, 1895, 27–28.

114. Ibid., January 14, 1895, 44.

115. Ibid., January 23, 1895, 69.

116. "This Court Has Faith in Lawyer," *Denver Post,* July 12, 1906, 2.

117. Claire Ortiz Hill website, http://rancho.pancho.pagesperso-orange.fr, accessed January 31, 2017.

118. Juan Bautista Lobato, "Hispanic Legislators," Richard Castro Papers, Special Collections Department, Auraria Library, Denver.

119. Morris F. Taylor, "Fort Massachusetts," *Colorado Magazine* 45, no. 2 (Spring 1968): 130–31, 139.

120. Simmons, *San Luis Valley,* 131. "J. B. Doyle and Company ran a Military Express elsewhere in Colorado." Simmons references the Colorado clippings file at the Hart Library, History Colorado Center; *Rocky Mountain News,* February 6, 1861, and *Cañon City Times,* May 4, 1861.

121. According to the military circular, "Mexican soldiers of Mexican lineage . . . were to be employed as Expressmen"; the Quartermaster Department furnished them with horses. NARA, Washington, DC, Letters and Telegrams Received, 1860–1880, Fort Garland, 1860–1887, "Circular," September 23, 1862, M1120, RG 393, box 1.

122. Lobato, "Hispanic Legislators," Richard Castro Papers, Special Collections Department, Auraria Library, Denver.

123. Salazar and Yost, *Our Lady of Guadalupe Church,* Marriages, 7. Reference to Church Marriage Register, 13.

124. Salazar, *Our Lady of Guadalupe Church Baptismal Registry,* 29–30. Reference to Church Baptismal Register, 80.

125. Ibid., 27–28, Reference to Church Baptismal Register, 152.

126. Ibid., 29–30. Reference to Church Baptismal Register, 213.

127. Salazar and Yost, *Our Lady of Guadalupe Church,* Baptisms, 5. Reference to Church Baptismal Register, vol. 3, 43.

128. Ibid., Baptisms, 5. Reference to Church Baptismal Register, vol. 3, 43. Deaths, 18. Reference to Church Burial Register, 64.

129. Ibid., Deaths, 18. Reference to Church Burial Register, 84.

130. Ibid., Deaths, 17. Reference to Church Burial Register, 105.

131. David Gonzales, *Bautismos de Nuevo Mexico Mission de Santa Clara 1729–1805* (Pueblo, CO: Genealogical Society of Hispanic America, 1995), Roll 12, Baptisms, 38.

132. Stoller and Steele, *Diary of the Jesuit Residence*, 202n24. By 1872, the church had obtained an organ.

133. Hart Library, History Colorado Center, CWA, Conejos County, Charles E. Gibson, Jr., 1933–1934a, 115. The bell was replaced when it fell from the tower. The original bell was later repaired and placed in a new church at Mesitas. It was later "traded [to] Beers Bros., of Antonito" for a new bell.

134. Salazar and Yost, *Our Lady of Guadalupe Church*, Deaths: 19. Reference to Church Burial Register, 77.

135. Stoller and Steele, *Diary of the Jesuit Residence*, 34–35.

136. Martinez, *San de los Caballeros Baptisms*, 215.

137. Ibid.

138. Interview with Hope Yost, Denver, April 17, 2004.

139. Denver Public Library, Western History and Genealogy Department, Samuel E. Brown (Browne), M91, January 18, 1864: item 3.

140. *Marriages from the Church of Santo Tomas Apostol de Abiquiu*, 4.

141. Stauter, *100 Years in Colorado's Oldest Parish*, 10.

142. Jesús María Velásquez served as mayordomo in 1859; in 1860 P. Vigil was the mayordomo. Several additional items appear on an 1860 inventory, including a description of the house. Stoller and Steele, *Diary of the Jesuit Residence*, 21–24, 192, 195, 197n110, 199–201.

143. Stauter, *100 Years in Colorado's Oldest Parish*, 8a.

144. "Lista de Personas que Forman la Compania de milicianos de los Conejos," January 17, 1860, Territorial Archives of New Mexico, Muster Rolls, Roll 85.

145. Tucker, *Otto Mears and the San Juans*, 13

146. Salazar and Yost, *Our Lady of Guadalupe Church*, Marriages, 7. Reference to Church Marriage Register, 13.

147. Ibid. Marriages, 16. Reference to Church Marriage Register, 98.

148. Olmsted and Baca, *New Mexico Baptisms, Church of Santo Tomas de Abiquiu* (Albuquerque: New Mexico Genealogical Society, 2000), 205.

149. Our Lady of Guadalupe Church Baptismal Register, 238.

150. Salazar and Yost, *Our Lady of Guadalupe Church*, Marriages, 7. Reference to Church Marriage Register, 36.

151. Our Lady of Guadalupe Church Burial Registry, 238.

152. Salazar and Yost, *Our Lady of Guadalupe Church*, Marriages, 12. Reference to Church Marriage Register, 12.

332 APPENDIX A: THE HISPANO TERRITORIAL ASSEMBLYMEN

153. Juan José Mascarenas was the San José alcalde for the Cenisero settlement. NARA, Washington, DC, Registers of Letters Received and Letters Received by Headquarters, Department of New Mexico 1854–1865, Maj. Gillespie to Alcaldes and Soto Alcaldes regarding Military Census at Conejos, November 3, 1862, RG 393, M1120, Roll 18.

154. NARA, Washington, DC, Letters Received by the Office of Indian Affairs 1824–1881, "Notes of Interview between Maj. Mayer and Headmen of Ute Indians," August 25, 1862, Roll 197; Letters Regarding the Superintendent of Indian Affairs, Gov. Evans to W. P. Bacon, December 16, 1862, and "Hearing Testimony," December 29, 1862–January 15, 1863, Roll 197; Letters Received by Headquarters, Department of New Mexico 1854–1865, Maj. Gillespie to Capt. Cutler, March 4, 1863, Roll 19.

155. Denver Public Library, Western History and Genealogy Department, Samuel E. Brown (Browne), M 91, January 18, 1864: item 3.

156. "Taos Marriages," April 21, 1856.

157. Colorado, County Marriage Records and State Index, 1862–2006 for Francisco Sanchez, ancestry.com, accessed April 17, 2019.

158. Lorraine Martinez, personal communication, October 17, 2013.

159. "Find a Grave Index, 1600s–Current," memorial for Francisco Sanchez, ancestry.com, accessed April 17, 2019.

160. Olmsted and Baca, *New Mexico Baptisms Church of Santo Tomas de Abiquiu* (Albuquerque: New Mexico Genealogical Society, 2000), vol. 2, 1821–1824; 1794; 1817–1853; 1837–1850, 79.

161. NARA, Washington, DC, Registers of Letters Received and Letters Received by Headquarters, Department of New Mexico 1854–1865, Maj. Gillespie to Alcaldes and Soto Alcaldes regarding Military Census at Conejos, November 3, 1862, RG 393, M1120, Roll 18.

162. "Protest against the St. Vrain Grant," *Pueblo Colorado Chieftain*, March 23, 1871, 3.

163. Steele, *Folk and Church in New Mexico*, 89. According to the corrido, Suaso was playing dice when he was killed by José Córdova; this is incorrect: he was killed by Eulogio Perea. "La Veta: The Suaso Murder—Personal-Gold Discoveries," *Pueblo Daily Chieftain*, September 6, 1876, 4; and "Hon. Silverio Suaso of Huerfano County Murdered," *Pueblo Daily Chieftain*, September 7, 1876.

164. Salazar, *Our Lady of Guadalupe Church Baptismal Registry*, 65–66. Reference to Church Baptismal Register, 103.

165. López-Tushar, *People of El Valle*, 80.

166. The other two commissioners were Ferdinand Meyer and Juan de Jesús Bernál. Stoller, "Grants of Desperation," 30, 35. Olibama López-Tushar, *People of El Valle*: 33–34.

167. Costilla County Court Records, County Clerk's Office, Map Filing, Tracts 357 and 369, Book 98, 85.

168. Pedro Rafael Trujillo, "Hispanic Legislators," Richard Castro Papers, Special Collections Department, Auraria Library, Denver.

169. 1880 US Census, Costilla County, Colorado, p. 251A, Schedule 1, 31, lines 45–49, Household 46, Dwelling 443, ancestry.com. Trujillo, "Hispanic Legislators," Richard Castro Papers, Special Collections Department, Auraria Library, Denver.

170. *Report of the State Engineer to the Governor of Colorado for the Years 1883 and 1884* (Denver: Times Company, State Printers, 1885).

171. Trujillo, "Hispanic Legislators," Richard Castro Papers, Special Collections Department, Auraria Library, Denver.

172. López-Tushar, *People of El Valle*, 80.

173. *Marriages from the Church of Santo Tomas Apostol de Abiquiu*, 29.

174. Martinez, *Taos Baptisms*, 662.

175. Hall, *Portrait and Biographical Record*, 197. See also "Sketches of Early Pioneers in Huerfano County," Louis B. Sporleder Collection, Denver Public Library, Western History and Genealogy Department, WH916, box 2, FF 22, 333.

176. Katherine L. Craig, Report of the State Superintendent of Public Instruction of the State of Colorado, 1907–1908, 15. In his biography, Valdez wrote that he taught in the first private school in Germanes (Hermanes) Plaza during the winter of 1867–68. See also "Sketches of Early Pioneers in Huerfano County," Louis B. Sporleder Collection, Denver Public Library, 335.

177. His brother Juan Bautista Valdez and their father, Mariano de Jesús Valdez, traveled by horse and buggy to teach in schools throughout Huerfano and Costilla Counties. "15th Annual Centennial Families Calendar," printed by the First National Bank of Trinidad, CO. According to the obituary published in the December 27, 1894, issue of the *Walsenburg World*, Mariano de Jesus Valdez encouraged all of his children to "aspire to honored and useful lives."

178. "Sketches of Early Pioneers in Huerfano County," Louis B. Sporleder Collection, Denver Public Library, 335–36.

179. Hall, *Portrait and Biographical Record*, 197.

180. "Judge Valdez County Pioneer Dies Thursday, Was Former Mayor and First County Assessor," *Walsenburg World*, July 21, 1927, 1.

181. Hall, *Portrait and Biographical Record*, 198.

182. *General Laws of the Territory of Colorado, 1874*, February 11, 1874, 97–98.

183. Colorado Springs Pioneers Museum, Craigin Collection, Early Far West, Notebook 6, 2.

184. Hall, Frank. *Portrait and Biographical Record of the State of Colorado: Containing Portraits and Biographies of Many Well Known Citizens of the Past and Present*. Chicago: Chapman Publishing, 1899: 197.

185. Delaney, *All Our Yesterdays*, 52.

186. James Farr, recorded interview with Paul Krier and Howard Delaney, Walsenburg, CO, October 1963, sound cassette tape 2 of 2, side B; original with Howard Delaney.

187. "Judge Valdez County Pioneer Dies Thursday," *Walsenburg World*, July 21, 1927, 1. See also Sánchez, *Forgotten Cucharenos of the Lower Valley*, 57–58.

188. Torres, Holy Trinity Church Marriage Registry, 3–46; reference to Church Marriage Register, vol. 1, 80, entry 1.

189. Nuestra Señora de los Siete Dolores, Registros de Matrimoniales, Book 1, 277.

190. Pino, *Our Lady of Sorrows*, 181. Reference to Church Baptismal Register, 144, entry 1005.

191. "Judge Valdez County Pioneer Dies Thursday," *Walsenburg World*, July 21, 1927, 1.

192. Nuestra Señora de los Siete Dolores, Registros de Matrimoniales, Book 1, 122.

193. Pino, *Our Lady of Sorrows*, 190. Reference to Church Baptismal Register, 137, entry 955.

194. Ibid., 187. Reference to Church Baptismal Register, 163, entry 1140.

195. Ibid., 278. Reference to Church Baptismal Register, 12, entry 82.

196. *Walsenburg World*, July 21, 1927, 1.

197. Martinez, *San Juan de los Caballeros*, 624.

198. Hart Library, History Colorado Center, Colorado Writers Project, "An Interesting Trip," Charles E. Gibson, Jr., PAM 349, 77.

199. Ibid. "Luis Valdez," interview by Charles E. Gibson Jr., 97.

200. *General Laws of the Territory of New Mexico, 1851–52* (Santa Fe, 1852), July 9, 1851. See also Twitchell, *Leading Facts of New Mexican History*, "San Miguel County," 4:216.

201. "Lista de Personas que Forman la Compania de milicianos de los Conejos," January 17, 1860, Territorial Archives of New Mexico, New Mexico Archives and Records Center, Roll 85.

202. Stoller and Steele, *Diary of the Jesuit Residence*, 45, 94, 132, 186. In 1873 "Rafael Cabeza (Lafayette Head), Manuel Sabino Salazar, and Celedonio Valdes [sic] carried a canopy over the eight young ladies with the statue of Our Lady of Guadalupe." In 1874 Celedonio (sic) Valdez, M. S. Salazar, and Captain Julian Espinosa carried the canopy.

203. Stauter, *100 Years in Colorado's Oldest Parish*, 7a.

204. Stoller and Steele, *Diary of the Jesuit Residence*, 21–24, 192, 195, 197n11, 199–201.

205. Stauter, *100 Years in Colorado's Oldest Parish*, 8a.

206. Denver Public Library, Western History and Genealogy Department, Samuel E. Brown (Browne), M 91, January 18, 1864: item 3.

207. Santa Clara Baptisms, Marriages, Deaths, Roll 12, Baptisms, 5.

208. Salazar and Yost, *Our Lady of Guadalupe Church*, Marriages, 5. Reference to Church Marriage Register, 6.

209. Maestas, "Jose Seledon Valdez Family," 49–50.

210. Santa Clara Baptisms, Marriages, Deaths, Roll 12, Baptisms, 37.

211. Colorado Legislator Biographies, http://www.leg.state.co.us/lcs/leghist.nsf /LegHistory.xsp?OpenDatabase, accessed October 1, 2017.

212. Stoller and Steele, *Diary of the Jesuit Residence*, 37n65.

213. Keleher, *Turmoil in New Mexico*, 138n93.

214. Rodgers Library, University of New Mexico at Highlands, James W. Arrott Collection, Department of New Mexico Letters, Sender to Receiver, RG 98, 178–79. Stores for Captain Velasquez's New Mexico Volunteers were to be sent "across from Fort Union to Capt. Burgwin."

215. "Lista de Personas que Forman la Compania de milicianos de los Conejos," January 17, 1860, Territorial Archives of New Mexico, New Mexico Archives and Records Center, Roll 85.

216. Stauter, *100 Years in Colorado's Oldest Parish*, 9–10.

217. In 1860 P. Vigil served as church mayordomo. Several additional items appear on an 1860 inventory, including a description of the priest's house. See also Stoller and Steele, *Diary of the Jesuit Residence*, 197.

218. Stauter, *100 Years in Colorado's Oldest Parish*, 21.

219. "I have spoken the language for a good many years as well . . . as any interpreter that [can] be found in the county." NARA, Washington, DC, Letters Received by the Office of Indian Affairs, 1824–1881, Colorado Superintendency, 1861–1864, "Velasquez, J. M. testimony," December 30, 1862, M234, RG 75, Roll 197.

220. Office of Indian Affairs, 1824–1881, Letters of the Colorado Superintendency, Roll 197, Frames 169–218. Velasquez also stated, "There are but two or three good interpreters . . . They are difficult to get . . . One is the United States Interpreter for the Abiquiu Agency [in] New Mexico. The other, Jesús M. Sanches; [Head's] present interpreter, [Nemecio Lucero]; and myself." Letters Received by the Office of Indian Affairs, 1824–1881, Colorado Superintendency, 1861–1864, Evans to Dole, September 16, 1862, M234, RG 75, Roll 197.

221. NARA, Washington, DC, Letters Receivedby the Office of Indian Affairs, 1824–1881, Colorado Superintendency, 1861–1864, John Evans to Charles Mix, February 18, 1862, M234, Roll 197.

222. Kelsey, *Frontier Capitalist*, 132.

223. NARA, Washington, DC, Letters Received by the Office of Indian Affairs, 1824–1881, "Notes of Interview between Maj. Mayer and Headmen of Ute Indians," August 25, 1862, Roll 197; Letters Regarding the Superintendent of Indian Affairs, Gov. Evans to W. P. Bacon, December 16, 1862, and "Hearing Testimony,"

December 29, 1862–January 15, 1863, Roll 197; Letters Received by Headquarters, Department of New Mexico 1854–1865, Maj. Gillespie to Capt. Cutler, March 4, 1863, Roll 19.

224. Juan José Mascarenas was the San José alcalde for the Cenisero settlement. Registers of Letters Received and Letters Received by Headquarters, Department of New Mexico 1854–1865, Maj. Gillespie to Alcaldes and Soto Alcaldes regarding Military Census at Conejos, November 3, 1862, RG 393, M1120, Roll 18.

225. John Lawrence, of Saguache, wrote the bill "while in Denver acting as interpreter for the Mexican members of the legislature." The bill provided for the appointment of Nathan Russell, Captain Kerber, and José Prudencio García as commissioners. It was later discovered that "Kerber lived too far away." Martin, *Frontier Eyewitness*, 4.

226. Salazar and Yost, *Our Lady of Guadalupe Church*, Marriages, 16. Reference to Church Marriage Register, 76.

227. Ibid., Deaths, 44. Reference to Church Burial Register, 8.

228. Ibid., Deaths, 43. Reference to Church Burial Register, 77.

229. Stoller and Steele, *Diary of the Jesuit Residence*, 41nn69–70, and 81, 83, 90, 108, 116.

230. *House Journal of the Territory of Colorado, Ninth Session, 1872*, February 8, 1872, 201 (relating to Velasquez).

231. Hart Library, History Colorado Center, "Colorado Business Directory;" 1875, Conejos, no page number.

232. Salazar and Yost, *Our Lady of Guadalupe Church*, Marriages, 16. Reference to Church Marriage Register, 76.

233. Ibid., Baptisms, 12. Reference to Church Baptismal Register, vol. 3, 72.

234. Ibid., Deaths, 44. Reference to Church Burial Register, 83.

235. Fisher, *Spanish Textile Tradition of New Mexico and Colorado*, 45.

236. Colorado Territorial Tax, 1863, Division 10, Costilla and Conejos Counties, ancestry.com, accessed February 17, 2000.

237. Costilla County Commissioners, Costilla County Records, Book 1, April 7, 1864, 6, and April 3, 1865, 16.

238. "Costilla County against Annexation," *Colorado Chieftain*, March 3, 1870, 1, col. 5. The males in attendance elected Dario Gallegos chair and Fred Walsen, of Huerfano County, secretary. Other Hispano officials in attendance were José Ignacio Ortega and José Nasario Gallegos.

Appendix B

Timeline of Hispano Colorado

Hispano Timeline of Colorado

Year	Notable Events
Spanish Colonial Period	
1540	Francisco Coronado first introduces Churro sheep to New Spain.
1598	Juan de Oñate enters New Mexico, claims land for Spain.
1692	Diego de Vargas crosses the Río Costilla.
1776	Francisco Domínguez and Silvestre Escalante explore an overland route to the California missions. They cross present-day Colorado.
1777	Spain sends a large shipment of cannons, tents, grenades, muskets and balls, gunpowder, bayonets, and uniforms to the British American colonies in support of their independence from England.
1779	Governor Juan Bautista de Anza crosses the Rio Costilla, then known as the Rio Datil. Captain Bernardo Miera y Pacheco draws a map of New Mexico that includes the southern part of present-day Colorado.
1780	Spanish King Carlos III decrees that "his vassals in America" will contribute a one-time *donativo* (donation) of one peso to help the American colonies in their war of independence from England. In New Spain citizens from areas in California, New Mexico, and Texas donate. The Province of New Mexico donates 3,677 pesos, 247 of which were donated by soldiers of the Santa Fe Presidio.

DOI: 10.5876/9781607329145.c012

1818	Second Lieutenant José de Arce, of the Spanish Presidio at Santa Fe, patrols southern Colorado to the Río Napeste (Arkansas River) in search of foreign intruders.
1819	The Adams-Oñis Treaty clarifies the border between the United States and Spain at the Río Napeste (Arkansas River).

Mexican Period

1821	Mexico wins independence from Spain on September 27, ending the Spanish colonial period. Nuevo México is now a province of Mexico.
1833	The Guadalupe (Conejos) Land Grant is issued to forty families. Settlement is attempted along the Río Conejos, but the settlers are driven off by the Utes.
1843	The Conejos Land Grand is reissued. Settlers are driven off by the Navajos.
1844	Charles Beaubien requests a grant of land (Sangre de Cristo) under his son's name.
1846	The US war with Mexico begins.
1846	Brigadier General Stephen W. Kearny enters Santa Fé on September 22 and establishes the Kearny Code of government in New Mexico.
	Kearny appoints Charles Bent governor of New Mexico and Charles Beaubien a judge on the New Mexico Supreme Court.
1847	Taos Massacre. Charles Beaubien become the sole owner of the Sangre de Cristo Land Grant.

American Period

1848	The United States wins its war with Mexico. The Treaty of Guadalupe Hidalgo is signed on February 2 with certain provisions declared by the United States to protect former Mexican land, language, and religion.
	Beaubien establishes the Costilla settlement along the Río Costilla of the Sange de Cristo. Settlers are permanently resettled along the Río Conejos on the Conejos Land Grant.
1850	Congress establishes the Territory of New Mexico.
1851	On April 9 Hispanos establish San Luis del Río Culebra, a settlement north of the Costilla settlement.
	The New Mexico Territorial Legislature establishes the Office of Translator on June 19.
1852	Construction is completed on the People's Ditch, a hand-dug acequia in the San Luis Valley.
	Fort Massachusetts is established at the request of Charles Beaubien.
1853	Sparse settlements are established along the Huerfano and Arkansas Rivers.
1854	Settlers at El Pueblo are attacked by the Utes.
	Conejos settlers arrive and begin digging acequias to irrigate their crops.
	Congress creates the Office of Surveyor General for New Mexico.
1856	On July 17 Beaubien leases land to the US Army for the creation of Fort Garland. The lease is for twenty-five years at a rate of one dollar a year.
1858	The first governmental township survey of the Conejos Land Grant is made, including Townships 33North through 36North, Ranges 10E through 11E.
1859	Miners flock to the Pikes Peak area in search of gold.

1859 (cont'd)	William Newton Byers publishes the first issue of the *Rocky Mountain News* on April 23 in Denver.

Anglo miners illegally form Jefferson Territory on October 25. They include New Mexico's "notch" in its new territorial boundaries.

Fort Garland replaces Fort Massachusetts.

1860	On January 17 the Conejos Militia of New Mexico is formed under Captain Jesús María Velásquez of Conejos. Hispanos in the "notch" still look to New Mexico for governance.

Jefferson Territory's statehood advocates convene in Golden, but Congress denies statehood.

Congress approves the Sangre de Cristo Land Grant.

Colorado Territorial Period

1861	On February 28 Congress establishes the Territory of Colorado, including a portion of New Mexico Territory's northern area. The change affects 7,000 Hispanos living in the "notch."

The US Civil War begins on April 12.

The Conejos Ute Indian Agency at Conejos is established on April 15, with Lafayette Head as agent.

President Abraham Lincoln appoints William Gilpin governor of Colorado Territory on May 21.

On July 3 Hispanos file a claim for the Conejos Land Grant with the surveyor general's office in New Mexico Territory. No action is taken.

Governor Gilpin establishes three judicial districts for the territory on July 10. The territory holds its first census: total population = 25,371. The population of Hispanos is understated when compared with 1860 New Mexico census data for the same area.

The first territorial election is held on August 19. José Víctor García is elected to represent Conejos County, and Jesús María Barela is elected to represent Costilla County in the Territorial House of Representatives. No Hispanos are elected from Huerfano County, and none is elected to the Territorial Council (Senate).

The Colorado Territorial Assembly meets in its first session on September 9. Representatives García and Barela are absent. Once they arrive, no arrangements are made for a translator. García requests two translated copies of the House rules, but none is received. The *Rocky Mountain News* publishes a Spanish translation of the Governor's Message.

The Territorial House of Representatives approves an act on October 11 to use English common law.

On November 7 the Colorado Territorial Assembly enacts several civil, criminal, real estate, stock grazing, and tax laws that impact Hispano life and land. Guadalupe County changes its name to Conejos County. Settlers continue to refer to its county seat as Guadalupe rather than Conejos. A translation of the laws not printed.

1862	On February 17 New Mexico delegate John Sebrie Watts sells 99,289 acres, in the fourth parcel of the Luis María Baca Land Grant in Colorado Territory, to William Gilpin for thirty cents an acre.

Colonel John Chivington takes command in Colorado Territory on April 4.

Vivián Espinosa and his mother, María Gertrudis Chávez, serve as godparents in a baptism on April 27.

1862
(cont'd)
The Conejos Land Grant is not recommended for congressional confirmation; in consequence, four men die in Conejos in land disputes in May.

On May 30 Representatives García and Barela ask Celestino Domínguez to write a letter to obtain federal money to print the Spanish translation of the territorial statutes. The US Treasurer fails to acknowledge that these Spanish speakers were annexed from New Mexico Territory; nor does he realize that they are citizens of the United States by provision of the 1848 Treaty of Guadalupe Hidalgo.

Governor Gilpin is removed from office in April due to excessive spending of territorial funds.

Only Anglos, no "Mexicans," are recruited at Julesburg in April and May for US military service in the Colorado Volunteers.

Congress enacts the Internal Revenue Act on July 1.

The second legislative session designates Golden as the new capital on July 11.

On July 15 Governor John Evans officially approves the decision to return the territorial assembly to Denver.

On July 30 the Costilla County clerk writes to Major Mayer at Fort Garland regarding a "revolt among these people."

In August Representative José Francisco Gallegos is mysteriously found dead on the Conejos plaza with "a rope around his neck."

Merchant F. W. Postoff writes two letters to Major Mayer on August 4, stating there is dissatisfaction among the "mex." regarding the laws.

Postoff sends Major Mayer a third letter on August 8 about the "secret meetings held by the Mex."

Major Mayer meets with leading Hispanos on August 17 regarding their loyalty to the Union. Mayer reports to headquarters in New Mexico Territory, "All of which I did not believe." He also notifies headquarters about Hispanos' "disposition to resist" taxation.

Newspaper reports on August 21 that the "Mexicans . . . are holding secret meetings and organizing for an armed resistance to the collection of taxes, etc."

Newspaper reports on August 27 of "impending insurgent activities."

Tax Day held in Colorado Territory on September 1.

Newspaper reports on September 4: "Threatening murmurs continue to be heard from the Mexicans."

Newspaper reports on September 5 that Lieutenant Hodt has found secret meetings in Conejos.

On October 7 Major Archibald Gillespie is ordered to take a military census in Conejos.

The second session of the territorial assembly ends on October 18 after forty days. The translation of the laws is not printed.

In November Colonel Chivington is placed in charge of the Military District of Colorado.

Fort Garland troops seize two muskets from a Mr. Gallegos on November 6. The following day they seize two more muskets and a Halls carbine rifle from two men identified only as "Mexicans."

In December the Espinosa brothers of Conejos allegedly rob a wagon between Santa Fe and Galisteo, New Mexico.

1862
(cont'd)   Lieutenant Hodt is ordered to Conejos on December 27 with twenty-five troopers "to compel obedience." Four Hispanos are arrested. Settler Francisco Gallegos is indicted as a disloyal citizen by the Third Judicial District Court for an inflammatory speech he made.

The first of three hearings is held on December 29 to determine if Indian agent Lafayette Head withheld goods from the Utes, sold government property, and employed an interpreter who could not speak Ute.

1863   Lieutenant Hodt arrives at the Espinosa home in Conejos on January 15 under the pretense of conscripting men into the Union Army for the Civil War.

On January 20 Hodt returns to arrest the Espinosas in San Rafael district. An altercation ensues.

The New Mexico Territorial Assembly approves a joint resolution on January 24 requesting land and its people in the southern part of Colorado Territory be restored to New Mexico due to a "total lack of proper administration of justice," printing laws only in English, and ties of "ancestry, nativity, and association to New Mexico."

Conejos County voters select Servilleta as the permanent location for their county seat. The selection is not approved, as no elections were sanctioned that year. The vote cannot be verified as the county clerk did not understand the law about retaining the list of voters.

Congress divides New Mexico Territory in half to create Arizona Territory.

Congress kills the Colorado statehood bill.

In March General Carleton of the New Mexico Military District formally states that Fort Garland belongs to the Military Department of Missouri.

Newspaper report on March 19: "Greasers" have been growing restless about taxation.

John McCannon's California Gulch posse shoots Vivian Espinosa. One shot removes his face.

On May 11 the Beaubien Document is created, giving right of access to settlers.

Governor Evans arrives at Fort Garland on September 28 with presidential secretary John George Nicolay; Simeon Whitely, Ute agent for western bands; and Dr. Michael Steck, New Mexico Indian agent for the Ute Treaty Council at Conejos.

The Espinosa "gang" is hunted down in October and violently killed.

The Ute Treaty Council is held at Conejos on October 7.

Charles Beaubien makes deeds to settlers on his Sangre de Cristo Land Grant on November 11. By the 1861 territorial law, these deeds are invalid because Beaubien failed to record the land boundaries and list the settlers by name.

1864   Golden City becomes the capital of the territory.

On January 18 Conejos citizens petition to replace Indian agent Lafayette Head due to malfeasance.

Major Archibald Gillespie, Military District of New Mexico, submits a final report of the military census of Conejos County.

The county seat of Huerfano County is changed from Autobees to Badito on February 16.

The Colorado Territorial Assembly passes a law on February 25 prohibiting the pasturing of animals within the limits of Denver or Golden or any town or village in Costilla or Huerfano Counties.

1864
(cont'd)

Costilla County's seat is changed on February 26 from Costilla to San Luis.

Celestino Domínguez finally receives payment on March 9 for his translations of the 1861 territorial session laws.

The territorial assembly passes a law on March 11 authorizing county commissioners to levy a property tax for road improvements and maintenance. Able-bodied men between the ages of eighteen and fifty owe five dollars a year. In lieu of payment, a laborer, using his own tools, can provide two days of labor on the county's public highway.

On April 7 Charles Beaubien sells all but a one-sixth interest in the Sangre de Cristo Land Grant to William Gilpin for $15,000. Gilpin then works with foreign investors to promote the land.

A hearing is held on April 18 in Conejos to examine claims about Agent Head's inappropriate actions, questionable character, and vengeful nature.

Governor Evans issues a proclamation on August 11 authorizing all citizens to arm themselves and hunt down hostile Indians.

The Colorado statehood initiative fails on September 13. The Hispano vote helps defeat the initiative.

On November 29 the Sand Creek Massacre of Cheyenne and Arapahos in southeastern Colorado is led by Colonel Chivington, as sanctioned by Governr Evans.

A petition is signed on December 27 and forwarded to New Mexico delegate Perea, asking for the notch to be placed in that territory's jurisdiction.

Session laws of the first, second, and third sessions (1861, 1862, and 1863) are finally printed in Spanish.

1865

The population of Huerfano County is 371; only 35 people are Anglo.

The US Civil War ends on April 9.

Under pressure from President Andrew Johnson, Governor Evans resigns his position on August 1 as Colorado territorial governor.

On September 5 another Colorado statehood initiative fails, 1,285 to 125. Hispanos voted against statehood: Conejos County (1 vote for, 465 against), Costilla County (25 for, 563 against), Huerfano County (98 for, 257 against).

1866

Alexander Cummings is named governor of Colorado Territory.

The territorial assembly creates Las Animas County from Huerfano County on February 9. Trinidad is selected as the county seat.

The territorial assembly creates Saguache County in December.

1867

Denver is established as the territorial capital.

Laws of the fourth, fifth, and sixth sessions (1864, 1865, and 1866) of the territorial assembly are finally printed in Spanish.

The New Mexico surveyor general forwards to Colorado's surveyor general all documents relating to grants in Colorado Territory.

1868

The Hispano vote successfully blocks a statehood initiative.

Laws of the seventh session (1867) are printed in Spanish.

1869

Due to the Darling survey of the Colorado southern boundary, the town of Costilla is returned to New Mexico Territory.

Silver is discovered, encouraging additional immigration into Colorado.

1870   On January 4 territorial auditor N. F. Cheeseman initiates the first discussion about the expense to translate statutes. English-only proposals are started.

Teofilo Trujillo of Costilla County experiences intimidation and violence from Anglo cattlemen.

In Huerfano County two Anglos severely injure herders of Juan Vallejos and mutilate his sheep.

Bent County is created.

1871   Thirteen-year-old Donaciano Sánchez is hanged by vigilantes in Saguache on January 9.

The Sangre de Cristo Land Grant is divided by William Gilpin into the Trinchera Estates and the Costilla Estates.

1872   On January 29 citizen Albert W. Archibald contests Las Animas County's election of a Hispano representative. The Territorial House holds a hearing and votes in support of Archibald over representative-elect Lorenzo Abeyta.

The territorial assembly passes a fence law on February 8 requiring milled fencing.

On May 12 Pueblo's *Daily Chieftain* reports that Mexicans are "willing to sell" their irrigated lands; "Americans" are "anxious to have whites as neighbors."

Codified (indexed) laws from the legislature's first through ninth sessions (1861–72) are printed in Spanish.

1873   The majority population of Las Animas County remains Spanish-speaking.

La Plaza de los Leones in Huerfano County is officially named Walsenburgh on June 16, later spelled Walsenburg.

William Blackmore visits the Guadalupe settlement on November 3 and meets with José Seledonio Valdez to negotiate a business arrangement.

1874   The Brunot Treaty opens Ute lands in the San Juan country to Anglo miners.

Lafayette Head is elected to represent Conejos and Costilla Counties in the Territorial House.

The territorial assembly creates Rio Grande County.

The territorial assembly passes a law on February 11 prohibiting the injury or death of livestock and herders.

In June Pueblo's *Daily Chieftain* reports that "In time . . . the Mexican and his worthless stock will disappear from these beautiful and fertile mesas and valleys."

1875   The population of Colorado Territory is approximately 100,000.

The United States opens a land office in Del Norte. Land grants are treated as public domain. Because the Conejos Land Grant had not yet been confirmed, some Hispanos apply for homesteads in three townships located on the Conejos grant in an effort to retain their granted land.

Colorado Statehood Period

1876   Colorado becomes the thirty-eighth state of the Union on August 1.

Appendix C

Territorial Governors and Delegates

Jefferson Territorial Governors, 1860–61

Governor	Party Affiliation	Years Served
L. W. Bliss, acting	Republican	1859
Robert Williamson Steele	Democrat	1859–60

Jefferson Territorial Delegate, 1859–60

Delegate	Party Affiliation	Years Served
Beverly D. Williams	Union	1859–60

Colorado Territorial Governors, 1861–75

Governor	Party Affiliation	Years Served
William Gilpin	Republican	1861–62
John Evans	Republican	1862–65
Alexander Cummings	Republican	1865–67
Alexander Cameron Hunt	Republican	1867–69
Edward C. McCook	Republican	1869–73
Samuel E. Elbert	Republican	1873–74
Edward C. McCook	Republican	1874–75
John L. Routt	Republican	1875–76

DOI: 10.5876/9781607329145.c013

Colorado Territorial Delegates, 1861–67

Delegate	Party Affiliation	Years Served
Hiram Pitt Bennet	Republican	1861–65
Allen Alexander Bradford	Republican	1866–67

New Mexico Territorial Governors, 1857–75

Governor	Party Affiliation	Years Served
Abraham Rencher	Democrat	1857–61
Henry Connelly	Democrat	1861–66
Robert Byington Mitchell	Democrat	1866–69
William Anderson Pile	Republican	1869–71
Marsh Giddings	Republican	1871–75

New Mexico Territorial Delegates, 1856–67

Governor	Party Affiliation	Years Served
Miguel Antonio Otero	Democrat	1856–61
John Sebrie Watts	Republican	1861–63
Francisco Perea	Republican	1863–65
José Francisco Chaves	Republican	1865–67

Appendix D

Glossary of Spanish Terms

abajo: below.

acequia: irrigation ditch.

alcalde: mayor or type of court system used in New Mexico and early southern Colorado.

alguacil: constable or sheriff.

almud: one quart.

anunciador: announcer.

aprobadas: approved or passed.

arriba: above.

asamblea: assembly.

blanca: white.

boggy: buggy.

boguecito: small buggy.

californios: Californians, people from California.

DOI: 10.5876/9781607329145.c014

cañon: canyon.

cantares: songs.

chile colorau: red chile.

Churro: a long-legged hardy sheep with long silky hair.

colorado: ruddy or reddish, as of ground, rock, or silt

comancheros: unlicensed traders.

compadres: parents and godparents.

compadrazco: co-parenthood or the reciprocal relationship between a godparent or godparents and the godchild and his or her parents.

comunidád: community.

conejos: rabbits; name of a county name and a settlement. The term also applied to the swift current of the river of the same name.

corrido: ballad.

costilla: rib; name of a county name and a settlement.

cuartilla/o: one pint.

diedad: diety.

Don/Doña: honorific title for a respected gentleman/lady.

donativo: donation.

en junta: as a group.

fandango: dance or celebratory event.

fanega: measure of volume equivalent to a bushel and a half.

frasco: a liquid measure equal to 2.5 quarts.

fraternidad: fraternity, brotherhood.

función: feast day.

gente: people.

gordo: fat, heavy.

huérfano: orphan; name of a lone butte near Walsenburg and the county in which it is found.

isla: island.

jacal: building constructed of upright cedar logs.

joya: jewel.

juez: judge.

juntas de indignación: grassroots or "indignation" meetings.

Las Ánimas: the souls; name of a county.

La Junta: the junction; name of a town.

legislativa: legislative.

leyes: laws.

leones: lions; in reference to the Leon family who settled La Plaza de los Leones in Huérfano County.

lucero: sunrise; also a surname.

mayordomo: ditch boss, caretaker, or event coordinator.

merced: commons.

mesas: tables; flat mountaintops.

montosa: mountainous.

morada: meetinghouse.

mosca: housefly; name of town in Costilla County.

nuestra: our.

nuevomexicanos: New Mexicans; people living in New Mexico or those New Mexicans who were annexed into Colorado Territory.

parciante: farmer or irrigator.

patrón: boss.

penitente: a member of a religious society or brotherhood that supported and aided the community; male members practiced self-flagellation during the Lenten season.

peón: contract laborer.

plaza: the main or central area of a town or settlement.

poblador: farmer.

posada: room/board.

progreso: progress.

pública: public.

pueblo: people; name of a settlement and a county of the same name. In New Mexico it refers to the villages of nonnomadic indigenous nations.

pulgada: one inch.

reglas: rules.

república: republic.

resolución: resolution.

revisado: revised; referring to indexed or codified statutes.

Río Arriba: literally, "river above"; a reference to the area located north of Santa Fe.

San: Saint.

sangre: blood.

sello: seal.

sesiones: sessions.

Sierra de la Grullas: literally, Mountain Chain of the Cranes, the San Juan Mountains of southwest Colorado.

sin: without.

territorio: territory.

tilma: cloak.

trinidád: trinity.

vara: measure of length equivalent to about 33.3 inches.

vecinos: neighbors.

vega: commons area used for gathering wood; sometimes referred to as a sierra.

zaguan: entrance.

zorro: fox.

Bibliography

Abbott, Carl, Stephen J. Leonard, and David McComb. *Colorado: A History of the Centennial State*. 3rd ed. Boulder: University Press of Colorado, 1994. 37, 55–56, 266.

Adams, David Wallace, and Crista DeLuzio, eds. *On the Borders of Love and Power: Families and Kinship in the Intercultural American Southwest*. Berkeley: University of California Press, 2012.

Andrews, Paul D., and Nancy L. Humphry. "El Patrón de Trinidad: Don Felipe de Jesus Baca." *Colorado Heritage* (Winter 2004): 15, 47–48.

Armstrong, Robert D. "'Clothed with the Authority': A Dispute over Public Printing in Colorado Territory." *The Papers of the Bibliographical Society of America* 93, no. 3 (September 1999): 359–77. http://www.jstor.org/stable/24304297.

Baker, James H., ed. *History of Colorado*. 5 vols. Denver: Linderman, 1927.

Baxter, John. *Dividing New Mexico's Water*. Albuquerque: University of New Mexico Press, 1997.

Berwanger, Eugene H. *The Rise of the Centennial State: Colorado Territory, 1861–76*. Urbana: University of Illinois Press, 2007.

Beshoar, Michael. *All about Trinidad and Las Animas County, Colorado: Their History, Industries, Resources, Etc.* Denver: Times Printing House, 1882.

DOI: 10.5876/9781607329145.c015

Boessenecker, John. *Bandido: The Life and Times of Tiburcio Vasquez*. Norman: University of Oklahoma Press, 2012.

Bohning, Larry. "Wilbur Fisk Stone." *Colorado Lawyer* 31, no. 7 (July 2002): 23–26.

Boyd, Elizabeth, and Robin Farwell Gavin. *Saints and Saint Makers of New Mexico*, Appendix D, "Legends of Few Localized Santos." Santa Fe: Western Edge Press, 1998.

Brayer, Herbert O. *William Blackmore: The Spanish-Mexican Land Grants of New Mexico and Colorado 1863–1878*. 2 vols. Denver: Bradford Robinson, 1949.

Broadhead, Edward. *Ceran: St. Vrain, 1802–1870*. Pueblo, CO: Pueblo County Historical Society, 1987.

Campa, Arthur Leon. *Hispanic Culture in the Southwest*. Norman: University of Oklahoma Press, 1993.

Carr, Ralph. "Private Land Claims in Colorado." *Colorado Magazine* 25, no. 1 (1948): 10–30.

Carrigan, William D., and Clive Webb. *Forgotten Dead: Mob Violence against Mexicans in the United States, 1848–1928*. Oxford, UK: Oxford University Press, 2013.

Castro, Richard. "Senator Casimiro Barela: Draft First Colorado Constitution." *Nuestras Raices* 2, no. 4 (October 1990): 154–55.

Castro, Richard T. "Shaping the Law of the Land." *Ranch and Range* 1, no. 8 (August 1900): 7.

Chang, Glenn K.M. "Leading the Way: The Prospector in the Trans-Mississippi West." *Journal of the West* (April 1981): 31–37.

Cobos, Rubén. *A Dictionary of New Mexico and Southern Colorado Spanish*. Santa Fe: Museum of New Mexico Press, 1983.

Collins, George W. "Colorado's Territorial Secretaries." *Colorado Magazine* 43, no. 2 (Summer 1996): 195–96.

Colorado Cattlemen's Centennial Commission. "Partners in Perfection." In *The Co-Operative Century: Colorado Cattlemen's Association 100th Anniversary Issue*, 13. Denver: Colorado Cattlemen's Association, 1967.

Colorado Historic Newspapers Collection. https://www.coloradohistoricnewspapers.org.

Colorado Society of Hispanic Genealogy. *Hispanic Pioneers in Colorado and New Mexico*. Denver, CO: Colorado Society of Hispanic Genealogy, 2010.

Colville, Ruth Marie. *La Vereda: A Trail through Time*. Alamosa, CO: San Luis Valley Historical Society, 1996.

Convery, William J. "Reckless Men of Both Races: The Trinidad War of 1867–68." *Colorado Heritage*, no. 10 (2004): 19–35.

Crawford, Ivan C. "The Leadville Muleskinner." *Colorado Magazine* 35, no. 3 (July 1958): 178–86.

Crimmins, Colonel M. L. "Fort Massachusetts, First United States Military Post in Colorado." *Colorado Magazine* 14, no. 4 (July 1937): 128–35.

Crofutt, George A. *Croffutt's Grip-Sack Guide of Colorado*. Vol. 2. 2nd ed. Boulder, CO: Johnson Books, 1981.

de Oñis, José. *The Hispanic Contribution to the State of Colorado*. Boulder, CO: Westview Press, 1965.

Decker, Peter R. *The Utes Must Go*. Golden, CO: Fulcrum Pub., 2004.

Delaney, Howard L. *All Our Yesterdays: The Story of St. Mary Parish, Walsenburg, Colorado*. Walsenburg, CO: Consolidated Publishing Company, 1944.

Delgado, Richard. "The Law of the Noose: A History of Latino Lynching." *Harvard Civil Rights–Civil Liberties Law Review* 44 (2009): 304.

Denver Public Library. *Nothing Is Long Ago: A Documentary History of Colorado, 1776–1976*. Denver: Denver Public Library, 1976.

Deutsch, Sarah. *No Separate Refuge: Culture, Class, and Gender on an Anglo-Hispanic Frontier in the American Southwest, 1880–1940*. New York: Oxford University Press, 1987.

Dill, R. G. "History of Lake County." In *History of the Arkansas Valley, Colorado*, ed. O. L. Baskin, 213. Chicago: O. L. Baskin & Co., 1881.

Downing, Finis E. "With the Ute Peace Delegation of 1863, Across the Plains and at Conejos." *Colorado Magazine* 22, no. 5 (1945): 193–205.

Eberhart, Perry. *Ghosts of the Colorado Plains*. Athens, OH: Swallow Press, 1986.

Ebright, Malcolm. "Introduction." In *Spanish and Mexican Land Grants and the Law*, ed. Malcolm Ebright, 4. Minneapolis, MN: Journal of the West, 1988.

Ebright, Malcolm. *Land Grants and Lawsuits in New Mexico*. Albuquerque: University of New Mexico Press, 1994.

Ebright, Malcolm. "Sharing the Shortages: Water Litigation and Regulation in Hispanic New Mexico, 1600–1850." *New Mexico Historical Review* 76, no. 1 (January 2001): 11, 15–17.

Ellis, Anne. *The Life of an Ordinary Woman*. Boston: Houghton Mifflin Co., 1929.

Ellis, Elmer. "Colorado's First Fight for Statehood, 1865–1868." *Colorado Magazine* 8, no. 1 (January 1931): 23–30.

Erickson, David L. *Early Justice and the Formation of the Colorado Bar*. Denver: CLE in Colorado, Inc., 2008.

Espinosa, J. Manuel. "The Neapolitan Jesuits on the Colorado Frontier, 1868–1919." *Colorado Magazine* 15, no. 2 (March 1938): 64–72.

Esquibel, José Antonio. "Rio de los Conejos Grantees, 1843." *El Farolito: Journal of the Olibama Lopez-Tushar Research Group* 14, no. 3 (2011): 13.

Everett, Derek R. *Creating the American West: Boundaries and Borderlands*. Norman: University of Oklahoma Press, 2014.

Farr, James. Recorded interview with Paul Krier and Howard Delaney, Walsenburg, CO, October 1963, sound cassette tape 2 of 2, side B; original with Howard Delaney.

Fedynskyj, Jurij. "State Session Laws in Non-English Languages: A Chapter of American Legal History." *Indiana Law Journal* 46, no. 4 (Summer 1971): 463–78. http://www.repository.law.indiana.edu.

Fernandez, José Emilio. *The Biography of Casimiro Barela*. Albuquerque: University of New Mexico Press, 2003.

Fisher, Nora. *Spanish Textile Tradition of New Mexico and Colorado*. Santa Fe: Museum of New Mexico Press, 1979.

Frazier, J. L. "Prologue to Colorado Territory." *Colorado Magazine* 38, no. 3 (July 1961): 161–73.

Galindo, Rene, and Jami Vigil. "Language Restrictionism Revisited: The Case against Colorado's 2000 Anti-Bilingual Education Initiative." *Harvard Latino Law Review* 7 (Spring 2004): 27–61.

Giddens, Paul H. "Letters of S. Newton Pettis, Associate Justice of the Colorado Supreme Court, Written in 1861." *Colorado Magazine* 15, no. 1 (January 1938): 3–14.

Gómez, Laura E. "Off-White in an Age of White Supremacy: Mexican Elites and the Rights of Indians and Blacks in Nineteenth-Century New Mexico." In *"Colored Men" and "Hombres Aquí": Hernandez v. Texas and the Emergency of Mexican-American Lawyering*, ed. Michael A. Olivas, 1–40. Houston: Arte Public Press, 2014.

Gonzales, Nicki. "La Sierra and the San Luis Land Rights Struggle." *Colorado Heritage* (March–April 2015): 26–27.

Gonzales, Phillip B. *Política: Nuevomexicanos and American Political Incorporation, 1821–1910*. Lincoln: University of Nebraska Press, 2016.

Gonzales, Phillip, and Virginia Sánchez. "Displaced in Place: Nuevomexicanos on the Northern Side of the Colorado–New Mexico Border, 1850–1875." *New Mexico Historical Review* 93, no. 3 (Summer 2018): 263–301.

Gonzalez, Deena J. *Refusing the Favor: The Spanish-Mexican Women of Santa Fe 1820–1880*. New York: Oxford University Press, 1999.

Guice, John D.W. *The Rocky Mountain Bench: The Territorial Supreme Courts of Colorado, Montana, and Wyoming, 1861–1890*. New Haven, CT: Yale University Press, 1972.

Gundy, Lloyd. "Of Mines and Men." *Colorado Magazine* (Winter 2003): 38–47.

Hafen, LeRoy R. *Colorado and Its People: A Narrative and Topical History of the Centennial State*. Vol. 1. New York: Lewis Historical Publishing, 1948.

Hafen, LeRoy R. "Colorado's First Legislative Assembly." *Colorado Magazine* 21, no. 1 (January 1944): 41–50.

Hafen, LeRoy R. *Colorado: The Story of a Western Commonwealth*. Denver: Peerless Publishing, 1933.

Hafen, LeRoy R. *French Fur Traders and Voyageurs in the American West*. Glendale, CA: A. H. Clark Co., 1995.

Hafen, LeRoy R. "Letters of George M. Willing, Delegate of Jefferson Territory." *Colorado Magazine* 17, no. 5 (September 1940): 184–89.

Hafen, LeRoy R. "Status of the San Luis Valley, 1850–1861." *Colorado Magazine* 3, no. 2 (May 1926): 46–49.

Hafen, LeRoy R. "Steps to Statehood in Colorado." *Colorado Magazine* 3, no. 3 (August 1926): 97–110.

Hall, Frank. "History of Costilla County." *Colorado Magazine* 5, no. 4 (August 1928): 140–43.

Hall, Frank. *History of the State of Colorado.* 4 vols. Chicago: Blakely Printing Co., 1891.

Hall, Frank. *Portrait and Biographical Record of the State of Colorado: Containing Portraits and Biographies of Many Well Known Citizens of the Past and Present.* Chicago: Chapman Publishing, 1899.

Harper, William Lee. "A History of New Mexico Election Laws." MA thesis, University of New Mexico, 1927.

Kane, John L., Jr., and Sharon Marks Elfenbein. "Colorado: The Territorial and District Courts." In *The Federal Courts of the Tenth Circuit: A History,* ed. James K. Logan, 38–78. Denver: US Court of Appeals for the Tenth Circuit, 1992.

Keleher, William A. *Turmoil in New Mexico 1846–1868.* Albuquerque: University of New Mexico Press, 1982.

Kelly, Lawrence C. *Navajo Roundup: Selected Correspondence of Kit Carson's Expedition against the Navajo, 1863–1865.* Boulder, CO: Pruett, 1990.

Kelsey, Harry E., Jr. *Frontier Capitalist: The Life of John Evans.* Denver: Historical Society of Colorado, 1969.

Kessell, John L. *Kiva, Cross, and Crown.* Washington, DC: National Park Service, 1987.

Knowlton, Clark S. "The Town of Las Vegas Community Land Grant: An Anglo-American Coup d'État." In *Spanish and Mexican Land Grants in New Mexico and Colorado,* ed. John R. Van Ness and Christine M. Van Ness, 12–28. Manhattan, KS: Sunflower University Press, 1980.

Langum, David J. *Law and Community on the Mexican California Frontier.* Norman: University of Oklahoma Press, 1987.

Lamar, Howard Roberts. "Colorado: The Centennial State in the Bicentennial Year." *Colorado Magazine* 53, no. 2 (1976): 109–28.

Lamar, Howard Roberts. *The Far Southwest 1846–1912: A Territorial History.* Rev. ed. Albuquerque: University of New Mexico Press, 2000.

Lambert, Ruth. *The Wooden Canvas: Arborglyphs as Reflections of Hispano Life along the Pine-Piedra Stock Driveway.* Durango, CO: San Juan Mountains Association Press, 2014.

Lecompte, Janet. "John Lawrence of Saguache." *Colorado Magazine* 55, no. 2 (Spring–Summer 1978): 133–60.

Lecompte, Janet. "Sand Creek." *Colorado Magazine* 41 (Fall 1964): 315–35.

Leonard, Stephen J. *Lynching in Colorado, 1859–1919.* Boulder: University Press of Colorado, 2002.

López-Tushar, Olibama. *The People of El Valle: A History of the Spanish Colonials in the San Luis Valley.* 3rd ed. Pueblo, CO: El Escritorio, 1997.

López-Tushar, Olibama. "The Spanish Heritage in the San Luis Valley." MA thesis, University of Denver, 1942.

Maestas, Eugene. "Jose Seledon Valdez Family." *Colorado Hispanic Genealogist* 5, no. 4 (2008): 40–49.

Martin, Bernice. *Frontier Eyewitness: Diary of John Lawrence, 1867–1908*. Denver: Colorado Endowment for the Humanities, 1990.

Martinez, Maria Clara. *Extracts of 1865–1881 Birth and Marriage Records of Parroquia de San Miguel, Costilla, New Mexico*. Self-published, n.d.

Martinez, Maria Clara. *Nuestra Señora de los Dolores, Arroyo Hondo, NM, 1852–1865*. Self-published, n.d.

Martinez, Thomas D. *San Juan de los Caballeros Baptisms 1726–1870*. Self-published, 1994.

Martinez, Thomas D. *Taos Baptisms: 1701–1852*. Self-published, 2000.

McCourt, Purnee A. "The Conejos Land Grant of Southern Colorado." *Colorado Magazine* 52, no. 1 (Winter 1975): 37–40.

McHendrie, A. W. "Trinidad and Its Environs." *Colorado Magazine* 6, no. 5 (September 1929): 159–70.

McMenamy, Claire. "Our Lady of Guadalupe at Conejos, Colorado." *Colorado Magazine* 17, no. 9 (September 1940): 180–81.

Mead, Frances Harvey. *Conejos County*. Colorado Springs, CO: Century One Press, 1984.

Meketa, Jacqueline Dorgan. *Legacy of Honor: The Life of Rafael Chacon, A Nineteenth-Century New Mexican*. Albuquerque: University of New Mexico Press, 1986.

Miller, Darlis A. *Soldiers and Settlers: Military Supply in the Southwest, 1861–1885*. Albuquerque: University of New Mexico Press, 1989.

Mondragon-Valdez, María. "Challenging Domination: Local Resistance on the Sangre de Cristo Land Grant." PhD diss., University of New Mexico, 2006.

Murray, Robert B. "The Supreme Court of Colorado Territory." *Colorado Magazine* 44, no. 1 (1967): 20–34.

National Park Service. "Trujillo Homesteads: Teofilo Trujillo Homestead 5AL791; Pedro Trujillo Homestead 5AL706." National Historic Landmark Nomination Form. 2011.

National Park Service. "Trujillo Homestead, Alamosa County, CO." National Register of Historic Places Registration Form, Continuation Sheet. 2000.

Nieto-Phillips, John M. *The Language of Blood: The Making of Spanish-American Identity in New Mexico, 1880s–1930s*. Albuquerque: University of New Mexico Press, 2004.

Noel, Thomas J. *Colorado Catholicism and the Archdiocese of Denver, 1857–1989*. Boulder: University Press of Colorado, 1989.

Oliva, Leo E. *Fort Union and the Frontier Army in the Southwest*. Santa Fe: Division of History, National Park Service, US Department of the Interior, 1993.

Olmsted, Virginia Langham, and Evelyn Lujan Baca. *New Mexico Baptisms, Church of Santo Tomas de Abiquiu*. Albuquerque: University of New Mexico Press, 2000.

Parker, Cynthia Ann. *Empire of the Summer Moon: Quanah Parker and the Rise and Fall of the Comanches, the Most Powerful Indian Tribe in American History*. New York: Scribner, 2010.

Parkhill, Forbes. *The Law Goes West*. Denver: Sage Books, 1956.

Paul, Rodman W. "The Spanish Americans in the Southwest, 1848–1900." In *The Frontier Challenge*, ed. John G. Clark. Lawrence: University of Kansas Press, 1971.

Paxson, Frederic L. "The Territory of Colorado." *American Historical Association* 12, no. 1 (October 1906): 53–65.

Perkins, James E. *Tom Tobin Frontiersman*. Pueblo West, CO: Herodotus Press, 1999.

Pettit Jan. *Utes: The Mountain People*. Colorado Springs, CO: Century One Press, 1982.

Pino, Theresa. *Our Lady of Sorrows/St. Mary Church, Walsenburg, CO*. Vol. 1, *Baptisms: July 23, 1870–May 12, 1878*. Self-published, n.d.

Pino, Theresa. *Our Lady of Sorrows/St. Mary Church, Walsenburg, CO*. Vol. 2, *Baptisms: May 15, 1878–April 05, 1886*. Self-published, n.d.

Price, Charles F. *Season of Terror: The Espinosas in Central Colorado, March–October 1863*. Boulder: University Press of Colorado, 2014.

Quintana, Frances Leon. *Pobladores: Hispanic Americans on the Ute Frontier*. Notre Dame, IL: University of Notre Dame Press, 1974.

Rau, Patricia Sanchez. *The Conejos Land Grant: Grantees of 1842–1843, Plus an Addendum of 1833 Grantees*. Self-published, 2014.

Rivera, José A. *Acequia Culture: Water, Land, and Community in the Southwest*. Albuquerque: University of New Mexico Press, 1998.

Rodriguez, Sylvia. "Procession and Sacred Landscape in New Mexico." *New Mexico Historical Review* 77, no. 1 (Winter 2002): 1–26.

Safford, Jeffrey J. "Three Brothers in Arms: The Philbrooks and the Civil War in the West." *New Mexico Historical Review* 88, no. 3 (Summer 2013): 321–40.

Salazar, David H. *Our Lady of Guadalupe Baptismal Registry, Conejos, Colorado, 1861–1868*. Denver: Colorado Society of Hispanic Genealogy, 1992.

Salazar, David H., and Hope Yost. *Our Lady of Guadalupe Church: Baptism 1868–1871, Marriage 1860–1881, Death 1860–1896*. Denver: Colorado Society of Hispanic Genealogy, 1998.

Sanchez, Joseph P. *Early Hispanic Colorado 1678–1900*. Albuquerque, NM: Rio Grande Books, 2015.

Sánchez, Virginia. *Forgotten Cuchareños of the Lower Valley*. Charleston, NC: History Press, 2010.

Sánchez, Virginia. "Linked by Water, Linked by Blood: Madrid Ditch No. 2 in Cucharas, Colorado, 1884–1903." *New Mexico Historical Review* 86, no. 4 (Fall 2011): 429–59.

Sánchez, Virginia. "Survival of Captivity: Hybrid Identities, Gender, and Culture in Territorial Colorado." In *Nación Genízara: Ethnogenesis, Place, and Identity in New Mexico*, ed. Moises Gonzales and Enrique R. Lamadrid. Albuquerque: University of New Mexico Press, 2019.

Sánchez, Virginia. *Survivors of Captivity: Genealogies of Known Captive Indians in Southern Colorado, 1860–1880*. Self-published, 2014.

Scott, Bob. *Tom Tobin and the Bloody Espinosas: The Story of America's First Serial Killers and the Man Who Stopped Them.* Baltimore, MD: Publish America, 2004.

Scott, P. G. "Diary of a Freighting Trip from Kit Carson to Trinidad in 1870." *Colorado Magazine* 8, no. 4 (July 1931): 146–54.

Secrest, Clark. "The Bloody Espinosas: Avenging Angels of the Conejos." *Colorado Heritage* (Autumn 2000): 11–17.

Shaw, Dorothy Price, and Janet Shaw LeCompte. "Huerfano Butte." *Colorado Magazine* 27, no. 2 (April 1950): 81–88.

Shawcroft, Gladys. "Biographical Sketches of Early Conejos County Settlers." *San Luis Valley Historian* 2, no. 1 (Winter 1970): 28–30.

Simmons, Laurie, and Thomas H. Simmons. *Town of Saguache and Cochetopa Corridor: Historic Resources Survey, 2000.* Denver: Front Range Research Associates, 2001.

Simmons, Virginia McConnell. *The San Luis Valley: Land of the Six-Armed Cross.* 2nd ed. Niwot: University Press of Colorado, 1999.

Simmons, Virginia McConnell. *The Ute Indians of Utah, Colorado, and New Mexico.* Niwot: University Press of Colorado, 2011.

Smiley, Jerome C. *History of Denver: With Outlines of the Earlier History of the Rocky Mountain Country.* Denver: J. H. Williamson, 1901.

Sporleder, Louis B. "Description of Plaza de los Leones." *Colorado Magazine* 10, no. 1 (January 1933): 28–38.

"The Statehood Celebration of 1876." *Colorado Magazine* 28, no. 3 (July 1951): 165–66.

Stauter, Monsignor Patrick C. *100 Years in Colorado's Oldest Parish.* Denver: St. Cajetan's Press, 1958.

Steele, Thomas J. *Folk and Church in New Mexico.* Colorado Springs: Hulbert Center for Southwest Studies, Colorado College, 1993.

Stein, Mark. *How the States Got Their Shapes Too: The People behind the Borderlines.* Washington, DC: Smithsonian Books, 2011.

Steinel, Alvin T., and D. W. Working. *History of Agriculture in Colorado.* Fort Collins, CO: State Agricultural College, 1926.

Stoller, Marianne L. "Grants of Desperation, Lands of Speculation: Mexican Period Land Grants in Colorado." In *Spanish and Mexican Land Grants in New Mexico and Colorado*, ed. John R. Van Ness and Christine M. Van Ness, 22–39. Manhattan, KS: Sunflower University Press, 1980.

Stoller, Marianne L. "Preliminary Manuscript on the History of the Sangre de Cristo Land Grant and the Claims on the People of the Culebra River Villages on Their Lands" Unpublished manuscript, 1978 (on file with author).

Stoller, Marianne L. "Spanish-Americans, Their Servants and Sheep: A Culture History of Weaving in Southern Colorado." In *Spanish Textile Tradition of New Mexico and Colorado*, ed. Sarah Nestor. Santa Fe: Museum of New Mexico Press, 1979.

Stoller, Marianne L., and Thomas J. Steele. *Diary of the Jesuit Residence of Our Lady of Guadalupe Parish, Conejos, Colorado, December 1871–December 1875.* Colorado College Studies 19. Colorado Springs: Colorado College, 1982.

Stratton, Joanna L. *Pioneer Women: Voices from the Kansas Frontier.* New York: Simon and Schuster, 1981.

Svaldi, David P. "The Rocky Mountain News and the Indians." *Journal of the West* (1984).

Sweig, Sheldon S. "The Civil Administration of Governor William Gilpin." *Colorado Magazine* 31, no. 3 (July 1954): 179–93.

"Taos Marriages." *Family History Library.* Microfilm 0017017, April 21, 1856. https://ldsgenealogy.com/cgi-bin/FHL2-NM.cgi?308057_Index_to_Taos_marriages_ (1770-1860).

Taylor, Morris L. *Trinidad, Colorado Territory.* Trinidad, CO: Trinidad State Junior College, 1966.

Taylor, William B., and Elliott West. "Patron Leadership at the Crossroads: Southern Colorado in the Late Nineteenth Century." *Pacific Historical Review* 42, no. 3 (August 1973): 339.

Teeuwen, Randall, ed. *La Cultura Constante de San Luis.* San Luis, CO: San Luis Museum Cultural and Commercial Center, 1985.

Thompson, Jerry. *A Civil War History of the New Mexico Volunteers and Militia.* Albuquerque: University of New Mexico Press, 2015.

Tobin, Thomas T. "The Capture of the Espinosas." *Colorado Magazine* 9, no. 2 (1932): 59–66.

Tórrez, Robert J. *New Mexico in 1876–1877: A Newspaperman's View.* Albuquerque: Rio Grande Books, 2007.

Trujillo, Jose E. "History of Atanacio Trujillo." *Nuestras Raices* 2 (1990): 55–58.

Tucker, E. F. *Otto Mears and the San Juans.* Montrose, CO: Western Reflections Publishing, 2003.

Twitchell, Ralph Eme. *Leading Facts of New Mexico History.* Albuquerque: Horn and Wallace, 1963.

US War Department. *Official Records of the War of the Rebellion.* Vol. 22. Washington, DC: Government Printing Office, 1880–1901.

Vallmar, E. R. "Religious Processions and Penitente Activities at Conejos, 1874." *Colorado Magazine* 31, no. 3 (1945): 172–79.

Van Diest, E. C. "Early History of Costilla County." *Colorado Magazine* 5, no. 4 (August 1929): 142.

Vandenbusche, Duane. "Life at a Frontier Post: Fort Garland." *Colorado Magazine* 43, no. 2 (Spring 1966): 132–48.

Van Ness, John R., and Christine M. Van Ness. *Spanish and Mexican Land Grants in New Mexico and Colorado.* Manhattan, KS: Sunflower University Press, 1980.

Van Nuys, Frank. *Americanizing the West: Race, Immigrants, and Citizenship, 1890–1930.* Lawrence: University Press of Kansas, 2002.

Westphall, Victor. *Mercedes Reales: Hispanic Land Grants of the Upper Rio Grande Region*. Albuquerque: University of New Mexico Press, 1983.

White, William R. "Illegal Fencing on the Colorado Range." *Colorado Magazine* 52, no. 2 (1975): 93–113.

Wilson, O. Meredith. *The Denver and Rio Grande Project, 1870–1901*. Salt Lake City, UT: Howe Brothers Publishers, 1982.

About the Author

Virginia Sánchez, an independent scholar living in Colorado, has always been fascinated by the history of the Southwest, specifically New Mexico and southern Colorado. She has deep roots in northern New Mexico, as her ancestors date to Juan de Oñate's entrance into the region in 1598. She earned a Bachelor of Arts degree from the University of Wyoming and a Master of Arts degree from the University of Colorado at Denver.

Virginia found very few books about southern Colorado's Hispano settlements, which resulted in her first book about Cucharas, a small settlement northeast of Walsenburg in Huerfano County. *Forgotten Cuchareños of the Lower Cuchara Valley* discusses the Hispano-Indio community, its acequia systems, and the changes wrought by the coming of the Denver and Rio Grande Railroad to the area. Now in its second printing, her book received the 2011 Miles History Award from History Colorado. From her research, she also wrote an article about an acequia ledger, "Linked by Water, Linked by Blood: Madrid Ditch No. 2 in Cucharas, Colorado, 1884–1903" (*New Mexico Historical Review*, 2011).

Virginia continued her research about the enslaved Hispano and Indio people who lived in southern Colorado between 1861 and 1870. This resulted in a self-published genealogical reference book, *Survivors of Captivity: Genealogies of Known Enslaved Indigenous in Southern Colorado, 1860–1870*. Now many descendants of those who were enslaved have available documented information about their ancestors' lives and the owners they served. The book is presently in many libraries in southern Colorado and New Mexico.

With Philip Gonzales, PhD, Virginia coauthored "Displaced in Place: Nuevomexicanos on the Northern Side of the Colorado–New Mexico Border, 1850–1875" (*New Mexico Historical Review*, 2018). The congressional discussions outlined in the article present new information about why New Mexico lost much of its northern territory to Colorado and the impacts on the Hispanos affected by this action. This article won the 2018 Gilberto Espinosa award for Best Article in the *New Mexico Historical Review*.

Virginia is a contributing author to a 2019 book from the University of New Mexico Press, *Nación Genízara: Ethnogenesis, Place, and Identity in New Mexico*, edited by Moises Gonzales and Enrique R. Lamadrid. Her chapter, "Survival of Captivity: Hybrid Identities, Gender, and Culture in Territorial Colorado," discusses indigenous identity in southern Colorado.

Articles Virginia has written have appeared in *Colorado Heritage*, the *New Mexico Magazine, Annals of Wyoming*, and *Colorado Water*. She has presented her research to several historical and genealogical societies in Colorado and New Mexico. She is a member of the Colorado Historical Society and the New Mexico Historical Society. In 2012 the Hispanic Annual Salute recognized her for her contributions to the Colorado Hispano community in the area of history. In 2013 Colorado governor John Hickenlooper appointed her to serve on the Colorado Historical Records Advisory Board.

Index